DENISE LEVERTOV

DENISE LEVERTOV

A POET'S LIFE

Dana Greene

UNIVERSITY OF ILLINOIS PRESS : URBANA, CHICAGO, AND SPRINGFIELD

FRONTISPIECE: Denise Levertov, Somerville, Massachusetts, 1974.
© Arthur Furst, used with permission.

Library of Congress Cataloging-in-Publication Data
Greene, Dana.
Denise Levertov : a poet's life / Dana Greene.
p.   cm.
Includes bibliographical references and index.
ISBN 978-0-252-03710-8 (cloth : alk. paper)
ISBN 978-0-252-09421-7 (electronic)
1. Levertov, Denise, 1923–1997.
2. Poets, American—20th century—Biography.
3. Jewish Christians—Biography.
4. Levertov, Denise, 1923–1997—Criticism and interpretation.
I. Title.
PS3562.E8876Z67   2012
811'.54—dc23 [B]   2012023708

For Richard

  with love

CONTENTS

CREDITS

A WORD OF GRATITUDE

Ruskin wrote, "To see clearly is poetry, prophecy and religion, all in one." Denise Levertov would have resonated with this trinity of expressions; her life and work embodied all three. I have had the good fortune to be in conversation with many who knew her as poet, prophet, or witness, and they have shared not only details of her life but, to use Rilke's word, their own "in-seeing" into their complex friend. But the reality is that most friends knew her from one time, place, or vantage point, hence their remembrance is partial. When taken collectively, however, their reflections have been immensely valuable in giving me access to a person I did not know. Although not knowing Denise Levertov might be construed as my deficit, I have actually experienced it as an asset. Personal experience of another, while it brings a certain kind of knowing, can also be an impediment as one confronts the difficult and knotty aspects of a person's life. I hope I have capitalized on this asset and minimized my deficit through dialogue with these generous informants.

I take full responsibility for the content of this biography, but it could not have come to life without the input of the many persons who agreed to be interviewed. To each one I am grateful: Emily Archer, Rose Marie Berger, Wendell Berry, Murray Bodo, Craig Boly, Jalair Box, Yarrow Cleaves, Jane Comerfort, Jack Costello, George Dardess, John Dear, Judith Dunbar, Lou Oma Durand, Barbara Epler, Grey Foster, Barbara Fussiner, Albert Gelpi, Barbara Gelpi, Shalom Goldman, Nikolai Goodman, Sam Green, Joan Hallisey, Sam Hamill, Mark Jenkins, Lee Kapfer, Maggie Kimball, Paul Lacey, Joanna Macy, Colleen McElroy, Marlene Muller, Kathleen Norris, Mary Randlett, Rick Rapport, Peggy Rosenthal, Jessica Schwartz, David Shaddock, Maureen Smith, Richard Strudwick, Valerie Trueblood, Jan Wallace, Emily Warn, Edwin Weihe, and Kevin Young, and for written statements provided by George Quasha, Carol Rainey, and Ian Reid.

Thanks go as well to those institutions and persons who supported this book's creation in a variety of ways: The Emory University Marion and Al Heilbrun Emeritus Fellowship, the Collegeville Institute, and the staff of the Stanford University Archives, particularly Polly Armstrong and Mattie Taormina, who guard a cache of hundreds of boxes of raw materials, which are the lifeblood for the biographer. I am especially grateful to Paul Lacey and Valerie Trueblood of the Denise Levertov Literary Trust, and to Emily Archer, Murray Bodo, Boaz Michael, Marlene Muller, Ronald Schuchard, David Shaddock, and Valerie Trueblood for sharing privately held materials. Special thanks go to Amy Benson Brown, Gloria Dworet, Albert Gelpi, Paul Lacey, Harry Marten, Angela Alaimo O'Donnell, Gretchen Schulz, and Valerie Trueblood, who read the manuscript and offered suggestions, although again, they are absolved of any responsibility for the final outcome.

One of the deepest pleasures of my life has been being sequestered for several years in my "scriptorium" writing this book. What has made this solitude even richer has been the support and companionship of so many persons who believed this biography needed to be written. They include: Peggy Barlett, Allanah Beh, Merrill Carrington, Starr Costello, Kathleen Fischer, Michael Glaser, Joyce Glover, Susan Henry-Crowe, Catherine Howett, Fay Key, Carol Wilkinson Martin, Ann Mauney, Robert Morneau, Kathleen O'Connor, Bob Silliman, Kathleen Staudt, Tony Stoneburner, Bonnie Thurston, Marcia Wade, and Liz Ward.

For many years my double life as a biographer, one living in the "skin" of her subject, had to be endured by others. For their forbearance I am grateful to my daughters, Justin Greene, Kristin Blackman, Lauren Greene-Roesel, and Ryan Greene-Roesel; my sisters, Karen Greene and Mary Greene Kyle; and my husband, Richard Roesel, to whom owing most, I dedicate this book. What is written here would not have been possible without his love, friendship, critique, and endless good humor.

DENISE LEVERTOV

PROLOGUE

Ars longa, vita brevis.
HIPPOCRATES

Furtively, Denny Levertoff[1] dug out the poems she had stashed between sofa cushions and sent them off to T. S. Eliot, editor of *Criterion*. Her parents knew nothing of this until weeks later when Eliot's response arrived.[2] It was 1936, and she was only twelve, but desire and embryonic talent had already coalesced in a "secret destiny." She was an artist, and for the next six decades that ambition would direct her life.

Levertov published her first book of poems at age twenty-three, but it was not until she married and came to America that she found her poetic voice, helped by the likes of William Carlos Williams, Robert Duncan, and Robert Creeley. Unlike the American Eliot who immigrated to England and made his future there, Levertov left England and was acclaimed in America. She became what Kenneth Rexroth said was "the most subtly skillful poet of her generation, the most profound, . . . and the most moving."[3] Author of twenty-four volumes of poetry, four of essays, and eight translations, Levertov was lauded and honored.[4] Shortly before her death in 1997, the woman who claimed no country as home was nominated to be America's poet laureate.[5]

Denise Levertov was the quintessential romantic. She wanted to live vividly, intensely, passionately, and on a heroic scale. She wanted the persistence of Cézanne and the depth and generosity of Rilke. But she baffled herself and was baffling to others. Urbane and sophisticated, she was also childlike and irksome. She was exquisitely attentive and present, and paradoxically complex and elusive. What remains of Denise Levertov is her work. *Ars longa, vita brevis.*

Immigrating to America made all the difference in Levertov's life, but she insisted no country would define her. She was a creature of the "borderland" and a pilgrim. Ordinary life was her subject, and language itself was her only home, her "Jerusalem." She refused all limiting designations of place or culture.[6] The only distinction she wanted was "poet in the world," one whose work it was to prophetically "awaken sleepers."

Levertov's peripatetic and tumultuous life took many turns, dimming, but never extinguishing her "secret destiny," which she believed had been transmitted through her Russian Jewish and Celtic forebears, those she called her "illustrious ancestors." This poetic vocation was one of the continuities in her life, as was her prophetic commitment to explore what she called "the eternal questions." She did this as a pilgrim, one on a journey who was not constrained by boundaries.

The evidences of Levertov as poet, prophet, and pilgrim are all there in the public record — the interviews, essays, and poetry. But what is obscure, only hinted at, is the conflict and torment she both endured and created in her attempts to deal with her own psyche, her relationships with family, friends, lovers, colleagues, and the historical times in which she lived. This underside of life influenced her prodigious creative work over her long career. Once she acclimated herself to America, the dreamy lyric poetry of her early years gave way to the joy and wonder of ordinary life. By the late 1960s and early 1970s, however, her poems began to engage the issues of her times. Vehement and strident, her poetry of protest was both acclaimed and criticized. The end of both the Vietnam War and her marriage left her mentally fatigued and emotionally fragile. She spoke metaphorically of a distortion of her inner eyes. Gradually, over the span of a decade, she emerged with new energy. The crystalline and luminous poetry of her last years stands as final witness to a lifetime of searching for the mystery embedded in life itself. Through all the vagaries of life and art, her response was that of a "primary wonder."

A constant for Levertov was her fidelity to imagination as the most important artistic faculty "[T]o believe," she wrote:

> as an artist, in *inspiration* or *the intuitive*, to know that without Imagination . . . no amount of acquired craft or scholarship or of brilliant reasoning will suffice, is to live with the door of one's life open to the transcendent, the numinous. Not every artist, clearly, acknowledges that fact — yet all, in the creative act, experience mystery. The concept of "inspiration" presupposes a power that enters an individual and is

not a personal attribute; and it is linked to a view of the artist's life as one of obedience to a vocation.[7]

For Levertov imagination was a "form of grace, unmerited, unattainable, amazing, and freely given. It was with awe that any who received it must respond."[8] She did respond by continuing to live with the door of her life open. The space carved out in her by her early solitude allowed "the power of poetry to play" in her, but it also created a vulnerability. Her openness cost her dearly, yet as the wellspring of her inspiration it shaped her, bending her to a life in obedience to poetry itself.

The unfolding of Levertov's "destiny" resulted in a voluminous poetic corpus. It was this work, not her life, she wanted remembered. She explicitly dismissed most biographies of poets as "sensational," "prurient," "overly subjective," and "gossipy." They were created with the help of heirs and psychiatrists and gave into the temptation to "suppress," "invent," or "judge."[9] She wanted none of it. For her any consideration of the life distorted and added little to the understanding of the poet's achievement.

And yet Levertov herself belied this Solomonic choice between life and art. For her the interaction between the two was continuous. As she attested: "Both life and poetry fade, wilt, shrink, when they are divorced."[10] It was from life itself that her art emerged. "I have always . . . written out of my own experience."[11] "I have always tended to reflect in my poems the places and the experiences of my life."[12]

> I've always written about what I was living. When I've been in the country, I've written about the country, when I've been in love I've written about being in love, and when I've been on demonstrations, I've written about that. . . . [Y]ou write about what you live. If one is what one eats, one's poems are what one does.[13]

For Levertov, poems not only emanated from life but reflected it. They were evidences of full, engaged living, what she would later call "testimonies of lived life."

Since the poet and the poem are bound in dialogue, one might argue that biography is the appropriate forum for exploring both. Certainly, Levertov provided ample opportunity for this exploration. The public Levertov is revealed in her writing and the more than twenty-five interviews she gave during her lifetime. The private person, Denise, is there in an archival treasure trove of diaries, notebooks, correspondence, and drafts in process. Here are described her relationships with fellow poets, antiwar and environmental allies, devoted students, academic colleagues, religious companions, and a varied assortment of friends and lovers. Although these materials must be used with caution since they can reflect her response in the moment and not necessarily be conclusive pronouncements, nonetheless it is in this great welter of information that one finds not only the shards of a life but the close interrelationship between her life and art. Here her inner and outer worlds are revealed. Irrespective of her suspicion about biography, these artifacts attest to the fact that she purposely left the makings of precisely the kind of biography she wanted: one that centered on the work as a creation of life itself. This biography is a first attempt to illustrate the powerful interconnections of Denise Levertov's life and work and to demonstrate what fellow poet and friend, Eavan Boland, predicted: "In every time there are just a few poets whose work — for its sheer lyric conscience — carries poetry safely into the future. Denise Levertov . . . is one of them."[14]

1

"A Definite and Peculiar Destiny"
1923–1946

In the work of a living poet the dominant personal myth may, in early or even in mature work, be only half formed; the poet himself does not yet know the whole story — if he did, he would stop writing. . . . Yet from the first his bent, his cast of imagination, has declared itself.
"THE SENSE OF PILGRIMAGE"[1]

From a very young age Denise Levertov had a definite sense of her "peculiar destiny," a personal myth that derived from her ancestors, Schneour (Schneur) Zalman, the Rav of Northern White Russia,[2] who was reputed to understand the language of birds, and Angell Jones of Mold, a Welsh tailor, who stitched meditations into coats and britches. She believed that these ancient ones were joined to her by a "taut" line across almost three centuries. They inspired her to make, as these ancestors did

> poems direct as what the birds said,
> hard as a floor, sound as a bench,
> mysterious as the silence when the tailor
> would pause with his needle in the air.[3]

The legacy of these two visionaries[4] was transmitted to her by her parents, the Welsh-born Beatrice Spooner-Jones, descendant of Angell Jones, and the Russian, Feivel Levertoff, whose ancestor was Schneour Zalman.

Angell Jones lived in northeast Wales on the River Alyn. His shop on High Street in Mold was not only his work site but the place where this Methodist preacher taught his apprentices scripture as well as the skills of the tailor. For a time David Owen, later acclaimed as one of Wales's greatest novelists, worked with Jones as an impoverished apprentice. The tailor's craft was handed down by Jones to his sons, and one grandson, Walter Spooner-Jones of Caernarvon, turned his manual dexterity to surgery, working as a junior doctor for a mining company in Abercanaid. Spooner-Jones married Margaret Griffiths, and soon after in 1885, Beatrice was born. When Beatrice was two and a half, her mother died in childbirth and her father remarried. It was not a fortuitous match in that the new wife became addicted to drugs and young Beatrice was neglected for several years. When she was ten, her stepmother died, and two years later her father did as well, leaving her an orphan at age twelve. At that point she was taken in by relatives, the Reverend David Oliver, Congregational minister of Holywell, and his wife, Bess, who cared for her and provided a good education. She had lessons in painting and voice, attended secondary and teacher training school, and absorbed the tenor of the Oliver household, which was strict, orderly, and deeply religious. But as an orphan Beatrice felt set apart from the other Oliver children.[5] Although she loved the natural beauty of Wales, she longed for a more adventurous life. Her dream was to teach in Paris, but that was considered unacceptable work for a young woman. In the end she secured a position at a Scottish Mission school for girls in Constantinople, arriving there on the Orient Express. In that distant, exotic city Beatrice Spooner-Jones would meet Feivel Levertoff, her future husband.

If Beatrice Spooner-Jones's early life was tragic, it was matched by that of Feivel Levertoff, who traced his heritage back to a rabbi of Lyady, Schneour Zalman, born in 1745 and later founder of Habad, an offshoot of Hasidism. By 1800, Zalman had been arrested several times, imprisoned in St. Petersburg by civil authorities, and denounced as a heretic by religious ones. He taught a consciousness of God's presence in all things and affirmed that even the most humble Jew had intellectual access to the divine. He believed life was worship and service and that all beings contained sparks of God. He embraced the material world in order to restore it to his creator. The exaltation and joyfulness of Habad were expressed in story, dance, and song. Three generations hence, Feivel Levertoff would transmit to his children the stories of this ancestor, Schneour Zalman.

Feivel Levertoff was born in either 1875 or 1878 in Orsha, what is now Belarus, to Shaul (Saul) and Batya Levertoff. According to one rendering, Feivel was related to Schneour Zalman through the paternal line as his great-grandson. Another story is that Zalman was Feivel's mother's uncle.[6] Stories of his early life focused on his religious identity and the conflict it caused within his family. One day the young Feivel found a scrap of paper written in Hebrew that told the story of a young man, much like himself, who proclaimed scripture in the temple. When Feivel's father discovered the paper, he incinerated it and admonished his bewildered son never to read such a thing again. Another story relates to Feivel's purchase of a copy of the Christian testament for which he also incurred his father's wrath. An ardent and deeply devout student, Feivel's early rabbinic education was in a local seminary, but because Jews were prohibited from studying in the university, he had to leave Russia. He traveled to Konigsberg, Prussia, where the freer university environment was much to his liking. It was there he became convinced that Jesus of Nazareth was the long-sought messiah. His family was appalled, declared him mad, and disowned him. Nonetheless Feivel became a Christian, believing that by doing so he would be more fully Jewish. He took a new name, Paul, after the most ardent follower of the messiah.

Paul Philip Levertoff, who always conceived of himself as a Jewish-Christian, joined the staff of the Hebrew Christian Testimony to Israel in 1901 and traveled throughout Europe and the Mediterranean, all the while engaging in scholarly writing. In 1910, he went to Constantinople to give a series of lectures and there met Beatrice Spooner-Jones. He was thirty-two years old, and she seven years his junior. For Denise Levertov this encounter was freighted with meaning. It was not merely the meeting of her parents but the joining of the distant ancestral heritage of Angell Jones and Schneour Zalman. As she put it: "Thus Celt and Jew met in Byzantium."[7] Through this fortuitous meeting Angell Jones and Schneour Zalman would enter the twentieth century. The "taut" line between these "illustrious ancestors" and Denise Levertov was established.

Although Beatrice's adopted family was not enthusiastic about her prospective husband — he was a foreigner and had no secure income — she and Paul, accompanied by a chaperone, returned to London and married in 1911. It was the union of two deeply religious orphans and their Celtic, Russian, Jewish, and Christian lineages.

The early years of their marriage were neither settled nor easy. First they moved to Warsaw and then to Leipzig where Paul Levertoff taught Hebrew and rabbinics at a postgraduate institute for Jewish missions. He remained there during the Great War, carving out a successful career as a teacher and prolific scholar, even though for a time he was under house arrest as a foreigner. A daughter, Phillipa, was born in 1911 but died within less than a year. The loss of this first child was crushing, particularly to Paul Levertoff. Living in a strange country with no close friends, he became depressed and ill. The grieving Beatrice Levertoff was given some consolation by a trip to visit relatives in Wales. A token from that trip was a leather strap provided by sympathetic seamen to hold together her damaged luggage. This strap would travel with Beatrice throughout the rest of her life, and would be passed down to Denise as she traversed the world.

While in Leipzig, a few months prior to the outbreak of war in 1914, Beatrice gave birth to a second daughter, Olga. This baby became a healing presence for Paul Levertoff. He doted on her while Beatrice turned increasingly to the preoccupations of domestic life.

When the war was over, the Levertoffs, who were the equivalent of displaced persons, traveled from Germany to Denmark, finally settling in Wales where Paul worked for three years as subwarden at St. Deiniol's, a theological library in Hawarden. During this time he was ordained a priest in the Church of England by the Rev. John Dubuisson, later Dean of St. Asaph's Cathedral.

Paul Levertoff's next move would be permanent. In his midforties he was appointed Director of the East London Fund for Jews and pastor of Holy Trinity on Old Nichol Street in Shoreditch, a Hebrew-Christian church where Jews believing in Jesus could worship. Holy Trinity was unlike other Anglican churches. It had no fixed congregation and no endowment, so Reverend Levertoff's salary was paid by a church organization dedicated to fostering Jewish-Christian relationships. Since the church did not have a vicarage, the family moved initially to Lenox Gardens in Ilford where their third daughter was born on October 24th, 1923. With the assistance of a midwife, Priscilla Denise was delivered just as the school bell rang at 9:15 A.M. at the nearby Highland Elementary School. Paul Levertoff was forty-five years old at the time and Beatrice thirty-eight. Olga was nine.

Eight months after Denise's birth the Levertoffs bought an 1890s, five-bedroom, brick, semidetached house at 5 Mansfield Road in Ilford not far from Lenox Gardens and nearby Cranbrook Road, the main street, and close to the large Valentine and Wanstead parks. Ilford, in the far northeast section of what is now the borough of Redbridge, a suburb of London, was experiencing substantial growth, and by 1931 it had a population of some 131,000. The Levertoff home was like those nearby, but had a few distinctive features. There were no blinds on the bay windows in the front or the French windows in the back, so passersby could see into the house, and the two gardens, a small one in the front and a larger one in the back, were both wild and unkempt although opulent and brilliant with color.[8] The Levertoffs lived in this house until Paul Levertoff's death in 1954.[9]

In this quotidian world the Levertoffs were, as Denise wrote, "exotic birds in the plain English coppice of Ilford, Essex."[10] Paul Levertoff was small in stature, lean, with bushy hair, brows, and beard, and piercing eyes; he was above all a scholar, deeply committed, complex, mystical, emotionally distant, and otherworldly. It was he who dominated the Levertoff household. Although a member of the Anglican clergy, he was a man set apart. His first

FIGURE 1. (1a) Paul Phillip Levertoff, circa 1910. (Source unknown.) (1b) Beatrice Spooner-Jones. Levertoff Special Collections, Stanford University.

language was not English, and he did not have an English education. The Church of England did not quite know what to do with him. His vocation was both to Jews (to show that Christianity was not alien to them) and to Gentiles (to point out the Jewish origins of Christianity and thereby suggest that anti-Semitism was incompatible with Christian life). Each Saturday morning at 11 A.M. he led a liturgy of psalms and songs and offered a service of Holy Communion in Hebrew. He later published this original Hebrew-Christian liturgy as *The Order of Service of the Meal of the Holy King*. He had few congregants, but he persevered for years in his mission. On Sundays he would preach at Christian churches in greater London. But he considered himself first a scholar and translator. He worked at home in an unkempt up-stairs study, watched over by an almost lifesize stone statue of the preaching Jesus. Initially Beatrice served as his secretary, but as Olga matured she internalized his religious vision and became his amanuensis. As an ecumenist, Levertoff was a member of several organizations — the Society for the Study of Religions, the Aristotelian Society, and the League of St. Alban and St. Sergius. But his energy was principally dedicated to scholarship. He was author of *The Son of Man, The Life of St. Paul, Israel's Religion and Destiny, The Religious Ideas of Hasidism, Old Testament Prophecy and the Religions of the East, Love and the Messianic Age*, and *Messianic Hope*, among others. He translated

The Confessions of Augustine and *The Gospel of Matthew* into Hebrew, and *The Zohar*, the medieval Spanish guide to mystical Jewish thought, into English. At the center of his belief was the notion that the love of God and of one's fellows was the essence of the Messianic tradition. The Law was given in order to bring forth the union of God and Israel; the Messianic age would perfect that union. Joy was the revelation of God within; compassion was the response to others and always led to service on their behalf.

Beatrice Levertoff was a small, portly woman with wavy hair who was well-dressed and wore dashing hats. It was said she had a "Jewish soul," meaning she was welcoming and generous. As a painter and a naturalist, she was a "a pointer-outer," one attentive to wildflowers, birds, and clouds, exclaiming upon their beauty and teaching her daughters their names. As a vocalist whose special talent was singing Lieder, she encouraged her daughters' artistic life. But there was an air of otherworldliness and naivety about her; Denise later claimed her mother was "a virtual innocent."[11]

Olga was an accomplished pianist, who especially loved Liszt, Chopin, and Bach. Denise, who took lessons in both painting and ballet, acknowledged her mother's influence in inculcating her love of nature: she "taught me to look; / to name the flowers when I was still close to the ground, / my face level with theirs."[12] Later in life, Denise speculated that if her mother had grown up in a large happy family, her habit of observation might not have developed and hence not been passed down to her. Denise attested: "I could not ever have been a poet without that vision she imparted."[13]

Enamored of Sir Walter Scott, Beatrice also had a deep appreciation of history, of archeological ruins, of churches, roads, and burial grounds. She unlocked the natural and created beauty of the English countryside for Olga and Denise. If Paul Levertoff gave his daughters gifts of "eloquence" and "fervor," Beatrice gave them "Welsh intensity and a lyric feeling for nature."

The Levertoff household was a hive of activity. Since neither daughter attended school, everyone was generally at home. They had few connections to the surrounding community and no extended family with whom they regularly interacted. Their Welsh, Russian, and Jewish cultural origins set them apart. Nonetheless, wayfarers of every sort — Jewish booksellers, Russian and German scholars, musicians, and Jewish refugees all passed through their home. Denise remembers the visits of the Russian theologians, G. P. Fedotov and Sergei Bulgakov. Both parents were interested in the important issues of the interwar period. Paul Levertoff protested Mussolini's invasion of Abyssinia, and both he and Olga condemned Britain's lack of support for Republican forces during the Spanish Civil War. Beatrice canvassed for establishment of the League of Nations and worked to find housing and employment for refugees.

Everyone in the family read, to themselves and to others. Every room of the house was filled with books, some of which were bought by Paul Levertoff as a secondhand "lot" from Sotheby's. Others came from the local public library where Miss Farmery, the librarian, sequestered new book arrivals until the Levertoffs could claim them. In this way Olga and Denise absorbed great literature by osmosis. Hearing books read aloud night after night, they developed an ear for language, and Denise later attested that this practice was the origin of her ability to read well in public.[14] They read most of the nineteenth-century English novelists, especially enjoying Jane Austen and George Eliot, and many Russian ones as well; Beatrice read the whole of *War and Peace* to her daughters. As a young child Denise's imagination was spurred by Bunyan, Beatrix Potter, and Hans Andersen. Later she read Carlyle and Chekhov, Ibsen, and Turgenev, but she especially loved the English poets — Henry Vaughan, George Herbert, Thomas Traherne, Wordsworth, and Keats. She said she carried Tennyson everywhere, stuck under an armpit for months on end. In her late teens she read the letters of both Keats and Rilke. From the time she was young, she claimed to share an affinity with Keats; like him she too wanted to be a great English poet.[15] Rilke's poetry and letters also would prove to be instrumental in developing her poetic vocation. Later she wrote: "Though my favorite poets were all men, I had enough faith in myself, or more precisely enough awe at the magic I knew sometimes worked through me, not to worry about that. . . . I didn't suppose my gender to be an obstacle to anything I really wanted to do."[16]

The Levertoffs were writers. Reverend Levertoff was a prolific author, and Mrs. Levertoff wrote a novella and a children's book. Olga began writing her own books when she was twenty-three. Denise claimed that when she was five she conceived of her first poem and dictated it to Olga.[17] By age eight she knew she was an artist. She insisted her life would not be dull, that it would be a story, an adventure. Writing proved to be the way to realize that aspiration.

It was Olga who introduced Denise to contemporary theater and to modern poetry, especially T. S. Eliot It must have been that connection, as well as Denise's knowledge that her father served on a committee with Eliot, that prompted her to send her poems off to him for review. Audacious or naive as she was, Eliot responded, cementing more firmly her sense of destiny.[18] Her prodigious output of poems was testimony that she followed his advice: learn languages, do translation, and above all continue to write.

Although the Levertoffs were able to impart many of their values to their daughters, these ardent and religious parents were incapable of inculcating a sense of religious piety in either of them. For a time Olga went to morning services, but her principal religious expression was intellectual. She joined her father in his research and writing; later she expressed her values in various forms of social protest. Although Denise admitted that she loved the beauty of the liturgy, the stained glass windows of churches, religious music, and the language of the King James Bible and the Book of Common Prayer, at about age thirteen she severed any ties with formal religion. For her religion was an embarrassment and a restriction. Her parents offered no opposition. Nonetheless she absorbed Christian culture through art, music, and literature, and she had a very strong consciousness and pride in being Jewish, although the Jewish community considered her family defectors. In their eyes Paul Levertoff was either a traitor or insane.[19]

Denny (pronounced Dinny) recalled an idyllic early solitary childhood, one filled with a sense of wonder and joy. Since she did not attend school,[20] she had few friends except for Olga, who was nine years her senior and her confidant.[21] Denise was naturally shy and understood that she was different from other children. But her sense of difference did not mean she felt less or better than they. What she did experience was a sense that her life had a special meaning. Her solitude denied her the experience of friendship, and consequently she was an awkward friend, even though she desired the intimacy of companions.[22] Later in life she regretfully recalled her first, and one of her only, childhood friendships, with Jean Rankin, a kindred spirit with whom she created The Adventure Seekers, a secret society. One of their favorite means of communication was to leave notes for each other in a rabbit hole in the local park. Their friendship was challenged when Jean refused to carry on their childhood cavorting in streams, condemning it as unladylike. Denny was outraged at this silliness, and when Jean refused to relent, she broke off the friendship, refusing to forgive and forget even after being petitioned by Jean and her family.[23] Denise's principled stance, her certitude that she was right, manifested itself early in life and remained part of her character. Only years later would she recognize her treatment of Jean as hard-hearted and unforgiving. As one who cherished and longed for friendship, Denise nonetheless could be a difficult friend.

As a child she was chubby, but she thinned out as she grew. Her hair was dark and curly, and she had what Beatrice called "shoe-button eyes," black and intense with no light in them. Her gaptooth smile, a sign of good luck,[24] was inherited from her mother. From an early age she carried a brown

FIGURE 2. Denise Levertoff, circa 1925. Special Collections, Stanford University.

glove-leather homunculus doll called "Monkey" with her, a permanent source of security and protection. Her education from about age five was under the direction of her mother and included lessons in reading and writing and listening to BBC school broadcasts. Although pleasurable for Denise, this training was unmethodical and eclectic. Denise later confessed that she was a scientific and mathematical "moron." Having never learned to multiply she was forced to keep a multiplication table at the ready for consultation.[25] After age twelve she was free to pursue whatever studies she liked. She traveled to London by herself on the tube, making regular visits to the cultural treasure trove, the Victoria and Albert Museum, where she relished being alone with art in its empty rooms. At age thirteen she saw Cézanne's Le Lac D'Annecy in the National Gallery of Art and took out a book on the artist from the Ilford library. She was attracted by Cézanne's work, and later when she read Rilke's Letters about this French painter, her attraction deepened. She would return to Cézanne again and again for inspiration. She studied French, and for five years took classes in ballet, spurred on by Olga. Sometimes she waited around Covent Garden hoping to encounter dancers entering and exiting the building. Although ballet allowed her to develop the elegant carriage of a dancer and express the joy and ecstasy she felt as a young girl, it never fully captured her imagination. Olga was the one who insisted that Denise study ballet, and at one point she actually stole the tuition money for her sister's lessons from their father's desk, concocting a story that Denise had received a dance scholarship.

Art, reading, and exploring nature and the English countryside occupied and inspired the young Denny. Her diaries and notebooks of this period are filled with reproductions of Cézanne's paintings, short descriptions of books she had read and those she planned to read, pen-and-ink sketches of a variety of subjects, lists of flowers and the meanings of their names, and of course, poems, all recorded in a cursive handwriting almost identical to that of her mother, who taught her the script. Her young mind was being formed to pay attention to and engage with her immediate surroundings. The absence of formal and systematic training conspired to ensure that her vocation as poet would go unchallenged.

With pride she claimed: "I am Essex-born." Although she dreamed of faraway countries, tracing voyages with her fingers in the family atlas, she loved the places of her childhood best — the little streams of Valentine and Wanstead parks, Cranbrook Wash, and Seven Kings on the High Road of Ilford where her birth was recorded.[26] She lived at the western end of the county far from London, an idyllic place for exploration. Sometimes she and Oggie, as she affectionately called her, would go on tramps, singing hymns as they went, often returning home after dark. The English national pastime of walking was deeply formative of Denise, prompting the opportunity for observation and a bodily movement that inculcated attention to rhythm. Sometimes the sisters would go to Valentine Park, dig up the taproots of the great trees and play underground for hours accompanied by their dog. It was there in Valentine Park that Denise confirmed her belief in other orders of being, in this case when she insisted that a little man — two feet high and dressed in a one-piece garment and a peaked cap — came out of the woods and clambered to the other side of the park.[27] Later she would write that she always had the sense that there was more to ordinary life than meets the eye, there was always the possibility of "entertaining angels unawares."[28]

Denise recognized that both the English countryside and the English language were formative of her, but she did not consider herself English, perhaps because of her "mish-mash" heritage, perhaps because she did not have a formal English education. Later on she claimed that she was a kind of "mongrel,"[29] a Jew among Christians, a goy among Jews, a Celt among Anglo-Saxons, a Russian among Celts, and vice versa. Among her school-going peers she was an exception, an anomaly,[30] one to be envied for her freedom from the constraints of the school room.

She usually described her early years as blissful. She had the affection of her mother and the companionship of her sister. The awe-filled spirit of Hasidism, expressed in dance, song, and ritual was an important aspect of family life imparted by her father. But there was a dark undercurrent in this seemingly idyllic world, epitomized in a few early childhood experiences. Once in an adventurous romp with friends in a beautiful vacant garden, an old tramp suddenly appeared. "A devil in paradise" was there to terrorize them. Later she wrote of this as "a revelation of how intimately opposites live, their mysterious simultaneity, their knife-edge union: the Janus face of human experience."[31] Another experience was even more shattering.[32] In this case she recalled a delightful day hiking with two German Jewish refugees, Gerhardt and Anna. This was one of Denise's first important experiences of shared friendship outside her family. The day was spent in nature enjoying laughter and singing and the sweetness of emergent friendship. However, as the hikers climbed into a hay-filled barn, a curved scythe blade was discovered dangerously thrusting through the hay. Their bliss-filled moment was destroyed. No one was hurt, but in the midst of beauty and delight a threat was revealed. Fearful, stunned, and chastened, Denise and her friends returned home. Joy and horror were juxtaposed in that moment. Both were real. The experience was seared in Denise's mind; it represented a central theme of her life, the conjoining of fears and promises, joy and sorrow. At age ten she had no way of knowing that this preoccupation would follow her throughout her life. It was a sign, however, that her Edenic life was about to end.

Denny's relationship with Olga was changing as she entered early adolescence and Olga her adult years. Oggie had been Denny's "confidante in all things." It was to Oggie that she dictated her first poem and to whom she showed her poems before she sent them off to Eliot. It was Oggie who harassed her to study ballet. It was to Oggie that she confessed that she wanted to join the Communist Party. She was rejected as under age but was encouraged to sell the *Daily Worker* on Saturday mornings in Ilford. Her parents never knew of this; only Oggie did.

As the much-older sibling, Olga vied for Denise's admiration and affection. Confidants, they were nonetheless vastly different in temperament. Denise was shy and introverted. She described herself as "a quiet mouse" who "preferred to be inconspicuous," one who created a "secret life."[33] Olga, on the other hand, was fierce, passionate, bossy, and dominating. She was an organizer, an intellectual with prodigious energy. Her emotions fluctuated. Denny could remember Olga banging on the piano for hours, pouring out her anger over an injustice or a suffering. If Reverend Levertoff's work set the tenor of the household, it was Olga's personality that dominated. From the very beginning Olga was the apple of her father's eye, a consolation after the death of little Phillipa. Paul Levertoff took great satisfaction in his precocious oldest daughter. His praise of her intellect, artistry, and moral probity bordered on adulation, and he forgave her every transgression. Father and daughter were allies, companions in scholarship and public protest.

The alliance of these two was powerful. Beatrice responded by giving her attention to Denise. This rivaled Olga's claim on her younger sister's affection, but it also established Beatrice and Denise as allies. As a consequence Denise spent considerable time with her mother, and it was her understanding and approval that anchored Denise's security and happiness. When that approval was withheld, however, Denise felt judged, controlled, and dominated. Her mother's affection was real, but it came at a cost. As Denise entered adolescence, she came to see her mother as naive and prudish, dependent and controlling. She withdrew from her and increasingly refused to share her thoughts with her. With her father she shared even less affection. As a very young child she recalled turning wild and fighting him to put her down when he would attempt to hug her.[34] She wanted a different kind of father; the one she had did not measure up.[35] In general she found him to be remote, preoccupied with his work, and inaccessible to her. As she saw it, he had contradictory characteristics. He was good and wise, but also childish, weak, humorless, and intolerant. He could be tyrannical to those at home and generous to outsiders.[36] It was only after his death that Denise would begin to appreciate his scholarly contributions and remember his sometimes joyful Hasidic expressions of delight.

Seen from the outside, the ethos of the Levertoff family appeared strong and consistent. Yet under the surface there were complex emotional relationships and conflicting family values, both of which would have a formative impact on Denise. In reflecting on her upbringing, she saw two strands of thought and feeling in her family. One was narrow, judgmental, and conscience-oriented; the other humane, unconventional, and book-loving.[37] The family's emotional dynamic was divided: father and Olga, mother and Denise or father, mother and Denise. As an emotional entity the Levertoff family did not exist.[38] Only in their activities — evening reading, morning prayers, and the occasional family expedition — were they a family vis-à-vis the outside world. Often they were divided. Generally, Denise recounted an idealized childhood, but she also acknowledged there were "tremendous domestic arguments and periodic full-scale 'rows' and even real tragedy."[39]

In her adolescence Denise offered the typical canard against parental inadequacy; they had not prepared her to live in the world. They were too old, too innocent, and too expectant that their daughter would behave as they did and have their values. In short, she believed her parents were incapable of parenting her.[40] Her response was to withdraw and to foster her special identity. Her solitary excursions, her daydreaming, her inner life of paintings, poems, and stories were her means of escape.[41]

From birth Olga was an enchanting child, gifted, precocious, and — by the age of eight — totally loquacious and persuasive. She studied piano and was enamored of ballet, having once seen Anna Pavlova perform. Her only formal schooling was less than a year of instruction at Our Lady of Zion Catholic boarding school for girls, which she left because of illness. Olga was energetic and inventive, zealous and intellectual. Always interested in theater, she joined a touring theatrical troupe and then organized her own amateur dramatic company. As her father's secretary she became very involved in his work and studied Greek and theology. She published her first book, *The Wailing Wall*, in 1937 with A. R. Mowbray and Company, an Anglican publishing house. It was hailed as a penetrating and original contribution to the Christian approach to the Jews. Like her father, Olga believed that the values of Judaism — its mystical elements, insights, and imagination — would be transformed and fulfilled in Christian faith. Like him she maintained the *Zohar* was the most important work of medieval Jewry, one which showed the inner meaning of the tradition's mystical thought.

Although seemingly allied with her father, in her teenage years Olga began to challenge parental affection. A pattern of consistent lying began when she was about twelve or thirteen, and she became increasingly strong-willed and dominant. By the time she entered her twenties she had a variety of suitors. She became engaged to one, Stan Robertson, who worked at the Communist Party headquarters in Ilford. Her father made it clear that this match was unacceptable. He had done likewise with an earlier suitor, a thirty-year-old gypsy singer. But what came next was to severely challenge him and Beatrice.[42]

Prior to the Spanish Civil War Olga and her father protested Britain's lack of support for Spanish Republican forces. During the war Olga volunteered and went to Spain to assist the anti-Fascists. There she met and fell in love with Tom Strudwick, a "cockney" Communist with a hardscrabble life, who was the age of her mother. To make matters worse, Strudwick was married to Emily Colgate with whom he had several children. When Olga returned to Ilford, there were serious battles between her and her parents who were shocked and embarrassed by their daughter's liaison with Strudwick. Initially Olga and Strudwick ran away together; the Levertoffs did not know of their whereabouts. When they returned, Paul Levertoff found a place for them to live since Olga was pregnant with the first of their four children.[43] In chronicling her sister's life during this chaotic period, Denise admits that reconstruction is difficult. Apparently Olga and Strudwick stayed together until 1945, but during these years Olga left two of her young children in Denise's care for a summer while, according to Denise, Olga, wearying of domestic life, was off having a love affair with a woman. At some point, Denise was not sure when, her sister was sent to jail for embezzlement for almost a year. In explaining her incarceration, Olga insisted that she was innocent and was only shielding the real perpetrator.[44] The details of Olga's life were elusive. As Denise wrote: "She was such a mixture of altruism, deception, willfulness and fantasy that it is impossible to know" the truth about her. [45]

Parted now from Strudwick and in her late twenties, Olga would spin out of control, bewildering both her parents and her sister. She would disappear for a while and then return and ask to borrow money. All the while she kept up her theater work and her interest in Christian-Socialism, Communism, and anti-Fascism. Brilliant, perceptive, and persuasive, she continued to write. In 1942 she published her second book, *The Jews in a Christian Social Order*. In this she emphasized Judaism's corrective value for Christianity. She argued that Judaism, with its emphasis on history and "this-worldliness," could serve as a counterforce to Christianity's otherworldliness and toleration of terrible evil. She pointed to the fact that Christianity had an anti-Semitic history, and that it was Christianity itself that stood between the Jews and Christ. To her, the conversion of the Jews would be possible only when Christians returned to the Jewish Christianity of the first century, with its revolutionary interpretation of the Gospel. Authentic Christianity needed to reject a shallow mysticism and ally itself with those who suffered and were downtrodden — namely European Jews.

During the war years when Olga's life became increasingly chaotic, Denise continued to live with her parents. She was determined to be neither another Olga nor her mother's ideal daughter. For a time she attend the Legat School of Russian Ballet in London, but at age sixteen, when war broke out in the early fall of 1939, she went to live in Beaconsfield in Buckinghamshire about twenty-five miles outside the city where the school had relocated. She stayed almost a year, returning to her family's home in the fall of 1940. During this time she wrote to her parents frequently, addressing them as "Twain," and regaling them with tales of the crowded dormitories with their curtained windows and the motley group of characters living at the school — dancers, refugees, Russian exiles, and misfits of various kinds — all under the watchful eye of Madame, the eccentric Russian teacher who ran the place. She wrote of the weather; the places she visited during her free time; her lessons in French, German, and Russian; and the long hours of ballet practice. Apparently the air raids never bothered her. She worried about Olga and lamented that her sister never wrote. She insisted she was not looking for a mate, which must have relieved her parents, who were still reeling from Olga's escapades.[46] Her hope was to travel, first to Europe and then to America. She signed her letters in girlish form with xxxx kisses and decorated the stationary with little sketches.

Denise's year at the ballet school was a strange experience, but it did provide the opportunity to be away from her parents.[47] She wandered freely and had time to read and write poetry. She had the good fortune to be able to visit the Herbert Read household, which was right next to the school and was filled with paintings and books. Read, curator of the Victoria and Albert Museum, was an art critic and poet. Their brief encounter would lead to greater engagement in the years to come.[48]

Curiously, it was not fear of the bombing or war or missing her family that Denise remembered from that year in Buckinghamshire. Rather it was the day she walked out of ballet class. In early spring of 1940, she spontaneously and resolutely gave up on ballet. She left the practice room, shed her ballet clothes, dressed, and knowing full well that there would be consequences for her actions, took to the road, singing and kicking up stones. She realized that even after five years of practice she did not want to be a ballerina. That was Olga's aspiration for her. She walked for miles, free and happy, returning to the dormitory after dark, aware that Madame would be furious. Although she remained at the school through the summer before returning to Ilford, the die had been cast. Her future was not with dance, although it would leave its mark. Ballet gave her an elegant carriage, deepened her appreciation of rhythm, and allowed her to experience being both creator and created simultaneously.[49] Much later she would write of her memories of dance:

> the joy of leaping, of moving by
> leaps and bounds, of gliding
> to leap, and gliding
> to leap becomes, while it lasts,
> heart pounding, breath hurting,
> the deepest, the only joy.[50]

FIGURE 3. Denise Levertoff, 1940. Special Collections, Stanford University.

Most of all her year at ballet school gave her independence from family, al-lowing her to assert herself. By age seventeen she was clear: she was a poet.

In late May of 1940, she heard artillery pound from across the Channel at Dunkirk. In response she wrote the two-stanza poem "Listening to Distant Guns," which was not about the war but her adolescent experience of two realities,[51] evident in her psyche since childhood — the tranquility of nature and the horror of battle — juxtaposed one against another. She was elated when the poem appeared in the 1940 issue of *Poetry Quarterly*, which was under the direction of Charles Wrey Gardiner. It was her first publication.

In the fall of 1940, Denise returned to Ilford and remained there for the next year. She was marking time by painting, playing the piano, help-ing around the house, reading voraciously, and continuing to write poems. During this time she deepened her friendship with Rebecca (Betty or Bet) Mitchell with whom she often attended theater performances. They became lifelong friends. When Denise began to worry that her poetic intensity was diminishing, Bet scoffed at her,[52] and when Bet became ill and needed to use a wheelchair, the two of them would read Chekhov together on Hampstead Heath. For them Chekhov was an artist with an objective and balanced vi-sion of the world. He saw injustice and barbarity, but he had compassion for the world's brokenness. He acknowledged that humans were an evolv-ing species but that among them were forerunners who had been given a glimpse of a positive future.[53] Denise admired Chekhov's hopefulness and equanimity, but he would soon be eclipsed by one who would guide her as a poet — Rainer Maria Rilke.

In October 1942, Denise turned eighteen, but she was still underage for military conscription, which applied to both males and females. Since she had a romantic idea of living the rural life, she volunteered to serve in the Women's Land Army and to work on a farm. Although this removed her from her family, she hated the work and promptly quit. Fearing her imminent conscription as a munitions factory worker, she joined the Civil Nursing Reserve and for several years served as a replacement nurse in five different nursing facilities in and around London. Nursing was hard, unpleasant, and exhausting, and she had neither talent nor inclination for it, but it did give her the opportunity to live away from her parents again. In the process she lost her naivety and her virginity. It proved to be her coming of age. In hospital work she encountered poverty (something she had never known before) illness, and death. She recalled her experience of looking earnestly into the faces of those who were dying. It was there that she learned that the "music . . . had stopped, and left / a heavy thick silence in its place."[54]

It was not merely the drudgery and ugliness of hospital work that gnawed at her but the idle chatter that made it difficult to write poetry. Even in these extraordinarily difficult circumstances she learned that human virtue could emerge,[55] but the truth was nursing was not something she enjoyed. After her first year she was both restless and unwilling to sit for the examinations required for further training. Instead she elected to work as an assistant nurse during her final years of service.

Caught up in the routine of work and the effort to avoid the endless rules that governed every aspect of her life, she and her peers, who were generally tougher and more worldly than she was, had great fun trying to outwit the ever-present hospital authorities who made them miserable. All the while she continued to turn out poems, which were published in small magazines such as *Poetry Quarterly*, *Voices*, *Outposts*, and *Gangrel*.

Given the demands of nursing, Denise found scant support for her creative life. However, one affirmation came at Easter 1941, when her father gave her a copy of a bilingual edition of *Fifty Selected Poems* by Rainer Maria Rilke. Soon after, she acquired Rilke's *Letters to a Young Poet*, which captured her imagination and strengthened her belief that she could be a poet. From Rilke she learned that the poetic vocation demanded a modicum of talent and persistence and a willingness to read, write, and experience life deeply. It was not Rilke's style or technique, but his visions, like those of Chekhov, that impressed her. Rilke confirmed what she intuited: the poet wrote from necessity, in order to fulfill his being. External affirmation did not matter. Central to poetry was solitude; it was the only means by which the poet could experience the solitude of the other. In the chattering world of the hospital, Rilke's message was a balm. He became one of her earliest mentors, and even into her seventies she wrote variations on his poems, what she called "Rilking."

Her friendship with others fueled her desire to write poetry. Herbert Read, whom she had met briefly when she was in ballet school, graciously read and critiqued her poems. Charles Wrey Gardiner, editor of *Poetry Quarterly*, began to include more of her work in his publication and to introduce her to Bohemian artists.[56] In her time off from the hospital, she frequented London's Café Royal, a gathering place for artists and Jews. She went there alone, drank coffee, smoked, read books, and met fascinating and bizarre people. This subculture was completely antithetical to both the world of the hospital and that of the Levertoff household. She knew her parents would be horrified by her social life, so she told them nothing.

Later, reflecting on this period of her life, she acknowledged being out of her depth. She confessed to having grown up in an environment that had no sense of Eros. Whatever she knew about romance came from Olga or from literature and art. When she left her family, she claimed to be "defiant & curious" but "unawakened," meaning that her sexual emotions were as of yet "false and sentimental."[57]

One of her new male acquaintances was Bill Rillock, a Communist who also enjoyed music and poetry. She claimed they "were delightfully, 'lyrically' in love for a few weeks." When with her encouragement he became more amorous, she became frightened. Later she analyzed this liaison as "stylized, expected, and rootless in a way."[58] The affair was over quickly and Rillock drifted away, but other affairs followed.

Stimulated by the company of visual artists and having studied drawing when she was younger,[59] she enrolled in an art class at London Polytechnic. From an early age she had expressed interest in painting,[60] and she believed that somehow she could be both poet and painter. This infatuation ended soon, however, when she became besotted with what she called "one of the loves of her life," a young man who was only a few years older than she was.[61] She gave up art to spend every spare moment with Stephen Peet, who had been in the Friends' Ambulance Service and was captured and spent time in a prisoner-of-war camp. Peet, who would go on to be an acclaimed documentary filmmaker, became a lifelong friend and lover.[62] Apparently, at one point in their relationship she was concerned that she might be pregnant. If that had come to pass her parents would have been horrified; they could not endure another experience like the one to which Olga had subjected them.[63]

With a demanding nursing schedule and an active social life, Denise nonetheless continued to write and publish poems throughout the entire period of the war. In 1945, a kindly editor at Sylvan Press suggested she compile her poems into a book-length manuscript, but the Press soon went out of business. When she went to retrieve her manuscript she was buoyed by having learned that she had landed a new nursing job, and with new confidence she walked to the nearby offices of the Cresset Press, maneuvered herself into the publisher's office, and asked to have her manuscript considered for publication. A few days later Cresset's editor, John Hayward, called to say her work had been accepted. She was overcome with gratitude. Finally her "secret destiny" was being realized. She remembered going to a church in Soho to kneel in awe of what was happening to her.[64] This was a first indication of the good fortune that would occur repeatedly in her life.

The Double Image, her little collection of thirty-one poems, was the only one of her books to appear with her family name — Levertoff. A year later Olga's book of poetry, *The Rage of Days*, appeared. In response, Denise changed her family name. Henceforth she would be Denise Levertov. She subsequently recognized the foolishness of this name change,[65] but in the moment she clearly must have wanted to distinguish herself from her sister who was increasingly unpredictable and bizarre in her behavior. Perhaps she also did not want a rival poet in the family. Poetry was *her* domain.

The book's title, *The Double Image*, as well as its organization into two parts — "Fears" and "Promises" — suggested a tension between two realities. Although written during the war, war was not its subject. The subject of war would emerge some twenty years later when it would become a powerful defining event in her life and poetry.

The poems of *The Double Image* are more interesting biographically than poetically. They illustrate her late adolescent understanding of the world as filled both with Edenic joy and portents of violence and evil, the former to be celebrated, the latter to be resisted. Writing in traditional style, she explored the Romantic themes of solitude, self, myth, nature, love, death, and the passage of time. She would say later that her early poems had "in them the seeds of everything that I've done since."[66] The volume's opening poem, "Childhood's End," describes the ending of a paradisiacal youth: "The world alive with love, where leaves tremble, / . . . marking miraculous hours, / is burning round the children where they lie."[67] Other poems reiterate this same theme of the "double image." In "Christmas 1944" she asks: "Who can be happy while the wind recounts / its long sagas of sorrow?"[68] In "To Death," the poem she considered the best in the collection, she metaphorically describes death as an "enviable prince," "eloquent, just, and mighty," one who entered with riches, whose image wore brocade. Death will receive his eager bride, life, who will bring him "a glittering dowry of desire and dreams."[69]

The "double image" became a hallmark of Levertov's poetry. Her early apprehension of life was of joy and wonder, inculcated by her mother and her father, the lover of nature and the fervent Hasidic Jew. She learned to express these emotions in what she called "primal speech," an original, primitive "Ur-language," which showed itself in "triumphant, / wondering, infant utterance."[70] But if she knew bliss from her earliest childhood, she learned of fear and sorrow through both close observation of life and her Hasidic heritage, which urged her to confront the reality of evil. As one living between cultures, she had acute power to see. Her vision was dual. Life was driven by "fears" and by "promises." Olga knew this, as did her orphaned, exiled parents.

The Double Image was published in 1946, but it was not until Kenneth Rexroth included six of her poems in his anthology, *The New British Poets*, in 1949 that her first book received attention.[71] Ironically she discovered a copy of Rexroth's *The Signature of All Things* at the same time she received his letter requesting permission to include a few of her poems in his anthology.[72] Of course she was pleased. Rexroth continued to be a great supporter. He considered her "the baby of the New Romanticism," and her poetry "wistful" like Matthew Arnold's "Dover Beach" or like "the earliest poetry of Rilke or some of the more melancholy songs of Brahms."[73]

To have published a book at age twenty-three was a considerable achievement, but Levertov knew she could not pay her way as a poet. After the war she took a series of dead-end jobs, first in an antique store owned by the father of her friend Betty Mitchell, and then in a book shop where she was incapable of making correct change. Neither was satisfactory employment. At this point she had few options. Although the intent had been for her to attend a university, the war eliminated that possibility. She certainly had no talent or interest in nursing. Postwar London was a dreary place. What confronted her now was a need for work and a way to pursue her life as a poet.

After she broke up with Stephen Peet, she fell in love again, this time with Norman (En) Potter, who would go on to be a successful designer and writer. She affectionately called him "Colin"; he called her "Kristin."[74] It was through En that she met George Woodcock, the poet anarchist, who subsequently reintroduced her to Herbert Read.

In late 1946, Denise decided to take a job as an au pair in Reeuwijk, Holland,[75] with the family of Jerry and Divi Lavies, friends of George Woodcock. She indicated that her plan was to stay there for three months and then to return to England, possibly to marry En.[76] Given that she was apparently in love with En, her departure is difficult to understand. Although she gave no reason for her decision, various factors may have influenced her. She had for some time nurtured a dream of visiting Europe and then America, a place not decimated by war, what she called "the only place fit to enjoy life."[77] Her job prospects in England were bleak, and leaving the country meant that she could escape the problems of Olga and the oversight of parents. But there may have been other reasons to explain her departure.

In early January 1947, Levertov set sail for Holland. It was a brutally cold winter. Fortunately she had a heavy raincoat cinched with a red and white leather Moroccan belt, a discard she found at George Woodcock's flat. The coat offered protection, and her "Monkey," which she took with her, gave solace. Two books, *The Double Image* and Rilke's *Selected Letters*, would provide inspiration. She was leaving behind the problems of family life and the dreariness of postwar England. A new life was at hand, and she greeted it expectantly, buoyed by a sense of destiny and the shining light of her "illustrious ancestors." She could not have known that Europe would provide her a way to America and that America would make her a new kind of poet. Later in her life she realized that her childhood had "foreshadowed" everything that would take place in her adult life.[78] Now that childhood was over.

2

In Search of Voice

1947–1955

And I believe fervently that the poet's first obligation is to his own voice — to find it and use it.

DENISE LEVERTOV TO WILLIAM CARLOS WILLIAMS[1]

The girl who sailed for Holland in January 1947 was barely twenty-three. She left England presumably for adventure, but in doing so she also escaped. She had no suspicion that by year's end her life would change irrevocably.

Her hastily arranged job as an au pair was seemingly a means to an end — the opportunity to travel. But the adventure began inauspiciously. Holland was cold, damp, and ravaged by war. She did not like the food or the Dutch, whom she considered tactless and dull.[2] Her employers were kind, however, and her work of giving English lessons to three teenage children was not taxing. But she was bored, stuck in a house by herself for most of the day in the village of Reeuwijk in a peat-harvesting area near The Hague. At times the boredom was relieved by visits to The Hague, Rotterdam, Haarlem, and Amsterdam, where she reveled in the beauty of the Rembrandts and Vermeers discovered in the art museums of these cities. All in all, she did not regret her decision to come to Holland.

The Levertoffs complained that she wrote infrequently. Terrified at causing her parents further grief — they had had plenty with Olga — and fearing their anger, she offered the excuse that she had the flu. But the reason was otherwise. She was pregnant. Having gone a couple of months without menstruating, she now had morning nausea. The father of the child was En Potter, who was in England and at this point intended to marry Caroline Quennell, one of Denise's friends. It is impossible to know whether Denise suspected a pregnancy prior to her departure for Holland. Although it was unlikely that she did, it would explain the hastily arranged job as an au pair at the home of friends of George Woodcock, who was Potter's friend. Abortion was illegal and hence dangerous in both England and Holland, but at least in Holland, no one would know of her calamity, especially not her parents.

Her diary for February 1947 includes her poem, "The Annunciation."[3] Years later after a reencounter with Potter she wrote another poem, "A Woman Meets an Old Lover." The first draft of the poem reads:

> He who seemed always
> to take & not give, who took me
> so long to forget,
> remembered everything I had so long forgotten.
> Would our child, I had let it be born, [sic]
> have cursed or blessed us?

In its final published form the last sentence of the poem was deleted.[4] Her parents never learned of her clandestine abortion, but it understandably increased her vulnerability. Only later would she acknowledge what had befallen her and how miserable she was. She describes it as a time of "evil," "pain & bankruptcy,"[5] the worst period of her life.[6]

After the death of both of her parents Levertov wrote a fictionalized account of her abortion in a story entitled "Recoveries."[7] Every detail of this dreamlike story matches the record of her brief stay in Holland. The story, told in the third person, is of an English girl who considers herself a poet and who goes to Holland to work as an au pair. The girl is described as "ignorant and naïve and accustomed to behave with dreamy rashness" yet not "without knowledge of possibility." She is at first immobilized by her pregnancy, fearing "the dramatic, tragic, naïve intensity of her elderly parents." For more than a month she lives in a passive state, not knowing what to do. She plods through the cold, gray days without anyone in whom to confide her secret. For weeks she vacillates between believing there is a "ring of protective magic around her" and concluding that she is dreaming and will awake from this nightmare. Finally she tells her employers she needs to see a doctor. Although the girl has previously known sorrow, she has never faced a disaster of this magnitude. Confronted with giving birth or having an abortion, the girl chooses the latter and then takes to her bed, refusing to eat, wanting only to die. But within days she realizes the disaster has passed, and her sense of joy and happiness returns, as well as a "sense of absolute identification with her earliest memories, of seeing things when she was two or three years old with the self-same eyes she looked out of now, a feeling of the continuity of that past with the long future she was walking towards."[8]

What the girl learns is that disaster, while part of life, is not permanent. The incident has been lived through and is over. If "Recoveries" was a fictive but public revelation of her secret, it came many years afterward. In fact, in the aftermath of the actual abortion, Levertov alternated between being miserable or in denial, although to the end of her life she maintained that her decision to abort was the right one.[9] That decision was clearly congruent with her tenaciously held belief that she was a poet and would permit nothing to interfere with that.

Throughout this difficult time she had the companionship of her homunculus, "Monkey," to which she told everything. She called him "pardoner," because he was forgiving and never turned against her. Her only fear was that she might lose him.[10] She also had the solace of Betty Mitchell who found out about the abortion from their mutual friend Caroline, En's girlfriend. Apparently Denise had written to Caroline telling her of the pregnancy and blaming herself; Caroline then told Betty. In a letter written at the end of March 1947, Betty offered to help Denise in this "difficult sexual and emotional muddle." She claimed that it was ridiculous for Denise to blame herself, and that she did not think badly of her. Betty assured her that Caroline, who now had to decide whether or not to marry En, was not angry with her either.[11] Believing that Denise had been associated with unhappy people for too long, Betty urged her to get to know some "simple, real" people, those who were "rooted to the earth." She was skeptical of Denise's plan to travel to America and urged her not to go.[12] A few months later Betty would meet "her dear sister" Denise, and they would travel together in Europe.

At the end of March Denise informed her parents that she was leaving Holland for Paris. Her mood was carefree, and she urged them not to worry about her, promising not to do anything stupid. She was sure that she could find a place to stay in Paris and that she would look for some kind of relief work while she was there. Both Kenneth Rexroth and John Hayward provided Parisian contacts for her.

Because Rexroth had been in touch with her about including some of her poems in his forthcoming *The New British Poets,* Levertov continued to correspond with him while she was in Holland. Although he was seventeen years her senior, she shared her misery and her lonely decision to have an abortion with him. Initially Rexroth was unsympathetic, but when she informed him she wanted to go to Paris, he sent her contact information for French and Russian intellectuals and anarchosyndicalists living there. Rexroth, soon to be separated from his second wife, was utterly charmed by Levertov.[13] As early as February 1947, he wrote Charles Wrey Gardiner in England that he could fall "madly in love with her."[14] Although Levertov and Rexroth would not meet until 1949, he was obviously besotted with her, signing his letters "with love and kisses" and exchanging photographs. She assured him that he was "one of the most important people" to her, and when he indicated he might return to America, Levertov confessed that she hoped to go there as well.[15] Later Rexroth wrote Robert Creeley saying that Levertov was "something they only turn out once in 100 years, one of the few people I ever completely loved at first sight. . . . Everybody, at least all men, who know her speak of her as though they once seen Dante's B[eatr]ice plain."[16]

Denise arrived in Paris in mid-April, and when her money ran out she took a job for a few weeks as a nursemaid. This turned out to be a kind of "slavery," which she escaped only with the help of a friend of Herbert Read. Nonetheless, she was delighted to be in Paris where she explored Montmartre at night, attended concerts, visited museums, and continued to read Rilke. She was leading the life of an artist and was pleased when she learned that a review of *The Double Image* had appeared in *Poetry Quarterly*. She assured "Twain," her parents, that she was having a great time, and playfully signed her letters "Tittles and Monkey." Paris clearly revived her spirits, but the memory of the past months was not obliterated. In her poem "Solace," dated Paris 1947 and dedicated to "N.P.," Norman En Potter, she recalls memory, indifference, and longing.[17] Years later, reflecting on this brief sojourn in Paris, she wrote that N. P. was in her mind like some sort of a "Demon Lover," someone she "couldn't bear not to love."[18]

Denise intended to spend a year in Paris, but as it turned out she stayed less than four months. During that time the news from home was dominated by Olga, whom Denise believed was deranged and no longer responsible for her actions. She urged her parents to take in Olga's children, volunteering to return to London herself to tend them. However, she added that she really did not want to do this.[19] Denise's halfhearted offer went nowhere; if it had, her future and her "secret destiny" might have been compromised. She must have known that to return home was to be stifled.

By early May, thanks to one of Herbert Read's friends who worked with the British Council, Denise secured regular employment in the Hertford British Hospital in Paris. But this came to an abrupt end after only two months when she was fired, ostensibly for not reporting as an honor guard for the visit of the British ambassador. She claimed innocence, but the decision was final. In a letter to her parents she explained that now she could travel in Europe and perhaps go to America.[20] By early August Denise and Betty, who had come over from England, headed to Provence.

Denise was thrilled by this opportunity, even though she had very little money and was reluctant to ask her parents for support, not wanting to be "un-independent" and "Olgaish." She and Betty went first to Avignon and then to Aix-en-Provence, sleeping in haylofts and fields and traveling by hitching rides. They were unafraid and enjoyed themselves immensely. Years later Denise recalled one discreet experience from their travels, a few moments of solace in a village church in Montelimar. In the cool dim interior they heard a choir of cloistered nuns singing a cappella. One single lush voice of an unknown nun rose above the others. She wrote, "we were awed to think of this treasure so hidden."[21]

Three weeks after leaving Paris Denise and Bet arrived in Geneva. They stayed first at a youth hostel and then rented a flat together. Both had secured employment: Denise caring for a baby and teaching English for Berlitz with aspirations of offering ballet lessons; Bet working in a government nursery. By mid-August Denise, fearful that if she returned to England she would not get out again, wrote her parents telling them that she and Bet were settled in Geneva and that she was eager to see the many marvels of the world. Almost as an afterthought she added that they had met a Russian-American from Harvard who might come to visit them when he passed through England. Probably to assuage any parental concern, she wrote she was "not romantic about anyone."[22]

She was, of course, enjoying the company of men in this stimulating Geneva environment. Stephen Peet was there, after working a stint in Czechoslovakia, as were Mitchell Ira Goodman, the Russian-American she had mentioned to her parents, and Stan Karnow, an American journalist who knew Goodman from Harvard. Karnow, in his recollections of this Geneva cabal, referred to Denise Levertov as "a spirited young English woman."[23] Within a short period of time Denise and Mitch paired off as a couple as did Stephen Peet and Bet Mitchell.

Denise and Mitch met initially at the Geneva youth hostel. She quickly began to learn the important particulars of his life. He was her age, born in Brooklyn, New York, and the son of Irving and Adele Rush Goodman. He had a younger brother, Howie, who was in college. At age thirteen Mitch's father emigrated from Latvia and became a successful haberdasher on Canal Street in New York. In the Depression his father lost his money but scraped by financially. His mother, much more highly educated than her husband

FIGURE 4. Mitchell Goodman,
circa 1950. Special Collections,
Stanford University.

and from a well-heeled family of furriers, worked as a schoolteacher. Since
the Goodmans' finances were limited, Mitch enrolled in Harvard as a full-
scholarship student. After university he trained as an artillery officer and
was discharged from the army at the rank of second lieutenant having never
served in combat. Supported by the GI Bill, he enrolled in a doctoral program in labor economics at Harvard and expected to take his exams in the
fall of 1947. In order to augment his small stipend, he wrote newspaper articles about his impressions of Europe. Denise provided additional detail
about Mitch to her parents. He was of Jewish heritage and of a leftist political bent. Physically he was tall, dark, and while she did not think him handsome, neither was he ordinary or sloppy-looking; in fact she thought him
the "cleanest" person she had ever met, always looking well-ironed. He had
an intelligent look about him, a high forehead, and large sad eyes in which
she said one could see all of the tragedy of the Jewish people.[24]

Denise's mid-August letter to Twain about settling into Geneva was followed by a postcard in mid-September and then a letter a month later asking
them for their blessing on her intent to marry Mitch. They had known each
other for two months. He proposed, and she tentatively agreed but wanted
her parents' concurrence. She confessed that she was not romantically in
love with Goodman but that she could visualize their marriage as "something good and happy." She laid out the pros and cons of this arrangement
and added that he had "a real damn-good-honest-to-goodness *character*"
and that Bet thought so, too. Character, she thought, was a sane quality, especially since charm did not have much behind it. She included the detail

that Mitch had pursued her. Initially he left Geneva to return to the United States, but when he reached the French border he returned to look for her.[25] For Denise this was obviously an important sign that he had taken the lead. The Levertoffs responded to Denise's request for agreement to her decision with a telegram that read: "Mazeltov."

Denise's volley back to Twain was to say she and Mitch would be getting married soon at the registry office in Paris with their friends as witnesses. Since it would not be a church wedding, she discouraged them from attending. She added that Mitch was "so real and genuine" that she felt calm and confident in this decision to marry. Seemingly amazed by this positive turn of events, she wrote her parents that when she left England for Holland the previous January, she was "drearily & silently in love with somebody" and if anyone would have told her of her bright future now, she would have laughed.[26]

For his part, Mitch said he came alive when he was with Denise, and his friend Karnow described him as "smitten" with her. The fact that she was of Jewish parentage and her father was a scholar would impress his parents. She already had a first publication to boot. Denise came to their relationship more by default and with the burden of the abortion some seven months earlier. In her calculus Mitch represented above all protection and security, even if she was not conscious of this at the time. Years later she admitted as much and also admitted her fear of angering or disappointing her parents. She wrote in her diary:

> Coming after my experience with En & in Holland, my marriage with M definitely did have an element of grasping at security—because it was marriage—even tho' the bad sexual beginning made it so totally chancy. If I ask "why then did he marry me?" (i.e., if I was not sexually stimulating to him) he might justifiably ask "what was the true basis of your apparent blind faith in me, in everything turning out ok? Were you *using* me to get security after your fright?" I think to a certain extent I was, & I think I was wrong & foolish not to get things worked out between us sexually *before* marriage, the way people do nowadays & a bolder less scared-of-parents person wd have then.[27]

Since she was not sexually attracted to Mitch, there might have been other reasons to marry him. She must have suspected Mitch would be a good spouse. He was educated, had an income, was Jewish and an American, and impressed her as someone of character who would not abandon her. They shared the same intellectual and political orientation. She might have thought: Why not marry? She was not giving up anything, not a job or university, and she was avoiding a return to England, which would bring with it the oversight of parents and the problems of Olga and her children. Marriage, at least, was an anchor. She could continue to write poems and deepen her understanding of her craft. Unfortunately, intervening circumstances would make it impossible for her to produce another volume of poetry for the next nine years.

A little more than three months after they met, Denise and Mitch married on December 2, 1947. There is no evidence of the planned Paris wedding; rather they returned to Ilford where their marriage was registered at the Seven Kings Registry Office. Afterward Paul Levertoff offered Jewish and Christian prayers and blessings at home on Mansfield Road.[28]

During the winter of 1948, they returned to Paris where Mitch enrolled at the Sorbonne, the GI Bill providing them with some limited income. Postwar Paris was still very much in a period of recovery, with labor unrest, food shortages, political instability, and ideological conflict. The city swarmed with immigrants and displaced persons eager to move on to a better life. Psychologically, the French were coping with their complicity with the Nazis and simultaneously attempting to reestablish a new artistic and cultural future. The newly married Goodmans reveled in the city's Bohemian life and took up residence in cheap hotels in the Latin Quarter. For Denise it was a period of discovery and incubation of the seeds of a new poetic life. Norman Mailer, a Harvard acquaintance of Mitch's recalling that winter in Paris, wrote that Denise was "a charming and most attractive dark-haired English girl with a characteristic space between her two front teeth. Everyone called her Dinny. Everyone in Paris liked her. She was pure as a bird, delicate yet firm in conscience." She was the "cheerful wife of the gloomy . . . tall, powerful, handsome, dark-haired" Mitch. Only years later did Mailer realize this "Dinny" was an "exceptional and splendid poet."[29]

It was in Paris that Levertov discovered the poets of America. She had read Whitman and Dickinson; Frost, Sandburg, and Pound in anthologized form; and of course she knew Rexroth's *The Signature of All Things*. But that was all. In the American bookstore on the Rue Soufflot near the Sorbonne, she purchased William Carlos Williams's *Selected Poems*, and elsewhere found a copy of Wallace Stevens's *the Blue Guitar*. Although she was influenced minimally by Stevens's work, Williams was another matter. She read his poems but did not yet understand their rhythmic structure. She explained later: "[T]hough I knew with mysterious certainty that his work would became an essential part of my life, I had not yet heard enough American speech to be able to hear his rhythms properly; his poems were a part of the future, recognized but held in reserve."[30] As Rilke had fostered her vocation as poet, Williams would guide her in her craft; but that help was yet to come.

Although Denise and Mitch planned to remain in Paris, apparently the desire to see Europe before it went "up in smoke again" supplanted their hope to stay in the city. To leave was also indication that Mitch had given up his doctoral work. They began a peripatetic life. In spring 1948 they traveled to Prague but decided it would be too cold there so they left for Florence, which they used as a base to visit Verona, Pisa, Lucca, and Venice. In Florence they frequented the U.S. Information Service library on Via Tornabuoni. There, in an issue of *Poetry*, (Chicago), Levertov found a review by Muriel Rukeyser of Robert Duncan's *Heavenly City, Earthly City*. When Levertov left Florence she took the magazine with her, the first step toward an intimate relationship with an important mentor in Duncan and a friend in Rukeyser.[31]

Florence, too, proved to be cold and damp, so like nomads they headed south to Rome, Naples, and Taormina. In Sicily, Levertov encountered the shrouded Mount Etna, one of the great mountains to claim her attention over her lifetime. Earlier in her life on a hunt for mushrooms with her mother in the Welsh countryside, she was startled to see a mountain looming some fifty miles away out of the landscape. Here was Eryi, Snowdon, "home / of eagles, resting place of / Merlin, core of Wales."[32] Later Provence's Mont Sainte Victoire, Cézanne's beloved subject, would inspire her, and toward the end of her life the elusive Mount Rainier on the edge of North America would draw her in.

Once the cold weather abated, the Goodmans left Sicily to return again to Paris. Although they loved the City of Light, claiming it gave them a heightened sense of both individuality and anonymity,[33] by the end of May 1948, they decided to move to New York. America was home for Mitch, and Denise had always wanted to go there. Family would welcome them and there would be work. Before they left Paris, however, they met James Laughlin, editor at New Directions publishing house, who was visiting there. He invited them to look him up once they arrived on the other side of the Atlantic. Again, it was Rexroth who arranged this important connection.

As they moved about, Denise did not correspond regularly with her parents. Feeling abandoned and shut out, Twain complained. In order to make amends she began to write them long descriptive letters about her travels and her happy marriage. She told them that she was writing poetry and had cut back on her smoking. She shared with her mother the secret that right after her marriage she experienced a miscarriage but this had worked to bring her and Mitch closer together.[34] Since her parents were beleaguered by the demands of Olga and her children, Denise urged them to leave England in order to protect themselves. Mitch sometimes appended notes to his wife's letters, explaining how intensely involved they were with each other and how their togetherness helped them love life to the fullest.

In her diaries Denise recorded other observations about Mitch, herself, and their relationship. She saw Mitch as a person who was generous of mind and heart, modest, and full of self-respect; he was not neurotic or religiously or socially prejudiced, qualities she believed characterized most English and European men. Mitch made her life joyful, particularly compared to the pain she experienced in Holland. In the entries of this period she confronted her own profound sense of insecurity. She saw herself as defensive and hysterical, undeserving of Mitch. Although he should "despise" her, she hoped she could grow more deserving of him over time. "The fact he has chosen to love me," she wrote, "gives me self-respect." And as an aside, but a portent of what was to come, she recorded that Rilke said that married people should not become absorbed in each other but should have a relationship with the society in which they live.[35]

Having decided to leave Europe for America, in September 1948 the Goodmans first went to England to visit the Levertoffs, adding a side trip to Wales. Finally at the end of October they boarded an army ship for New York City. At age twenty-five Denise was finally on her way to America, and her joy was double in that she knew she was pregnant.

But New York City was a shock. Initially they rented a hotel room in Greenwich Village, the center of Bohemian culture in America. Beginning in the 1940s the Village attracted international artists of every sort. Actors, musicians, writers, and painters flocked there. Cafes sprang up everywhere, providing opportunities for writers, particularly poets, to read their work. Although the Village was the lively capital of alternative culture, Levertov encountered it as dirty, littered, and decaying with drunks lying in the streets. The place overwhelmed her. She found the city alien and terrifying, and she was not at all sure she had arrived in the place of her dreams. A few years later in the poem "An Innocent," she wrote of some of her impressions, recalling a scavenger picking through refuse and his rebuke of those who watched him.[36]

The Goodmans soon rented a little three-room walkup apartment at 52 Barrow Street for fourteen dollars a month. They painted the place, trying to make it their own, but there were inconveniences. The toilet was in the hall, and the shower was rigged up over the kitchen sink. In order to climb in, one had to stand on a chair. Denise did not enjoy housework, but she learned to cook and that gave her some pleasure. They were welcomed by Mitch's parents and brother and an assortment of his Harvard friends, including Robert Creeley. Denise made her first American woman friend, Barbara Bank, who would later marry the painter Howard Fussiner. Another new friend was Al Kresch, whose artistic work Denise memorialized in a poem, "Kresch's Studio."[37] Her relationships with painters, those in the past like Cézanne and in the present like Fussiner and Kresch, give indication of her lifelong interest in the visual arts.

Since their apartment was small, Denise and Mitch went out frequently to the library, concerts, and museums. They haunted bookstores, and on a side table in the nearby Phoenix Bookshop on Cornelia Street Denise found a copy of Robert Duncan's *Heavenly City, Earthly City*, marking the commencement of years of admiration for this poet she would later call "master" and "mentor."

Although they had very limited resources, Denise and Mitch always found enough money to do what they enjoyed. They were happy given there was so much to think about, to see, to write, to read, and, of course, there was preparation for the baby, who was due to arrive soon.[38]

During this period the Levertoffs' letters from England were full of lament about Olga. In 1945 Olga, who had now parted from Tom Strudwick, deposited her three younger children in Catholic orphanages near Leeds. She never saw them again, and the three lived as orphans until the age of majority.[39] Olga continued to care for her eldest daughter Iris,[40] and at one point in the early 1950s the two of them lived with the Levertoffs in Ilford. But mostly Olga was out of touch, disappearing without word. Given her parents' difficult situation, Denise lobbied to have them visit New York. She tried to secure a teaching position for her father at Union Theological Seminary and opportunities for him to preach in New York City, but nothing came of this.

One of the big events of 1949 was the publication of Rexroth's anthology, *The New British Poets*, which included six of Denise's poems and mention of her in the introduction.[41] Rexroth hailed her as an up-and-coming young British poet, although by this point she had cast her lot on the other side of the Atlantic and it would be there that she would re-create herself not as an American poet but as sui generis.

Levertov's transition to America would be made possible by several mentors — Robert Creeley, William Carlos Williams, and Robert Duncan — but

Rexroth was her first advocate, the one who connected her with James Laughlin and hence to New Directions, the press that subsequently would publish almost all of her work. Disappointed when he learned Levertov had married,[42] Rexroth finally met Denise and Mitch in person when he visited in New York in April 1949. A year or so later he wrote to Creeley, "maybe I am jealous of her husband."[43] Although disappointed he had not snagged Denise as his wife, Rexroth remained her supporter, much as he was of other women poets.[44]

Denise and Mitch waited expectantly throughout the spring of 1949 for the delivery of their child, the second big event of the year. Before the birth, Denise wrote the poem "Who He Was," in which she rejoices in this baby, who she knows will experience darkness but hopes will have love as a constant in his life.[45] On June 11, 1949, Nikolai Gregor Goodman was born. He was a chubby baby with a big appetite. Soon after Denise left the hospital they headed to Vermont. This was the beginning of their summer vacation routine. Mitch would buy an old car at the beginning of the summer and they would head for New England. This particular summer they visited the Creeleys in the White Mountains of New Hampshire and spent the rest of the summer in Maine, returning to Barrow Street in September, at which point Mitch sold the car. Since they lived on GI Bill allotments, money was very limited. Mitch had been trying to get an advance from a publisher, but as a stop-gap he sold clocks at Macy's department store, hoping that he would soon find employment with the Department of Welfare.

Baby Nik flourished. He sang and talked and gave his parents pleasure. Although Mitch's parents sometimes helped care for him on the weekends, the cumulative pressures of the baby, very little money, and the demands of city life were overwhelming, particularly for Denise. She felt oppressed by the stupid, vulgar, and materialistic hordes of people in the city. She was exhausted, depressed, and numb and complained that six months after Nik's birth she had written only one poem. By March 1950, she was feeling a bit improved, but she had great anxiety about Mitch's future. She saw their lives being diminished by ordinary minutia. They had no time for rest and no solitude to appreciate beauty. Their senses of seeing and hearing were less intense, and their sexual encounters less frequent. She feared Mitch was being "drawn under" by their lives and that she had hurt him by her bad temper. In her diary she admonished herself to be aware when she felt her "black venom rising" lest she hurt him and kill his gentle and sweet loving nature. At that point they had been married two and a half years.[46]

Life did not improve. She described the period after Nik's birth as "a drab nightmare." When he began to walk, they found their apartment cramped; neither of them could do any substantial writing. Wanting to move, they fixed on southern France as a place where they could have greater leisure to write. In July 1950, Mitch sent a letter to the Levertoffs asking if they would make them a loan so that they could travel to London and introduce them to their grandson. They would then go on to Provence.

The visit to England was mixed. Denise claimed that the best part was seeing Olga and feeling close to her and not finding her "crazy or maddening or jealousy-provoking." But her parents were sad. Her father had great anxiety about impending old age, and Denise thought Beatrice was judgmental of her as a mother. She wrote, "I came to mother full of love — & she I know waited as full of it — but there was some barrier almost of *dislike* on her part, I seemed to feel — hurtful & numbing."[47] After this visit, Paul Levertoff became ill, and letters from both her parents seemed cold. Denise hoped that her parents' planned visit with them in Europe would be a happier experience.

The year in Provence was beneficial, and Denise's spirits improved. It was during this time she began recording her dreams, a practice she kept up for decades. They lived in Puyricard, a village outside of Aix-en-Provence where natural beauty, the vistas of the towering Mont Sainte Victoire, and the ease of life were therapeutic. Mitch produced travel articles for the *New York Times*, Denise wrote poetry, and Nik attended a little school run by nuns. One of Denise's memories from that year was her eight-kilometer bicycle ride into Aix-en-Provence one hot summer day to visit Cézanne's studio. Finding the place much as he left it in 1906, her childhood memory of discovering Cézanne and his joy of making art was reignited.[48] It was Cézanne's vocational tenacity, expressed in preoccupation with Mont Sainte Victoire, which would inspire her throughout her life.[49]

One of the important events of this year was her relationship with Robert Creeley and Ann Mackinnon, who rented a house near their village. The two couples had visited several times in New England, but this proximity allowed them to spend many leisurely hours in an orchard in conversation — Robert with Mitch about prose; Robert with Denise about poetry.[50] In her memoir of this period Ann Mackinnon described Denise as beautiful with dreamlike qualities but also strident. Mackinnon allowed that she thought her husband was in love with Denise and that Mitch was "kindly," "vague," and "a bit lazy."[51]

Creeley proved to be an early and important advocate for Levertov. He introduced her to Ezra Pound, whose extreme political views she tried to ignore — and to Cid Corman, poet and founder of the new poetry magazine *Origin*. Thanks to Creeley's support, Corman agreed to publish one of Levertov's poems in the 1951 issue of his magazine. Others followed in 1952, and in 1953, six more appeared in subsequent issues.[52] Creeley also suggested Denise contact his friend, William Carlos Williams, the acclaimed Modernist poet and pediatrician. She seized on this idea and sent an unannounced letter to Williams, much as she had to Eliot years earlier. Williams responded with humility to her missive of admiration. Although Creeley obviously helped her, his attitude toward Levertov was complex, and there was tension between them. He was sexually attracted to her but found her irritating, hostile, excessively self-confident, and too bourgeois. As time went on they each began to distrust the other.[53]

The Goodmans left Puyricard in August 1951 and moved to Sori near Genoa on the Ligurian coast. After much delay, the Levertoffs came to visit for twelve days in January 1952, right before Denise and Mitch were to return again to New York. It was a good visit, but unbeknown to Denise it would be the last time she would see her father.

The Goodmans returned to America reluctantly. New York City was a very expensive place to live, and Denise thought the country had a "disgusting political atmosphere." On arrival they stayed initially with Mitch's parents in the Flatbush area of Brooklyn, but Denise hated this arrangement and felt suffocated. They soon moved back to Barrow Street. Nik was almost three now and in school a full day. Mitch and Denise shared household duties: he did the dishes, made the beds, and did the shopping. She prepared supper, washed the clothes, and put Nik to bed. Financially, life was difficult. To help with expenses and pay the seventeen dollar-a-month rent, Denise began working at St. Vincent's Hospital and then at a cancer hospital. However, she found nursing too preoccupying and looked for other employment — first as a proofreader, which was easier and calmer, and then as an after-school child-tender. Although bored and frustrated by these menial jobs, she was grateful that they allowed her to Americanize her speech.

For his part Mitch worked on his novel and wrote travel articles. He turned down a civil service job in New Jersey ostensibly because they did not want to transfer Nik from his school. Their financial situation continued to be perilous and was made more so by Mitch's parents' need for financial support. As they could, they tried to supplement his parents' income. Denise's parents also had difficult problems. Both of them had been ill and needed surgery — her father for a hernia and her mother for gallstones — and they continued to be preoccupied with Olga. Denise urged her parents to leave

Olga, whom she referred to as "a self-inflicted torture" to herself, and to sell their house and move to Vermont. As if this double parental concern were not enough for them, Nik, now four years old, was in a general state of revolt most of the time, throwing tantrums and screaming.

Some relief came the following year. They moved to 249 West 15th Street near Chelsea to the same building in which Barbara Bank had an apartment. The place had more room than their Barrow Street apartment, but it was in a rough neighborhood, as Denise's poem "15th Street" indicates.[54] In letters to her husband Denise wrote of how his love and respect made her feel capable of almost anything, strengthening her core, self-respect, and courage.[55] She recorded a specific incident that expressed her husband's love. Heartbroken and weeping at the loss of her beloved "Monkey," Mitch, in an effort to console her, put up flyers at subway stops, placed an ad in the *Herald Tribune*, and spent hours searching for this "pardoner." Lamentably, "Monkey" never materialized.[56] One tension between them was Denise's desire to have her husband finish his novel, *The End of It*. He procrastinated interminably. He would leave the city for the country in order to write and then would want Denise to come and be with him. He suggested that she quit her job, their principal source of income, so that he would not be alone.[57] It was a great relief when Little Brown took a first option on his book and advanced him three hundred and fifty dollars.[58]

The significant events of the year for Levertov involved the beginning of two friendships that would change her personal and professional life. She had corresponded with William Carlos Williams since the end of 1951, but she did not meet him until two years later when she took a bus to his home in Rutherford, New Jersey. At this time he was a seventy-year-old, well-established medical doctor and important American poet. Since she disliked using the telephone, her argument being that gesture was necessary for communication and hence the caller needed to see her,[59] she mostly was in touch with Williams by letter or in person. Their friendship continued in this way for ten years until Williams's death in 1963. Reflecting on his impact on her, she wrote, "I was reading a great deal and taking in at each breath the air of American life. William Carlos Williams became the most powerful influence on my poetry at that time."[60] The elderly Williams was very fond of her, and she considered him a "wonderful friend" and a "gateway" into her development as a poet.[61]

Her other friendship, in this case with Robert Duncan, was more intense. Levertov had admired Duncan's work ever since she first read Rukeyser's review of his *Heavenly City, Earthly City*. Their friendship began when Duncan read her poem "The Shifting,"[62] in *Origin,* and wrote her a humorous fan letter-poem. Perplexed by the letter and thinking it mocked her poem, she was nonetheless intrigued by the cryptic signature, "R. D." She sent an inquiry as to whether R. D. might really be *the* Robert Duncan.[63] It was, and a friendship of poetic intimacy began, mostly carried out through a voluminous correspondence that included more than 450 letters. Although from the beginning, unspoken differences existed between the two, these went unexplored. For twenty years Levertov had in Duncan a mentor and confidant of inestimable value, one who helped her develop as a poet.

Levertov's incipient connection with American poets was strengthened when her poem "Merritt Parkway" appeared in 1954 in the newly established *Black Mountain Review.*[64] Edited by Creeley, the *Review* was an off-shoot of the Black Mountain College experiment in North Carolina.[65] Although it had only seven issues, the *Review* fostered interest in the so-called Black Mountain poets who clustered around Charles Olson and included Duncan, Creeley, Levertov, and Hilda Morley, among others.[66]

Just as Levertov was expanding her connections in the artistic world, she and Mitch were besieged by a welter of problems. During 1954 and 1955, Paul Levertoff died and Beatrice came to live with them; their financial situation remained tenuous, Nik was increasingly difficult to control, and tension frayed their marriage.

Denise learned of the seriousness of her father's condition in January 1954. In May she wrote her mother to say that she and Mitch could come to England only for an emergency and to tell her father that they would read all his books, something she had previously refused to do. In a letter to her father written a few months before his death she confessed:

> [Y]ou know my feelings about religion are pretty indefinite and I hate hypocrisy & dishonesty. I am unable to practice the forms of what I don't wholeheartedly believe, even if I respect it, and even if emotionally I have the impulse to do so; however Nik insisted that I deliver aloud a formal prayer, so I looked up a Collect for the sick & read it to him much to his satisfaction and mine.[67]

In another letter, written from Vermont where they were summering, Denise wrote that she admired her mother for her courage and she loved her "Daddy" and would remember all he had said to her.[68] On August 2nd a telegram arrived informing her that her father had died on July 31st and would be buried on August 5th. Denise wrote tearfully to her mother of her resentment toward Mitch for not being able to provide money for her to go to England for the funeral. When asked to contribute to the fund for Reverend Levertoff's brass memorial, they declined, saying the money would be better spent to bring Mrs. Levertoff to America.[69]

Paul Levertoff had always been a distant, remote figure to his daughter. She wanted protection and engagement from him, but this was never forthcoming. In the poem "In Obedience," which she called "an elegy for my father," she wrote,

> I dance
> for joy, only for joy
> while you lie dying, into whose eyes
> I looked seldom enough, all the years,
> seldom with candid love.   Let my dance
> be mourning then,
> now that I love you too late.[70]

Without knowing of his dying, Denise danced for her father in Vermont. At the same time, he apparently rose from his bed and did the same. Olga Levertoff records this same phenomenon — "the death-dance of one holy Jew!" in her poem "The Ballad of My Father":

> *My father danced a Hassidic dance the day before he died.*
> *His daughters they were far away, his wife was by his side.*
> . . . .
> *So he danced in his joy as he did when a boy*
> *and as often he danced for me.*[71]

While Olga remembered a father who danced for her, Denise remembered her inability to respond with affection. She loved him, indeed, too late.

After her father's death Denise's religious skepticism softened. Although she wrote, "I must say the organized church is as unattractive to me as ever,"[72] his death brought a modification of her views. Now instead of being "regretfully skeptical" she claimed to be "tentatively non-skeptical."[73] The principal consequence of this attitude was that she and Mitch developed a greater interest in Hasidism and began to read her father's writings as she had promised. For the first time in his life Mitch began to think of himself as Jewish. For Denise's thirty-first birthday he gave her a two-volume set of *Tales of the Hasidim,* by the Jewish mystical philosopher Martin Buber.

When they told Norman Mailer of this find, he purchased both volumes. The Goodmans were particularly delighted to find in *Tales of Hasidim* a substantial amount of material on Schneour Zalman, Denise's ancestor. *Tales* stimulated Mitch and her to read the Bible and other books by Buber, as well as to join a Jewish book club.[74] Many years later she attested to the importance of the Hasidic sense of wonder in her life. She told an interviewer:

> Hasidism has given me since childhood a sense of marvels, of wonder. The Hasidim were a bit like the Franciscans; although in both movements there was also a very great strain of asceticism, yet along with it there was recognition and joy in the physical world. And a sense of wonder at creation, and I think I've always felt something like that . . . I think that's what poems are all about.[75]

Two of her subsequent books of poetry, *The Jacob's Ladder* and *O Taste and See*, clearly reflect the influence of her new appreciation of the Hasidic tradition passed down through her father from her "illustrious" ancestor Schneour Zalman.

Denise's main preoccupations after her father's death were Nik's continued erratic behavior, their poor financial situation, and the integration of her mother into their family life. This dismal situation was relieved a bit by a visit in early 1955 by Robert Duncan, who stopped in New York on his way from San Francisco to Mallorca with his partner, the painter Jess Collins. Their animated conversation invigorated Levertov, and she was sorry to see them leave. Her friendship with Duncan would be her touchstone, and Collins would collaborate with her subsequently in illustrating her little book, *Five Poems*.

But family problems persisted. When Nik was five years old, reports from his school indicated that he had bad social-relations skills and outbursts of anger. Denise worried that if he did not improve, he would need to see a psychiatric social worker. Fortunately Trinity School provided such assistance. Gradually Nik improved and was a bit easier to handle. But in a letter to Williams she confided that she was afraid that Nik's life would be "stormy," as he took "everything pretty hard."[76]

Their financial situation remained bleak. Mitch's freelance writing had become less dependable, and in early 1955, since he was almost finished with his novel, he thought about getting a job, but nothing came of this. Denise, in the meantime, found employment in a greeting-card store. Even though office jobs paid more, this one was less boring.

Denise's big project was helping her seventy-year-old mother extricate herself from England to America. To expedite her mother's visa, Denise became a naturalized citizen. She later wrote that she regretted this but then thought of Williams, Wallace Stevens, and Jefferson,[77] Americans she admired. Prior to her arrival, Beatrice wrote affectionate letters to her daughter and son-in-law addressing them as "Twain Junior" or "Darling Trio," or in the case of Denise, "Tit Darling." But Beatrice had ambivalent feelings about leaving England. On the one hand she was concerned about Olga; on the other she wanted to escape her eldest daughter's problems. Denise assured her that just because one could have pity for Olga as a "schizophrenic,"[78] one was not obliged to help her. In fact she now considered Olga beyond their help. Beatrice was also reluctant to be a burden on Denise and Mitch, but Denise argued that she would be a great help as a built-in babysitter. Privately, Denise worried that they all might not get along, especially because of her poor housekeeping skills. But as it turned out, housekeeping proved to be the least of the problems. Beatrice arrived in New York in early May but soon after became ill and needed two operations. Convinced that her mother would not be happy in the city — it was too ugly, dirty, and noisy, and without a garden — Denise and Mitch decided at the end of June 1955 to move again, this time to Guadalajara, Mexico, where they hoped to have more time to be creative and to live more inexpensively.

Before their departure they headed to Vermont for the summer. Beatrice was out of the hospital and on the mend, but Nik contracted chicken pox and had no one with whom to play. Because he was constantly under foot, neither Mitch nor Denise got much work accomplished. They left Vermont and returned to New York in September. Throughout this period Denise was studying Spanish in preparation for their departure to Mexico.

Levertov found it difficult to write during the years of Nik's childhood. She confessed to Williams that this was because she let herself get bogged down by the roles of mother and housewife, which "exasperate, defeat, & bore" her. She contended that her desire to be honest led her to refuse to write unless she had something to say, and because she lacked an interesting mind and was unintelligent, and only "erratically possessed," her creative output was minimal.[79]

Although she felt trapped by the conditions of her life, others were urging her to take on new projects. Earlier Cid Corman proposed she compile her poems into a book, which he would publish with *Origin Editions* in Paris, but lack of funding ensured that the project never came to fruition. Subsequently, Williams and Creeley encouraged her to develop a collection of poems, and Rexroth indicated he would suggest to James Laughlin at New Directions that he publish her work. Encouraged by this support, she applied for a Guggenheim Foundation Grant and asked Williams for a recommendation. While not yet successful in the grant process, her confidence, fragile for so many years, was now increasing. This preliminary request for support from Guggenheim, repeated later, would ultimately come to a positive result.

Mitch, on the other hand, was not having such good fortune. The Little Brown publishing option had fallen through, and now he did not have a publisher for his novel. He traveled to Europe in the fall of 1955 and sent letters to Denise affirming not only his affection for her but the fact that apart from her he did not feel whole. Because of her, Mitch said he was a new person; meeting her was a new beginning for his life.[80]

Denise's affection for Mitch was more erratic. Prior to their leaving for Mexico she had a two-week affair with John Day, a man who unbeknown to her had loved her for a long time. She confessed to falling in love with him even though she knew she would probably never see him again. She "unburdened" herself about this affair to both Williams and Duncan in letters she wrote soon after her arrival in Guadalajara. She came to realize, however, that she loved Mitch, was committed to their marriage and to the care of Nik, and was sure she would live through all of this. Nonetheless she was confused and miserable.[81] A year later she wrote to Duncan, remembering the anniversary of her parting from John Day "on the corner of Christopher St. & 7th Avenue W."[82] In her poem "The Third Dimension," in which she recalls this affair, she explores the limits of simple honesty: "[B]ut love / cracked me open / / and I'm / alive to / tell the tale but not / honestly:"[83] Years later when an interviewer queried her about this poem, she said it "was a poem about falling in love with someone although I still loved my husband, and about the inexplicableness of this. It wasn't 'mystical.' It was just about how complicated life is."[84]

This affair is revelatory of Levertov's own self-understanding and the state of her marriage to Mitch, who might well have had his own liaisons, although Denise does not mention this in her diaries. Denise was profoundly insecure, something she recognized in herself. This insecurity manifested itself in her "black venom" rages when she felt her world out of control, but also in her deep need for external approval. When someone, especially a male, took the lead and expressed admiration for her as a poet and a woman, she responded passionately. Years later she wrote in her diary about her affair with John Day: "The charm of JD was definitely that he woo'd me, took the lead. What was wrong with it was that though he seemed to have devotion to me he didn't have a very full image of who I was, so the 'acceptance' was somehow lacking."[85] What she wanted was to be pursued, and unfortunately Mitch, who was increasingly depressed as Denise's success increased, was incapable of doing that. This impossible dynamic was at the heart of their marital problems, which were already full blown before they left for Mexico.

Over the next five years Levertov finally came into her own. She would publish four books of poetry and be included in Donald Allen's pioneering study, *The New American Poetry*, the only woman among the fifteen poets to contribute a statement on poetics. Her early years in America were ones of incubation, of developing the techniques of her craft, and of making important contacts in the world of American poetry. One of the most important factors in her ascendancy was the support she received from mentors.

Herbert Read, John Hayward, and Charles Wrey Gardiner were early advocates for her in England. Kenneth Rexroth, Cid Corman, James Laughlin, William Carlos Williams, Robert Creeley, and Robert Duncan were their American counterparts. But these expressions of support and inspiration were built on a foundation that she carried with her from her early life. She could not have responded to the opportunities that America offered unless she had been prepared and willing to become a new kind of poet. Her greatest preparation came through Rilke, her constant companion since 1941.

Although she was influenced in her youth by the poetry of Keats, Wordsworth, Blake, Tennyson, and later Gerard Manley Hopkins, it was Rilke who had primacy; it was he who shaped her ideas about the nature of her craft and the vocation of poet. References to Rilke riddled her poetry and prose, and she continued to refer to him throughout her life. In a later essay, "Rilke as Mentor," she recognized her profound debt to him:

> Thus all the useful and marvelously stimulating technical and aesthetic tendencies that I came upon in the 1950s were absorbed into a ground prepared not only by my English and European cultural background in general but more particularly by Rilke's concept of the artist's task — a serious, indeed a lofty, concept.[86]

Beginning in 1947, Denise made an index of Rilke's *Selected Letters*, mining them for inspiration to sustain and reinforce the ideas she held instinctually. From him she absorbed the notion that the poet wrote from necessity and that each poem and each of its lines "needed" to be written. Rilke confirmed her sense that solitude was imperative for the poet's inner development and ability to grasp the otherness of life. She characterized Rilke's style as "reverent, passionate, and comprehensive." His reverence led him to concrete and sensuous images; his passion brought him to internalize experience; and his comprehensiveness helped him bridge the gap between art and life. Rilke was the single most profound poetic influence in her life.

If Levertov had been asked for the second most important influence of this early period, she would have responded: Williams. Later she wrote it was in him that she found "a Franciscan sense of wonder that illumines what is accounted ordinary"[87] When she first came to America, she was somewhat embarrassed by the vague, dreamy poems of *The Double Image*, what she considered creations of her adolescent mind. She came to admire the American poets — Wallace Stevens, Pound, Emerson, and Whitman, although she found the American-born Eliot lacking vitality in diction and rhythm[88] — but none of them offered what she needed. She was flummoxed by American speech patterns, rhythms, and usage and wanted to find a way to write naturally, to embrace ordinary subjects and discover what was already there in concrete experience. In short, she wanted her new life in America and her art to intersect, but she had neither the language nor know-how to do this. She was immediately attracted to Williams with his interest in the local, the present, and the lives and speech of ordinary people.[89] Williams became her model for anchoring poetry in life and using the vernacular in service of her craft. His importance was that "he showed us the rhythms of speech *as poetry*."[90] If Williams changed her poetry, he also changed her life. It was he who showed her how one could be a poet while leading an ordinary life. She said:

> [H]e helped me deal with being a grown woman, with a husband and baby and very little money, in a strange country, a strange city (New York) and a language which, though ostensibly the same in which I had grown up, was in fact different in pace, rhythm, and nuance.[91]

Incapacitated by a stroke, Williams nonetheless continued to serve as both a father figure and mentor urging her to "practice, practice, and practice." He warned her of the great personal cost of being a poet, especially for a woman:

> It may be that women are different from men in that, they may have to strip themselves barer than men do, the history of Sappho seems to indicate it — nothing held back, absolutely nothing, complete incon-

tinence, but the cost is exorbitant. Women can rarely do it, they are physically ruined. Not that they should not be but the cost is more than can endure. And nothing less than completely laying themselves bare is any good.[92]

Williams knew the rigors of the poetic life, and he was well aware that women faced particular burdens. The most notable American poets in the 1950s were men. H. D. (Hilda Doolittle), Marianne Moore, Louise Bogan, and Elizabeth Bishop were the exceptions. Publishers and editors were men too. In the new generation of American poets of the fifties, Levertov was unique — foreign born and female — she stood almost alone in a world in which contemporary feminism had not yet been born.[93]

As she acknowledged her debt to Rilke in a series of essays, she would do the same for Williams.[94] She would also give public praise to another mentor, Robert Duncan.[95] Erudite, cosmopolitan, and opinionated, Duncan was a poet, public intellectual, and key figure in the San Francisco Renaissance of the 1950s. He was a force to be reckoned with. Duncan, along with Charles Olson, Robert Creeley, Levertov, and a few others, came to be called Black Mountain poets. All had been influenced by Williams and Pound, were published in *Origin* and *The Black Mountain Review*, were opposed to the closed form of poetry associated with the New Critics, and were committed to the ideas articulated by Olson, namely to "projective verse," which put emphasis on the process of writing itself, and "composition by field," which deemphasized subjectivity and projected a poem's energy directly to the reader.

Otherwise the conjoining of this diverse group was tenuous. In fact Levertov never visited Black Mountain College and met with these fellow poets only on rare occasions.

Of this group Duncan had the greatest stature in Levertov's estimate. She admired his vast knowledge and was encouraged by their agreement on poetic concerns, but this did not explain her personal affection for him, which bordered on awe. She said: "No matter what anybody else said and however much praise and approval I got from other quarters, if I didn't have his, it didn't mean much to me. He was like my touchstone."[96] Although years later this intimate relationship would change dramatically, in her early years in America Levertov would continually seek Duncan's professional and personal approval.

By the end of 1955, Levertov's long period of incubation as a poet was over. Grounded in the inspiration of Rilke, she came to America and found her poetic voice thanks to Williams and a coterie of contemporary poets who sustained her. Increasingly she was clear about her vocation, and her technical command of her craft improved. As she indicated later, she believed coming to America where poetry was very much alive was crucial for her development.[97] Levertov would now express herself in an outpouring of poems and the honing of her poetic vision. The next years would be crucial to the making of Levertov as a poet.

The Making of a Poet
1956–1961

> I believe poets are instruments on which the power of poetry plays.
> "STATEMENT ON POETICS"[1]

High in the mountains of Greece a perilous road leads to Delphi, the sacred center of the world, the place where heaven and earth meet. There in 1961 Denise Levertov took her "final vows" to poetry at the shrine of Apollo, praying that the flame of the poem be kept alive in her. Although she became violently ill when she drank water from a nearby brackish spring, she nonetheless sang and danced. She speculated that perhaps it was not Apollo who heard her, but another god, Dionysus, the one she claimed as name-patron.[2] She was thirty-eight, and the power of poetry played in her. Her vocation was irrevocable.

The years prior to this vocational clarity were filled not only with the cares of family life but the opportunity to acclimate herself in America and to hone her craft. After the publication of *The Double Image*, Levertov episodically wrote poems for a number of small magazines, but beginning in the mid-1950s a torrent of writing poured forth. Within six years she published *Here and Now* (1956), *Overland to the Islands* (1958), *With Eyes at the Back of Our Heads* (1960), and *The Jacob's Ladder* (1961). This productivity led to her being lauded as one of the "new American poets." She had talent and tenacity, but she also had access to mentors and abundant good fortune.

Levertov began corresponding with William Carlos Williams in 1951. Several years later, after *Here and Now* was published, he confessed that he was "a little in awe of her" and had not realized how good a poet she was.[3] He claimed she had "the perfect driving disposition for a poet, and I think the depth of human experience on which to draw from." "The poet is the only one who has not lost his way and you are a poet. We must look to you. Keep

on doing what you are already doing for us."[4] He said he felt closer to Levertov than to any other modern poet.[5]

When Williams read *With Eyes at the Back of Our Heads*, he wrestled with
deciphering her secret:

> It may be druidic or perhaps an hebraic [*sic*] recrudescence but it's
> impressive and good for the art of poetry. You have the head for it, an
> impressive head which I have been long conscious of but that's only an
> accessory phenomenon, that curious artistic ability that flares in the
> words themselves is the thing to be treasured. It may at any time be
> lost, see that it isn't at any cost![6]

In his 1960 recommendation of Levertov for a Guggenheim Fellowship,
her second application, Williams indicated that ultimately she would be
considered "one of the most distinguished artists of her time."[7] Such accolades must have gone a long way to win her the Fellowship.

Robert Duncan, in his preface to *Overland to the Islands*, was effusive in
his praise: "In the dance of word and phrase to express feeling, in the interior music of vowels, in subtlety of changing tempo within the form, in the
whole supple control in freedom, she excels."[8]

Kenneth Rexroth, who Levertov called her "discoverer," described her
as "wise," "humane," "unique," "incomparable," the best of the new poets,
one with "an infallible ear," "a clear, sparse, immediate and vibrant" style, a
Neo-Romantic, and the leader of the generation of revolt against Eliot and
his ilk.[9]

Support for Levertov by these mentor poets was paralleled by encouragement from publishers. Levertov suspected it was Rexroth who brought
her work to the attention of Weldon Kees. Although Kees agreed to publish
her work, his unexpected suicidal death in 1955 meant her manuscript was
in limbo until it was picked up about a year later, again at the suggestion
of Rexroth, by Larry Ferling, aka Lawrence Ferlinghetti. Ferlinghetti, a
Beat poet and publisher, wanted to include Levertov in his new City Lights
Pocket Series. Jonathan Williams, himself a poet who had been influenced
by Williams, Pound, Olson, and Creeley, also hoped to publish her work.
In an effort to respond to both of these men, Levertov offered Ferlinghetti
first choice of her poems and gave the remainder, plus some new work, to
Jonathan Williams.[10] But her real breakthrough occurred, again thanks to
Rexroth, when James Laughlin, founder of New Directions, a publishing
house for avant-garde poetry and prose, brought out her *With Eyes at the*

Back of Our Heads. The opening poem of this volume would win the Bess Hokin Prize for poetry, a portent of Levertov's future success. The volume's title had its origin in a saying of Beatrice Levertoff, but for the poet herself, "the eyes in the back of our heads" referred to the inner eyes.[11] Supported by these mentors and publishers, Denise Levertov was now a poet to be watched. But it was her inclusion in Donald Allen's anthology, *The New American Poetry*, in 1960 that cemented her reputation.

Levertov's status as a "new American poet" was built on the one hundred and fifty poems she managed to write while living in New York, New England, and then Mexico during the period 1956 through 1961. The source of inspiration for these poems was her life experience. These places, and her joys, sorrows, successes, failures, tensions, and pleasures, and those of her husband and son, were all inextricably connected; they were the substance of her life and the stimulus to her creativity.

The Goodmans arrived in Guadalajara in January 1956. Their aspiration was for a less expensive way of life, more room for their expanded family — Mrs. Levertoff moved there with them — and the experience of greater tranquillity and beauty. They rented the "Pink Circle House," at 1915 Florencia on the edge of town, right at the crossroad where Indians and cowboys, bikes, cattle, and donkeys all intersected. Although the burnt landscape reflected Levertov's own exhausted feelings, she soon came to enjoy living there. She developed a daily pattern of sitting at the kitchen window, from which she had a view of the mountains, and writing. When possible she went swimming and practiced ballet. Nik attended a little school, and Mitch, who wrote travel articles for *Atlantic Monthly*, had easy access to his beat of Central America and the Caribbean. It seemed a good move. One of the highlights of the year was the publication of *Here and Now*. It was a modest little book, but Robert Creeley claimed it was "a veritable quantum leap" from *The Double Image*,[12] and Rexroth praised it as full of integrity and "polished in the vitals of a powerful creative sensibility."[13]

If life in Guadalajara had a negative it was that it was more expensive than they expected and the city's population was growing rapidly, especially with Americans. One of these Americans was Virginia Barrett, who had married a Mexican and whose child attended kindergarten with Nik. Barrett and Levertov became friends, a relationship that lasted for almost forty years.

After about five months the Goodmans decided to move again, this time to Guanajuato, where they hoped living would be less expensive, more Europeanlike, and a place where Mitch might find some new work. But the move never materialized. Since both Nik and Mitch wanted to leave Guadalajara, they finally decided to relocate in Oaxaca. When they first arrived in August 1957, their house on Crespo was not yet fully constructed; consequently, for several months they lived in the finished portions while the rest of the house continued to be built around them.

Mitch's restlessness, depression, and insecurity worsened during their sojourn in Mexico. He later characterized this period as one of a downward spiral and a falling apart.[14] In some measure his troubles must have been associated with the fact that his novel was rejected again, this time by Random House. Another source of tension was the daily presence of Mrs. Levertoff. Several years later Denise, reflecting back on the tension between her mother and husband, wrote that she did not think that Mitch's feeling toward her mother could be characterized as jealousy, so much as a desire for conjugal privacy. Apparently Mitch was unwilling to have his mother-in-law deprive him of his wife's attention. Denise admitted that when they were all living together in Guadalajara a good deal of tension did build up and was not expressed.[15] This abated somewhat when Mrs. Levertoff went off to Oaxaca to study Spanish for a few weeks and decided to stay on there with her host family, the Abascals, serving as an adopted grandmother to their children. Given the Goodmans' family dynamic, Beatrice Levertoff's departure was understandable. She continued to live on with the Abascals for the next twenty years, an orphan of sorts once again.

Levertov called her two-year sojourn in Mexico "a long convalescence"; it was as well a time of germination for many of her poems. When Mitch, Nik, and she moved to Oaxaca, she explored the rich Toltec archeological treasures of the area and investigated her local surroundings. In the nearby Church of Santo Domingo she encountered frescos depicting subjects from both the Old and New Testaments. She was impressed particularly by a fresco of Jacob's dream and his ladder to heaven, an image that would be central to one of her later poems.[16]

Levertov captured the evocative sensuality and rich cultural heritage of the country in her "Five Poems from Mexico"[17] and wrote of her experience of living there in other poems. In "A Supermarket in Guadalajara, Mexico," she described the lively spirit of the place:

> In the supermercado the music
>   sweet as the hot afternoon
> wanders among the watermelons,
> . . . .

hovers like flies round the butchers
. . . as they dreamily
sharpen their knives; and the beautiful
girl cashiers, relaxed
in the lap of the hot afternoon,
breathe in time to the music
whether they know it or not—
at the glossy supermercado,
the super supermercado.[18]

She anthropomorphized the Mexican peppertrees: "The peppertrees. The peppertrees!" They "stand aside in diffidence"; they "shiver a little"; they are "restless, twitching / thin leaves in the light."[19] The indigenous cultural heritage provided inspiration for her poem/translation "The Artist," which was based on a Toltec Codex and was subsequently admired by Thomas Merton.[20] In this she contrasted the carrion artist, who worked at random, sneered at people, and was careless and defrauded, with the true artist, who *"draws out all from his heart, / works with delight, makes things with calm, with sagacity."* This true artist *"maintains dialogue with his heart, meets things with his / mind."*[21]

Although burdened with personal problems — a difficult mother, a disgruntled husband, and a troublesome child — during the late 1950s Levertov continued to express in her poetry the joy and delight of ordinary life. In "Laying the Dust" she wrote of the commonplace act of reducing dust by throwing water on it, of the "sweet smell" that rises, of the flashing water that arches and leaps.[22] She wrote of the effort to live intensely:

Let the rain plunge radiant
through sulky thunder
rage on rooftops
let it scissor and bounce its denials
on concrete slabs and black
roadways. Flood the streets. . . .
. . . .
Drown us, lose us,
rain, let us loose, so,
to lose ourselves, to career
up the plunge of the hill.[23]

In another poem she wrote: "If we're here let's be here now."[24] She summed up her central insight: "You know, I'm telling you, what I love best / is life. I love life!"[25]

For Levertov wonder and awe were experienced in ordinary life and in engagement with the natural world. In "Notes on a Scale" she speaks of the trees instructing her,[26] and in "Come into Animal Presence," of what animals have taught her:

> What is this joy? That no animal
> falters, but knows what it must do?
> That the snake has no blemish,
> that the rabbit inspects his strange surroundings
> in white star-silence? The llama
> rests in dignity, the armadillo
> has some intention to pursue in the palm-forest.[27]

Mexico allowed Levertov not only to experience a new culture but to reencounter joy and wonder. But this sojourn would end, not because of her, but because Mitch wanted to return to New York. Even though their financial situation was more stable in Mexico, he felt cut off from friends and colleagues. Beat poets Allen Ginsberg, Gregory Corso, and Jack Kerouac, as well as Peter and Lafcadio Orlovsky visited Guadalajara for one evening,[28] but only Robert Creeley came to see them in Oaxaca. Additionally, both she and Mitch had been ill—he with hepatitis, she with malaria. Nik did not like his school, and Irving Goodman, Mitch's father who was in Brooklyn, was worried about his own financial situation, having recently been forced to retire. There were reasons to leave Mexico, but Denise did it reluctantly.

Marital tension predated their move to Mexico, continued through the two years they lived there, and accompanied them back to New York. Unspoken anxiety existed around the fact that Goodman considered his travel writing "hack" work and that his book still had not found a publisher. There was tension as well around her brief liaison with John Day. In fact Levertov wrote Duncan that it took a year for her to reestablish her marriage after this affair. Apparently Levertov also wanted another child, but she told Duncan she did not think they would have one.[29] As she saw it, their problems stemmed from Mitch. He was possessive and did not want her to work; he did not want her to cut her hair. Her gregariousness and many friends were "irritating" to him.[30] For his part, Goodman believed that being in Mexico had opened him up a bit after years of shutting himself down. He attested that Denise was his most important connection with life, that she gave him life.[31]

Marital discord and the demands of domestic and artistic life exacerbated Levertov's already conflicted sense of herself as a poet and a woman.[32] This tension was expressed episodically in her poems of this period. In "The Earthwoman and the Waterwoman," she juxtaposed the domestic and the artistic self. Earthwoman has "oaktree arms," and her children are well fed. Waterwoman sings "gay songs in a sad voice" and "goes dancing in the misty lit-up town / in dragonfly dresses and blue shoes." Her children are "spindle thin."[33]

In another poem, "Dogwood," Levertov writes graphically of the strain between her artistic and domestic self. She writes of a sink full of dishes, no hot water, an unswept floor, a scarcity of money, a sleeping Nikolai, a Mitch who is sick. Each lament is followed by the dismissive, "Oh well." She feels compelled to choose: she can hear music or admire the beauty of the dogwood or try to please husband and Duncan. She tries to do it all: "Oh well, Early to bed, and I'll get up / early and put / a shine on everything and write / a letter to Duncan later that will shine too / with moonshine. Can I make it? Oh well."[34]

In a powerful poem, "The Goddess," Levertov reveals the lie the poet has been living and how the Goddess, who spoke truth, flung her across the room until she finally lay outside "Lie Castle" in the cold, with mud-splattered lips. The poet had tasted the power of the Goddess, who had plucked her from close rooms and given her power to speak again in her own tongue.[35]

Levertov's early poems of self-identity and conflict are juxtaposed against others in which joy is the dominant theme.[36] This sentiment is best expressed in "The Wife," which ends: "I don't stop to ask myself / Do I love him? but / laugh for joy."[37]

Even though her husband and son were thrilled to leave Mexico and return to New York, it took time for Levertov to adjust to the idea. She realized the move needed to happen for Mitch's sake because he was incapacitated by living away from his home base. Although she was as yet unaware of Nik's physical malady, she concluded he, now age nine, might be happier in New York as well, and hence easier to manage. She consoled herself by remembering that living in Mexico did have negatives: the pace of life was very slow and it was remote. Nonetheless, she was reluctant to leave. On departure she wrote to Duncan:

O Mexico! Now, about to leave, how I love thee — thy kind people, thy tortillas, black frijoles, & especially the small-town bands of musicos blithely, seriously, exquisitely discordant — andandand — vale, land of melancholy joys and joyous melancholy — adios —...[38]

As compensation for the move, Denise and Mitch agreed that on return to America they would spend their weekends scouring the Hudson Valley around Bear Mountain looking for a place to live outside New York City.

In January 1958, they returned to the United States via what Denise considered one of the world's most beautiful cities — San Francisco. This circuitous route to the East Coast was taken so that she could give a reading at the San Francisco Poetry Center where Duncan was director. Her well-received presentation was preceded by a glowing introduction by Duncan. But at a postreading party honoring her, the San Francisco poet Jack Spicer read a poem expressing his extreme misogyny. Although Levertov said nothing at the time, she would subsequently write her own poem in response.[39] Aside from Spicer's affront, the occasion did have positive outcomes. Eve Triem, a poet and friend of Duncan, was there and she and Levertov became friends,[40] and in celebration Duncan published her little chapbook, *Five Poems*, illustrated by Jess Collins.[41]

The Poetry Center reading was a first for Levertov. She was a natural for such an event in that she had presence, was an excellent public reader, and as a woman poet, was a unique phenomenon. Her intensity, seriousness of purpose, and urgency were coupled with a joyfulness, and her lovely modulated voice, with its slight foreign accent, made her alluring to her American audience.[42] Breath and body communicated the meaning of her words. Her carriage was elegant, and she projected a cultivated personage, reflecting what Rexroth claimed she had: a wisdom and humanism older than the Renaissance.[43] Her appearance at the San Francisco Poetry Center was just the first of many more to come. Readings would become a staple of her life, bringing in revenue, cultivating a "public," and affirming the importance of poetry in the lives of her listeners.

The Goodmans left San Francisco for New York, settled into their old apartment on West 15th Street, while Nik matriculated at nearby P.S. 41. Their reentry into New York was not easy. Denise thought the City was cold and dirty, "an alien and terrifying place."[44] She complained to Duncan that their lives were "gloomy and sordid." They had the flu and bed bugs to boot. But their social life and connection with others did improve, although Denise and Mitch responded differently to this improvement. In reporting to

Duncan about their attendance at a party, she wrote: "Wish he were able to enjoy such things, I always feel guilty and rather a fool for having had fun when he hasn't."[45] While living in Maine that summer, Denise indicated that her husband's state was still fragile. "We are not depressed here," she wrote Duncan, "that is, Mitch is still in a very delicate emotional state but is getting better & relaxing; sleeps a lot too, which he needs."[46] However, another blow came to Goodman on their return from Maine when he found out that his novel had been rejected again, this time by New Directions.[47]

Levertov's professional life, on the other hand, had taken off. After the publication of *Here and Now* in 1956, *Overland to the Islands* appeared two years later. It was an elegant little book with a preface by Robert Duncan. Its beautiful white cover, decorated with threads of green and blue, was designed by her friend, the New York figurative painter Albert Kresch. In a review of this volume the poet and critic Hayden Carruth commended Levertov as "skillful, unlabored, close to nature."[48]

Soon after, James Laughlin agreed to publish *With Eyes at the Back of Our Heads*. This was a major coup, ensuring that her work would be marketed by an established New York publishing house. Although the book still carried the mark of Williams, filled as it was with poetry of "the immediate"[49] and "the here and now," it also illustrated a beginning independence from him, which would be more fully evident in *The Jacob's Ladder*.

The return to New York offered Levertov a livelier artistic environment as well as the possibility of new friendships with women poets.[50] She met Adrienne Rich through Alfred Conrad, Rich's husband, who had been a classmate of Goodman's at Harvard. The relationship between Levertov and Rich would deepen when Levertov, under the sponsorship of the Radcliffe Institute, lived in Cambridge for two years where Rich resided. It was through Rich that Levertov would meet Albert and Barbara Gelpi, with whom her life would subsequently intersect in important ways.[51] Although Rich was six years younger than Levertov and American-born, they shared a Jewish heritage, a struggle to make their way as young female poets, and the concerns of motherhood. Their admiration was mutual. In a generous act Levertov agreed to care for Rich's two young sons while Rich was away for a week or two. This was no small gift from a woman who found domesticity and child care taxing. In 1961, Rich published the poem "The Roofwalker" and dedicated it to Levertov.

Although supportive friends, Levertov and Rich differed on a number of issues. Rich was partial to Whitman and Wallace Stevens and was less enthusiastic about Williams and the Black Mountain poets, especially Duncan, whom she was introduced to by Levertov. When Rich commented that parts of Levertov's poem on Boris Pasternak were "sentimental," Levertov wrote: "I think it is the rationalist in you that is objecting to the mystic in me."[52] Nonetheless these two women poets drew strength and confidence from their mutual exchanges. They reviewed each other's drafts of poems, discussed their favorite poets and mentors, and debated their differences on poetics. Although there is no evidence explaining their estrangement, their correspondence ended in the mid-1960s, One can imagine that Rich's decision to separate from her husband,[53] her increasingly insistent feminism, and her public acknowledgment of her homosexuality in 1976 must have set Levertov on edge. It would be years before there would be rapprochement between them.

Levertov's friendship with the poet, translator, and political activist Muriel Rukeyser took a different course. She first encountered Rukeyser years earlier when she read her review of Duncan's *Heavenly City, Earthly City*, but they did not meet until 1961 when they both gave readings at Columbia University. Levertov wrote Duncan that their "meeting was like a thunderclap, we practically rushed into each others' arms." She said Rukeyser, a large woman, was "a quite wonderful Giantess, a kind of Great Mother terrible & encompassing."[54] Rukeyser was older than Levertov, and although not much in direct contact, they shared friendship, motherhood, political worldviews, and poetic sensibilities, even though Levertov did not consider Rukeyser an excellent poet." Their friendship was consolidated first in 1965, when they worked together to launch Writers and Artists against the War in Vietnam, and later in 1972, when they traveled together to Southeast Asia. Levertov considered Rukeyser a generous friend, who "more than any other poet I know of (including Pablo Neruda) consistently fused lyricism and overt social and political concern."[56] In 1967, Levertov published the poem "The Unknown," dedicating it to her friend.[57] For her part Rukeyser pushed through Levertov's election to membership in the American Academy of Arts and Letters. After Rukeyser's death in 1980, Levertov wrote a poem in Rukeyser's memory describing her as "a cathedral," one who "didn't despair, / grieved, worked, / moved beyond shame, / / fought forty years more."[58] In the late 1950s and early 1960s Levertov's friendships with Rich and Rukeyser sustained her as she negotiated the world of poetry where as yet there were few women.

After a few very difficult years of marriage, 1960 and 1961 seemed a relatively positive time for the Goodmans. The summer of 1960 was particularly happy, although there were debilitating sorrows. Mitch's mother, Adele

Goodman, whom Levertov admired, had a stroke in January 1960, and her subsequent death a month later exhausted both Mitch and her. In a letter to Duncan she wrote that this death illustrated one of her worst faults: a "lack of patience for long run goodness."[59] There was also the issue of the care of Irving Goodman, who suffered from incipient dementia. He lived with them for six months, but subsequently was moved to a nursing home where he died in January 1966.

Even though his marital relationship had improved, Goodman was not happy living in New York City; he found it "destructive" to him. He wanted to be alone and in nature. Since he liked being in Maine, they purchased an old farmhouse with a fieldstone fence on some forty-five acres of overgrown pasture and woodland in Temple. Mt. Blue was visible in the distance. The house had seven rooms, no heating or plumbing, and was four miles from the nearest post office.[60] They bought the place for thirty-five hundred dollars and planned to restore it and live there permanently after Nik finished primary school. As it turned out, until 1972 they spent large portions of each summer there, but never lived in the house year-round. During holidays and in the summer they always welcomed fellow writers and students to the farmhouse, engaging them in conversation and taking them to hunt mushrooms in the woods. In time they built a well-equipped writing studio for Mitch near the house, while Denise continued to use the kitchen table as her writing space.

Two months after they purchased the Temple property, they moved to another apartment in the city at 277 Greenwich Street near Washington Market, which was larger than their previous apartment and had hardwood floors and big windows. They loved it. Their only neighbors were the jazz musician Race Newton and his wife.

Given that their finances were limited, Levertov felt an increasing obligation to contribute to the family's meager income, but Goodman did not want her to work. One source of earnings was her poetry readings, which she began to do more frequently. In 1960, she did readings at Princeton, Yale, Harvard, and New York University, and the following year she toured midwestern and West Coast colleges and appeared again at the Poetry Center in San Francisco where she stayed with Duncan and Collins. She was guaranteed an additional fifty dollars a month working for a short stint as poetry editor of the *Nation*. She also agreed to give some lectures at the School of Visual Arts for which she would be well paid. And then there were prizes. The Bess Hokin Prize, awarded by *Poetry* (Chicago) in November 1960 meant an additional one hundred dollars, part of which she spent on a new

Olympia portable typewriter. The following year she was surprised when the Longview Foundation presented her with an award and the princely sum of three hundred dollars. And finally, Mitch had some good news. In January 1961 Horizon agreed to publish his novel, *The End of It*, with an advance of five hundred dollars and future options on his next two books. These windfalls convinced Levertov they could patch together enough money to allow Goodman to give up "hack" work and take an unencumbered year in which to write.

For both economic and psychological reasons they were elated by the news of the Horizon contract. *The End of It* was set in Italy in 1944 and explored the nature of war and satirized the society that had waged it. Although not autobiographical—Mitch never served in the European theater because he was asthmatic—its main character is a soldier who falls in love with a foreign woman who helps him come alive. Well-written and dramatic, the novel is not about this individual soldier but the military-industrial machine of war. The blurbs on the book's cover by William Carlos Williams, Norman Mailer, and Galway Kinnell undoubtedly helped sales. The book was reissued twice, having been reviewed in *Harper's*, the *New York Times*, and *Time*. At last Mitch had achieved some success and his spirits improved, but not for long.

Mitch's depression had been a strain on their relationship for years. Denise wanted her husband to be happy and felt responsible for ensuring this, but she did not want his depression to destroy her as a person and poet. She was convinced that he was jealous of her success and harbored resentments against her, although she admitted she was "ignorant, obtuse, unkind & confused" in her relationship with him and that she did not bring her sensitive, perceptive self to their marriage. The tension between them was summarized in their difficult sexual relationship. She wrote in her diary that while Mitch was good and kind to her and others and that she took pleasure in his appearance and pride in his being an artist, she felt no passion for him. The circular argument linked her lack of passion to his lack of sexual confidence, and his lack of confidence to his sense of inadequacy as compared to her.[61]

In her ruminations Levertov also attempted to unravel her complex relationship with both her parents and her son. These preoccupations were major themes in her diaries for decades. She believed that her tremendous need of approval from others resulted both from the lack of her father's affection and her mother's unconscious attempt to dominate her. When she had her mother's approval, she was secure and happy; when she did not, she was wretched. As she saw it, in her late childhood and teens she was the one who sought to love others, but she herself was not loved. When others thought well of her, she developed self-confidence. Unable to discuss these matters with her parents, she turned to Mitch as the first person to whom she could reveal herself. He was a "bridge" between her and the outside world.[62]

In Levertov's eyes her mother had a tendency to become emotionally dependent on one person, and now with the death of Paul Levertoff, Denise was that person. Initially she hoped her mother's last years would be happy ones, but she came to see this as an impossibility. She urged her mother to find new friends.[63] And she did. When the Goodmans returned to New York, Beatrice Levertoff stayed on in Mexico living with the Abascals.[64]

Levertov was hopeful about her relationship with Nik, who was nearing twelve. She recognized that she was responsible for much of the poor interaction between them and resolved to stop nagging him since she thought she might be recapitulating her own childhood — that is, requiring that he earn her approval so that she could dominate him.

Strained in her relationships with her husband and mother, she determined to improve her relationship with her son and to focus on her own creative life. In late 1961, shortly after having returned from Delphi, she recorded this entry in her diary:

> One feeling I have sometimes is a sort of grim resignation, i.e., Oh well, if I can't satisfy or be satisfied in my marriage I will give myself to that in which I can give & receive satisfaction — not "the literary life" in the busy-busy sense but "the life of the mind" and the life of the creative imagination. And meanwhile work to improve as Nik's mother because there I *do* believe in the possibilities. Am I saying I don't believe, hope, in the possibilities for me & M? No, I don't think I'm saying that: only that I don't feel myself capable of *changing* that situation radically; and that I feel radical change must come from M himself — he must get at the bottom of why he is so unconfident & learn to function better sexually on the most practical physical plane — I think I would respond to that change. But meanwhile instead of moping I feel like plunging doggedly into those areas where things *do* work out for me.[65]

The area where things did work out for her was in writing poetry. She knew she had a strange and wonderful gift that allowed poems to be spoken through her and that this had an effect on others. Nonetheless by 1961, Levertov was aware of a gap between her private and public life. "I know I am not in my most private life anything like as wise & good as they imagine

yet I see that it is given me to act & speak wisely and goodly among strang-
ers."[66] This disparity between her own self-understanding and what others
thought of her would haunt her for many decades.

Levertov was also conscious of another gap, this time between her poetry
and its connection to life's suffering. The source of this awareness was at
least in part the Hasidic tradition, which transmitted from her father was
reinvigorated by her encounter with Buber. Its mandate was to fuse "the
burning" of desire with service to the world, to live a life of fervor and joy
as one worked to oppose evil and injustice and hence reconnect the scattered
sparks of the divine. This influence is manifested in the poems of *The Jacob's
Ladder* published in 1961. The book's central poem, "The Jacob's Ladder,"
was inspired by the fresco she saw in the Church of Santo Domingo in Oaxaca. In it she describes the ladder and the human volition needed to climb it:

> The stairway is not
> a thing of gleaming strands
> a radiant evanescence
> for angels' feet that only glance in their tread, and need not
> touch the stone.
>
> It is of stone....
> . . . .
> A stairway of sharp
> angles, solidly built....
> . . . .
> and a man climbing
> must scrape his knees, and bring
> the grip of his hands into play. . ."[77]

In another poem from this volume, "During the Eichmann Trial," she
expresses her concern for justice in the world. Although the poem was not
principally about Eichmann but the human capacity for evil, it is the only
poem in which she refers directly to the persecution of the Jewish people. In
it she both calls forth human empathy and indicts all of humanity as equally
capable of heinous deeds. Referring to Eichmann she writes:

> He had not looked,
> pitiful man whom none

pity, whom all
must pity if they look

into their own face . . . .

He stands

isolate in a bulletproof
witness-stand of glass,
a cage, where we may view
ourselves, an apparition

telling us something he
does not know: we are members
one of another.[68]

In "During the Eichmann Trail," Levertov expanded her understanding of the role of imagination. Earlier she conceived of this human capacity in Keatsian terms: "We are faithful / only to the imagination. *What the / imagination / seizes / as beauty must be truth*."[69] But in this poem she suggests that imagination is the birthplace of empathy and compassion, the means by which a shared sense of responsibility for evil in the world is deepened. In a subsequent essay she explains this linkage:

> The imagination of what it is to *be* those other forms of life that want to live is the only way to recognition; and it is that imaginative recognition that brings compassion to birth. Man's capacity for evil, then, is less a positive capacity, for all its horrendous activity, than a failure to develop man's most human function, the imagination, to its fullness, and consequently a failure to develop compassion.[70]

In another poem, "A Common Ground," she points to humanity's shared unity, which derives not from common speech,

but the uncommon speech of paradise,
tongue in which oracles
speak to beggars and pilgrims:
. . . .

> speech akin to the light
> with which at day's end and day's
> renewal, mountains
> sing to each other across the cold valleys.[71]

The language of poetry, this "speech of paradise," was a tool for creating "common ground" and compassion among people. It was as well the means by which one awakened to the "authentic." In "Matins," named for the first prayer of the monastic hours, Levertov calls on "Marvelous Truth," in its many guises, to "confront us" to "dwell / in our crowded hearts / our steaming bathrooms, kitchens full of / things to be done, the / ordinary streets." She petitions "Marvelous Truth": "Thrust close your smile / that we know you, terrible joy." "Marvelous Truth" leads to the authentic.

> That's it,
> that's joy, it's always
> a recognition, the known
> appearing fully itself, and
> more itself than one knew.
> ....
> The authentic! It rolls
> just out of reach, beyond
> running feet and
> stretching fingers, down
> the green slope and into
> the black waves of the sea.[72]

Levertov believed there was joy in a fidelity to truth and authenticity, but there was a dark side to life to be confronted as well. In her long poem "Three Meditations" she acknowledges the reality of evil. Using a quotation from Ibsen — "The task of the poet is to make clear to *himself*, and thereby to others, the temporal and eternal questions"[73] — she poses the question: How does one live with joy and wonder and confront the evil in oneself and in the world? For Levertov the internal and external question is the same: "the same problems, the same tyrannies, injustices, hopes, and mercies act and react and demand resolution."[74] Each of her three meditations offers direction. In the first she urges:

Live
in thy fingertips and in thy
hair's rising; hunger
be thine, food
be thine . . .
Breathe deep of
evening, be with the
rivers of tumult, sharpen
thy wits to know power and be
humble.

In a dramatic second mediation she juxtaposes external and internal evil, the political and the personal:

Barbarians
throng the straight roads of
my empire, converging on black Rome.
There is darkness in me...
. . . .
Who sent the child
sobbing to bed, and woke it
later to comfort it?
      I,I,I, I.
I multitude, I tyrant,
I angel, I you, you
world, ...

She proposes in her third meditation a means to deal with evil: "authentic" self lets no evil enter.

We breathe an ill wind,...
. . . .
bringing the poet
back to song
as before . . . .

to drive away devils,
response to

the wonder that
as before
shows a double face,

to be
what he is
being his virtue

filling his whole space
so no devil
may enter.[75]

The Jacob's Ladder set Levertov on a new course as a serious poet. She was now more than a disciple of Williams and a member of the Black Mountain poets. She was unique, and she wanted it that way. Of course, she was still very much allied with Robert Duncan with whom she shared the closest friendship and whom she admired and depended on. She expressed her adulation of him in her poem "Homage":

To lay garlands at your feet
because you stand
dark in the light, or lucent
in the dark air of the mind's world
solitary in your empire of magic, undiminished.[76]

Duncan's feelings for her were equally worshipful. He wrote that he loved her and that she was his companion in art and his poetic conscience. Her actual presence, her being with him, was a pure joy and everlasting delight.[77] They clearly helped each other as fellow poets, but the fundamental differences between them went unexplored, at least for a time.

Although she had not yet established her independence from Duncan, a few years before Williams's death in 1963, she gradually began to announce her poetic differences with him. Obviously she cherished Williams as a friend, but she began to experiment poetically. When he criticized her poem "The Jacob's Ladder" for not being written in the American idiom, she responded that while his first commitment was to that idiom, hers was not. She allowed that "The Jacob's Ladder" had to be the way it was written "because *it sounds the way I think and feel about it.*" She went on to explain that she did not grow up as an American or as English but that her home atmosphere was European. While admitting to not having deep local roots, she argued she could be at home everywhere and nowhere. She believed "fervently that the poet's first obligation was to his own voice — to find it and use it," and she tenderly chided Williams not to think of her defecting from him but to consider her "a special case." And then to close her defense she added the line: "I'm a later naturalized, second-class citizen, not an all-American girl, & I'm darned if I'm going to pretend to be anything else or throw out what other cultural influences I have in my system, whatever *anyone* says."[78]

Williams must have had some inchoate sense that *The Jacob's Ladder* was different from her three previous volumes that had so clearly reflected his influence. In her earlier work, Levertov attempted to portray the energy within things, but the poems of *The Jacob's Ladder* pointed beyond the thing itself to a reality in which form and content were fused and imagination acted to illuminate a deeper meaning. Although Williams had served her well, she had now moved beyond him to new terrain.

It was at this point in the mid-1960s that Duncan introduced Levertov to his friend H. D. Although they met twice and only exchanged a few letters prior to H. D.'s death in September 1961, Levertov's letters to her indicate her sense of privilege in knowing this woman poet. Part of their exchange included H. D. giving Levertov a copy of her *Bid Me To Live*, the story of the difficult life of a woman writer during World War I. This gift captivated Levertov who called it "a beautiful and completely absorbing book," one that deepened her understanding of what it meant to be a woman artist in the world of men.[79] In an essay of appreciation of H. D., Levertov lyrically described what this "old one" offered: "doors, ways in, tunnels through" to the interpenetration of "past and present, of mundane reality and intangible reality." H. D. showed a way "to penetrate mystery," that is, "the Hiddenness," "the Other Side."[80] Although their relationship was short-lived, Levertov believed that it was only at this point in her life that she was capable of absorbing H. D.'s genius.[81]

A new way forward, the pilgrim way to which Rilke introduced her and which H. D. modeled, was opening before her. What she reaffirmed was that her poetry would be a celebration of mystery, something she acknowledged was the most consistent theme of her poetry from its beginning.[82] The poems of *The Jacob's Ladder* were evidence of that reaffirmation.

To honor H. D. at her death, Williams in his waning, and Ezra Pound on his reclusive exile in Italy, Levertov wrote the poem "September 1961." It serves as testament of her gratitude to these "great ones."

This is the year the old ones,
the old great ones
leave us alone on the road.

The road leads to the sea.
We have the words in our pockets,
obscure directions. The old ones

have taken away the light of their presence,
we see it moving away over a hill
off to one side.

They are not dying,
they are withdrawn
into a painful privacy

learning to live without words.[83]

Without the inspiration of Williams, Pound, and H. D., Levertov might never have been able to plumb the experience of quotidian life and create the poems of immediacy and mystery that characterize this period. She now had a body of work on which she could reflect. And it was precisely that reflection she now undertook.

In a letter to Duncan written in 1961, Levertov confessed that she had been preoccupied with the formulation of poetic theory, and although she worried that might keep her from writing poetry for a while, she concluded "perhaps there are times in one's life when one *must define* to oneself & to others what one is after."[84] Levertov had arrived at that time. Over the next several years, stimulated by other poets and her own desire to clarify her views on her craft, she would produce a number of essays on poetics.

It was not that she had not thought about poetics previously, but it was of minor interest compared to her emphasis on developing poetic technique. In an early poem, "Overland to the Islands," she expressed an incipient form of poetics. In it she describes the method of the artist, analogizing it to the instinctual behavior of a dog, which she might first have learned from her childhood pet. The emphasis is on movement and sensuality. Following this canine behavior, the poet and the reader will arrive "overland to the islands," a magical place.

Let's go-much as that dog goes,
Intently haphazard.

. . . .

         Under his feet
rocks and mud, his imagination, sniffing,
engaged in its perceptions — dancing
edgeways, there's nothing
the dog disdains on his way,
nevertheless he
keeps moving, changing
pace and approach but
not direction — 'every step an arrival.'[85]

Much like the dog, the poet goes "intently haphazard," using the senses and imagination, disdaining nothing. "'Every step an arrival,'" a phrase borrowed from Rilke, signaled Levertov's attempt to bring together the poet/pilgrim's search with living in the "here and now." This was the way both to make a poem and to live fully.

The spur to seriously reflect on her poetics came when Donald Allen, who had been introduced to her by Duncan in 1956, invited her to be included in his anthology *The New American Poetry*. Allen's intent was to celebrate an emerging group of young avant-garde and experimental poets, whom he considered the twentieth century's second phase of America's rich poetic heritage. This volume was developed in response to the more conservative and traditional anthology, *New Poets of England and America*, edited by Donald Hall, which appeared three years earlier.[86] Allen's anthology proved to be highly influential; by 1999, it had sold 100,000 copies.[87] Nonetheless, Levertov ultimately came to feel that inclusion in the anthology might have had negative implications as well, allying her too closely to these new experimental poets.[88] But for the moment it was high acclaim.

For purposes of organization Allen divided the various contemporary American poets into five somewhat artificially arranged groups: the Black Mountain poets; the San Francisco Renaissance; the Beat Generation; the New York poets; and a catchall group who did not fit into the other categories. Each poet contributed several poems; of the forty-four contributors, only four — Levertov, Helen Adam, Madeline Gleason, and Barbara Guest, were women. Some fifteen also submitted statements on poetics, including Charles Olson, Robert Duncan, Robert Creeley, Lawrence Ferlinghetti,

Jack Spicer, Jack Kerouac, Allen Ginsberg, Frank O'Hara, Gary Snyder, and LeRoi Jones, along with some lesser lights. Levertov was the only woman among this group. Their statements were eclectic, one notable being Olson's, which set out his ideas about projective verse and his famous proclamation, one he attributed to Creeley, that "Form is never more than an extension of content."

Levertov's statement on poetics was brief and brimming with energy. It was not theoretical but read more like a credo and gave evidence of both her sophistication and self-confidence. In embryonic form it contained her extensive reflection on the craft of poetry, a subject she would return to in the next decade. A few years earlier she had insisted she lacked a "masculine mind" and consequently was confined to the "immediate," unable to write prose or create a system of general ideas.[89] Her statement on poetics put the lie to that claim.

As she explained to Duncan, her intent was "to define to oneself & to others what (she was) after." She began in this way:

> I believe poets are instruments on which the power of poetry plays.
> But they are also *makers*, craftsmen: It is given to the seer to see, but it
> is then his responsibility to communicate what he sees, that they who
> cannot see may see, since we are "members one of another."[90]

In these two brief sentences Levertov expresses her understanding of the task of the poet and the poet's relationship to both the power given and the duty expected. These notions had broad implications for the way she practiced her craft and her sense of obligation to others. Hers was a poetry that led inevitably to engagement with the world.

The focus of her second paragraph is narrower and centers on the technical craft of poetry. She wrote:

> I believe every space and comma is a living part of the poem and has
> its function, just as every muscle and pore of the body has its function.
> And the way the lines are broken is a functioning part essential to the
> poem's life.

In the third paragraph of her poetic credo she considers the relationship between form and content. "I believe," she wrote,

> content determines form, and yet that content is discovered only *in*
> form. Like everything living, it is a mystery. The revelation of form
> itself can be a deep joy; yet I think form *as means* should never obtrude,

whether from intention or carelessness, between the reader and the essential force of the poem, it must be so fused with that force.[91]

Although she continued to augment her ideas about the aim, method, form, and content of poetry, it was the final paragraph of her statement that would cause consternation and ultimately require an explanation. As written in 1959, this paragraph read:

> I do not believe that a violent imitation of the horrors of our times is the concern of poetry. Horrors are taken for granted. Disorder is ordinary. People in general take more and more "in their stride" — hides grow thicker. I long for poems of an inner harmony in utter contrast to the chaos in which they exist. Insofar as poetry has a social function it is to awaken sleepers by other means than shock.

Levertov's poetry in the subsequent 1960s and early 1970s seemed to many to be in direct contradiction to this statement in which she clearly separates contemporary events and the concern of poetry. As the "horrors" of the Vietnam war increased and the "disorder" in her personal life augmented, Levertov did not take these events "in stride." Rather her psychic life began to unravel, her marriage disintegrate, and her poetry became more strident and didactic. While she might "long for poems of an inner harmony," few would be forthcoming. Her poems shocked, and she meant them to do so.

Her statement of poetics ended with a single line, a salute to those who were friends and who had helped her to become the poet that she was. She wrote: "I think of Robert Duncan and Robert Creeley as the chief poets among my contemporaries." But those friendships, too, would be challenged.

As the decade of the 1960s began, Denise Levertov was considered a poet of great promise. Her early years in America provided a period of incubation for the making of Levertov the poet. She discovered her voice, honed her poetic technique, reflected on her craft, and achieved considerable recognition. It was no wonder that in the summer of 1961, with Nik in summer camp and Mitch commissioned to write a travel article on Greece, that she went with him and visited Delphi.[92] Her success as a poet seemed assured and she made her vow to poetry.

4

"A Cataract Filming Over My Inner Eyes"
1962-1967

It is hard to be an artist in this time because it is hard to be human:
"WRITERS TAKE SIDES ON VIETNAM"[1]

How to be an artist and person — how to live with joy and sorrow in difficult times — this was the conundrum that dominated Denise Levertov's life for more than a decade. Her resolution was to be "poet in the world," but this was costly. She longed for "claritas," but war on the macrocosmic level and marital discord in the microcosm distorted her vision.

The decade of the 1960s began well enough. It was an auspicious time to be a poet. Poetry magazines, publishing houses, poetry readings, and writer-in-residence programs at colleges and universities proliferated, allowing for greater exposure for poets, especially for women, who previously had little opportunity for recognition of their talent. Levertov benefited from these circumstances.[2]

Positive reviews of *The Jacob's Ladder* and her inclusion in *The New American Poetry* enhanced her visibility. She was in demand as a poet, and in 1961, was granted a coveted Guggenheim Fellowship. In addition to its prestige, the accompanying monetary award allowed her some luxuries: a new washing machine, dryer, and dishwasher. Each made domestic life simpler.

Tensions in her marriage and family life had temporarily abated. The Goodmans spent a blissful summer in rural Maine, eating from the garden and enjoying the seclusion,[3] although Denise sometimes chafed at the fact that she was dependent on Mitch to transport her everywhere. She had never learned to drive and suspected Mitch liked it that way. Mitch too was happy. His novel had been reviewed positively, and Denise was delighted for him, hoping that this literary success might provide him, now age thirty-eight, with a fresh start as a writer. Nik, now ready for high school, had been

FIGURE 5. Denise Levertov, 1962.
Dante Levi. Special Collections,
Stanford University.

given a tuition scholarship to Putney, a boarding school in Vermont. For all
of them it was a good summer.

But the memories of these idyllic months faded quickly. Nik's adjustment
to Putney was not easy, and Denise was constantly concerned for him. She
worried about his erratic academic performance and his choice of friends.
Counselors remarked on his lack of social engagement, but she remained
confident of his idealistic nature and his ability to empathize with others,
particularly those who did not fit in. She wanted to feel proud of Nik, but
could not. Neither could she feel proud of Mitch,[4] whose depression led
him to see a Jungian therapist beginning in the early 1960s. By 1963, Denise
sought out Ann van Waveren, her own Jungian therapist. Together, husband
and wife read and discussed Jung's writings and their individual dream life.
Levertov was convinced that this gave them a bond that held their marriage together for several years.[5] In her diary she made copious notes on her
dreams, analyzing them and sometimes sharing them with others.

In 1963, with Guggenheim support ended, Levertov contributed to the
family's finances through her poetry readings by working as poetry editor
for the *Nation*, staying until early 1965 when Hayden Carruth took over, and
by serving as a consultant first for Wesleyan University Press and a year later
for W. W. Norton.

These last two assignments give some evidence of her prickliness and independence. At Wesleyan she defended the poetry of James Dickey, who subsequently asked her to be his literary executor replacing Donald Hall. Even though Levertov had never met Dickey, she agreed to his request, but then retracted it after they met. In a letter to Duncan she complained that she had been put in a "false position" and that Dickey was not to be trusted and had no soul.[6] At Norton she acquired new poets like the Canadian Margaret Avison,[7] but she also had run-ins with others, in this case the previous editor of *Origin*, Cid Corman. Their tussle occurred over Levertov's insistence that Corman not be allowed to select what she considered inferior poems for a forthcoming Norton collection of poetry. Name-calling ensued. Corman said she was mean, bossy, and arrogant; she called him "bitter, vain, malicious & pathetic." Although she ultimately apologized, she was proud of her ability to assert her views. She wrote that she often upset some of her best friends, including Duncan and Creeley. "I did appall them, often," she wrote, "but I kept my pride & independence. I expressed my genuine eclecticism, & kept their love & respect too."[8]

Her independence is also evident in her relationship with George Oppen, an older poet with whom she shared political commitments, artistic commonalities, and a respect for both Pound and Williams. Oppen was fascinated with feminine consciousness and wanted to encourage and support its development. Fixated on Levertov, he praised her poetry, especially "Matins" and later "Relearning the Alphabet," but he also offered instruction that Levertov interpreted as paternalism. Worried that she could not be mother, activist, and poet, he urged her to stop writing for a while. He was also concerned that the political rhetoric expressed in her poem on the Eichmann trial obscured poetic truth. After one argument Oppen was convinced that Levertov expressed her anger at him in a poem in which she identified him as an old blind cuckoo bird. In response he wrote a poem critical of her feminine pragmatism.[9] Such paternal instruction was not well-received by Levertov. This set-to with Oppen was a portent of another instance of paternal instruction by the much admired Duncan. But that was yet in the future.

Levertov was reunited with Duncan and Creeley at the Vancouver Poetry Conference in August 1963, the first time all major Black Mountain poets were together in one place. She used the opportunity to publicly express her gratitude to Creeley for helping her transition to America.[10] Being with these kindred spirits, especially her beloved Duncan, energized her. She returned to New York elated.

But the year had its sorrows. Earlier in the spring William Carlos Williams died, and in July Denise received a letter from her sister expressing her bewilderment at what she perceived as an effort on the part of their mother and Denise to "un-love" her. Olga pleaded for all of them to renew trust in each other again.[11] Then in October Denise learned that Olga was seriously ill with cancer. According to Denise's telling, Olga asked her to delay visiting her in England until her health improved.[12] Five months later, Olga, ravaged in body and spirit, was dead at age forty-nine. Mrs. Levertoff assured Denise that her husband had forgiven Olga prior to his own death.[13] But neither Denise nor her mother had actually seen Olga for a decade, and Olga's estranged children learned of their mother's death only after the fact.

In the midst of these personal sorrows, a teaching opportunity opened for Levertov. Beginning in 1964, she taught a thirteen-week evening course called "The Craft of Poetry" at the New York City YM-YWCA Poetry Center. For the next three decades she would teach regularly at both private and public colleges and universities as a writer-in-residence, as an adjunct faculty member, and finally as a tenured professor. Teaching supplemented her income, made her an itinerant who moved about, and brought her in contact with young people and their ideas. Since she was an "untaught teacher," she had to work hard in the classroom; however, she maintained that being uncontaminated by school herself, she was closer to her students and able to understand them better than other teachers.[14]

Levertov took teaching seriously even though she warned serious writers against taking it on as a full-time occupation, contending it would diminish their opportunity for creative work. Artists needed work that did not absorb all of their attention.[15] Nonetheless, as a part-time teacher she respected her students, demanded they work hard, and engaged with them outside the classroom. She insisted that the poet's craft required precision and demanded the same from her students. Dogmatic and tenacious in argument, Levertov had little empathy for the thin-skinned who could not withstand her often withering criticism. She resonated best with students who wanted to learn and believed they could learn something from her. She was realistic about what she could teach them — certainly not inspiration. Her hope was to help them find their "voice," to be better readers of poetry, and to provide standards by which they could evaluate poems. Although rigorous in her expectations, she was a generous teacher. She kept in contact with students over the years, supported them by writing recommendations, congratulated them on their successes, and invited them to her home, creating what one former student called a "Deniversity," a hospitable place to discuss poetry.[16]

During the mid-1960s she taught at Drew University in nearby Madison, New Jersey, a position she landed through the help of Barbara and Howard Fussiner,[17] at City College of New York, and then for the entire academic year of 1966-67, at Vassar College in Poughkeepsie, New York, for which she was paid the handsome sum of nine thousand dollars. Because in each setting she had different kinds of students, she tailored her teaching to accommodate their needs.

The Drew students were docile, at least as compared to the adults she taught at the Poetry Center Workshop in New York. They also lacked a sense of community, something Levertov tried to counter by reducing her own authority and building up an *esprit de corps* among them. Their lack of community was brought home to her when one of her students committed suicide at the end of term. In response she wrote a letter to her class members urging them not to be discouraged, saying that life was complex and unpredictable, that joy would return, and that they needed each other to be alive.[18] Among all these early teaching assignments, Levertov especially enjoyed her experience at Vassar. She lived on campus and hence had access to women friends and interesting and responsive students. She had no domestic chores and none of the anxieties of family life.[19]

During this same period Goodman taught at City College and at Hofstra and Drew, but teaching did not fulfill him. In letters to his wife he wrote that he was losing a sense of what he must do, that he needed to get back to himself, to come into his own.[20]

Levertov, on the other hand, felt energized by her teaching and by recent accolades for her work. In 1964, she was named an honorary scholar at the Radcliffe Institute, a position she held through 1966. The three thousand dollars per year Radcliffe stipend was augmented by teaching, consulting, prizes and awards, and poetry readings. In 1964, she won the Harriet Monroe Memorial Prize and the Inez Boulton Prize, and the following year she received the Morton Dauwen Zabel Prize given by *Poetry* (Chicago) and the American Institute of Arts and Letters Award, which brought with it twenty-five hundred dollars. In 1964 alone, she gave poetry readings at Choate, Dartmouth, Wesleyan, Colgate, Goucher, and Colby. She was lauded, applauded, and bringing in income.

Levertov conceived of herself as poet who also explored the craft of poetry and explained it to others through lectures, essays, and interviews. An interview in 1963 with David Ossman indicates that she had firmly solidified her principal ideas and was able to communicate them to a general audience. Among the fourteen poets interviewed by Ossman, Levertov was sui generis, the lone woman.[21] In this interview she defined poetry as a gift and a responsibility, not to oneself, but to poetry itself. It demanded craftsmanship and an ability to write "objectively" about the immediate and the concrete. A poem had to arise from a deep level within the poet lest it not be alive. Although poetry could not leave out intelligence, it did not begin there.

In the mid-to-late 1960s, in essays and lectures, Levertov continued her foray into poetics. She explored the poet's psychological condition and dealt with issues of craft. In "Origins of a Poem" she demonstrates her ability to explain the intimate relationship between the genesis of a poem and the task of the poet. She describes the origin of a poem in this way:

> The progression seems clear to me: from Reverence for Life to Attention to Life, from Attention to Life to a highly developed Seeing and Hearing, from Seeing and Hearing (faculties almost indistinguishable for the poet) to the Discovery and Revelation of Form, from Form to Song.[22]

The poet arrives finally at music, which is the quality of song within speech itself. "Writing poetry," she wrote, "is a process of discovery, revealing *inherent* music, the music of correspondences, and the music of inscape."[23]

Levertov suggests in this essay that the life experience of the poet and the creation of the poem are intimately intertwined. Citing Heidegger, she insists that to be human is to be a "conversation"; communion is the basis for living humanly. The poet's development flows from a progressive deepening of one's human sensibilities, and the poem emerges from the poet's dialogue with the self.[24]

Levertov's early reflections on organic poetry were first presented in a lecture entitled "Asking the Fact for the Form" given at Wabash College in 1962,[25] were reiterated at the Vancouver conference the following year, and found their way into print soon after in "Some Notes on Organic Form." In this essay she describes organic poetry, the relationship between the poem's form and content, and how each is discovered and revealed. Her intent is to differentiate between "free verse" and organic poetry, to clarify her views vis-à-vis Charles Olsen, and to wrestle with some of Duncan's suggestions and ideas. She admitted, however, that in this regard Duncan might consider what she understood about organic poetry to be rudimentary since so much of it had come to her through him.[26]

In defining "organic poetry" Levertov starts from the assumption that the poet intuits "an order, a form beyond forms, in which forms partake."[27]

Organic poetry discovers and reveals the order that is already there. Human creations, including poems, are "analogies, resemblances, natural allegories" of that order and those forms.

In order to elucidate these ideas, Levertov borrows the notion of "inscape" from Gerard Manley Hopkins. "Inscape" is the intrinsic inner form in an object and objects in relation to each other. It is being in the thing itself, a manifestation of incarnation. "Instress," another of Hopkins's inventions, is the poet's experience of the perception of "inscape."[28] In short, organic poetry searches out and reveals "inscape" through the experience of "instress."

Above all, organic poetry is a process that begins with an intense experience that "demands" the poet speak. As the poet meditates and muses on this experience, not as a solitary but "in the presence of a god," feeling "warms" intellect, words come, offering a way into the poem. Elements of the poet's being are brought into communion with the poem in which content and form dynamically interact. In a process of "crystallization of the elements of experience," words come and the poem is born.

Levertov acknowledges that organic poetry and free verse are similar in that both share a freedom from preexisting models of meter, but she points out that they use this freedom for different ends. Free verse insists on freedom from all bondages, while organic poetry places itself under the strict laws of "inscape," discovered by "instress."[29] Free verse, she writes, is failed organic poetry in that it arises when the poet's attention is "switched off" before the intrinsic form of the experience is revealed.

Earlier, Levertov had taken on Charles Olsen's claim that form was never more than an *extension* of content by insisting that "[f]orm is never more than the *revelation* of content." This point is reiterated again. For her the source and the end of poetry were not language, which is merely the means for the revelation of content. The difference is important,[30] although one not fully appreciated at that point because both Duncan and Creeley appeared to have assented to this seemingly minor modification. Her essay on organic poetry is her attempt to state as clearly as possible her understanding of the relationship between language and meaning. In it she makes reference to several cases of Duncan's influence, but she strains to find a tentative consensus between his ideas and hers.

Although Duncan praised "Some Notes on Organic Form," he also acknowledged that his experience of form was less stable than hers,[31] and that he thought of his poetry as "linguistic" rather than organic.[32] But both poets wanted to claim complementarity in their views, even though differences did exist between them. For Duncan there was no meaning independent or prior to its creation through language. For Levertov, the poet discovered and revealed meaning that was prior to language. However, at this point this fissure remained unexplored. Only in retrospect did the full implications of these differences become evident.

In "Some Notes on Organic Form" Levertov suggests that form and technique work together to give birth to the poem. This notion is examined more fully in "Line-Breaks, Stanza-Spaces, and the Inner Voice," first given as an interview and then published in the same year as her essay on organic poetry.[33] In this she defines the function of these technical devices as the means by which the poet's inner voice emerges not as speech but as song. Techniques are used to record what she calls the inner voice of the poet. Among them she gives pride of place to the line-break, that small hiatus in ongoing perception, like a half comma, which is the source of both melody and pitch pattern bringing a poem close to music.[34]

More than a decade later Levertov returned to explicate these poetic techniques.[35] In these later essays she explores indentation, capitalization, and interruption of clauses in nonmetrical poetry. But the line-break continues to take precedence over all of them. She calls it the poet's most important tool, one producing subtle and precise effects. It is the line-break that makes possible exploratory poetry — that is poetry that reveals the thinking/feeling process that gives birth to the poem. The most important function of this tool is rhythmic. As a parallel form of punctuation, the line-break records the subtle movement among perceptions. Combined with indentation, it makes possible a record of hesitations and pauses that invite the reader to intimately participate in the poem. In addition, the line-break allows for various melodies to emerge and hence different meanings to be apprehended. Of all the tools of the poetic craft, Levertov insisted that the line-break was preeminent.

In order to illustrate how organic poetry proceeds, how these techniques work, and how the poet enters the poem, Levertov reconstructs the process of writing her poem "The Tulips."[36] She describes receiving a bunch of red tulips that gradually wither and become "wild blue." The silence within her gives rise to a pause. The tulips' petals are "winglike," reminding her of "jack rabbit ears." The tulips are near the window, and when its pane rattles, the petals fall. And we listen for that small sound.[37] In exploring the creation of another poem, "The Son," she links memory, experience, and knowledge of the human condition. She waits for words to find her, details to assert themselves, images to arise. Digressions are abandoned, variant words are attempted. And all of this is produced in an intense dreamy and sensuous state. The emergent poem requires not only laborious work on her part, but a quality of what Keats called "Negative Capability," a kind of "intense passivity" during which words find the poet. She admits that this "passionate patience" is the basis of her own poetry, the opportunity for words to be given.[38]

In another essay, "Notebook Pages," Levertov draws a close connection between the song in a thing and the melody in the poet herself, confirming that the experience of the poet and the created work are directly linked. "The *being* of things," she writes,

> has inscape, has melody, which the poet picks up as one voice picks up, and sings, a song from another, and transmits, transposes it, into tones others can hear. And *in his doing so* lies the inscape and melody of the poet's *own* being.[39]

Levertov's articulation of poetics had consequences for her own craft. *O Taste and See*, her sixth volume of poetry, appeared at this same time. In reviewing this collection, Albert Gelpi claimed that in its poems one could see Levertov's "combination of integrity and energy and technical control that allows her to hold her pivotal place at the spinning center of contemporary poetry."[40] If Williams showed "the rhythm of speech *as* poetry" and H. D. provided "doors, ways in, tunnels through" "to penetrate mystery," Levertov could now use the "obscure directions" of these masters to explore her own inner experience. *Here and Now* focused on the external world, and *The Jacob's Ladder* on a deeper meaning in things. In *O Taste and See*, she plumbed her own inner life as an artist and woman.

In this volume Levertov reverses Wordsworth's "the world is too much with us" and claims instead that "[t]he world is / not with us enough," encouraging the reader to "taste and see." The way through to this world was to take it into oneself, to "bite, / savor, chew, swallow, transform / / into our flesh."[41] In another poem she speaks of her desire to replace God, "to worship *mortal*."[42] In "Claritas" she analogizes the artist with the sparrow who strives "in hope and / good faith to make his notes / ever more precise, closer / to what he knows."[43]

What was closer to what she knew was her own roiling inner conflict as woman and artist. In *O Taste and See* Levertov writes with directness and insight about marriage, sex, and erotic longing, concluding the volume with three "runes": know your world; know yourself; know that if "you would grow, go straight up or deep down."[44] In *O Taste and See* Levertov was going "deep down" in order to discover the world and herself simultaneously.

O Taste and See contains poems of erotic ecstasy and the divided self. The volume opens with the wild, compelling "The Song of Ishtar," a paean of praise to copulation in which "[i]n the black of desire / we rock and grunt, grunt and / shine" when the "great shining shines through me / . . . and breaks in silver bubbles."[45] In "Love Song" the body is analogized to a landscape on which sexual longing is acted out. In "Eros at Temple Stream" she speaks of bodies on fire. In "A Psalm Praising the Hair on Man's Body" she honors the ruff of breast and groin. But the power of *O Taste and See* is in the poems related to woman's split self.

The theme of the divided woman was evident in Levertov's early volumes. In *Here and Now* "earthwoman" and "waterwoman" are juxtaposed. In *With Eyes at the Back of Our Heads* the wife is portrayed as compliant. In the poems of *O Taste and See* the split in woman continues to be acknowledged, along with a bitter attack on women themselves and recognition of the sorrow of marriage. In "In Mind" Levertov pits an innocent, unadorned, kind woman who has no imagination, against the moon-ridden girl, who knows strange songs but is not kind.[46] In "Hypocrite Women" she responds to Jack Spicer's misogynist poem. She castigates women as hypocrites, herself included, for not speaking of their own doubts, but consoling men in theirs, and for having pared down their dreams "like toenails," "like ends of split hair."[47] In two of her poems about marriage she expresses both the sorrow of unfulfilled communion and fear of lost freedom. There is an "ache of marriage," but her plea is, "Don't lock me in wedlock, I want / marriage, an / encounter — ."[48]

For the next decade, in both her life and poetry, Levertov wrestled with marriage, her perceived lack of freedom, and her desire for intense, passionate, and life-giving relationship. Pulled in one direction and then another, she considered feminist issues in her work but rejected the designation of feminist for herself. She was not to be categorized. She insisted that the issue of being a female artist did not influence her work. When she writes, "It is hard to be an artist in this time because it is hard to be human," she is referring to the difficulty of artistic life in time of war; however, this might just as well have been said about her inability to navigate the shoals of gender and artistic integration.

By the mid-1960s the Goodmans' marriage began to unravel. There was less and less "encounter" between them.[49] Although in the past Denise felt responsible for Mitch's well-being as husband and writer, she was now giving up on this. She had a "dreadful anxiety" about him and no longer felt as if she knew what was best for him and his work, even though she believed he was potentially a great writer and artist.[50]

Other encounters filled the emotional gap in her life. Teaching gave her satisfaction, as did her relationship with Duncan, whom she met a few times in San Francisco, in Vancouver in 1963, and again in April 1964 at a reading sponsored by the Academy of American Poets at the Guggenheim Museum in New York City. But since they were seldom together in person, it was their almost weekly correspondence that cemented their intimate, affectionate, and professionally rewarding friendship.

Their relationship was complex. Duncan was involved in a longtime homosexual liaison with Jess Collins, whom Levertov respected and admired. She adulated Duncan, and he bolstered her sense of worth as a poet. Each became the emotional and intellectual center for the other, so much so that Levertov claimed that Goodman was jealous of their friendship.[51] In July 1962, Levertov records a dream in which she tenderly put her head on Duncan's chest as he put his arms around her and stroked her hair saying "I am your Shepherd." A few lines later she comments on Mitch's sexual failure.[52] In 1964, she wrote to Duncan: "Robert: I love you. I love your work, & at the same time in my very slow growth . . . have *just* come to the point where I can dare to 'disagree' with someone I so much admire."[53] Neither she nor he saw her proclamation of beginning independence as any kind of break. Duncan wrote back a few weeks later saying:

> So don't grieve. I can't imagine not loving you, and love can find no offense in misunderstanding. Nor in disagreements, which we've often had. But I do know what you can fear, for there are times when I've not heard from you when I think "O now she has turnd [*sic*] away. I've lost my place in her heart."[54]

Levertov's tentative assertion that she had finally come to the point where she could "disagree" with Duncan was not a statement of emotional estrangement. Her attachment to him remained strong. In her diary of 1965 she records another dream in which a young girl sends a marriage proposal to Duncan. In the dream, Levertov tries to dissuade the girl from sending the letter, but can not explain why. Later in analyzing the dream, she wrote that she had a certain flirtation pleasure in identifying with this young girl.[55] In April 1966 she wrote Duncan a letter-poem, which concluded:

"Love"?—I love you but
I love
                another, as you do.
Love I send, but I send it
in another word.
                Longing?
                        Poetry.[56]

Although their intimate friendship was not expressed sexually, theirs was an "encounter" full of a desire that nurtured and sustained each of them. However by 1966, consciously or unconsciously, Levertov found a way to establish an incipient intellectual independence from the man she both publicly and privately acknowledged as "her Master." In a letter to Duncan and in a published statement advertising one of his books she suggested that he was a powerful presence, "mountain-like," one who could best be emulated by one "being more oneself."[57]

During the early 1960s Levertov was emotionally absorbed by marital tension and poetic friendship. However, her initial political activity dates from this period as well. Unlike many other activists, she did not begin her political engagement in the civil rights movement.[58] Rather it was increasing national paranoia toward the Soviet Union and the call for compulsory air-raid drills, the construction of defense shelters, and the testing of nuclear weapons that prompted her participation in a City Hall Park action in New York City in 1960 at which twenty-nine people were arrested, including Dorothy Day, the cofounder of the Catholic Worker movement. The following year in April 1961, both she and Mitch took part in another demonstration in which participants wore buttons urging "Stop the Testing" and carried banners reading "Peace is our only Shelter." Both were arrested, and so began their long string of protest activities and arrests, which were monitored by the Federal Bureau of Investigation.[59]

It was the buildup of U.S. military influence in Southeast Asia, however, that deepened Levertov's engagement in antiwar activity. In 1964 when she was asked to help organize an antiwar protest, she agreed but added she really had no idea how to do this. Ultimately, nothing came of the request; however, the following year after the escalation of hostilities over the Gulf of Tonkin incident, she dreamed she needed to engage in antiwar work. In April she and her friend Muriel Rukeyser solicited support from writers and artists for a New York Times advertisement against the war. Five hundred people signed on, and from among that group, Levertov and Rukeyser organized Writers and Artists Protest Against the Vietnam War.[60] It was only after Levertov began her opposition to the Vietnam war that Goodman joined that effort in which he would ultimately come to play a major role.

Antiwar work energized both Goodman and Levertov, but it did not improve their marriage. Levertov gained emotional satisfaction not from shared engagement with her husband but from the friendship and common purpose she had with others, particularly student activists, who were often more than twenty years her junior. With them she came alive.

At this point she was constantly preoccupied by the war, and this had consequences for her writing. As she indicated to an interviewer, "I couldn't write anything *but* a political poem because this was what was on my mind night and day."[61] Her first antiwar poem, "Life at War," was published in 1966. Its title signified the pervasive nature of war and how it transformed life itself. In creating the poem, she followed the approach taken in *O Taste and See:* an event is taken into the body of the poet and is experienced there. What does war do? It numbs, gets "caught in the chest"; its grits pock the lungs; the imagination becomes "filmed over with the gray filth of it." Her lament is that humans, capable of language, mercy, and kindness, are responsible for a war in which entrails run out, breasts are broken open, and skinned penises are discarded in gullies.[62] Life is at war with itself. Indeed, "it is hard to be an artist in this difficult time because it is hard to be human."

During the mid-1960s Levertov's frenetic antiwar activity left her psychologically fragile. Her diary documents her deteriorating relationship with Mitch and her increasing vulnerability. In these entries her full, open handwriting changed markedly, giving visual evidence of her overwrought anxiety.[63]

Now in her early forties Levertov was emotionally needy, and she knew it. A few years earlier she had admitted that if she were affirmed by a male, she would think him in love with her and she would be stirred erotically.[64] It was no different now.

Levertov came to realize that she enjoyed living apart from Mitch; teaching at Vassar convinced her of that. In an effort to encourage their separation, she indirectly suggested that he have an affair; after all she was suspicious he had had one while he was teaching at Stanford, and much to her surprise she was not jealous.[65] While she recognized Mitch was determined and sweet, his lack of self-confidence, which she worried might be actually slowing his mental processes, made her incapable of respecting him as an artist. Feeling ambivalent toward him, she would then be ashamed of her lack of faith and patience with him.

As she reflected on their marriage, Levertov sometimes admitted that she too might have contributed to its slow disintegration. In her diaries she claimed she had a "dark side," which was petulant, hysterical, cold, and malevolent, but then she would quickly add that she believed Mitch was actively and deliberately depriving her of an erotic life. Twice she recorded an almost identical fantasy: Mitch would propose divorce and she would agree only to realize that she was too old and that no one would want to marry her. He had taken the best years of her life

To her mind her relationship with her father helped explain her feelings toward her husband. As a child she resented her father's preoccupation with his work and his inability to express affection for her. Without paternal comfort or solace, she suspected she demanded greater affection from Mitch to make up for it.[66] She analogized her "tough" response toward her father with her attitude toward Mitch, who lacked erotic affection for her.[67]

Seeing no exit from her marital dilemma, Levertov wrote that she felt close to insanity. In early 1967, anxious about both her marriage and the escalation of the war, she wrote Duncan: "I was as near a sort of crackup as I have ever been at the beginning of Jan. — but we went to Puerto Rico for 10 days & I pulled myself together."[68]

As if she were not fretful enough, Levertov felt a pressing need to come to terms with the life and death of her brilliant, compassionate, yet troubled sister. But, of course, the memory of Olga was tangled in the complex relationships within the Levertoff family: her father's early adoration of Olga; her mother's fear and probable resentment toward her oldest daughter; Denise's own acolyte relationship with her sister; and her mother's undue control of her.[69] Aside from Denise's analysis of her family dynamic, the fact was that as soon as they were able, both sisters left home, escaping the influence of parents. Olga ran away with a lover, and Denise left first for underage civilian service and then for Holland and marriage to Mitch, all in short order.

In her soul-searching about her sister, what emerged were the "Olga Poems," in which Levertov not only wrestled with the meaning of Olga's life and death but with her own demons. The "Olga Poems" were in part autobiographical.

Olga, a powerful and manipulative personality, led a dissolute life and prompted bewilderment and fear on the part of her entire family. In pondering this life, Denise ricocheted between resentment and grief. She castigated Olga for her "ruthless" stridency,[70] but her own stridency was full-blown at this point. Some years later when Levertov reread her entries on her sister's life, she wrote in pencil as a sidebar: "So odd to read this 20 yrs later & realize how *like* Olga I became & in many ways still am."[71] The fact is that the structure of the personality of these two sisters, especially their sense of responsibility for defeating evil in the world, was similar. For Levertov to write poems about Olga was in some sense to confront herself.

Levertov saw her sister's life as a "maze," an impossible jumble of events, although many others remembered her as a "magnetic and wonderful person"[72] who helped organize and served as the secretary of the Yellow Star Movement, an organization opposing racial and anti-Semitic injustice. In her last years Olga participated in antinuclear demonstrations and reasserted her Christian-Socialist ideas, although in the end she might have allied herself with Judaism since her gravestone was inscribed with a Star of David.

Denise brought all of her ambivalence and emotion about her sister to bear in the "Olga Poems," which were appropriately included in *The Sorrow Dance*. These poems focused on Levertov's remembrances of the times and places they shared. However, her positive memories of her sister were overshadowed by the dread she encountered in the one she called the "Black One," the "incubus," one who "browbeat" and "wanted to shout the world to its senses," whose will, rage, insistence, and manipulation were aimed at bringing in the reign of a just world order. For Olga, this quest became a mania, disordering her life. But Levertov asserted that through it all "a white candle" burned in Olga's heart. As she imagines her sister dying, her body consumed by cancer, pain, and drugs,[73] she asks rhetorically:

> Through the years of humiliation,
> of paranoia and blackmail and near-starvation, losing
> the love of those you loved, one after another,
> parents, lovers, children, idolized friends, what kept
> compassion's candle alight in you?[74]

While the enigma of Olga remained, Levertov could have asked this same question of herself: What would keep compassion's candle burning in her as she confronted the inhumanity of war?

Levertov's memories of her sister did not quickly abate. After participating in an antiwar demonstration in Times Square in 1966 in which she wore a locket — "reliquary" — for Olga, she recorded three experiences that reminded her of her sister. In the poem "A Note to Olga,"[75] Levertov remembers the brokenness of her sister's life, but she interprets that life as a testimony of engagement with an unjust world.

What is remarkable about this period in Levertov's life was her ability to simultaneously engage in protest activity and write prolifically. Her major publications in 1967 were *In Praise of Krishna: Songs from the Bengali* and *The Sorrow Dance*.[76] The former was Levertov's first major work of translation, which she undertook with Edward C. Dimock, whom she met through her friend Bonnie Crown at the Asia Society.[77] It was as if at last she were responding to Eliot's suggestion, made long ago, that translation would make her a better poet. Other translations would follow.[78]

Her volume of poems *The Sorrow Dance* contained what Levertov would later call her first attempt at poetry *"on the edge of darkness."*[79] Many of its poems — "A Lamentation," "Olga Poems," "A Note to Olga," "Life At War," and "The Mutes" — are written in "grief-language." In "The Mutes" she writes of the groans of men ogling women. Theirs is "language stricken, sickened, cast-down / in decrepitude." It gives evidence that "'[l]ife after life after life goes by / / without poetry, / without seemliness, / without love.'"[80] Others, such as "What Were They Like," "Two Variations," "Altars in the Street," and "Life at War" refer specifically to the Vietnam War.

Although most of the poems of *The Sorrow Dance* are dark, a few speak of "a jubilation echoing from wonder." In two psalm poems, Levertov attempts to find a way to hold together the opposites of sorrow and hope by searching for an answer "not behind but within" reality itself. In "Psalm Concerning the Castle" she depicts the castle as a place of growth where imagination can flourish. In litany form she petitions: "let that country where (the castle) / stands be within me, let me be where it is."[81] In "City Psalm," she confronts injustice head on. It is a poem resulting, she said, not from LSD, which she admitted to having used, but from an un-induced experience made possible because she was a medium for poetry itself.[82] In this masterful poem, Levertov's "claritas" of vision shines through violence and war:

> The killings continue, each second
> pain and misfortune extend themselves
> in the genetic chain, injustice is done knowingly, and the air
> bears the dust of decayed hopes,
> ....

But then she suggests a way through:

I have seen
not behind but within, within the
dull grief, a gleam
·····················
an abode of mercy,
have heard not behind but within noise
a humming . . .
Nothing was changed, all was revealed otherwise;
not that horror was not, not that the killings did not continue, . . .
···
but that as if transparent all disclosed
an otherness that was blesse'd, that was bliss.
I saw Paradise in the dust of the streets.

Because of its darkness, *The Sorrow Dance* provoked criticism, but even her biting critic Robert Bly, writing under the pseudonym "Crunk," commended some of her war poetry as "private poems whose movement was at times magnificent."[83]

As Levertov continued to write poems, she also continued to explore the poetic vocation. In a lecture given in 1967 she reiterated the theme of the need for the interaction of life and art lest both be diminished. She also sketched out the obligations of the writer

[to] take personal and active responsibility for his words, whatever they are, and to acknowledge their potential influence on the lives of others. . . . When words penetrate deep into us they change the chemistry of the soul, of the imagination. We have no right to do that to people if we don't share the consequences.[84]

If the work of poetry was to celebrate life, then the poet must have total involvement in life in order to preserve it. To be poet was to be "poet in the world." Trying to live into this appellation, Levertov wrote political poetry and engaged in extensive opposition to the war.

Family life went on. The Goodmans spent the summer of 1967 in Maine. Nik was off in Europe prior to enrolling in the Rhode Island School of Design where he had been awarded a scholarship. Mitch worked on antiwar organizing, and Denise dedicated herself to two projects and attended the Montreal Poetry Conference. She had some concern about participating in the conference because Ezra Pound was slated to give opening remarks and she was fearful of becoming embroiled in the public protest over his appear-

FIGURE 6. Nikolai Gregor Goodman, circa 1966. Special Collections, Stanford University.

ance. As one of the "great ones," Pound had obviously inspired her. A few years earlier when she presented a paper at a Pound symposium, she tried to minimize the impact of his "racist and rightist" ideas on her,[85] arguing that they were "abhorrent" to her and an "aberration" in him. She attested that her personal contact with Pound had been "marked by kindness and probity" and that his legacy to her was that he taught her to not accept "received ideas without question." As it turned out, Pound canceled his appearance in Montreal; she was relieved. Nonetheless the incident is instructive as an example of a dilemma Levertov would increasingly face, namely how to respond when her admiration for a poet's work conflicted with the poet's political views. From here on, she would insist that she could not and would not praise anyone with the wrong politics. "I've come to be more and more intolerant of people whom I can't respect politically," she said in 1973, "and to feel in fact that there are situations in which tolerance is not a virtue. I have a poem about it. It says 'O tolerance, what crimes have been committed in thy name.'"[86]

As the decade moved toward its end and the war raged on, Levertov became less tolerant and more engaged in protest on the streets and in her writing and speaking. She spent the summer of 1967 compiling and editing "Out of the War Shadow," the 1968 War Resisters League calendar and anthology of poetry. Dedicated to the recently deceased A. J. Muste, pacifist and antiwar activist, the calendar included poems by many of her friends: Hayden Carruth, Robert Creeley, Barbara Deming, Robert Duncan, among others, as well as her own "Altars in the Street," a poem much beloved by Muste.

Another summer project was the development of a lecture to be given at a meeting of theologians and poets convened under the auspices of the Church Society for College Work at the Washington National Cathedral in October 1967. Among the select group of participants brought together to discuss myth, parable, and language, Levertov was the only woman. As she prepared her talk she reflected on the full sweep of her poetry from *The Double Image* through *The Sorrow Dance* and discovered, much to her delight, that from the beginning there was in her work a myth, a "plot behind the plot." Her presentation, published subsequently as "A Sense of Pilgrimage," traces the myth of pilgrimage through her life and work, linking the spirit of the here-and-now with the notion of quest. Conceiving of life as "a vale of soul-making," a term she borrowed from her beloved Keats, she recognized that its purpose was not so much to arrive at a destination as to hold to a purpose, to keep a candle alight all the way through life.[87] Although she did not offer Cézanne as an exemplar of such tenacity and "continuance," he would be referred to in her later work for precisely these attributes.

Perhaps because she was in a religious setting or because there were theologians in the group, Levertov offered a coda to her presentation indicating that she believed the rites and traditions of religious orthodoxy could have a positive poetic advantage, but that the reality was that most poets were agnostics or atheists. She referred to herself as a "sort of peripheral syncretist type,"[88] meaning she was not religiously orthodox. Not one to forego the opportunity to win support for the antiwar movement, Levertov distributed materials on conscientious objection to conference participants. Then after two days of scintillating discussion of myth and poetry she went directly across town to take part in an antiwar march that brought an estimated 70,000–100,000 antiwar demonstrators to the nation's capital. She persuaded Duncan, who also attended the meeting, to stay over to participate as well.

At this point Goodman, too, was heavily engaged in antiwar activity. His initial participation began in 1965, followed in February 1966 by his helping to organize World War II veterans in an antiwar march down Fifth Avenue in New York after which they burned their military discharge papers. A month later he lead a walkout at the National Book Award ceremony in Philharmonic Hall where Vice President Hubert Humphrey addressed the audience, and a few months after that while teaching in the Voice Project at Stanford University, he garnered some fifty faculty and staff signatures on a pledge of civil disobedience against the war. During the summer of 1967 while in Maine he drafted "A Call to Conscientious Resistance to the War," which brought him together with Noam Chomsky from MIT and

Rev. William Sloan Coffin from Yale. In the fall he helped organize an event that brought some one hundred persons together to turn in thousands of draft cards to the Justice Department. The leaders of this action, The Boston Five — William Sloan Coffin, chaplain; Dr. Benjamin Spock, noted pediatrician; Michael Ferber, Harvard graduate student; Marcus Raskin, writer; and Goodman, the organizer and detail man — were charged with violation of the Selective Service Law. The following day demonstrators rallied at the Lincoln Memorial, and later about 30,000 of them marched on the Pentagon.[89] Mitch Goodman was center stage as Americans, riveted to the television screen, watched protesters challenge the government and its war.

The final months of 1967 were a protracted period of waiting for indictments. Since Levertov was not teaching that semester, after the October demonstrations she traveled around the country giving poetry readings. These provided some income as well as an opportunity to stimulate interest in the antiwar movement. She went to Tucson, to Union College in East Kentucky, and then to the University of Kentucky at Lexington. It was then on to Chicago and to Winona, Minnesota, and St. Teresa's College where she met Sister Bernetta Quinn and spoke to contemplative nuns.[90]

While she was in Kentucky she stayed with the poet Wendell Berry and his wife, Tanya, and met the photographer Ralph Meatyard who arranged on December 10th for all of them to visit Thomas Merton, the Trappist monk and poet, at the nearby monastery of Gethsemane. As early as 1961, Merton had read some of Levertov's poetry and wrote the Nicaraguan poet and theologian, Ernesto Cardenal, that he thought her work was splendid.[91] The same year in correspondence with Mark van Doren, Merton said he had read Levertov's poem "The Artist" and found "[i]t is very fine, very spiritual in a broad, Jungian sort of way."[92] Prior to their meeting, Levertov's only contact with Merton had been a solicitation for one of his poems to be included in the War Resisters' League Calendar. After they met, Merton recorded in his journal that he found Levertov to be a warm person whom he liked very much and that he was grateful she shared with him her newly composed antiwar poem "Tenebrae."[93] Years later in reflecting back on their brief meeting, Levertov said they talked mostly about the peace movement, not about literature, and certainly not about anything religious since she had no religious commitment at the time.[94] There was no further substantive correspondence between them,[95] and a year to the day from their meeting, Merton died in a freak accident in Thailand. Twenty-five years later Levertov would publish "On a Theme by Thomas Merton."[96]

By 1968, Levertov's extensive antiwar work prompted an interviewer to ask whether her political action had an effect on her artistic life. She answered that actually it was the other way around. She said that as a poet she had for a long time said things in poems that had moral implications and she believed that one had an obligation as a human being to follow those moral implications with actions. "So I feel that it is poetry that has led me into political action and not political action which has caused me to write poems more overtly engaged than those I used to write."[97] For one who considered herself "poet in the world," her statement reflected the actual genesis of her antiwar engagement, but her answer was nonetheless evasive. Had her antiwar work affected her artistic life? Decidedly yes, as she herself revealed in "Advent 1966." In this poem she reports that the grim destruction of the war had devastated her poetic vision: "my clear caressive sight, my poet's sight I was given / that it might stir me to song, / is blurred. / / There is a cataract filming over / my inner eyes."[98]

While the consequences of her antiwar activity and her foray into political poetry were lamented by many, it was unclear at this point what the long-term effect would be. In the short term, however, she knew it meant that her "claritas" was distorted.

5

"Staying Alive"
1968-1971

There is despite my age something green & undeveloped about me.
DENISE LEVERTOV, DIARY, 1969[1]

As "poet in the world," Denise Levertov's writing reflected the great social upheaval in American society in the late 1960s. But that upheaval, focused as it was on the Vietnam War, does not explain her sense of personal anxiety. Overwrought, fretful, and needy, she contemplated an accidental suicide.[2] In a letter to Duncan she described her battered state:

Well, I am in pain and sometimes don't know where to turn, as if all salt had lost its savor, but perhaps indeed my life has deepened as it has darkened. I want to say Pray for me, but to whom. I don't know what god has afflicted me. Is it Eros? I thought so but now I'm not even sure.[3]

Her pain was exacerbated by the fact that she did not know its source or how to cure it. Now in her midforties, she had come to the surprising realization that there was something "green & undeveloped" in her. She wanted to be whole, to integrate her inner and outer life, but she had to deal not only with persons and circumstances that were beyond her control but with her own past. Her "undevelopment" impeded her ability to respond maturely to her situation, yet it was precisely this "greenness" that was the wellspring of her childlike wonder at life, the source of her poetic insight.

"Greenness" was the legacy of her protracted childhood. Solitude and protection from social intercourse allowed her imagination to flourish and her communion with the natural world to deepen. But this extended childhood was followed by an abbreviated adolescence. The usual maturation of young adulthood was foreshortened for her. By her own admission she was forced to grow up quickly. But in some ways her adolescence was also prolonged. Now well into middle age, she faced a series of difficult problems:

a war that raged on with no end in sight, a marriage in which she had no "encounter," a mentor who would shortly reject her poetry and warn her against the consequence of her political engagement, and a reputation that would be tarnished by what was called her "protest" poetry. Her flickering self-insight offered no solace or way through. During the four years between 1968 and 1971, Levertov was forced to grow in new ways. It was the nadir of her life. What she needed most was to "stay alive."

As 1968 began, Levertov had no inkling of what might transpire over the next year. Of course, she was anxious about Mitch's indictment, but other pressures were minimal. She had no teaching responsibilities or book deadline that year. A second grant from the American Academy of Arts and Letters and extensive poetry readings — she gave seventeen in a seven-month period — provided adequate financial support. And there would be a return visit to Puerto Rico and, after a hiatus of three years, a visit with her mother in Mexico. There would also be cause for celebration. She would have Mitch's little book of poems, *Light from under a Bushel*, printed privately, and Nik, who was studying at the Rhode Island School of Design, would make it through his first year, although he would lose his scholarship because of poor academic performance.

Nonetheless the year turned out to be one of the worst in her life. In the midst of strife and concerned over losing her poetic vision, Levertov continued to write.[4] The most haunting of her several poems published that year was "A Tree Telling of Orpheus," which was illustrated with four of her own pen-and-pencil drawings. Narrated in the voice of a tree, this compelling poem tells of the coming of the Thracian poet, Orpheus, and the transformation he wrought.[5] The tree recounts how the sound of the poet's voice penetrates its roots and shoots, telling of dreams and making it "deeply alert." "[I]n terror" "but not in doubt," the tree understands Orpheus's song. In response to his music, it wrenches itself from the soil, and with its brother trees follows the sound of the poet, who soon is gone. The trees wait, sure only that they have lived. Having seen and felt more, they are incapable now of returning to their former selves. What is rendered in this poem is the story of transformation, of permanent change and clarity emergent from a profound inner experience.

On the national level the event that galvanized Levertov was the war. The other significant events of the year — the assassinations of Martin Luther King and Robert Kennedy and the 1968 Democratic Convention — are not mentioned in her journals or poetry. She began the year with a speech at the Jeanette Rankin Brigade march in Washington D.C. in which more than five thousand women participated. This was followed by extensive travel to give poetry readings, which allowed her to meet with local war resisters to encourage their work.

While she waited for Mitch's trial to begin, she wrote "An Interim," a poem in which she speaks both of relishing the opportunity the trial would give her to "confront the war makers" and lamenting the war's destruction of life and of language. Quoting the military justification: "'It became necessary / to destroy the town to save it,'" she mourns this manipulation of language, which she calls the "mother of thought." She admonished her readers not to be heartsick for Goodman and her but for the crimes of war itself and the suffering of "the great savage saints of outrage," those who were sacrificing their lives in resistance, those in jail, and those who had immolated themselves.[6] "An Interim" like much of the poetry of this period, expressed a rage and vehemence that can only be explained as emanating from a personal battle with evil.

After six months, the trial of the "Boston Five" finally began in late May in Federal District Court. The defendants had become antiwar heroes, and some twenty-eight thousand people signed a statement of complicity agreeing to take their places. Although Marcus Raskin was acquitted, the other four were found guilty of conspiring to incite violation of the Selective Service Law and were sentenced on July 10th to two years in prison; Coffin, Spock, and Goodman were each fined five thousand dollars. On the following day, the U.S. Court of Appeals for the First Circuit in Boston overturned the convictions on technical grounds, and charges against Spock and Ferber were dismissed. Evidence against Goodman and Coffin could have led to a retrial, but the prosecution never pursued the matter.[7]

The trial and the ongoing war continued to take a psychic toll on Levertov, and her anxiety was compounded by her unsatisfactory relationship with Mitch. In the summer of 1968 she wrote in her diary:

What I need to learn is to acknowledge my own dark, Dionysian, irrational side, at the same time, if I don't want to hurt others & ruin all I hold most dear, *not* take refuge from it in mere retreat into a moralism that breaks down so easily & is not founded in deep conviction but only in the need to feel I'm on the right side; *but instead*, to discover some other kind of strength—a mature, skeptical even, gut-felt way to avoid disasters without denying the *existence* of impulses which, if followed, wd be destructive.[8]

A mature way was not to be found, at least in the short run. Her relationship with Mitch was made more complex by a recent infatuation with George Quasha, a handsome instructor in his late twenties at the State University of New York at Stony Brook. Quasha and Levertov shared interests in the work of Eugene Guillevic and Rilke but were also joined in their admiration for Duncan. Quasha was finishing up a dissertation on Duncan, and Levertov agreed to share her letters from Duncan with him. The first substantive encounter between them was in 1968 at an international poetry conference held at Stony Brook. Subsequently Levertov published an essay in *Stony Brook Magazine* edited by Quasha. Their aesthetic and emotional attraction led Levertov to a desire for sexual encounter. In two poems she expressed this longing. In "Mad Song" she claimed to cherish a "viper" within. She queried: "How am I to be cured against my will?"[9] In another she described herself as "a woman foolish with desire."[10] This emotionally freighted relationship with Quasha was not merely about the need for sexual intimacy but also about the desire to remain young, attractive, and the subject of adoration. It established a pattern that would be replicated several times in subsequent years.

Her diary entries for the summer of 1968 confirmed this experience. She wrote that sexual feeling between her and Mitch was totally in abeyance. Although she loved him, she was unable to share her powerful and secret fantasy life with him. She worried about aging and the loss of beauty and her determination to stave them off. While she felt that at this point she had recovered her sanity, she had no joy, which she attributed to inhibitions that kept her from living fully. The dilemma was how to follow her impulses to their logical conclusion, to be honest about her infatuation with Quasha with "its kisses and foolish letters," and to not hurt others, especially Mitch.[11]

Quasha's letters reveal his amorousness and gratitude for their relationship. He claimed to be "blessed to the point of speechlessness" and that he "could never be otherwise than *in* love with you."[12] In this relationship Quasha had not only an intimate connection to his hero Duncan but also the attraction of an established older woman poet. He was simultaneously flattered and thrown off balance as to how to negotiate this relationship with Levertov.

When Levertov finally talked with "darling" Mitch about Quasha, he was not angry. Her "infatuation" continued, and a mid-November visit with Quasha at Stony Brook was tumultuous for her. Alone in the Holiday Inn she wept, uncomprehending of her reaction of both shame and humiliation. If Quasha was confused by their relationship, she was too, tangled as it was with her love of Duncan. In her diary she wrote of feeling trapped between her love for Mitch and for Quasha, whom she described at this point as charming but devious and conceited, someone who was not attracted to her because of her advancing age.[13] Then in a startling self-revelatory entry she wrote that she realized how similar her love of Quasha was to her love of Duncan, with the difference that with the latter there was no hope of physical expression, whereas with Quasha there theoretically was. She concluded that she needed more than one love, but a triple love was untenable. Mitch would be her husband and sharer of daily life, but she would have to transfer her love of Duncan to Quasha in order for it to be fulfilled. As a consequence she only wrote episodically to Duncan.[14]

Whether Quasha served unconsciously in her mind as a surrogate for Duncan is unknown, but she nonetheless confessed to Duncan that she had been in an interior "maelstrom" since June, and although she could not write about it in a letter, she had written some poems about it. She confided that she was in pain, and although Mitch had been a "staff" on which she could lean, she feared leaning too hard.[15]

Apparently her pain did not subside. A month later she recorded cryptically in her diary that while she was in Tucson over Christmas, she thought of an accidental suicide.[16] Confused by the experiences of the last year, a few weeks later she recorded her insight about being "green & undeveloped."[17] During the coming months her relationship with Quasha deteriorated after he announced that he planned to marry. For his part Quasha attested that Levertov had affirmed something good in him and that he would always love her and hoped his thoughtlessness and indiscretion had not alienated her for good. But he confessed that, wanting not to hurt her, he found it difficult to be honest and direct with her.[18] There was melodrama as criticisms were lobbed one at the other: Levertov called him wayward and ungrateful; he said she was a woman of extremes. Soon after Quasha's marriage in May 1969, their correspondence ended.[19] In this and in subsequent relationships, Levertov had much at stake. What she considered rejection caused fury, not merely because she felt betrayed but also because her desire and need to feel young, attractive, and worthy of adoration was unrealized.

During the winter and spring terms of 1969, Levertov taught at the University of California, Berkeley, and lived near the campus on Stuart Street. She worked on several writing projects, the most important of which was a bilingual translation of selected poems of the little known French poet Eugene Guillevic. Her intent was not to reproduce Guillevic's work but to reconstitute the original in English as if he had been writing in that language.[20] In her long introduction to his life, Levertov compared Guillevic's simplicity of diction to that of William Carlos Williams and his indignity at the misuse of people with that of Antonio Machado. The work was well-received and resulted in her nomination as a finalist for the 1970 National Book Award in the category of translation.

In addition to the translation and several other projects,[21] Levertov finished a long poem after many months of intense effort. "Relearning the Alphabet" would become the centerpiece of a volume by the same name to be published the following year. Consumed by anger, outrage, and despair over the war and her personal life, she attempted to relearn joy with this poem. The alphabet itself provided the structure for the poem, moving through all twenty-six letters. "A" was for "a beginning;" "B" was for "to be," etc. Her hope was that by relearning the alphabet, letter by letter, word by word, she would "relearn the world," that is, return to the place of her origin as poet and reintegrate her inner and outer life. These aspirations were only partially successful.[22] Understandably, the poem had a quality of drifting, of being lost. She wrote of "stumbling back" to her origins, to her joy, her Jerusalem.[23] The nugget of affirmation in the poem was compromised further by other poems that were published with it. "An Interim," "From a Notebook," "Biafra," "The Gulf," all reflected despair and institutionalized evil.

Relearning the Alphabet was widely reviewed, but the verdict was mixed. Paul Zweig, writing in the *Nation*, panned it as "disappointing," filled with "incomplete poems," "sad" and "self-righteous."[24] Victor Contoski hailed certain of its poems as musical, especially "A Tree Telling of Orpheus" and "An Embroidery (II)," but said the book lacked balance, having more sorrow than joy.[25] On the other hand, Levertov's friend, Bernetta Quinn, applauded the poet's honesty and called her prophetic,[26] and Todd Gitlin saw a new creative energy emerging from its beautiful poems, "which take us to the place where the inner person meets the outer reality."[27]

Levertov's six months in Berkeley were artistically productive, and her teaching experience was therapeutic. As a result she claimed to feel younger, more confident, more open to suggestion, and less authoritarian.[28] In part this probably resulted from the fact that she felt more allied with students than with faculty. At the end of February she wrote Quasha a letter, which she never sent but in which she expressed her delight at being in a place where people had a broader conception of what was beautiful and attractive. She admitted this helped her have greater self-confidence. Although she was forty-five, she said she had the physical condition of a much younger woman. In comparing herself with other poets, she felt she was quite equitable in temperament, even though earlier in life she had had violent rages and was neurotically impatient. She attributed her slightly manic-depressive temperament to the fact that she was half Welsh in heritage and a Scorpio. Obviously emotional consistency could not be expected of her.[29] If she had explored her astrological sign, she would have found congruence with her own character. Scorpios are reputed to be passionate, dynamic, and observant, but also inflexible, suspicious, and fiercely independent.

The winter term at Berkeley began inauspiciously. She taught a general education course in reading and expository writing to thirty mostly uninterested students whom she considered ethically unprepared "savages," students who lacked any understanding of the issues of the Third World Strike that was roiling on campus. However, spring term was another matter. In an elective poetry and prose seminar, she had "intelligent," "sensitive," and "responsive," upper-level students,[30] with whom she experienced a profound sense of human communion and solidarity, not only in the classroom, but also in their collaborative participation in the defense of People's Park.

Student culture at the University of California at Berkeley in the late 1960s was unique. The Free Speech Movement was born there earlier in the decade, and by 1969 the university was a hotbed of civil rights and antiwar activity. In the spring of that year a major confrontation involving the university administration, the governor of California, and student activists occurred over the control of a newly acquired space near campus. Students wanted to claim the area as a people's park, a place where free speech would be allowed. They rallied to turn a muddy lot into a park, planting sod, flowers, shrubs, and vegetables. On the order of Governor Ronald Reagan, the police intervened to oust the students. Tear gas and billy clubs were used by the almost eight hundred police who patrolled the area. The fracas between police and students continued from late May through mid-June; one student was killed, and more than one hundred were injured. Levertov was deeply implicated in these events in that she and others gave inflammatory speeches at Sproul Plaza, which led directly to a march to People's Park and confrontation with the police.[31] She responded generously to her students who participated in these acts of civil disobedience, going as far as paying bail for one who was incarcerated in Santa Rita prison.[32]

Levertov's notes from these events became the basis for her poems. She recorded working together with her students, planting in the park, hauling debris to the dump, participating in daily rallies and marches, and confronting the police. She wrote of experiencing a new vision of a world of gentle and loving people, of the closing of the generation gap among those who undertook common work, and a profound learning that came from acting together in solidarity.[33]

Like thousands of others, Levertov was caught up in the youthful spirit of protest in which confrontation and hope were intertwined. Her "greenness" made her particularly susceptible to what for her seemed like joyful celebration and action on behalf of justice. She relished her sense of solidarity with students but at times was challenged by their excesses. At a Poetry Reading for the People's Park in which Duncan, Ferlinghetti, and others participated and she served as Master of Ceremonies, a student, dressed in costume as an eight-foot pink felt penis, jumped on stage and grabbed the microphone, announcing that he was "the People's Prick." The crowd erupted while the appalled Levertov tried unsuccessfully to gain control of the raucous audience. The student danced around her on the stage, but the forty-six-year-old English-born poet did not have the skills to control the occasion.[34]

Levertov departed Berkeley after the spring term, and in June gave the commencement address at Bennington College before heading back to Temple for the summer where she and Mitch enjoyed their farmhouse with its recently installed bathroom. It was a "lazy," "slack," and "negligent" time. Hayden Carruth and his wife visited, and Levertov wrote Duncan that her "infatuation or enchantment" with Quasha was over and that, just like in the fairy tales, it had lasted a year and a day.[35] The end of this "infatuation" and the solidarity she experienced while at Berkeley appeared to have at least stabilized her emotional life. The leisurely summer gave her the opportunity to write a clutch of ten short poems focused on the themes of tranquility and renewal; they reflected her reprieve after a demanding six months in California.[36]

By the beginning of the fall term, the Goodmans moved to a bay-fronted brick house at 177 Webster Street in East Boston, and Levertov began a new position as visiting professor at Massachusetts Institute of Technology. She enjoyed this teaching assignment, and to honor thirteen of her students she wrote "A New Year's Garland for My Students/MIT: 1969-70."[37] Again, she allied herself with student activists and engaged with them in antiwar protest. In 1970, she accompanied members of the Students for a Democratic Society, SDS, in a takeover of the office of the Institute's president, staying with them through the night during the occupation.[38]

One of her students was Richard Edelman, a neighborhood organizer who subsequently served as her secretary for a few years.[39] Her relationship with Edelman was paradigmatic of her penchant for idealizing talented male student artist/activists. She claimed Edelman was a "rare" person, a "naturally gifted poet," an "activist," and the student from whom she learned most. This admiration was based in the fact that she found in him a double "pulse," the "flame-pulse" of revolution and the "river pulse" of poetry. When these meshed, as she claimed they did in him, then "singing" began.[40]

Although Edelman was special, she had many student friends whom she met at the Institute, on marches or in political organizations. Since most were half her age, they made her feel young and full of life and reduced her anxiety about aging. With them she sensed a shared solidarity and communion; with them she connected to the "pulse" of life itself. As her marriage and long-established friendship with Duncan faltered, she grew more and more dependent on these students, especially Richard Edelman, to ensure her emotional well-being.

In November 1969, while teaching at MIT she participated in a demonstration at the Department of Justice in Washington, D.C. She memorialized that moment in a poem describing the experience of being overcome by tear gas and of "[w]anting it, wanting / with all my hunger this anguish, / this knowing in the body / . . . wanting it real."[41] Her desire for the physical internalization of anguish speaks of her yearning for experience, which made her actually feel alive.

Levertov was impelled both by a sense of righteousness against the war and a desire to experience ecstasy in opposing it. She wanted a vivid life. She later wrote to Duncan:

> I'd sooner spend my last days with the people who have courage & vision & are living their lives vividly right now, & not in a selfish way but always in relation to their sense of a need for a better life for others, even though they make lots of mistakes & are ignorant & often fall flat on their face. Like I do. . . . I'd sooner take the chance that my ideological understandings will become more sophisticated as I go along than wait inactively until I was perfectly sure all I did & all my friends did was morally, intellectually, etc., correct & justified. Because I cd. wait for ever. Meanwhile I have to live with myself, & I'm an impatient person.[42]

Levertov continued a demanding schedule of both political action and lecturing on poetics. In "Great Possessions," an elegant lecture given to the Society for the Arts, Religion, and Contemporary Culture in New York in January 1970,[43] she criticizes much of contemporary poetry and calls for a return to our "great possessions," the capacities for paying attention and having a passion for "the thing known," capacities inherent in each person. She argues that the role of the poet is to "translate" experience to readers and to transport them to other worlds. This is achieved when the poet brings to his work an "ecstatic attention" and an "intensity" that is able to penetrate to the reality of the thing itself. In illustration she quotes from a source that had influenced her own vocation as a poet — Rilke's *Selected Letters*:

> If a thing is to speak to you, you must for a certain time regard it as the only thing that exists, the unique phenomenon that your diligent and exclusive love has placed at the center of the universe, something the angels serve that very day upon that matchless spot.[44]

In her lecture Levertov claims an intimate relationship between the quality of the poet's life, i.e., its abundance and integrity, and the quality of one's poetry. Banal lives produce banal poetry, and sterile and banal poetry does not compel one to take risks and live fully. She suggests that poetry, with its experience of abundance, can be a revolutionary stimulus to life, providing the imaginative energy necessary to survive difficult times. And living in an abundant, life-giving way enriches one's inner self from which poetry flows. "Great Possessions" offers a compelling statement of poetry's ability to engage with the world and to meet the contemporary need to integrate inner and outer life.

In both her poetry and prose Levertov expropriated the antiwar term of "revolution." In "Great Possessions" she claimed poetry was inherently revolutionary, a stimulus to the unlived life. In a speech in April 1970, at an outdoor rally at the University of Massachusetts, a center of antiwar activity, she spoke of the "necessity of revolution." By this she meant not protest over a single issue but the need to take on the entire capitalistic, imperialist system. She said she had come to realize that the issues of war, poverty, racism, social injustice, and male chauvinism could not be compartmentalized; they were connected. Hope lay in the solidarity of all those who opposed these interconnected evils.[45] Later in her lengthy correspondence with Duncan she defended her use of the word "revolution" not as "threat," "vow," or "ultimatum" but as a statement of the need for "a changed society." Although she admitted that she did not know how that change might take place, she knew she wanted to be with those who lived into that aspiration, even though some of them believed armed struggle might be necessary to create a new society.[46]

Levertov's harsh rhetoric sometimes prompted strong opposition. A case

in point was her reception at Goucher College in Maryland in May 1970. After reading a few of her antiwar poems in the college chapel, she called on
her audience to remember those who also had suffered because of their opposition to racism and urged them to engage in militant resistance. Half the
audience walked out on her, and she was condemned for having desecrated
a holy place.[47]

After finishing the spring term at MIT, Levertov went to Colby College
in Maine where she was awarded an honorary degree, and then on to Boulder, Colorado, for two weeks before she left for Europe in early July. Her
European trip involved a stop in Italy on her way to Yugoslavia where she
was scheduled to give a reading. In "Part III," a section of her long poem
"Staying Alive," she writes of these travels, the sense of solidarity she experienced meeting Sudanese and Iraqis in Yugoslavia, her relief at being out of
the "writhing lava" of "Amerika," and her joyful return to England after an
absence of twenty years. England was her "nest," a place where she encountered gentle and kind people.[48] While in England, she returned to the haunts
of her childhood — to Ilford and Valentine Park — and visited her childhood
friend Bet and others who had known her over many years. Bet's advice to
her was to wait in darkness, to "Get down into your well, / / it's your well /
/ go deep into it / / into your own depth as into a poem."[49] This admonition
must have stirred in Levertov memories of her own poem "The Well," written many years earlier.[50] These encounters left her feeling refreshed, confident, and happy, relieved of the anxiety of aging and of sexual longing.[51]

Although she arrived back in Boston renewed, her solace dissipated quickly. She realized that her new position, a yearlong commitment as artist-in-
residence at Kirkland College in Clinton, New York, would not be felicitous.
She disliked the place and as a consequence spent as much time as possible
in Boston, interacting with students with whom she read poetry, listened to
guitar music, drank, and partied, thereby integrating herself into their lives.
Richard Edelman became a constant in those circles. Her relationship with
Mitch became more and more attenuated.

In June Mitch finished a writing project he had labored over for two years.
*The Movement toward a New America: The Beginnings of a Long Revolution: A
Collage — A What?* carried the citation "assembled by Mitchell Goodman, a
charter member of the Great Conspiracy, on behalf of The Movement."[52] He
thought of this not as a book but as a chronicle of people making their own
history. As he conceived it, The Movement had a life of its own, a complex
manner of thinking and being, and a unique state of mind that could be
grasped through the evidences it produced — letters, newspaper clippings,

flyers, cartoons, photographs, and alternative institutions and sources of information. His collection of artifacts resulted in a book almost eight hundred pages in length, a book that reflected the antiwar sentiments both he and Denise shared.

Although one might suspect this publication gave Goodman some pleasure, there is no evidence of an improvement in his emotional well-being or in his marital relationship. In early December he and Levertov sought out a Dr. Pearlman for marital counseling. Levertov's diary entries for this period reflected her continuing confusion about her marriage. According to her account, she admitted that she loved to be with Mitch and had never met anyone else with whom she wanted to spend her life, but she believed he had an underlying feeling of defeat and degradation. In their counseling session she said he spoke of humiliation and psychic castration.[53] While she realized that Mitch cared about her, she believed he also undermined her self-esteem by not seeing her as attractive or seductive and treating her as a poor creature who needed help. But others affirmed her as warm, inspirational, and lovable. Who was correct? she asked in her diary. Should she and Mitch separate? Was she not really a grown-up person? Why had she never learned to drive a car? Did her problems derive from the fact that she never made a definite break from her parents? Her questions indicated that she was confronting her "undevelopment" and her sense of being paralyzed.[54]

Her confusion is confirmed by a letter to Richard Edelman toward the end of 1970. As was often her custom she would write a diary entry or letter in order to both review and make sense of an issue. In this long letter to Edelman, which she never mailed, she reflects on the changes she had undergone during the last year and a half. The period began when, fearful of aging and becoming unattractive, she became infatuated with George Quasha. She described it as a time when she was unable to stop crying.[55] In retrospect she realized Quasha was a "creation of her imagination," an expression of her need to love others and not feel boxed in. However, the real catalyst for change in her consciousness occurred at Berkeley where she experienced comradeship; shared danger; and mutual, reciprocal relationship. That experience brought her to reevaluate her love of solitude and her possessions, the value she had placed on marriage, and her commitment to nonviolence. She felt like an adolescent who was challenging her long and passionately held assumptions. Although she knew of Mitch's love and concern for her she realized their intimacy was based not on pleasure but on problem-solving. Regarding her belief in nonviolence, it pained her to renounce it, but she hoped that after the revolution she and others could study and create true nonviolence. Nothing seemed stable as she attempted to develop a new consciousness; she convicted herself of "wanting the moon," of "wanting to enter a life not mine."

In this same letter Levertov confessed to loving Edelman, but she recognized they could not be lovers because such a relationship would be filled with guilt and would not end well. To pursue it would be very selfish and wrong on her part. Edelman's inability to love her was perfectly natural, and her personal turmoil was not his responsibility.[56]

In the midst of this emotional confusion Levertov left the country at Christmastime 1970 for a meeting with Russian intellectuals. She traveled to the Soviet Union, her luggage secured with the leather strap her mother had used on her trip from England to Wales more than fifty years before. The Cold War was at full throttle as she entered Moscow, the enemy's capital.

Scant information exists about this trip, but if her poem "Conversation in Moscow" accurately reflects her experience, it had a profound effect. The "conversation" took place at a late-night dinner attended by Levertov and four Russians — a poet, a historian, a biologist, and an interpreter. Fueled by red wine, their dialogue focused on the eternal questions of the human condition. They shared their common belief that they must not lose touch with the source of life, with "the mineshaft of passion," and with grief and delight, which were always entwined. Initially Levertov was taken aback by the comments of the historian who asserted they must in the end follow Christ. She thought he was joking, but he went on to explain he was speaking not of dogma and the corrupt church but of the spirit, of a "frail trust" in "The Way." She was touched by his wisdom.[57]

In January 1971, Levertov returned from Moscow to visit her mother for ten days in Mexico. By this time Mitch, who wrote he had a strong inclination to be with her and hoped they would get back together,[58] was spending most of his time alone in Maine. In May they moved from their East Boston residence to Brookline where they created a communal living arrangement with two other couples at 19 Brook Street. These accommodations were small — a bedroom and workroom — but sufficient. Levertov was happy living in this arrangement in that she had fewer domestic responsibilities and enjoyed the camaraderie. In the summer the Goodmans visited England together; however, Mitch was ill and returned home early in August. Denise stayed on until the beginning of October, visiting old friends and participating in a march from Trafalgar Square to the U.S. Embassy to protest the killing of George Jackson, the black revolutionary leader.[59] Although she felt more estranged from Mitch, in his letters addressed to "Deno," he indicated that he believed their relationship had changed for the better and that he felt close to her.[60]

The year 1971 proved to be doubly difficult. *To Stay Alive* was released. If *Relearning the Alphabet* had disappointed some readers, this volume dismayed even more of them. Its publication weakened Levertov's reputation. Only a few close friends and critics understood what she was attempting to convey. The other difficult issue was her break with Duncan after almost twenty years. In fact, these two episodes were linked. As Levertov's antiwar rhetoric escalated, it fueled animosity between her and her "master." Their differing view on the relationship between poetry and politics was only one factor that drove them apart. Reciprocal need complicated their relationship.

In her preface to *To Stay Alive* Levertov stated her purpose: to record her own inner/outer experience in America during the 1960s and early 1970s as historical happenings shared by others. Although she did not make the connection, *To Stay Alive* had a similar purpose to Goodman's *The Movement toward a New America;* both chronicled a piece of American history, both included prose and poetry based in actual historical events, and both were collages of very different sorts.[61] She said later that *To Stay Alive* was her only book that was an "enterprise," meaning that it was written as a book, rather than as a group of separate poems that she then arranged in book form.[62]

What was new in *To Stay Alive* was her acceptance of violent action on behalf of a righteous cause. Her heroes had always been those who disdained killing and embraced integrity, honesty, and love of life. But she had come to realize that their ranks needed to be expanded to include all who struggled against the "obscene system" that destroyed life, even those who did so violently.[63] This renunciation of nonviolence was clearly a break with her past and would inevitably have consequences.

The first section of *To Stay Alive* contained some of her previously published poems. Her new poems were in part violent, disjointed, and disunified. In one section, "Staying Alive," she makes clear that to affirm life means to embrace revolution; to do otherwise is to choose death.[64] In another section she quotes herself: only "anger was love." She then goes on to reject a canard Duncan hurled at her and conclude the poem reiterating her intent: to hold fast to her love of those who dare to struggle and reject the "unlived life." The poem is written in homage to those who choose to live fully: "O Holy innocents!" she wrote, "I have / no virtue but to praise / you who believe / life is possible."[65]

Three years after its publication Levertov's friend Hayden Carruth summarized some of the criticism leveled against *To Stay Alive*: it was self-righteous and filled with slogans; it built morale but was not artistic; it was bad prose, stale, boring, depressing, indulgent, and would not endure as poetry.[66] Others claimed it was a patchwork of all kinds of materials, in which the sense of evil overwhelmed the impulse to celebrate.[67] It was "bad confessional verse" written in "casual diary form," full of "righteous indignation," "uncompromising moral zeal," and a "self-important tone."[68] Its language was hard and intransigent, reflecting her alienation and the growing gap between her and her opposition.[69] It reflected the doubt and questioning of one who was unable to reconcile suffering with human perfection.[70] *To Stay Alive* was her most controversial book of poetry.

The more positive reviews came from those who understood what she was attempting. For them *To Stay Alive* was "open-ended," "exploratory," and raised questions but did not give answers. It was a transitional work in which she tried to understand reality in some new manner. While it had its affirmations, it offered no final resolution.[71] *To Stay Alive* was compared to Williams's "Paterson," a "montage" with a mixture of letters, prose, conversations, and lyric lines. As such it reflected the literature of the time.[72] Carruth admitted that while not an entirely successful work, its purposes were clear. It was a sequence about Levertov's life as a political activist, a historical exploration of the spirit of her times, an examination of artistic responsibility, and a creative attempt to capture the "inscape" of the late 1960s. He thought "Staying Alive," the volume's principal poem, was "one of the best products of the recent period of politically oriented vision among American poets."[73]

In language, structure, and subject, *To Stay Alive* jolted those who had admired and followed Levertov's work, especially Duncan. While both Levertov and Duncan opposed the Vietnam War, they had a strong difference of opinion over the relationship of poetry to particular historical events. This difference was brought to the foreground with Levertov's fierce antiwar rhetoric. Expressed succinctly, Duncan's view was that "the poet's role is not to oppose evil, but to imagine it."[74] For Levertov, on the other hand, poetry must engage the world and "awaken sleepers." Although she accepted that not all poets could or would write political poetry, any poetry written during a time of war would of necessity "be tinged with anguish."

The root cause of the intellectual disagreement between these longtime friends has been attributed to fundamental yet unacknowledged differences in their ethical and aesthetic world views, already there in incipient form in the early 1960s.[75] Some critics characterized Duncan as individualistic, anarchistic, and platonic, and Levertov as incarnational, monotheistic, communitarian, and socialist.[76] Others offered as explanation Duncan's hostility toward the official world of poetry, his penchant for attacking small matters, his health problems, his ideological intolerance, and his recalcitrance.[77] Still others cited their respective differences on the importance of the individual and the collective voice[78] or their various interpretations of spiritual traditions and the transcendent.[79] Another suggested that from the beginning Duncan and Levertov represented the polar opposites in organic poetry.[80] Whatever their disagreements, it was not inevitable that their friendship would fracture given they had lived with their differences for decades. Other factors contributed to the break between them, most notably the psychic need Duncan and Levertov had for each other.

Beginning in the late 1960s the relationship between these two poets had begun to fray; nonetheless, until 1971, Levertov continued to express admiration for her "master." As she became more personally active in antiwar activities, Duncan warned her against letting those actions take over her life. He feared for her well-being. He described her televised speech at the Rankin Brigade march in Washington as an "apparition of Denny in full ardor" aroused by the "demos" and unrecognizable to him.[81] As a Freudian he believed that antiwar supporters, including Levertov and Goodman, were afflicted by a Judaic-Puritanic covenant against the evil of war that subjected individual conscience to the superego. He said he was repelled by this.[82] Levertov did not directly respond to his comments but instead wrote less frequently. However, after reading a review by Duncan of the work of her friend Hayden Carruth, she complained of Duncan's unjustified and contentious attack on him and reminded him of Carruth's mental breakdown and ongoing depression. This was quintessential Levertov, responding sympathetically to friends and those in need of care. While she criticized Duncan, she wrote that she hoped their friendship would endure.[83] In October 1970, Duncan, who was teaching at the University of Santa Cruz, sent her a copy of his Santa Cruz Propositions in which he described Levertov as Kali, the Hindu goddess of destruction. Levertov was the violent "Mother-Righteousness," "Madame Outrage of the Central Committee," "Mother of Hell" "whirling" with "flashing eyes" calling for "Revolution or Death," announcing "only anger is Love." "She is dangerous."[84] Levertov did not respond immediately, and when she did it was to say that she had lost the Propositions and to please resend it. Her letter to him was without rancor,[85] although she took on his attacks in *To Stay Alive* when she wrote:

                    I am not Kali, I can't sustain for a day
      that anger.
                    'There comes
                              a time
                                  when only anger
                                                    is love' —
      I wrote it, but know such love
      only in flashes.[86]

When Duncan received a copy of *To Stay Alive* he wrote to try to convince
her of the rightness of his position, namely that revolutions had always been
oppressive to the artist; that there was no time in history in which there had
not been war; and that what was needed was to be faithful to poetry, to keep
language alive. He urged her to follow her friend Bet's advice, to go deep into
her own well.[87] Levertov shot back a reply asking whether Duncan believed
To Stay Alive was not innovative, whether his opposition was all ideological,
or whether he thought the quality of her work had deteriorated because of
her political involvement. If the latter, she was saddened to lose his approval
but not crushed because she no longer had the same kind of dependence on
him she once had.[88] In a quick succession of letters he wrote saying that in
the Santa Cruz Propositions he was responding to her as one possessed by
the demonic spirit of the mass. He accused her of moralizing, of wanting
punishment and reprisals — hence his denunciation of her as Kali. He indicated that to pull down the "obscene system" as she suggested would be to
destroy the entire human species because "insane greed" was everywhere in
human history.[89] In mid-October he wrote a long, meandering letter, both
defending his position and attacking her. The letter contained his reitera-
tion that a poem should not be used to say anything; it had its own meaning,
and the poet was to imagine evil, not oppose it. But woven together with
these legitimate claims about poetry were more of his personal attacks. For
Duncan her war poems should not be read as an experience of Vietnam "but
in relation to the deeply underlying consciousness of the woman as a victim in war with the Man." They were the product of a rage-filled defender
of women's liberation. He accused her of sloganeering and of refusing to
examine her own ideology, which was that of the vacuous, ignorant "innocent" she lionized.[90]

    Levertov wrote a long response to what she called the "hodge-podge" of
issues raised by Duncan making it clear that he had many misapprehen-

sions and that his "coerciveness," "dogmatism," "pontification," and "arrogance" were disturbing. He had no right to tell her what the experience at People's Park was like and no right to condemn her use of slogans; this was "BULLSHIT" and "DISGUSTINGLY ELITIST." She called his comments about her war poetry insulting, the result of his own projection, and warned him not to attribute his own "complexities of mind & of intention" to her. On the matter of defending women's liberation, she explained that although initially not fully aware of the problems facing women in society, she was now more sympathetic, but she had never been a member of any women's liberation group. In response to his attack against fellow antiwar protesters, she countered with her own estimate that they were people of courage and vision who wanted to create a new society. Her view was that people in general share a belief in people's capacity for goodness, and certainly in the Christian world, even skeptics and atheists have been affected by the concept of redeemability based on the notions of both the Incarnation and humans being made in the image of God.[91]

Duncan continued to correspond with her,[92] but Levertov, exhausted by the exchange, proposed that in "courtesy and good faith" they call a truce for a year and a day and stop discussing these issues. Nonetheless she was glad to have said what she did about his arrogance.[93]

The truce mostly worked; their correspondence diminished. Levertov made it clear to Duncan her dependency on him had ended, even though it had taken her a long time to outgrow it. She claimed to be more "centered" now but had no energy to respond to his letters.[94] In public statements she minimized their differences, saying that they shared much in common but that Duncan was a "mythologist" who had put her in a role she did not believe was true for her and hence had caused their "current and unusual block in communication."[95] But she had made her break. Their friendship seemed to end with a whimper, but within a few years Levertov's fury would be unleashed at what she considered Duncan's later betrayal.

Both Duncan and Levertov brought their complex personalities and their emotional need to their relationship. Levertov served Duncan's need for adulation. When the adulation ended he was obsessed. Because for Levertov intellectual and aesthetic communion were closely linked to sexual desire, being sexually attracted to Duncan was inevitable even though that attraction could not be realized. Duncan provided the passion she needed but did not get from her marriage. The fact that her relationships with him and Mitch were fading simultaneously pointed to a major transition in her life.

At least in her public statements, Levertov gave no indication that a major change was occurring in either her work or her life; rather, she saw continuity. In a 1972 interview she said:

> I do not feel that there is a marked difference between volume and volume (of my poetry), just as I feel that there is no essential difference between my "political" and "personal" poems (the political *is* personal and vice versa) and just as I feel definite continuity between the self I remember with long corkscrew curls at age five and myself now . . . the field has grown larger as I walked through it, . . . but yes, it is the same field.[96]

Although Levertov might have experienced some general continuity in work and life, in 1972 that statement was too facile to describe her actual situation. Her "field" had grown larger, the eternal questions had become more urgent, and the relationship of the poet to her world more complex. As poet she was compelled to "awaken sleepers," but to do so at that point in history was to come face to face with monumental human suffering and evil. Was it possible to write political poetry? Was the balanced relationship between lyric and didactic poetry achievable? Was poetry capable of taking on evil? Was it realistic to believe that evil was the absence of compassion and that compassion was developed by fostering imagination? Could the poet stand against the force of systemic malevolence? Was evil external and to be attacked or internal and to be diminished within the individual? And what was the price of taking on these questions?

Levertov continued to ask these questions while dealing with despair over the war and her personal relationships. The events of the last few years had tarnished her reputation as poet, brought her marriage to its near end, and undermined her most prized friendship. The resolution of these issues would take years. The only way through, the only way to stay alive, was to do what she always did — to write.

6

Endings

1972–1975

How gray and hard the brown feet of *the wretched of the earth.* . . .
How lively their conversation together.
How much of death they know.
I am tired of the "fine art of unhappiness."

"THE WEALTH OF THE DESTITUTE"[1]

The years between 1972 and 1975 were a period of critical endings for Levertov, an extraordinary time of emotional turmoil and confusion. Three cen-
trifugal forces — the end of the Vietnam War, her break with Duncan, and
her divorce from Mitch — could have overwhelmed her. In the end they did
not. She survived, and haltingly searched for a new life. Two books of poetry
appeared. *Footprints* (1972) and *The Freeing of the Dust* (1975) both attested
to her longing for freedom and desire to leave the past behind, and a collection of essays, *The Poet in the World* (1973), established her preeminence in
poetics. As she groped toward the future, Levertov carried a talisman with
her, a new understanding of her name Denise. Previously she assumed Denise derived from the Greek "Dionysus." Now to her delight she discovered
that in Hebrew its origin was in "Daleth," meaning "door," "entrance, exit
/ way through of / giving and receiving."[2] Obliquely she began to live into
this new self-understanding.

In 1972, the way forward was not clear, but at least she had some sense
of stability in that she was no longer as peripatetic. Although she made a
trip to Vietnam, gave poetry readings throughout the country, and taught
at the University of Cincinnati in spring 1973, she was anchored principally
at Tufts University in a regular faculty position. She and Mitch moved from
Brookline to 4 Glover Circle, near Davis Square, in Somerville, Massachusetts. Mitch usually resided in Maine, although for part of 1972 and for 1973,
he was in Mankato, Minnesota, where he served as Chair of Ideas at the state
university. But for Levertov Somerville was her permanent household from
1973 through 1988. This relative physical stability may have contributed to
her productivity.

For eight years the Vietnam War dominated Levertov's consciousness. In the fall of 1972, just prior to Richard Nixon's reelection, her emotional intensity reached a crescendo when she, Muriel Rukeyser, and Jane Hart, a fellow war resister and wife of U.S. Senator Philip Hart of Michigan, traveled to North Vietnam. The trip gave them a firsthand perspective on the war.[3] On return Levertov wrote a long, two-part report describing their experience, documenting both the horrors of war and the resilience of the Vietnamese people,[4] among whom she said she found a grace and gentleness. The intent was to present a summary of their experiences to a Senate committee, but when denied permission to do so, Levertov lay down on the floor of the Senate building, was arrested, and spent the night in jail.

Levertov's experience of the Vietnamese people reaffirmed her linkage of joy and sorrow. They were destitute, "the wretched of the earth," but they were also heroic and brought her to tire "of the 'fine art of unhappiness.'" Much like her experience with Russian colleagues in Moscow in 1971, she came away desiring to stay close to the source of life and accept the "paradoxical delight" of being alive.

But the horrors she encountered on the trip — maimed women and children, bomber pilots, and POWs — were deeply embedded in her psyche and hardened her opposition to the war. She produced a spate of antiwar poems; one, "A Poem at Christmas, 1972, during the Terror-Bombing of North Vietnam," was written soon after her return from Hanoi while holed up in a snowstorm in their farmhouse in Maine. In it she imagines a murder in which she, in the guise of a waitress at an inaugural dinner, stabs Kissinger and throws napalm in Nixon's face. "O, *to kill / the killers! / /* It is / to this extremity / / the infection of their evil / / thrusts us."[5] Years later she explained that the harsh language of some of her poetry was the result of her tendency to feel responsible for things done by "one's own kind."[6] Obviously this tendency alienated many of her readers.

But over the next year this harsh language diminished. In "Modes of Being," she juxtaposes the suffering of war with the joys of nature. Here she elucidates the paradox of the human condition: "Joy / is real, torture / is real, we strain to hold / a bridge between them open, / and fail, or all but fail."[7] It was this recognition of the need to bridge the poles of joy and sorrow that made "Modes of Being" one of her most compelling antiwar poems.

By early 1975, Communist troops took control of South Vietnam, and the last U.S. soldiers exited in ignominy. America was exhausted and humiliated; those who had opposed the war felt not jubilation, only relief that the end had come. Although Levertov never changed her view on the immorality of the war, she subsequently acknowledged that she got caught up in "the fierce, bitching trashing, 'off the pig'—shouting demonstrations of the late '60s, early '70s!"[8]

The end of war in 1975 meant the end of an extraordinary expenditure of her emotional and physical energy. But two other wrenching emotional experiences continued to drain her — the end of her relationships with both Duncan and Mitch.

Given the long friendship and the authentic caring between Duncan and Levertov, one might have expected only a diminished intensity between them. In fact Levertov's diary entries for this period indicate that she was on the cusp of learning something new about herself from the set-to with Duncan. Although he could be judgmental, she recognized she could be cold and hostile. She reflected that the tyranny she experienced might be self-imposed and not the fault of Duncan. It was she who had to free herself from him.[9] Duncan, too, seemed to have softened. He wrote that he hoped he might come to a "just reading" of her poetry.[10]

But the illusion of an ongoing friendship was shattered when Levertov read James Mersmann's *Out of the Vietnam Vortex: A Study of Poets and Poetry against the War* (1974) and discovered remarks from a 1969 interview with Duncan embedded in a footnote.[11] In that interview Duncan claimed Levertov had a neurotic motive in writing her political poetry, which was, to his lights, a form of sadism. Her reference to "a flayed penis" and her "disgusted sensuality" showed that her poetry was about sexual war against men and not the Vietnam War. Duncan continued to harbor these hostilities, reiterating them in his own 1973 notebook entries.[12]

When Levertov read the Duncan interview, she was furious at his disloyalty. Nonetheless, her public comments about him continued to be professional, albeit those of a dissenting colleague. In "Some Duncan Letters — A Memoir and a Critical Tribute" written in December 1975, she chronicled their long friendship, remembering particularly his intelligence, love, support, and solidarity, but noting they now each had taken "fierce" positions that were as yet unresolved.[13]

Deeply wounded by Duncan's comments, Levertov hoped he would apologize and offer a public retraction; however, none was forthcoming. Levertov had come to a point where she no longer needed Duncan's adulation. As a consequence, for all intents and purposes, she ended their relationship, unwilling to endure what she considered his autocratic tendencies. There would be one final flare of indignation at him and then, after his death in 1988, an attempted reconciliation.

Terminating this long relationship with her "master" was one thing, but ending almost thirty years of marriage with Mitch Goodman was another altogether. It was not that she and Goodman did not care about each other; they did. They also shared many interests and had similar views on the most important issues. Nonetheless from as early as the mid-1950s, there is evidence of real problems between them, even though separation was not discussed until 1970. After their trip to England in the summer of 1971, Mitch hoped for the healing of their relationship, but the following summer Levertov decided to separate. In her poem "Crosspurposes" she writes of their letters crossing in the mail — hers announcing her decision to part, his full of the desire to try again. Her poem concludes with the recognition that their union was irrevocably broken: they were looking past each other to different horizons.[14]

No formal action was taken to end the marriage. In January 1973, Levertov wrote that it might be best for Mitch if they parted; however she admitted she did not have energy to begin another separation or to give him more attention. She wrote in her diary that she hoped he would meet someone he cared about and would take the initiative to end their relationship himself.[15]

Goodman did take the initiative to meet someone he cared about. In spring 1973, he was teaching again at Mankato State University in Minnesota. This gave Levertov the opportunity to enjoy her independence and the freedom from what she perceived as her husband's protective paternalism. She wrote her mother that when she saw him in February he seemed to be growing and building a new life, but that it was too bad that it took their living apart to make that happen.[16] Unknown to Levertov, Mitch had begun a relationship with Sandy Gregor, a twenty-two-year-old undergraduate at the university. When the term ended, Goodman moved back to Boston and Gregor followed.[17] But the actual Levertov/Goodman divorce was still more than a year in the future.

Prior to their divorce, Levertov was under an immense amount of stress. She carried on several relationships during this period. Some were helpful; others contributed to her emotional roiling.

In the spring term of 1973 she taught at the University of Cincinnati[18] where she met Steven Blevins, "a hippy waif" student with an intense desire to learn to write poetry. When Blevins subsequently moved to Boston and needed a place to live, Levertov let him stay in her attic and hired him as her part-time secretary and handyman. Blevins, a homosexual, was a creative visual artist and poet with a great sense of humor. Levertov was grateful to have him in her life at this very difficult time.

Her relationship with Blevins gave her some stability as she negotiated her emotional attachment to Richard Edelman, which continued during this time. Although she and Edelman were never lovers, she was passionately in love with him, sometimes blurting this out in the presence of others.[19] She confided in her diary: "I know with a deep & private sense of pleasure, that no one loves him *more* than I do."[20] Other than her relationship with Nikolai, she said her friendship with Richard was the most precious thing in her life. Finally this infatuation ended when Edelman told her he was in love with someone else. She burst into tears. For his part Edelman assured her that he hoped to continue a loving relationship with both his wife and her.[21] Levertov always maintained that her love for him was authentic.[22]

As she vacillated about her marriage, Levertov carried on a number of brief affairs with younger men, but they went nowhere. It is unknown whether she was seeking release from pent-up sexual energy, affirming her feminine appeal to men, countering her fear of aging, claiming a right to equal sexual access, or following out the logical implications of her previous "open marriage." What is known is that she wanted "encounter." Sex was the quotidian way to such encounter, something she felt she never had with Mitch.

In an unpublished statement entitled "On Friends and Lovers," Levertov writes that she wants to be central to the life of someone, and that except for Steve Blevins, she is not central to anyone's life. All her friends and lovers want something from her — advice, encouragement, or sex — but none wants the mixture of these plus passion and devotion, which is what she considered love. Although she is willing to give everything, no one seems willing to match her devotion. "Why?" she queries. She has personality, character, good-enough looks. People are drawn to her; even women fall in love with her, though she is not in the least interested in them. Baffled and perplexed, she asks — is she too verbal, too much of a handful, too much Denise?[23] Her questions were rhetorical; nonetheless she had begun to ponder her own uneasy relationship with others, especially men. Levertov's endearing and difficult qualities were so intricately interwoven that it was almost impossible to extricate one from the other without destroying who she was. She described Olga's life as a "maze" and a "jumble." Hers was much the same. Although at this point she had greater self-understanding than at any other previous time, Levertov remained an immensely complex personality, especially to herself.

One of her brief infatuations of this time was with Ian Reid, a young Australian academic and poet. In some ways this relationship recapitulated her earlier liaison with George Quasha. Reid and Levertov corresponded beginning in 1971, and he interviewed her by mail the following year.[24] When he came to the United States in fall 1974 for a residency at Cornell University he and Levertov met for the first time in Boston. Their love affair began then and continued until June 1975 when Reid returned to Australia. But their meetings were few, and what sustained them was a rich and expansive epistolary relationship that influenced the writing of both of them. It is possible that this intense correspondence with Reid replaced Levertov's previous exchange with Duncan, which was now in abeyance.

Levertov and Reid were entranced with each other. Needy and lonely, she nonetheless recognized potential problems between them, namely the age gap, their different life circumstances, and Reid's marriage. Reid, for his part, was immature and out of his depth but lured by intellectual interaction with this acclaimed poet, all the while recognizing a talent gap between them. As Levertov continued to idealize him, he became concerned and began to pull back from the relationship, confessing that he was not as physically intense as she was; he urged her to continue her long-established relationship with Stephen Peet.[25]

It is clear that, as was so often the case, Levertov's ardent relationships fueled her creative life and erupted into poetry. In a long poem entitled "Modulations for Solo Voice,"[26] with the subtitle "Historia de un Amor," she chronicled her infatuation with the idealized Reid. The themes here are of a wayfarer coming from afar bringing one new life, creating longing, ecstasy, and then anger. The series closes with an epilogue contrasting what she thought she found, "fire," with the reality of what she had, only "the play of light on bright stones."[27]

Through all these many relationships Levertov's indecision about her marriage dragged on. In August 1974 she wrote Goodman saying that although she hoped for his happiness, she did not believe she could make him happy and consequently she wanted a divorce. But she was not resolute, suggesting that if he did not want to end the marriage, she would try again.[28] Finally she acknowledged their marriage was untenable and at last she filed for divorce.[29] She resented both that she had to be the one to end the marriage and that she had not been told about Mitch's affair with Sandy Gregor.

Levertov always blamed Goodman for the failure of their marriage. He, on the other hand, insisted no one was at fault and that they did the best they could given that their natures were incompatible and "sex deserted them," a reality he would always grieve.[30] Mitch did claim that Denise's "fevered" relationship with Richard Edelman had a part to play in their breakup. It was

FIGURE 7. Denise Levertov, 1975. Walnut Street Theatre, Philadelphia. Edward Schwartz. Special Collections, Stanford University.

his view that Edelman served as Levertov's lover, a young romantic revolutionary, a poet in need of a mentor, a representative of a new generation, and the second child she once wanted but never had.[31] Initially Edelman was a symptom of their disintegrating marriage, but to Mitch's mind, he became a cause. Unable to compete with him, Mitch said his confidence declined and he became depressed.[32] He suggested Denise needed to enter co-counseling as he had done.[33]

Finally on December 2, 1975, their twenty-sixth wedding anniversary, their divorce was finalized. Although the divorce proved painful for Nikolai, there was no visible rancor between them. In the settlement, Levertov was awarded the house in Somerville, and Goodman the farmhouse in Maine where he later would live with Sandy Gregor.[34] During this period, Goodman's financial situation was grim, and he asked Levertov for support. She complied, sometimes paying for his dental work, car repairs, or portions of his medical insurance.[35] Levertov's largess toward Goodman would continue long after their divorce.

Admitting that it had taken her a long time to mature, now at age fifty-one Levertov felt she had passed from youth to "genuine middle age." Her poems of this period reflect the reality of longing in a life without a husband.[36] Other lovers would continue to spur on her creative life. In 1975 she began another off-again, on-again, five-year relationship with Jon Lipsky,[37] whom she called "Brother in dreams; Sometime Lover, Friend, Imaginer." Like Levertov, Lipsky, who was in his early thirties and beginning a career as a playwright and acting instructor, was interested in dreams and attended a Jungian Institute studying with Levertov's Jungian therapist, Robert Bosnak. Levertov would dedicate a sequence of poems to Lipsky entitled "Life in the Forest." But it was only with Stephen Peet that she was able to sustain a long relationship. Between Peet and herself there was no generation gap, no false, medieval romanticism, just "mutual affection & respect & enjoyable light hearted sex."[38] Their episodic meetings would continue for many years.

Many of the poems of this period reflect again the theme of the divided female self. In "The Woman," Levertov queries the bridegroom — can he "endure / life with two brides?" One is "homespun," and hungers for the bridegroom, the other dresses "in crazy feathers" and wearies others and herself.[39] In "Divorcing," she describes a single garland of flowers and thorns twined round the necks of Siamese twins choking them. If severed could one survive without the other?[40] And in "Prayer for Revolutionary Love," she expresses her deepest hope that lovers might not put Eros in bondage, but rather be loyal to each other and to each other's work.[41] It was this same revolutionary hope in mutual love and work that she and Mitch had attempted. Their failure was fresh in her mind.

She was now a "woman alone," and she captured that sentiment in a poem by that name in which she celebrates the joy of sex: "[w]hen she cannot be sure / which of two lovers it was with whom she felt / this or that moment of pleasure, of something fiery / streaking from head to heels, the way the white / flame of a cascade streaks a mountainside."[42] In "A Woman Meets an Old Lover," she recalls a previous sexual encounter, a poignant affair she had thirty years before.[43] This was generated by her meeting a former lover, "Colin" En Potter, father of her aborted child, whom she now found much diminished.[44]

Levertov might grieve her loneliness, but she relished the solitude, which allowed for artistic productivity. Her first volume of poetry to be published after *To Stay Alive* was *Footprints*. She dedicated it to James Laughlin, publisher of New Directions. A slight volume with poems that were not particularly distinguished, *Footprints* represented nonetheless a submerged undercurrent of her lyric poetry, which existed side by side with the poems of *To Stay Alive*. Since its poems could not appropriately be incorporated into *To Stay Alive*, she included them in a separate volume. Many of them reflect a subdued happiness: "Nothing I see," she writes, "fails to give pleasure, / / no thirst for righteousness / dries my throat, I am silent / and happy, and troubled only / by my own happiness."[45] There are other poems that foreshadow her later interest in the relationship between human and nonhuman life. For example, in "The Life around Us" she writes of the coming of night, a phenomenon no human, but only the "sightless" trees, "without brain-cells" could know.[46]

Critics varied in their response to *Footprints*. One argued that it showed that Levertov's political poetry was something of the past, that it had not fundamentally damaged her writing and reputation.[47] Another lamented that an established poet like Levertov would participate in what the reviewer called "the Corn-Porn movement."[48] Although *Footprints* gave evidence that Levertov could still write lyric poetry, it did not prefigure the quality of her future work.

In 1975 at the point when her reputation hung in the balance, *The Freeing of the Dust* appeared.[49] It was a substantial volume of sixty-four poems, most of which related to the end of the war and the demise of her marriage. Levertov's friend Hayden Carruth nominated the book for the Lenore Marshall Poetry Prize. It won and brought in an award of thirty-five hundred dollars. Carruth's testimony was a form of vindication: "For twenty-five years Denise Levertov has been one of our most prominent poets. . . . Today she is a woman at the creation of her maturity, acute in perceptions, wise in responses, and an artist, moreover, whose technique has kept pace with her personal development."[50]

Nonetheless, *The Freeing of the Dust* was a transitional volume. It contained neither a clear vision nor a synthesis of her inner and outer life, but as its title indicates, its poems were about a freeing from the constraints of the past.

Levertov's major achievement of this period was the publication of *The Poet in the World*, a collection of some thirty essays, most of which had been published previously. If it was released to counter negative comments about her earlier poetry,[51] it did that. *The Poet in the World* advanced her stature. It was hailed as "an indispensable guide to modern aesthetics" and "one of the best books a poet has written about the poet's craft."[52] In the preface, Levertov laid out three reasons for its publication: the collection brought together

her scattered prose writing, it gave her something to refer people to when they inquired about the craft of poetry, and it let students know where she stood on a variety of issues.

The Poet in the World includes fictive pieces, a long essay on teaching, and several speeches and statements on the Vietnam War, as well as numerous essays on important poets — Williams, Pound, H. D., Creeley, Duncan, and Rilke. However, the essays on the craft of poetry and the vocation of the poet are its most significant.[53] These address a multitude of aesthetic questions: the origins of a poem, the centrality of inspiration, the relationship of the poet to the object and to the reader, the function of imagination, reverencing and paying attention, the revealing of inscape, the role of myth, and the responsibilities of the poet. In commenting on *The Poet in the World,* one reviewer remarked on the dignity, clarity, and intensity of Levertov's contribution and pointed out the "essential interrelatedness and mutual reinforcement of the meditative and the active" revealed in the book.[54] Hayden Carruth commented that in *The Poet in the World* Levertov brought together the "mystery" and "craft" of poetry and illustrated "the receptivity and creative energy which is [her] identity as a poet."[55]

If *The Poet in the World* is marred, it is by the inclusion of a postscript appended to her "Statement on Poetics," which had appeared earlier in *New American Poetry.*[56] In this postscript Levertov addresses the barrage of criticism she encountered from her earlier declaration, which read: "Insofar as poetry has a social function, it is to awaken sleepers by other means than shock." The reality was that her poetry, especially *To Stay Alive*, seemed intentionally to do just that, to shock readers. Levertov attempted to explain what she meant in her original statement. She was unpersuasive.

Nonetheless by 1975 in both her poetry and poetics Levertov had clarified for herself what it meant to be a "poet in the world." She did not see her political poetry as a mistake or aberration; rather it was her attempt to integrate her personal and public life. This hard-won clarification was made against a backdrop of her own great losses — of friendship and marriage — and her interior struggle to become a whole person. The way forward was not yet clear. There would be more loss to come and more anxiety over her lack of self-understanding. But she had come through. She had given up "the fine art of unhappiness," and now was open, as her Hebrew name "Daleth" implied, to the future and the "giving" and "receiving" it might offer.

1

Coming to a New Country
1976-1981

> Not yet, not yet —
> there is too much broken
> that must be mended,
>
> . . . .
>
> So much is unfolding that must
> complete its gesture,
> so much is in bud.
> "BEGINNERS"[1]

There was much broken, much that needed mending, not only in the world, but in Levertov's life. On January 4, 1976, on her way to visit her mother in Oaxaca, she recorded in her diary a reflection on her previous year. She noted she spent Christmas at the Yaddo artists' community in Saratoga Springs and New Year's at home in Somerville reading Simone Weil.[2] In chronicling the previous year's significant events, she listed: her divorce in December; the publication of *The Freeing of the Dust;* receiving tenure at Tufts; and her ongoing relationships with Jon Lipsky and Stephen Peet.[3] There was nothing in her jottings that gave indication of what would unfold for her at the end of the decade. But she was coming to a new country. There was so much "in bud."

The trauma of the last few years, while not over, seemed to be abating. The war had ended; her friendship with Duncan waned dramatically, although there was episodic contact between them; and her divorce ensured a different relationship with Mitch. Gradually her attention shifted, and by early 1978 she clearly felt she had entered some new phase in her life. "Well, I am certainly in a different time period from the one I was in, say, four or five years ago," she said.

> Perhaps it began with buying my house, or perhaps it began with deciding, definitively deciding, to end my marriage. I am not at all sure where to put the beginnings of it. But I know that I am in a phase of life which has to do with living alone, and with having a lot of freedom. All of my decisions now have to be my own decisions. . . .

But in any case, I am sure that there must be a myth which is about a person having come to a new country or a new mode of living.[4]

Certainly owning her house on Glover Circle in Somerville gave her a sense of stability, and divorce from Mitch allowed her to explore her erotic desires even more than before. Her relationships with younger men gave her sexual pleasure and affirmed a youthfulness that she had felt slipping away as she aged. Since the divorce was not acrimonious, her relationship with Mitch did not change substantially.

Goodman lived in the farmhouse in Temple, worked on local political issues, and wrote poetry and a second novel. He brought in very little money and sometimes relied on Levertov to supplement his finances in order to pay his medical bills and insurance. He continued to think of Denise, Nikolai, and himself as a family even though he now lived with Sandy Gregor. Although he indicated that he had no intention of marrying, he kept open that possibility.[5] Sandy Gregor, who was employed, described herself as having grown up in "an honest, upright, Protestant family in Minnesota and bearing all the marks of the experience. The diffidence the worst, . . . the sturdiness the best."[6] She and Levertov had a positive relationship and occasionally they visited each other. In 1980 Mitch and Sandy married, and when their son Matthew Orlando was born soon after, Mitch asked Levertov to help with the birth expenses.[7] Denise would cherish "Matty," frequently sending him presents, especially books, and keeping his photograph on her refrigerator. Mitch encouraged this, suggesting that Matty could serve as the second child she never had.

Neither Denise nor Mitch considered the end of their marriage a traumatic event. What hurt and puzzled them, however, was how Nikolai was responding to them. He had taken a five-year leave from his undergraduate studies at the Rhode Island School of Design but returned there in 1975. That year he met a graduate student with whom he subsequently lived and whom he ultimately married in 1984. Her chosen artistic name was Nefertiti, apparently because her profile resembled that of the Egyptian queen. She was a handsome African American woman and an accomplished graphic artist. The work of Nikolai, a watercolorist, and that of Nefertiti, a graphic illustrator, complemented each other.

What was bewildering to both parents was Nikolai's increasing resentment. Levertov blamed this on Nefertiti. In June 1977, Levertov wrote her son, apparently in response to some communication from him in which he laid out his disappointments with her, that she grieved and regretted her rages against him as a child, but that at the time her personal needs and the demands of her daily life were impossible. While she agreed that she did not help him grow and survive, she adamantly denied that she hindered or stifled him. His natural self was kind, but she conceded that she failed to teach him that "me first is not the way to self-fulfillment."[8] But Levertov also attributed her own failures as a mother to Mitch. The refrain was familiar: Mitch's lack of success produced lack of sexual confidence and that produced anxiety in her that was expressed in rages toward Nikolai.[9]

Mitch, on the other hand, believed that as "late developers" he and Denise contributed to their son's problems by overprotecting him and simultaneously being themselves excessively preoccupied with other matters.[10] For his part, Nikolai maintained that what he wanted was to force discussion of issues his parents refused to acknowledge. Since discussion did not take place, he withdrew from them for almost six years.

It is difficult to know the exact causes of this wrangling because some of the salient letters of the period are unavailable.[11] Whatever the immediate causes, Nikolai's retreat, perhaps exacerbated by Nefertiti, grew out of many years of difficult parent/child interaction. These relationships would take a different turn when several years later Nikolai became ill.

While troubled and befuddled by her son's distancing from and seeming punishment of her, Levertov confronted another difficult situation — her mother's declining health. An "orphaned" woman who lost her own parents as a child, her husband in 1954, and her eldest daughter ten years later, Beatrice Levertoff lived the last two decades of her life in an adopted household in a foreign country thousands of miles from her only daughter. But she was sturdy, had great mental acuity, and was engaged with life. She tramped the hills of Oaxaca, maintained a large, lush garden, read the *Guardian* and the *New York Times*, meticulously recorded events in her diary, painted, wrote poetry, prayed with scripture, corresponded with many people, including Nikolai and her other grandchildren, hosted Denise's friends who trouped through Mexico, and served as an emotional locus for others. But it was Denny's letters, presents, and visits that brought the most joy to her life. Denise usually visited twice a year, but at times the length between visits was extended; at one early point there was a three-year interval between her trips to Oaxaca.

While grateful to her mother, Denise admitted that she did not have a close relationship with her. She felt guilty about her mother's loneliness, particularly as Beatrice inched toward ninety and became increasingly deaf and blind, but she came to the conclusion that there was nothing she could do about this. She needed to earn a living and hence could not move to Mexico; it would be too expensive to live in a hotel there anyhow. But mostly, it would be an unbearable strain to have her mother live with her. She would have no freedom and it would cut off her sex life.[12] When Beatrice wrote two years before her death that she felt like dying, Denise responded that she wished she could spend more time with her but that was impossible since she had to work for a living. Even if she brought her mother to Somerville, she would not be happy because the weather was terrible and she was frequently traveling.[13] Denise's visits increased, but there was always some acrimony between them, and then there would be regret. After visits at Christmas 1975, summer 1976, and Christmas 1976, Denise wrote each time apologizing for being bossy or cross during their time together. Beatrice tried not to complain, but she was lonely; she believed that people loved her but really did not want her company.[14]

Denise admired her mother. She sometimes read her poems at poetry readings, wrote a biographical piece about her, and publicly acknowledged that without her mother's vision she would not have been a poet.[15] Politically mother and daughter were almost universally in agreement, and Beatrice supported her daughter's divorce, believing that Mitch was sick, selfish, and a victim of isolation.[16]

But Denise could not abide her mother's prudishness about sexuality. Since adolescence her mother's expectation was that her daughter be pure and good; that was the price of affection. When Denise plunged into the adult world, she was an innocent, but she quickly gained considerable sexual experience. Retrospectively, she recalled her embarrassment on her twenty-first birthday when her mother quoted a poem about a pure and virtuous girl and applied it to her. At that point Denise had participated in many "sordid adventures" and was actually living with En Potter. By her mother's standards she would have been "living in sin."[17]

In 1974, Denise finally got around to having an honest exchange with her mother about sexuality. She told Beatrice that she thought her disdainful and "disgusted" attitude toward sexual and other physical experiences was a distortion and heretical for a person of her religious persuasion. According to Denise, her mother explained her prudishness as a consequence of her Victorian upbringing.[18] Their exchanges on matters of sexuality must have continued because Beatrice wrote recalling her long-ago horror at Denise's interactions with "unsavory" companions and her daughter's statement that she might be pregnant with Stephen Peet's child. She confessed that she could not bear another experience in life like the one they had endured with

Olga.[19] Denise shot back: "I hate to impugn your memory, but you really have the Stephen story all wrong. Forget it, anyway — it is so long past. But that is not how it was or what I said, I assure you. I was much too scared of you to have said any such thing & I'd sooner have died than become pregnant!"[20] The reality was that although not pregnant with Peet's child, she had been with Potter's.

Beatrice Levertoff's view on sexuality was tangled with her understanding of religion. For her the spirit was good and the body a prison. Denise captures this enigma of her mother in a poem as one who loved the natural world but feared the body, a woman who taught her to name the flowers but to whom it had not been given

> to know the flesh as good in itself,
> as the flesh of a fruit is good. To her
> the human body has been a husk,
> a shell in which souls were prisoned.
> Yet, from within it, with how much gazing
> her life has paid tribute to the world's body![21]

Beatrice's dualistic worldview and her prudishness made Denise embarrassed about religion and unwilling to accept any of her mother's promptings about a reality that meant so much to her. For example, in the early 1970s Beatrice encouraged Denise to read the work of Teilhard de Chardin, the French Jesuit, but Denise resisted claiming his writing was too Christian and full of cosmic optimism.[22] She suggests that it was precisely her mother's devotion that made her unwilling to reveal her own skepticism about religion. So the conversation about religion was avoided, as was any final intimate sharing between them.

In early 1977, Beatrice became very weak. Denise visited twice in a three-month period. Then in May her mother had an accidental fall, which led to her hospitalization. Denise returned to Oaxaca once again. Her mother died several days later on June 8th, shortly before her ninety-third birthday. The funeral service was held in the small, ornate San Felipe Neri Church where Beatrice Levertoff had worshiped for twenty years. She was buried in the local cemetery. Denise, the Fussiners, and a few other friends attended the funeral. Although he revered his grandmother, Nikolai was not present. After the funeral Denise returned to Somerville but was ill all of July, and only in early August was able to function again. As a way of honoring her mother, she created The Beatrice Levertoff Memorial Foundation, which for several years funded a little center for the visually handicapped of Oaxaca. Denise's relationship with her mother and her death would haunt her and become a major subject of her subsequent poetry.

Feeling abandoned after her mother's death, Levertov was consoled by her friends. When she told Muriel Rukeyser she felt like "a middle-age orphan," Rukeyser responded, "Oh, I'll adopt you. You'll be my adopted something."[23] When Adrienne Rich read Levertov's poems about her mother's death, she contacted her offering her condolences. Rich commented that reading the poems reminded her of the days long ago when they communicated so freely. "Maybe we will not be friends again," she wrote, "yet I confess I would love to spend an evening with you, talking." She hoped they would have dinner together and try to describe their present worlds to each other. Apparently, Rich's olive branch was not accepted.[24]

A newer poet friend, Alice Walker, also contacted Levertov after she read the poems about Mrs. Levertoff's death. Since Walker was concerned about her own mother at this time, she appreciated these poems. In 1977, Levertov published "The Long Way Round," a poem about American racism, and dedicated it to Walker and Carolyn Taylor, both African American social activists. Walker, who was twenty-one years younger than Levertov, nonetheless felt at home with her and encouraged their friendship. At one point Walker introduced Levertov at a lecture, revealing her admiration for her as a fighter against racism, hypocrisy, and war. She called her a poet of fire, passion, and rage whose private life testified to what she wrote. In 1983, on the occasion of Levertov's sixtieth birthday, Walker dedicated the poem "On Sight" to her, but their correspondence abruptly and inexplicably ended after that time.[25]

Writing served as a means by which Levertov dealt with emotional topics. This was clearly the case with her grief and guilt over her mother's death. In "A Daughter (I)" she chronicles her final visits with her mother and their role reversal. Denise is now mother, yet she longs "for her mother to be mother again, / consoling, judging, forgiving"; Beatrice, now a helpless, half-blind, half-deaf child, blesses Denise and sends her away. "Tired and ashamed," the daughter sobs, but she does not return. Her love is "shrunken in her to a cube of pain / locked in her throat."[26]

"A Daughter (II)" recounts Denise's visit to her mother in the hospital, a place where oxygen hisses and nurses ply their trade. The time for communion between them is over. The daughter laments her mother's passing:

she knows she can't have: one minute
of communion, here in limbo.
                    All the years of it,
talk, laughter, letters. Yet something
went unsaid. And there's no place
to put whatever it was, now,
no more chance.[27]

Remembering this final lack of communion, Levertov recalled the child's rhyme she and her mother sang together. It was about "a soul-cake," one they were never able to share.[28] In "Death Psalm: O Lord of Mysteries," Levertov remembers her mother's long readying to die and death's unwillingness to come. In petition the poet asks:

O Lord of mysteries, how baffling, how clueless
is laggard death, disregarding
all that is set before it
            in the dignity of welcome — . . .
. . . .
laggard death, that shuffles
past the open gate,
past the open hand,
past the open,
            ancient,
            courteously waiting life.[29]

In the poem "Death in Mexico," Levertov establishes the garden as a metaphor for her mother's life. As Beatrice is taken away to the hospital on a stretcher, she is unaware that the garden she tended for twenty years — its roses, lilies, and begonias — is returning to nature. Its destruction is reminiscent of the passing of life. "Gardens vanish. She was an alien here, / as I am. Her death / was not Mexico's business."[30]

The tragedy was the unfulfilled expectations of her mother's life, the lack of intimate communication between them, and Denise's sense that she had abandoned the one who had given her life and a poet's vision. "If only, if only, I didn't feel I let mother down at the end," she wrote.[31] In a dream recorded after her mother's death, Denise notes her anguish at finding a supplicant who stayed all night in the mortuary near her mother's body hoping for payment. After finally removing him from the chapel, Denise returned to kiss her dead mother's lips. "But aah! Her mouth at my touch fell open & the black breath of death rose up to my nostrils & I backed away. Too late, again too late."[32] Her words here are evocative of her response to her father's death some twenty-three years earlier: "Let my dance / be mourning then, / now that I love you / too late." The death of Beatrice Levertoff in Mexico was traumatic for her daughter, whose sorrow and guilt continued for years.

With her husband gone, son remote, and mother deceased, Levertov was alone and lonely, but she now had time and energy to travel more widely. In the early 1970s she made trips to England, and after her divorce she considered moving there. In the summer of 1976, under the auspices of the Library of Congress, she and five other poets visited several English universities, and Levertov appended a side trip to Tours and to Rome. Although she always claimed that she was not rooted anywhere, she had many positive childhood memories of the English countryside. Visiting England and recalling those memories was therapeutic. One result was her composition of "Chekhov on the West Heath," which was requested by James McConkey of Cornell University to be presented at the Chekhov Festival in Ithaca. In this long poem she explored her early life during wartime and how she and Bet Mitchell rejoiced in reading Chekhov aloud on the Heath. In the midst of war's sorrow Chekhov gave hope and made them able to glimpse a distant future full of potential.[33]

Two years later, after her mother's death, Levertov made another trip to England, visiting St. James, Piccadilly, where she encountered William Blake's baptismal font, which she described in copious detail in another poem.[34] In 1979, and again in 1981, she traveled to Australia with a stopover in Tonga. She also visited Banff, Alberta, and in 1980 went to Sofia, Bulgaria, where she addressed both the Commission on the Environment and Energy at the World Peace Parliament and the International Meeting of Writers. She urged these groups to see the interrelationships between human warfare and war against nature, to foster nonviolence toward humanity and toward the earth, and to see the human species as part of the global ecosystem. These addresses prefigured a theme of much of her later writing, the need for humans to live in harmony with nature.[35]

Levertov's increased travel paralleled a renewed interest in reconnecting with Olga's children. Both she and Beatrice had begun corresponding with them a few years after Olga's death, but now Levertov had an opportunity to met them in person. Iris, the eldest, was separated from her three siblings, Julia, Richard, and Francesca. Orphaned at a very young age, these three youngest had no recollection of their mother.[36] Each had made his or her way in the world with varying success. Iris Glanville-Levers was married with children. Julia Strudwick was for a time a Jehovah's Witness, and among her siblings had the most difficult life and marriage. Understandably, she looked to her aunt for help and inspiration.[37] Richard Strudwick married and engaged in the local politics of Leeds; Francesca Weaver, whom Denise helped uncover her Jewish roots, married and lived in New Zealand.

Denise continued to reflect on what she called the "jigsaw" of Olga's life, sharing her memories with her nieces and nephew. With them she softened her own ambivalent evaluation of her sister. She described Olga as a woman with a vision of goodness who was capable of self-sacrifice and courage, but one who alienated others and was a terrible liar who believed her own lies. In Denise's mind Olga's negative characteristics resulted from having been given an impossibly high standard to live up to by her father who idolized her as a "wunderkind."[38]

Divorce allowed Levertov greater freedom to travel and more solitude; it did not alter her financial situation. She continued to earn money through poetry readings, and from 1976 to 1978 she served as poetry editor of the new progressive magazine, *Mother Jones*. But her chief means of support came from her employment at Tufts University, which began in 1973 with a visiting professorship that subsequently became a regular faculty position. Her abrupt resignation from Tufts after six years is illustrative both of her difficult relationship with academic colleagues and the high dudgeon with which she confronted difficult situations.

Levertov enjoyed teaching at Tufts and intended to remain there, but when the English Department hired a faculty member, who although appropriately credentialed, had in Levertov's estimation "intellect divorced from affect," she expressed "shock" at the outcome. This was something she could not tolerate. Given that her opposition prompted the accusation that she was attempting to blackmail her colleagues, she resigned from the faculty. In a letter to her colleagues, she subsequently explained that younger members of the department asked her to reconsider her decision without betraying poetry and her principles. As a consequence she decided to remain, enduring her "scruples" and "indignation," if henceforth decisions were made by all department members, not just those with tenure, and if steps were taken to make the department more democratic. While she was away for six weeks in Australia, some changes were made, but a colleague she admired resigned and she decided to leave. This time her explanation was that poetry and her political commitments had top priority in her life and that it was impossible to keep up regular teaching and meet these commitments simultaneously. She admitted that she probably would have resigned even if a question of "principle" about the department's "oligarchic structure" had not been involved, because for medical reasons, which she did not identify, it was better for her not to be in the cold winter climate of Massachusetts. In her diary she confided that she was dismayed at having caused a rift among the faculty, but she was confident that she had acted on principle even though that principle might have been misapplied in this case. She knew she could survive without Tufts, and she was euphoric that a new, open road was before her.[39]

After she left Tufts, other opportunities and recognitions did come to her. In the summer of 1979 she participated in Centrum, a writers' workshop in Port Townsend, Washington, where she delivered the "Craft Lecture,"[40] in which she discussed line-breaks, indentation, and scoring as techniques for writing "open verse." Robert Bly, Sam Hamill, Maxine Kumin, and some admiring students were in attendance. It was there that Levertov, who was a demanding teacher, had a falling out with Bly over her pedagogical techniques. When Bly publicly humiliated her, she stomped out saying she could not stand it anymore and subsequently refused to share the stage with him.[41] Her animus toward him would go on.

Soon after, thanks to a nomination by Muriel Rukeyser, she was elected to the American Academy of Arts and Letters, and for the next three years a string of employment opportunities fell into place. She was appointed writer-in-residence at Lake Forest College, Hendrix College, and the University of Sydney, and beginning in the fall of 1981 she took up a position as Fannie Hurst Professor at Brandeis University, a regular position she held through 1983. But the most significant offer came from Stanford University — a teaching assignment in its Creative Writing Program during winter term. In February 1981 she accepted the Stanford offer, calling the day of decision, a wonderful "Tommy-tot" day. She was again financially secure and able to permanently escape winter in the Northeast.

During the six-year period between the end of the Vietnam War and the beginning of her time at Stanford, Levertov continued to respond to the suffering and violence she encountered around her. This engagement followed from what she believed was poetry's social function — to open the reader to greater compassion. As she saw it, even if a poem was forgotten, it was remembered in body and mind making readers more empathetic, bringing about a "kind of chemical change" in them.[42] As "poet in the world," she attempted to foster this empathy. In "For Chile, 1977," she memorializes the regime of the ousted Salvador Allende and laments the takeover by

Augusto Pinochet. Chile was "a land where the winged mind / could alight," but executioners had arrived and "hopes are scorched."[43] In "Greeting to the Vietnamese Delegates to the U.N," she captures her sense of solidarity with the Vietnamese people, and in "On the 32nd Anniversary of the Bombing of Hiroshima and Nagasaki," she writes: "A new bomb, big one, drops / . . . And they tell us, *'With this / the war is over.'*"[44] In her prose she explores incidents of injustice such as the torture of the Korean political prisoner and poet Kim Chi Ha and the political ideology and spiritual underpinnings that gave him courage and patience to endure years of suffering.[45] But it was the assassination of Oscar Romero, Archbishop of San Salvador, in March 1980, that affected her most profoundly. Her "El Salvador: Requiem and Invocation" would appear a few years later.

Levertov gave priority to her writing, but her political activism did not cease. At a 1979 rally on Boston Common she spoke about the interconnections of the military draft, the arms race, and the development of nuclear power, and in March 1980, with some thirty-five thousand in attendance, she addressed an antidraft rally in Washington, D.C.[46] In an interview she acknowledged her fear of the escalating nuclear arms competition between the United States and the Soviet Union. She was worried, believing "[t]he worst thing is the nuclear threat. That is greater than all the massacres in the world because it is total massacre. . . . The nuclear threat is the central priority question. . . . We are getting closer and closer with the arms race to the virtual inevitability of a nuclear war. . . . Whether there is still a chance of success is something we don't really know. We feel that we must go on trying, but whether we can actually succeed is another question."[47]

This concern for the epic nuclear threat led her in June 1978 to participate with a Tufts University "affinity group" and some six thousand other demonstrators against the construction of the Seabrook nuclear power plant in New Hampshire. There she met Joanna Macy, who shared her concern for environmental destruction and military buildup. The two became friends, and both took part in the 1979 sit-in at the Nuclear Regulatory Commission. Mitch Goodman was also among the group of some two hundred people who protested for fifty-six hours on H Street in Washington, D.C. Levertov was arrested and spent long hours in a holding cell with supportive women activists, sharing food and the final "ecstasy" on hearing that construction on the plant had been suspended. This action spurred her to write the poem "About Political Action in Which Each Individual Acts from the Heart." In this she speaks of solitaries drawing close and the great energy that flowed "from solitude / and the great power from communion."[48]

According to Levertov's evaluation, her comrades in the antinuclear and environmental movements were of a different ilk than those she had known in the antiwar protests of the preceding decade. Neither "Flower-children" nor "Maoists," they were kind, disciplined, unpretentious, mature, and had "staying power."[49] These activists would play an increasingly important role in her life, giving her emotional stability and renewed inspiration. In them she found a new spirit of solidarity, what she called the "locus of my deepest hope."[50] In her poem "For the New Year, 1981," she commemorates this hope:

> I have a small grain of hope —
> one small crystal that gleams . . .
>
> I need more.
>
> I break off a fragment
> to send you.
>
> Please take
> this grain of a grain of hope
> so that mine won't shrink.
>
> Please share your fragment
> so that yours will grow.[51]

These same themes of hope and solidarity are reiterated a year later in the poem "Beginners":

> But we have only begun
> to love the earth.
> We have only begun
> to imagine the fullness of life.
> . . . .
> We have only begun to know
> the power that is in us if we would join
> our solitudes in the communion of struggle.[52]

Years before, Bet Mitchell had admonished Levertov to find new friends, those who were simple, real people who were "rooted in the earth." She had at last found such friends, and they would help her set new priorities. She claimed to previously have valued freedom highly but said she had now come to believe that peace and mercy were more important. When freedom was the primary goal, justice and mercy were subordinated.[53] She was coming to a deeper understanding of the potential power of nonviolence. "I think," she said a few years later,

> that the only way for a person who believes in the potential power of nonviolent action is to cling to that belief, not to be judgmental about people who in desperation are being led to take up arms, and to try to learn to be non-violent in one's own methods — and to just hang in there in this ambiguous position. . . . [O]ne cannot see a solution and yet one believes that in the long run a certain proffered solution, namely armed struggle, is inefficient, because it brings about a repetition of the very conditions it struggled against. . . . One has to keep on asking the questions; one has to keep on pointing to instances of creative non-violence where they have existed, and giving loving support in so far as one can to the poor and desperate.[54]

Extensively engaged as poet and activist, Levertov's emotional life continued to ricochet back and forth between elation and depression. She contacted her analyst Robbie Bosnak to ask whether she should see him again, but finally concluded she needed to deal with her anxiety herself. The impending nuclear catastrophe filled her with horror, and she felt paranoid. Again, she contemplated suicide, but decided that this would cause Mitch and Nikolai to grieve and hence it would be wrong to take such action. In the end she concluded it was creating poetry rather than seeking personal happiness that would give satisfaction.[55]

The perennial issue of her undesirability also continued to obsess her. She lamented she had no one in her life to give her courage and moral support and no male who was neither homosexual nor extremely young to escort her to places. "I can't help the . . . feeling," she wrote, "that people will think there's something wrong with me that I can't find a man — or will pity me . . . then my own appearance, every sign of aging especially in my face, is depressing to me & emphasizes my isolation."[56] A love relationship eluded her, and she worried that the sexual pleasure she had begun to enjoy might desert her, even though she thought of herself as an attractive woman who had a capacity for relaxed and cheerful sex.[57]

Retrospectively she chronicled the major events of the 1970s, listing her "many love affairs." She had relationships with Reid and Lipsky and other lovers, all of which failed. Nonetheless, she believed these affairs gave her a sense of confidence and diminished her sexual hunger.[58] The one lover she could rely on was Stephen Peet, but he lived in England, was married, traveled the world, and was generally not available. Nonetheless she considered him a cheerful paramour, the ideal man — handsome, uncomplicated, "low brow," "frank," "confident," and with a kind of "animal sexuality" that she did not find elsewhere. He was not intimidated by her. However, after a few days with him she said she felt "intellectually and spiritually undernourished."[59] Nonetheless, their relationship continued for years.

Now that she was unattached, friendship was even more important to her. But Levertov could be a difficult friend, oblivious as she was of the demands she made on others. One of her endearing qualities, however, was her generosity, not merely in terms of gift-giving and financially helping a raft of people — she said this was one of the great pleasures of her life — but also in terms of offering her contacts and connections to help others. She was especially magnanimous to artists and students, writing introductions, forewords, book-jacket blurbs, and recommendations for fellowships and grant applications.[60]

When she discovered artistic talent, she encouraged and nurtured it no matter the circumstances. A case in point is Jimmy Santiago Baca, a convict in an Arizona state prison. Their friendship began when Baca invited Levertov to give a poetry reading at the prison in July 1976. In the long process of fighting his conviction, Baca wrote poetry that Levertov critiqued and published in *Mother Jones*. After his release Baca returned to school, married, took up new employment, and continued to write poetry. In 1987, Levertov wrote an introduction to his *Martin; And, Meditations on the South Valley*, which was published by New Directions.[61]

Levertov's friendships with two other artists, Steve Blevins and Carol Rainey, began in the early 1970s when they met at the University of Cincinnati. What these friendships illustrate is not only Levertov's encouragement of the artistic talent of others but her complex attitudes toward homosexuality.

As Levertov extricated herself from her marriage, Blevins's presence was a balm in her troubled life. Their relationship on both sides was tender, loving, and adoring and lasted more than two decades. Levertov missed Blevins when she was away and forgave him everything when she was with him. She trusted him and discussed with him her relationships with Peet and Lipsky and meeting her old lover, En Potter. At one point in their friendship when Blevins lamented the drying up of his poetic inspiration, Levertov offered suggestions to stimulate his creativity — get himself out into wild nature, take a course at the poetry center — and then she added that she believed his focus on homoerotic images was draining rather than nourishing his artistic inspiration. In her view the images he had in his house separated sexuality from personhood, making the other a sex object. Any act that divided sexual sensation from emotion, feeling, and reverence for the other was blasphemous.[62] As she rejected her mother's denigration of sex, she also rejected sexual objectification. Nonetheless Blevins remained beloved to her. When he was diagnosed with AIDS she asked the Jesuit priest-poet Daniel Berrigan to minister to him before his death. In his memory she wrote an introduction and saw to the posthumous publication of Blevins's poems, *Dreams That Wake As Words.*

Levertov's meeting with Carol Rainey, a thirty-year-old graduate student, occurred when Denise was exhausted and emotionally fragile. After their encounter in Cincinnati Levertov and Rainey kept up an episodic correspondence, but then after a year of no contact, Levertov abruptly wrote her asking if she would be her literary executor. When Rainey informed Levertov that she was a lesbian, Levertov's response was tense and cold, but she indicated that she continued to want her to take up the position and move to Boston. After Rainey moved to Boston, Levertov then rescinded her offer, informing Rainey of this by mail. According to Rainey, this letter included Levertov's hope that she never see her again.[63] In a diary entry of this period, Levertov expressed her irritation with lesbianism and her justification for reneging on her offer to Rainey:

> I am not alone it seems in feeling that if one has a pleasant trip to the movies or eats dinner with a woman friend some feminist instantly jumps to the conclusion one is "gay." Apparently some speaker at a women's studies conference interpreted poems of mine that way! I must try to find out who it was. . . . How maddening. It is wretched. How nice the new sense of sisterhood & mutual appreciation of 10 years back was — and now it's (for the moment) half-ruined by this. All the subtle web of assumptions that goes along with it. And men being confused & socially hesitant because of it — . . . And if one were to write an open letter to the feminist community one wd be slandered as being some sort of Anita Bryant or something. It is a "no win" situation. But at least it confirms my sense that to have accepted Carol as my secretary would have been socially disastrous for me; & that others feel the same way relieves me a little of the sense of having been mean-

spirited about it. Some day Carol may read this, I suppose. It is the first time I've thought of that — & I'll dismiss the thought quickly for one's notebook must be for oneself alone, while one lives. Yet I wd like others in the future to know what a woman of my generation, divorced or otherwise single, has to experience in this supposedly "liberated" age. A liberation which merely assigns one new (& even more false than in the past) labels is no liberation. . . . The lesbian feminists create a new sexism, . . . God, I wish I had more good non-gay men friends, . . . — simply as *escorts!*[64]

In the process of resolving this issue, Levertov wrote a letter to Rainey, one she never mailed, in which she explained that she believed homosexual experience was a phase of adolescence from which some people were never extricated. If one were a lesbian, however, one needed to find a reciprocal partner and not fixate on a heterosexual. Although Levertov admitted that she might have sent Rainey the wrong signal, Rainey should not assume anything from it. She resolved that their friendship could go forward only when Rainey found someone to love and when Levertov herself was in a relationship with a man, not at "semi-loose ends as I am now."[65] After some time, Rainey wrote again sending Levertov her account of their complex relationship. Levertov responded warmly and generously to Rainey's artistic effort to explore a painful experience in her life but gave no indication that she had rethought her views on lesbianism. Although their correspondence abated, after a twenty-year hiatus they reestablished contact with each other. Levertov sent Rainey books, and Rainey wrote lengthy letters suggesting that even when they were estranged she believed they were together on the fundamental issues. Rainey's last letter to Levertov arrived about six weeks before Levertov's death.[66] Whether, in fact, Levertov ever resolved her relationship with Rainey is improbable.[67]

One of the consequences of Levertov's break with Rainey was that she was without a literary executor. Not wanting either Mitch or Nikolai in that capacity, she pursued other possibilities, settling ultimately on the Quaker Paul Lacey, professor of English at Earlham College. Lacey came to her attention when Fortress Press sent her a copy of his book, *The Inner War: Contemporary Poets in Review*, which included a chapter on her poetry.[68] Apparently she appreciated Lacey's sensitive interpretation of her work. They had never met, but always sure of her instincts, she wrote Lacey asking if he would serve as her literary executor. He suggested they first meet and then agreed to take on this responsibility but argued vociferously against depositing her archive at Earlham, which was her preference.

The exit of Carol Rainey from Levertov's life did not resolve her uneasiness about lesbianism. She was a single woman and did not want to be thought of as a lesbian. From her earliest days, and explicitly mentioned during her brief affair with John Day in 1957, she wanted to be "adored" by men. This need for male adoration also colored her view of feminism.

"Second wave" feminism had its proximate origin in the antiwar movement, but broke first into national consciousness with the 1963 publication of Betty Friedan's *The Feminine Mystique*. As the movement spread from universities to the homes of ordinary women, poetry became one of the principal vehicles through which a shared feminist consciousness was built up and sense of solidarity created. The women's poetry movement, linked as it was to the development of feminism, substantially changed the content of poetry, bringing women's experience front and center.

Levertov insisted that although she had come to appreciate some of the complaints of feminists, she was alienated from that movement itself. Her first priority had been opposition to the Vietnam War, and she resented feminists pulling back from that because of its *machismo* culture. She also said she could not abide the "self-pitying" of feminists who acted from white, middle-class privilege. Furthermore she was dismayed that in some places in the country feminism had been taken over by "radical Lesbians" who expected heterosexual women to be like them. When asked about her views on lesbianism by an interviewer, she responded: "I mean, I really like men (and they are half the human race after all). That doesn't mean I believe in their continued dominance of society."[69]

It is true; she did not want women's freedom curtailed. She condemned sexism and rejected the denigration and objectification of women. But she neither applied the critique of gender to society nor did she want to be identified as a feminist. To be so was to limit her scope and hem her in. She would have none of this. While she came to see the interconnections between social injustice at home and abroad in war, nuclear buildup, hunger, racism, and even male chauvinism, she did not include feminism as part of the solution.

On the other hand, she did explore many issues at the heart of feminist consciousness — women's split self-identity, the confines of marriage, the female desire for freedom, a woman's delight in sexual pleasure, and the mother-daughter relationship. But Levertov maintained that even if the subject matter of her poems might arise from the fact that she was a woman, that did not mean she wrote feminist poetry. She said: "I think there is poetry by women, but 'Women's Poetry' is used by some of the feminist groups to mean poetry by women for women. It limits the readership. I feel that the Arts always have transcended and must transcend gender. If it's a good work of art, then it's for anyone that wants it."[70] Several years later she announced: "I don't believe I have ever made an aesthetic decision based on my gender."[71]

It was not as if Levertov accepted gender relationships as they were. She realized there was a need for both men and women to become more human, more androgynous, which meant neither homosexual nor unisexual.[72] But as late as 1990 she affirmed her consistent refrain: "Since I started writing when I was five, this constant consciousness of 'I am a woman, I am a woman speaking as me' has never been part of my consciousness: it just isn't part of it. I am a human being. And I am *me*. . . . I'm not a woman poet; I'm not a man poet. I'm a *poet*, and that has always been my consciousness."[73]

What is remarkable about Levertov is that in the 1950s and early 1960s, an unpropitious time for any woman artist, she was able to achieve recognition in the male-dominated world of poetry. The fact that she was unable to fully respond to the changing values advanced by "second-wave" feminism at least in part is explained by the fact that her consciousness had been formed earlier in England in the 1930s and 1940s and not in America in the 1960s. In some ways she was more traditional and less affected by the American inclination toward gender equality. But she was incapable of embracing feminism for other reasons as well. The wellspring of her artistic identity stemmed not from any sense of equality with others but from her unique inherited ancestral "destiny." If she had claimed she was a feminist she might have allied herself with all women and hence threatened her distinctive self-understanding. She also seemed oblivious to the fact that she owed much of her good fortune to male poets and publishers on both sides of the Atlantic, making it possible for her to often be the lone woman poet among them. If she had claimed to be a feminist, it might have challenged that privilege or alienated males who were hostile to feminists. Ironically, as a woman poet she continued to be haunted by traditional female concerns — her failures as mother, as daughter, as lover.

If Levertov eschewed being called a "woman" poet, her resistance to being a "confessional" poet was equally strong, although some critics convicted her of precisely that.[74] As she saw it, autobiographical subject matter could contribute to poetry as long as it was transformed and was not egocentric and self-referential, characteristics she found in confessional poetry. In a 1979 interview she said of the poem:

> Even though its subject matter may be personal you will have wrought out of that subject matter something which corresponds to the experience of others, because we are not that different from one another at the deepest levels. In fact, it is precisely at the deepest levels that we are most alike.[75]

What defined confessional poetry for her was not the subject matter but how and for what end it was employed. She considered poetry neither therapy nor self-expression. Her point was graphically illustrated when she said:

> I don't think that a lot of confessional poetry *is* good poetry. . . . As I understand it, the confessional poem has as its motivational force the desire to *unburden* the poet of something which he or she finds oppressive. But the danger here is reducing a work of art simply into a process of *excretion*. A poem is not *vomit!* It is not even tears. It is something very different from a bodily purge.[76]

If not a "purge," what was poetry? From her first credo in Allen's *The New American Poetry* through her many lectures and essays on poetics, Levertov explained that the objective of the poet was the creation of an "autonomous structure" that had a life and meaning of its own. A poem was not the expression of the poet's subjective experience, but rather what resulted from a dialogue, a meeting of the poet and the "reader within." Stated otherwise, a poem was written in the presence of the "god"; this transformed it, making it correspond to the understanding of others. As such it could awaken readers because it corresponded to their experience.

Levertov took up the issue of confessional poetry again in an essay written in 1974 at the time of Anne Sexton's suicide. In this she rails against the destructive tendencies of the confessional poets — Plath, Lowell, Snodgrass, and Berryman, and, of course, Sexton. Her intent here is not so much to lay out her disagreement with their poetry as to counter the equating of creativity with death and self-destruction. Irrespective of Levertov's own fleeting conjuring of suicide, as a poet she stood clearly on the side of art affirming life. To underscore that poetry is life-giving, even in difficult situations, she quotes Thoreau: "'You must love the crust of earth on which you dwell. You must be able to extract nutriment out of a sand heap. Else you will have lived in vain.'" She writes that to identify love of death with creativity and love of poetry is to insult Sexton.[77]

Rejecting confessional poetry out of hand, Levertov was also eager to avoid overuse of the autobiographical, what she called "the dominant first-person singular of so much of American poetry — good and bad — of recent years."[78] She makes this point in the introductory note to her next volume, *Life in the Forest*, citing the influence of the Italian poet, Cesare Pavese. In her earlier war poetry she attempted to set her poems within a historical context, hence extending their universality. In *Life in the Forest* she consciously focuses on landscape and the use of the third person singular or first person plural. Although not always successful, this is her attempt to universalize her poems and set them apart from the work of the confessional poets.

The title — *Life in the Forest* — suggests the volume's content; the poet lives in the dark forest, yet there is life to be found there. Its poems survey life in its full continuum: love, sex, desire, loneliness, engagement with the world, loss, and death. The opening poem, "Human Being," sets the tone for what follows. From childhood the human is confronted with experiences of "ecstasy" and of "dull grief," "of kneel[ing] in awe of beauty," and of seeing those "who cannot learn / anything from suffering, / suffer." To be human is to drift on "murmuring currents of doubt and praise."[79] Although there is no reconciliation of opposites here, *Life in the Forest* represents a shift in Levertov's poetry toward a deeper search for meaning. Her perennial pursuit of "the double image" continues, albeit in more nuanced form.

In 1979, one year after *Life in the Forest* appeared, New Directions issued her *Collected Earlier Poems, 1940-1960*, which included poems from *The Double Image, Here and Now, Overland to the Islands*, and *With Eyes at the Back of Our Heads*, in addition to some of her very early uncollected poems. Included in the book is an author's note in which she details her early publishing history beginning with the portentous letter from T. S. Eliot up through James Laughlin's taking her on as a New Directions author.

Another collection, *Light Up the Cave*, was brought out in 1981 and included thirty-four of her essays written after the publication of *The Poet in the World*. The collection ranges widely, bringing together reminiscences of Rukeyser, Duncan, Herbert Read, and Beatrice Levertoff; paeans of praise for Rilke and Chekhov; and three fictive pieces with autobiographical themes. But it is in the essays on the craft of poetry and on political poetry that Levertov's strengths are in high relief. In "On the Function of the Line" and "Technique and Tune-Up"[80] she takes up and expands previous considerations of techniques used in nonmetrical forms of poetry. In a section on political poetry she attempts to explain its raison d'etre: to awaken "pity, terror, compassion and the conscience of leaders; and [to strengthen] the morale of persons working for a common cause."[81] Because most political poetry is written by active participants in political life, and because these poets desire an "osmosis" of their personal and public lives, Levertov argues that it is impossible for them to divide the didactic from the lyrical. Their poems are full of anguish but are intrinsically affirmative.[82] She claims that there is no inherent contradiction between poetry and revolutionary politics because they both follow from the same source, "a profound and generous passion for life."[83] A few years later in defense of her position she said:

> If artists, with their finely tuned receptors and their gift of reaching people, don't act on their deepest moral commandments, who on Earth should? They won't write bad poetry unless they're bad poets; good poets don't use poetry, poetry uses them. My didactic poetry should be judged by the same criteria as my lyric poetry; in my opinion, it won't be found wanting.[84]

Increasingly, Levertov's poetry was not found wanting. In the five years between 1976 and 1981 she published three volumes of poetry, and several long poems were brought out in limited editions.[85] One of these, "Mass for the Day of St. Thomas Didymus," first published in 1981, was a portent of things to come. The poem did not emerge ex nihilo, but rather its gestation was made possible by her experiences and friendships of this period. It was the act of writing itself, however, which was the midwife. Its publication indicated that she was no longer trying to "stay alive" but that she had "come to a new country." This assertion was prescient beyond her ability to yet comprehend.

8

"The Thread"
1982–1984

> Something is very gently,
> invisibly, silently,
> pulling at me-a thread
> or net of threads
> finer than cobweb and as
> elastic.
>
> . . . .
>
> but a stirring
> of wonder makes me
> catch my breath when I feel
> the tug of it when I thought
> it had loosened itself and gone.
>
> "THE THREAD"[1]

"The Thread," a poem of the 1960s, reflected Levertov's ongoing awareness of her vocation. In the early 1980s at age sixty, the tug was there again. In this case it was a silent ineluctable shift from the doubt that grounded her lifelong agnosticism toward a tentative religious faith. This resulted not from some dramatic conversion but from "faithful attention" to living out her vocation as a poet. Already by 1977 she was aware that writing had some link to what she understood as religious experience. When interviewed she said: "I would say that for me writing poetry, receiving it, is a religious experience. At least if one means by this that it is experiencing something that is deeper, different from, anything that your own thought and intelligence can experience in themselves. Writing itself can be a religious act, if one allows oneself to be put at its service. I don't mean to make a religion of poetry, no. But certainly we can assume what poetry is *not*—it is definitely not just an anthropocentric act."[2]

Levertov recognized the celebration of mystery as the most consistent theme of her poetry from the very beginning.[3] She discovered mystery in the "divine sparks" of the Hasidim and in her search for "inscape." The "negative capability" of Keats, the "disinterested intensity" of Rilke, the dialogical relationships of Buber, each brought her closer to its revelation. Her language attested to its presence. She spoke of hymns and psalms, of pilgrimage and communion, of a destiny. For her the poet was priest, and the poem, a temple. "The irresistible impulse of the soul" was praise. She sometimes used the language of religion, but its meaning was always literary and aesthetic. Earlier when asked what she meant by religion she responded: "The impulse to kneel in wonder. . . . .The impulse to kiss the ground . . . The sense of awe. The felt presence of some mysterious force, whether it be what one calls beauty, or perhaps just the sense of the unknown — I don't mean 'unknown' in the sense of we don't know what the future will bring. I mean the sense of numinous, whether it's in a small stone or a large mountain."[4]

The evidence of Levertov's search for mystery is everywhere in her writing, but she claimed not to have belief. She considered herself a "syncretist, or a dilettante of religions."[5] She distinguished between the primary religion of awe and faith and the philosophical and moral religion of institutions that were associated with belief, an established authority, and a preordained system of virtues. She was suspicious of the utilitarian need for religion that gave solace and led one to evade the eternal questions.[6] She would have no truck with such religion. At best she was agnostic. During the 1970s, however, the circumstances of her life began to change, removing previous obstacles to faith and offering new sources of inspiration. She was on new terrain.

Since she left home at age seventeen, Levertov moved in Bohemian circles of artists, activist, and academics, most of whom were areligious or antireligious. She married a person who had no religious interest except for a passing curiosity about cultural Judaism. Divorce from Mitch meant that she no longer needed to take his views into consideration, and her mother's death eliminated an irritant and an embarrassment over religion. With these impediments removed, the influence of new friends would have an impact.

Over the years her poetry attracted people who were concerned with spiritual matters. Although they offered a countervailing influence in her life, these friendships did not spur a personal interest in religion. Beginning in the 1960s she corresponded with the Canadian Christian poet Margaret Avison, whom she called the direct heir of George Herbert and Gerard Manley Hopkins.[7] In 1962, Eileen Egan, the Welsh-born director of Catholic Relief Services, contacted her about her poem "During the Eichmann Trial." Egan became a friend and confidant who invited Levertov to speak at the Catholic Worker several times beginning in the late 1970s and introduced her to the pacifist group, Pax Christi, to Dorothy Day, and to the young Jesuit activist John Dear. In late 1957 the poet Wendell Berry began a correspondence with Levertov, met her a few years later in New York, and lived for a time in the same apartment building as the Goodmans. Berry was her connection to Thomas Merton. At the same time Levertov and Bernetta Quinn, a Franciscan nun, social activist, and poet who taught at historically African American colleges, began a correspondence. By 1974, Levertov was in contact with the Catholic journalist Coleman McCarthy, and as early as 1959, she read poetry with the Jesuit poet Daniel Berrigan, whose "boyish adventurousness" she liked. Beginning in 1967, Tony Stoneburner — poet, author and Professor of English at Denison University — was writing her about participation in the seminar on poetry and theology held at the Washington National Cathedral. Others like the Dominican nun Mary Norbert Kob shared with Levertov her harsh treatment by parishioners for her antiwar opposition. Levertov met the Benedictine priest-poet Raymond Roseliep through her poet friend Eve Triem, a devout Episcopalian living in Seattle. Roseliep became a correspondent, as did the much overworked Canadian Montfort priest Gerry Pocock. Levertov encouraged high school teachers like Brother Joseph Chvala; graduate students like Maureen Smith, an English Catholic who subsequently wrote a book on Levertov and became a friend; and Joan Hallisey, another friend, who wrote a dissertation on Levertov and taught in Catholic colleges. One of Levertov's most important friendships was with the Franciscan priest Murray Bodo, who would later help her through difficult personal and religious issues.[8]

By the late 1970s Levertov also began to acquire new friends from among the ranks of the nuclear disarmament and environmental movements, some of whom were people with religious sensibilities. She found them to be persons with discipline and tenacity, who were "holistic" in approach, kind to each other, and able to find richness within the struggle itself. Unlike the Vietnam activists of the previous decade, these colleagues were not puritanical and did not believe that things had to get worse before they could get better.[9] Interaction with these friends challenged Levertov's assumption that religion was an "embarrassment" and "irrelevant."

Gradually she became more aware of the links between religious conviction and defense of human rights, especially as she explored the persecution of the Korean dissident Kim Chi Ha and the murder of Archbishop Oscar Romero.

For Levertov, the 1970s and early 1980s were "unprecedented times." Unlike the Vietnam War, which had been carried out through military combat in one part of Southeast Asia, the current stockpiling of nuclear weapons had global implications of the most catastrophic proportions, imperiling the human species and all of creation. She found it to be a terrifying time and believed that the odds of curtailing the impulse toward cataclysmic war were formidable. Despairing that this tide of destruction could be stemmed, she sought a source for renewed hope.

Levertov came to religion tentatively, doubting, embarrassed. Occasionally, she would attend a religious service, something she had generally eschewed since adolescence. In 1977, she recorded a visit to Assisi and then her participation in Christmas midnight mass at St. Anselmo's in Rome. These experiences moved her. "During the service I felt very emotional," she wrote: "It was the first time I was in a church for a service since Mother's funeral at San Felipe Neri in Oax. It was all brightly lit, not candle lit, I cd see. . . . I wish I cd take communion & yet felt as always it might be a hypocrisy only. I can't even truthfully say, Lord, I believe, help Thou my unbelief."[10]

The following Christmas Eve she was in Cambridge, Massachusetts, at a candlelight service at the Swedenborg Chapel of the Church of the New Jerusalem. She wrote that the experience was moving and "it seemed & still seems an opening up to faith."[11]

Gradual realignment of doubt and faith expressed itself in her poetry. In fact it was in the process of writing poetry that she first experienced this shift. Retrospectively, she claimed that the first poem to illustrate her redirection toward religion was "Human Being," the opening poem of Life in the Forest.[12] The poem captures the rhythm of walking through life, responding with doubt and awe, but never able to pass "the wall," the stumbling block of suffering. Nonetheless thanks are given for each day of life. Giving thanks became Levertov's way through the tangle of doubt.

By October 1979, the first semester after she resigned from Tufts, Levertov began writing a long poem in which she wrestled with what she called "the unknown." The poem, "Mass for the Day of St. Thomas Didymus," commemorated the apostle Thomas, who was suspected of being a twin, hence the appellation, didymus. Levertov, like Thomas, was a doubter, one of little faith, who needed to see and touch in order to know the truth. The idea for this poem came to Levertov a few years earlier when she attended a choral recital that was structured around the parts of the mass and included sections from various musical periods — medieval, renaissance, classical, baroque, and modern. This traditional liturgical structure allowed for a unified whole to be created out of distinctive musical styles. Inspired by this choral piece, Levertov conceived of a poem that would follow the same liturgical pattern but would be an "agnostic" mass, with each of its parts being a secular meditation. Kyrie was a cry for mercy and Gloria a song of praise. Credo, an alternative statement to the Nicene Creed, confessed belief in the earth and its dust. Sanctus announced that all is holy; Benedictus blessed the variety of expressions of the spirit; and Agnus Dei presented the lamb of God. By December 1979, Levertov finished the Benedictus; the Agnus Dei would be completed by early 1980.[13] Finally, in 1981 the long "Mass for the Day of St. Thomas Didymus" was published. Both aesthetically and biographically it is an important poem, a marker for understanding the last two decades of Levertov's life. She was very pleased with its outcome.[14]

And with reason. Its language is reminiscent of Hopkins, and its images — "dim star," "spark of remote light," "guttering candle" — reflect the Hasidic influence that she had so deeply internalized. "Mass" is a poem of both praise and lament, which calls on an unknown God who is both near and distant. The Kyrie opens with a petition to the "deep, remote unknown" to "have mercy on us" because we live in terror of what is known and unknown. The Gloria follows, praising the sun and snow, the night, the day. The Credo attests to both belief and doubt:

> I believe the earth
> exists, and
> in each minim mote
> of its dust the holy
> glow of thy candle.
> . . . .
> . . . I believe and
> interrupt my belief with
> doubt. I doubt and
> interrupt my doubt with belief. Be,
> belove'd, threatened world.[15]

Sanctus is a great hosanna to the "unknown," the "unknowable," and the Benedictus is a hymn of praise to the spirit, to all that is, to that which bears the spirit within it, to all being. The Benedictus concludes with a statement of hope: "the word / chose to become / flesh. In the blur of flesh / we bow, baffled."

But in the Agnus Dei, the final section of "Mass," Levertov poses a question. She presents the lamb of God, the innocent, defenseless creature as the one who takes away the sins of the world. While offering this confounding image of weakness, she queries her readers: Is it they who must hold this "shivering God" to their "icy hearts"? She rallies those who can respond, those who are yet human, to shield this defenseless lamb:

So be it.

> Come, rag of pungent
> quivering,
>> dim star.
>>> Let's try
>> if something human still
>> can shield you,
>>> spark
>> of remote light.[16]

In some sense this is a culmination of Levertov's decades of resistance to evil turned now not toward a God who protects humans, but vice versa. Humans are petitioned to protect a defenseless God.

Levertov recorded her experience of writing this poem over several months: "[W]hen I had arrived at the Agnus Dei I discovered myself to be in a different relationship to the material and to the liturgical form from that in which I had begun. The experience of writing the poem — the long swim through waters of unknown depth — had been also a conversion process."[17]

She did not elaborate on the nature of this conversion. Rather than an embrace of belief, what seems to have happened is a shift away from doubt. It was as if when parts of her past dropped away, Levertov was ready to take on some fuller exploration of the reality she always knew was there, the "something not behind but within." Levertov made it clear that writing "Mass" brought her to the point of understanding the Incarnation as something that engaged human volition and cooperation,[18] and by the end of 1980, she could write: "My feeling is hesitantly turning more toward religion (Christian) than ever before."[19] But this did not imply institutional affiliation or creedal adherence. Rather, her lifelong experience of wonder and awe was being reconfigured. The "thread" was "gently," "invisibly" tugging on her, pulling her in some new direction,

In order for her tentative faith to be strengthened, Levertov had to have confidence that it was not incompatible with her political beliefs and that it would not threaten her aesthetic freedom. What appeared to be central to moving her forward was her profound sense of gratitude for life and what that implied. A few years later she wrote in explanation:

> More and more strongly as the years have passed, and despite whatever grief and losses those years brought to my private life, despite, too, my constant and often intense awareness of the tensions, disasters, cruel-

ties and overwhelming threats of this period in history, I experienced a welling-up of gratitude for life itself and for the many extraordinary blessings of my own history . . . To what, to whom. Gratitude implies an object; & not merely an impersonal force but a giver having the option of *not* giving. A belief in blind chance, in luck, does not give rise to the sensation of gratitude as I experience it.[20]

"Baffled" Levertov nonetheless "bowed." Her decision was to begin to act as if she believed, without waiting for intellectual clarity.[21] What she called her "Pascalian wager" meant that she would try to act like a Christian in order to become one, even if, she was "unorthodox."[22]

It was not that she had found a way to reconcile the poles of "the double image," the terror and beauty, the "fears" and "promises." Rather, she came to acknowledge that this quest for reconciliation was an ongoing human effort. "One can't hold the full knowledge of that horror and of joy, . . . at the same moment. One wants to find a synthesis that will at least answer the question, 'How can this be?' And that's part of the human moral search, that is part of what it is to be human."[23] Nonetheless, as she became increasingly aware of the terror presented by the nuclear age, she was filled with anxiety. Her next volume, *Candles in Babylon*, included a section entitled "Age of Terror."

Candles in Babylon derived its name and that of its opening poem from the nursery rhyme incorporated in "To Minnie" by Robert Louis Stevenson. Levertov reencountered this rhyme in the late 1970s as she leafed through *A Child's Garden of Verses*. In "To Minnie" the innocent ask: How far it is to Babylon and can we get there by candle light and return home again?[24] *Candles in Babylon* is launched on the image of children holding their "shivering flames" crying "Sleepers Awake!" and hoping they can return to the calm of home from Babylon, symbol of all that evokes terror.[25]

The poems of *Candles in Babylon* waver between despair and hope. Some reflect cataclysmic destruction. In "Concurrence," Levertov describes morning glories, faultless and blue and "lit from within," and the pollution that will destroy them. In "What Could It Be" she tells of uranium being torn out of the flesh of Mother Earth in order that nations might kill. In "An English Field in the Nuclear Age," she writes of the beauty of the field and how all within it "holds its breath, for / this minute at least was / not the last." In "Unresolved" she attests that "[o]ur song is a bird that wants / to sing as it flies, to be / the wings of praise, but doubt / / binds tight its wire to hold down / flightbones, choke back breath. / We know no synthesis."[26]

These poems of despair are paired with beautiful lyric poems about nature, Eros, and hope. Levertov writes of clumps of irises that must be distributed lest they fail to flower and of the refusal to despair when there is so much to be realized. In "Writing in the Dark," she speaks of the necessity to have words pulled from the depths of unknowing, "words that may have the power / to make the sun rise again."[27]

Candles in Babylon ends with two poems that tilt the weight of the collection toward hope, "Mass for the Day of St. Thomas Didymus" and "The Many Mansions," the volume's concluding poem. In this latter she imparts a vision of the world of the white herons, a vision given the poet to share and pass along as an "amulet of mercy."[28] The basis of this poem was a dream recorded in the summer of 1980 in which she entered into a miniature landscape inhabited by two tiny white cranes. The dream convinced her that the infinite creativity of God implied the potential existence of thousands of alternative worlds. This gave solace because even if humans destroyed this world, another equally beautiful, duplicate world would be preserved because humans had not chosen to destroy it. In this way both the creativity of God and the freedom of man would be honored. It was this vision, this "amulet of mercy" that she wanted to pass "from hand to hand."[29]

Candles in Babylon appeared the same year Levertov began her permanent teaching position at Stanford where she would be in charge of the poetry workshop and the Stegner Poetry Fellows Program.[30] In addition to these winter term responsibilities, for the next two years she continued to teach fall term at Brandeis University, with her house in Somerville serving as her base. It was from there that Yarrow Cleaves, a poet who served as her secretary for many years, attempted to handle the minutia of Levertov's life: bills, appointments, correspondence, travel arrangements, and manuscript preparation, in addition to watering plants, picking up cleaning, and running errands. Like all her secretaries, Cleaves made Levertov's life and work possible, and although an exacting and sometime inflexible employer, Levertov encouraged her assistants to pursue their own work as poets.

The move from Boston to Palo Alto in winter was felicitous. Levertov was stunned by the beauty of the place with its sunshine, flowers, soft light, and wonderful skies. She loved living there and referred to herself as a "migrant bird" who, escaping the harsh winters of Massachusetts, returned each year to the same rented upper-level apartment at 624 Mayfield Avenue across from a small park. The apartment was large and light-filled, and through the window she could see several large trees. She had room for "the blackcat," that is, her piano, for her many books and her manual typewriter. In

Palo Alto she learned to knit,[31] took up the study of German, and continued piano lessons. She usually rode her bicycle to campus and relied on friends to trundle her from one distant place to another. These were happy years.

She had friends in the area. The poet Carolyn Kizer and her architect husband, John Woodbridge, were nearby in Berkeley, and Kenneth Rexroth was in Santa Barbara. She visited him shortly before he died in 1982. Levertov felt welcomed at Stanford and at ease with colleagues in the English Department, although in 1985 she unsuccessfully opposed the hiring of Marjorie Perloff based on disagreements over poetic principle. Perloff supported the so-called Language poets, and Levertov did not. During her first months in residence at Stanford, the University's Center for Research on Women held a conference to discuss how gender influenced the work and lives of sixteen women poets, including herself. Both Alicia Ostriker and her Stanford colleague, John Felstiner, critiqued her poetry, the latter arguing that her audience was both male and female.[32] There was consternation at the conference, however, when Levertov opposed certain claims about lesbianism.

It was during these Stanford years, unbeknown to most of her friends and colleagues, that Levertov's commitment to faith deepened.[33] In 1982, she heard a lecture by the sociologist, poet, and nonviolent activist Danilio Dolci, who worked on behalf of the poor in Mafiosi-infested Sicily.[34] She knew she was in the "presence of greatness" when she heard Dolci characterize himself as a midwife, one intent on bringing to birth the maximum creativity of all beings in order that the world would be saved from destruction. Dolci insisted that the eternal questions would never be answered definitively, but that one had to continue to bring forth the "natural resourcefulness" of humans and not be overcome by the horrors of the world. Levertov came away inspired, convinced that Dolci was "dropping seeds into my head." She resolved to do what she could to mitigate impending disasters, but not to constantly "feel" them. "In what spirit, then, to go on living?" she asked. "The way I feel at present, it is a matter of trying to live as humanly, & as gratefully (for all the love & beauty one continues to experience) as one can, from day to day, & of contributing all one can to attempting prevention of the horror; but at the same time I feel a certain amount of 'psychic numbing' in myself everyday, & feel it is *necessary* — without it I would be a quelling mass, a walking slough of despond."[35]

Her intent was to live gratefully, humanly, and calmly. She sought nourishment wherever she could find it. By the early 1980s she more regularly began to attend religious services. She writes that in Holy Week, 1981, she attended services at The Church of the Advent, an Anglo-Catholic Parish in Beacon Hill in Boston, and then dropped in at the Catholic Paulist Chapel. She took communion at these churches but felt self-conscious that she might be making a mistake. In her diary she tried to understand what "transubstantiation," the changing of bread into Christ's body, might mean. She concluded that "any reverent & joyful consumption of natural good . . . is a communion service. And looking, touching, listening, breathing in fragrance or freshness of clear air — they too are sacraments, ways in which to express 'remembrance.' This thought is perhaps the answer to prayer, for I did pray to *feel* the communion service."[36]

Unwilling to be hemmed in by any particular religious or theological orthodoxy, Levertov attended Anglican, Episcopalian, Presbyterian, and Catholic churches in Boston and Palo Alto. In London she attended St. James, Piccadilly; in Paris St. Merri; in Rome the Byzantine Rite church of Santa Maria in Cosmedian. Although she acknowledged there was some "vulgarity in my shopping around for the right place of worship," she could not enter a ready-made structure but had to find components and construct her own, hence her peripatetic Sunday observance and what she called her "do-it-yourself theology." She was, she said, by nature and heritage an artist, one who was "forever a stranger and pilgrim."[37] She was not about to be constrained by orthodoxy of any sort.

As a child Levertov experienced her earliest communion with nature. Among antiwar protesters, especially students, she encountered another form of communion, solidarity in common action. She searched, mostly unsuccessfully, for the intimacy of communion in sexual expression. Now, for the first time she could envision another possibility: solidarity, communion, and intimacy with others in common faith. But she had her requirements. She wanted a religious community that offered aesthetically beautiful liturgies — i.e., good music, art, and intelligent sermons — and one that engaged with the world in an active commitment to social justice. In the Boston area she found Emmanuel Episcopal Church, whose pastor Rev. Al Kershaw oversaw a strong social justice program as well as splendid musical offerings. She also attended St. James Episcopal Church in Cambridge and the Catholic Paulist Center, where social justice activities were a community mainstay. When she was in Boston, her "shopping around" for religious community was facilitated by Joan Hallisey, who was in charge of driving her hither and yon.

In Palo Alto she met Robert McAfee Brown, professor of religion at Stanford and associate pastor of the First Presbyterian Church, a place that offered sanctuary to Salvadoran refugees and other outreach to the poor.

Through Brown Levertov was introduced to Judith Dunbar, a faculty member at Santa Clara University, who for nine years was Levertov's Sunday companion when she was in California. Together they attended a variety of churches, including First Presbyterian, nearby Episcopal churches, and the Catholic St. Ann's Chapel, an intimate setting with a superlative choir led by William Mahrt.[38] Their practice was to attend a service and then have lunch and conversation about issues of theological and political concern. During Easter Week of 1982 after attending services at First Presbyterian, Levertov wrote in her diary that she was happy to be with people who were believers and what joy it would have brought her parents to see her there. They always said she would be "found" someday. She wondered if her "thread" was pulling her in this new direction.[39]

Grateful, engaged, and artistically productive, Levertov's renewed happiness was dimmed in July 1982 when she learned that Nikolai, now age thirty-three, had been diagnosed with a Medulloblastoma, a brain tumor that usually presents itself in childhood. His six-hour brain surgery at Beth Israel Hospital was followed by extensive radiation treatment. In all, the procedures were very costly, even after initial insurance coverage. As was so often the case, Denise paid the bill.

The relationship between Nikolai and his parents had been distant since their divorce, and in fact he had not seen them for several years prior to his hospitalization. His situation now was life-threatening, and Denise and Mitch stayed in contact with him during his many weeks of recovery. Denise was consumed with worry. Her fleeting recall of the words of John of the Cross — "In the evening of life we will be judged on love" — that she had seen over the doorway of the Marist Chapel at Kenmore Square in Boston, prompted her to ask herself how much love she had given to others, especially to Nikolai and her mother. She queried: Could she care for others and herself at the same time? She prayed for Nikolai during his illness and lamented that she had not been a committed Christian when he was growing up so that she could have transmitted some faith and a sense of community to him. She quickly realized, however, that Mitch would not have joined in this and hence a religious commitment might have created even more family conflict.[40]

Preoccupied by how she might have contributed to Nikolai's illness, she began to reread her diaries from earlier years. Now some seven years after the divorce, she again revisited her marriage. She believed that she had put immense energy into pleasing Mitch and making him happy and that he did not recognize her effort. He was selfish, needed to be the center of attention, and made all the major decisions, leaving her to deal with the consequences. As a result she had been angry and "crudely violent," "undisciplined," without nurturing gentleness toward Nikolai, and potentially, but never literally, an abuser of him. What she asked now was whether her anger contributed to Nikolai's fears and nightmares and whether this was linked to his cancer? In a poem, "During a Son's Dangerous Illness," she explores the grief of a menaced son whose potential death leads to touching eternal nothingness and "tasting, in fear, the / desolation of / survival."[41]

During Nikolai's hospitalization there was a brief "thaw" in the relationship between him and his parents, but communication between them faltered soon after. When Nefertiti observed to Denise that she did not see love between mother and son, Levertov retorted that it was "mutual insecurity" that explained this and that she was sure Nikolai had an underlying love for her even though he found her personality difficult. She admitted she wanted her son to acknowledge her love of him and to show that he loved and was loyal to her.[42]

Gradually Nikolai's health improved, although the illness and treatment took a great toll on him. Levertov attributed his healing to his own courage and, even though she felt patronized and condescended to by her daughter-in-law, she acknowledged that Nefertiti's support and devotion had been essential to her son's improvement. Nikolai and Nefertiti, who lived in Montclair, New Jersey, continued to be generally estranged from both Levertov and Goodman. Desperate to find a way through this taxing relationship, Levertov would seek counsel in negotiating these difficult shoals.

Now in her sixth decade Levertov realized she was happier without sex, if it was of the "superficial," "unemotional" kind.[43] This realization seemed to have been linked to her reflection on her perennial desire to be adored. She reviewed again who cherished her and who did not and concluded that at this point in her life it was friends and her public who loved her. She then followed with a telling comment about the gift of religious experience: "What is sought is the *experience* of the love of God—though it is true that there's the attempt to *love* God, to serve God, etc., to be the actor, i.e., yet what is desired is to really believe that God loves *you*—to *feel* it, to experience it & know one knows it."[44]

Levertov continued to wrestle with the issues of doubt and faith and with the intellectual conundrum of human suffering and a merciful God. Nonetheless, four years after writing "Mass for the Day of St. Thomas Didymus," she now spoke not of the human desire to love and protect God but of the desire to experience God's love.

Given the considerable energy Levertov was dedicating to religious reflection, one might assume that her commitment to social justice issues would abate. Although she made it clear she did not want the "foolish label"[45] of "poet of protest" applied to her, she did want to connect her new religious sensibilities with her social justice commitments. An invitation to do just that came when the composer Newell Hendricks asked her to write a libretto for an oratorio on a subject of her choosing. Having retained in her memory the horrific murder of Oscar Romero and four American religious workers in 1980, Levertov suggested El Salvador as a theme for a libretto text. Her intent was to illustrate the horror of the situation in El Salvador, to explain its causes, and to define these deaths in terms of martyrdom, namely that they carried a message.[46]

In preparation for writing, she researched the pre-Columbian history of Central America, secured copies of the letters of the Maryknoll religious workers and sermons of Romero, and read the poetry of Carolyn Forché, who had lived in El Salvador for several years. Levertov worked on the manuscript during her ten-day visit to the Banff Centre in Alberta, Canada, in August of 1982.[47] Her objective was to produce not a poem but an unfinished text around which Hendricks could compose an oratorio. Using Bach's "Passion" and the oratorios of Hayden and Handel as models, she designed a text with a narrator, a chorus representing the people of El Salvador, and the voices of Romero and the Maryknoll workers. The text moves from pre-Columbian times to the present, chronicling the suffering of the Salvadoran people. The responses of chorus and narrator are interspersed with prayers and litanies and long recitations of the names of the dead. Levertov's goal was to inspire faith and hope in her hearers by illustrating how suffering, born of injustice, could produce a vision of a new life.[48] The first public reading of "El Salvador: Requiem and Invocation" was given in April 1983 at the First Presbyterian Church in Palo Alto. It premiered a month later with the Back Bay Chorale and the Pro Arte Chamber Orchestra at Sanders Theatre in Cambridge, Massachusetts. It was, as she had hoped, a poem-prayer in which the religious and political merged one into the other.

Levertov acknowledged that writing the libretto had a positive influence on her. By focusing on the words of Romero, she was able "to stop making such a *fuss*, inside my mind, about various points of doubt."[49] She subsequently claimed that "El Salvador" and "Mass for the Day of St. Thomas

Didymus," among other poems, moved her from "shaky belief" closer to faith.[50]

At this point Levertov only tentatively expressed her religious sensibilities in her poetry. These were private matters, which she was hesitant to share lest she alienate readers. In 1983, she wrote that this had been

> a period when I've known — ever since last December, & more & more — the meaning of Grace. Little by little I gain a *little* sense of confidence in my own beliefs, know my own experience of God's goodness to me, & a little courage in beginning to acknowledge it. But it is not only cowardice that holds me from openly speaking of it in the sense that I wd only alienate many, it is better to try & live more gratefully so that they might wonder what is affecting me — & then I would have more credibility.[51]

She goes on to write a highly self-reflective observation:

> And at the same time that I experience this I am aware of how un-transformed I am — not in the least more willing to do good things politically, but rather feeling the impulse to live in & for art & nature & not *think* about all the horrors. And also, as I read (& have quoted in the Oratorio) about the love of the poor I become very much aware that I don't love the poor — I really am an intellectual snob, I guess, & I like to be with people of refined manners and developed minds. Yet at the same time I have a degree of faith I never had before, & a wish to try to earn some of the goodness I receive — & at the same time the recognition that Grace is by definition un-earnable.

Although these reflections occurred against a backdrop of the good fortune of money and honors,[52] more was at stake.

Levertov's experience of God's goodness, of her own faults and her desire to live a transformed life parallel the shift that occurred in her poetry starting in the early 1980s. Although lament always would be present, this period reflected a decided emphasis on a poetry of awe and praise, which flowed from her increasing sense of gratitude. She responded much like her mentor Rilke, who when asked, "What does a poet do?" answered: "I praise."[53]

The first of her books to convey an overt religious orientation was *Oblique Prayers*, which appeared in 1984. She admitted to her friend Kathleen Norris, who reviewed the volume, that these were not "announced" prayers but rather prayers that *sidled up to the reader*.[54] These prayer-poems, one of the original forms of poetry, met the human need to praise, beseech, and communicate, much as did incantation, magic, prayer, and religious ritual.

Levertov's anxiety over the destruction of the natural world and nuclear warfare is evident in the first section of the book. One poem is dedicated to Jonathan Schell, author of *The Fate of the Earth*; another, "Gathered by the River," written for Beatrice Hawley and her painter husband John Jagel, describes an event commemorating the anniversary of the bombing of Hiroshima and Nagasaki, during which candles are launched on the Charles River as the trees "ponder" "our strange doings, as if / well aware that if we fail, / we fail also for them: if our resolves and prayers are weak and fail / / there will be nothing left of their slow and innocent / wisdom."[55]

In another section, Levertov offers her translation of fourteen poems by the French poet Jean Joubert. Here, her purpose is to introduce the American public to a poet with whom she resonates deeply. But it is in the book's final section, "Of God and the Gods," that Levertov attempts to get at what Ruskin referred to as "the totality of spiritual powers delegated by the lord of the universe."[56] In these fifteen poems she returns to rivers that remember, to poplar and fig trees, to flowers and the earth-gods, and then moves seamlessly to poems that signal her newly acknowledged faith.[57] In these she reflects on an "awe so quiet / I don't know when it began," and of "a gratitude" that sings in her.[58] In the poem "Of Being," she revisits her awareness of mystery. She writes:

> I know this happiness
> is provisional:
> . . . .
> but ineluctable this shimmering
> of wind in the blue leaves:
> . . . .
> this need to dance,
> this need to kneel:
> this mystery:[59]

In a group of explicitly religious poems she explores her new faith. In "St. Peter and the Angel," she recalls Peter's miraculous escape from prison through the help of an angel and his sending forth on a mission with an understanding that "He himself must be / the key, now, to the next door, / the next terrors of freedom and joy." In "This Day" Levertov affirms the nearness of mystery and alludes to the Incarnation: "God's in the dust, / not sifted // out from confusion."[60] In "The Task," God is perceived in the great tundra wilderness, a weaver at the loom, absorbed in the task of fulfillment, oblivious to the petition of human voices, attentive only to the work and its completion. Levertov credited the inspiration for this poem to a friend's description of the Alaskan wilderness around Mount Denali and her own reading of the poetry of the fourteenth-century English mystic Julian of Norwich, who claimed to apprehend the plan of God.[61]

Levertov's unresolved tension between a God who is both near and remote is expressed in "The Avowal," dedicated to friends Carolyn Kizer and John Woodbridge. In this, she circumvents two images of the Divine — one as near, one as far — with the human avowal of grace. She writes of swimmers who are borne up by water and hawks by air, so one can float, "into Creator Spirit's deep embrace, / knowing no effort earns / that all-surrounding grace."[62] As nothing before, *Oblique Prayers* reveals Levertov's entry into the unexplored landscape of faith.

The early 1980s was a rich time for Levertov; she flourished in every regard. Honors came to her. She was one of the six first-time winners of the New York University Bobst Award for a lifetime of sustained achievement[63] and cohonored with the Shelley Memorial Award from the Poetry Society of America. Honorary degrees were bestowed by St. Michael's College in Vermont, Bates College, and St. Lawrence University. In 1983, her sixtieth birthday was celebrated with the publication of a *Festschrift*, *In Celebration: Anemos*, to which thirteen of her poet-friends contributed.[64]

And she was productive. *Candles in Babylon* appeared in 1982, *Oblique Prayers* two years later. In addition, in 1983 New Directions brought out a collection of her previously published poems from *The Jacob's Ladder*, *O Taste and See*, and *The Sorrow Dance*. At this same time a spate of essays appeared, including two on her mentor William Carlos Williams, which explored his prosody and technique,[65] and an "Autobiographical Sketch,"[66] one of her few such pieces.

One of the most important of this group of essays is "Poetry, Prophecy, Survival," in which Levertov elaborates the work of imagination. Earlier, in "Origins of a Poem," she defines imagination as an essential human capacity for inculcating empathy and compassion for the other. In "Great Possessions," she identifies imagination as the faculty that penetrates through the meaning of appearances. In "Poetry, Prophecy, Survival," she suggests that imagination can lift affliction by illuminating it and making it more comprehensible, separating the affliction from the self.

Levertov has a "sense of the interdependence of all things" and claims

FIGURE 8. Denise Levertov, 1983, Richmond, Ind. Copyright © David Geier, used with permission.

that poetry reveals the unity of this "trembling web of being." In what she calls these "unprecedented times" when the fate of this web of being hangs in the balance, poetry helps one survive; it gives witness, and like prophecy it "transforms experience and moves the receiver to new attitudes." Although poetry itself cannot bring about change, it stimulates the imagination, quickens a love of life and helps one find the energy to stop "the accelerating tumble . . . towards annihilation."[67]

In "Horses with Wings," first delivered at a conference at the University of Alabama entitled "What Is a Poet?," Levertov reiterates her belief that the poet must be vividly engaged in the world, always living with the door of life open. She explores several correspondences between the winged horse Pegasus and the poet. Like Pegasus, the poet inherits an unconscious, protean power, a potential for great passion and intensity. Both are capable of "thundering prophecy" and "delicate nuance." They are animal, intuitive and sensual, not intellectual beings. Both have wings. In the case of the poet this is the power of imagination, a form of grace to which he responds with awe. Like Pegasus, the poet is stern and demonic, and has a commitment to meticulous and energetic work.[68]

In another essay, "A Poet's View," Levertov continues a discussion of the role of imagination. Imagination achieves its purpose not by presenting "closing arguments" but rather through "testimonies," and "circumstantial evidences." It is the "perceptive organ," the one "which synergizes intellect, emotion and instinct" and makes it "possible, though not inevitable, to experience God."[69] Her claim is important, not only because it emphasizes imagination as the integrative human faculty, but because it points to its centrality for full human development. Imagination was the key to becoming fully alive, fully human, fully oneself.

In this same essay Levertov responds to a query put to her: What do you believe and how has that belief affected your work? In response she lays out her intellectual commitments to inspiration, a constancy of vision, an obligation "to work from within," a social responsibility, and a conviction to nurture one's creative gifts even if that might mean sacrifices in other areas. When asked about her faith, she is less forthcoming, but she does chronicle her incremental and episodic movement from agnosticism to faith.

She writes:

> Had I undergone a sudden dramatic conversion, I would probably find
> it easier to speak of this. But the movement has been gradual; indeed,
> I see how very gradual and continuous only when I look back at my
> own poetry, my private notebooks, and the many moments through
> decades when I stepped up to the threshold of faith only to turn away
> unable to pass over.[70]

She recounts how slowly the "unknown" began to be defined for her as God, and later as God revealed in the Incarnation, how she was strengthened in her resolve to live a life of faith even if she could not solve the paradox of suffering and a merciful God, and how as she learned of the engagement of churches in the work of justice her embarrassment about religion diminished. But by her own self-description she was an "unorthodox" Christian, whose faith might be seen "scandalous" to the traditional believer.[71]

A year or two later she spoke of her tentative faith and the hope it provided. Using the metaphor of "shoots," she said:

> Well, my religious faith is at best fragile, but if, in fact, that which I
> hope is true *is* true, then I think God's mercy may prevent the anni-

hilation of our planetary life, despite human stupidity and violence. I also have strongly that sense of . . . the first shoots of some different consciousness, of moral evolution.[72]

In the tangle of her long, complicated life, a "thread" had "gently, invisibly" pulled Levertov toward this new consciousness. Now her unorthodox faith would impel her toward personal and communal reconciliation.

9

"Making Peace"
1985-1988

> But peace, like a poem,
> is not there ahead of itself,
> can't be imagined before it is made,
> can't be known except
> in the words of its making,
> grammar of justice,
> syntax of mutual aid.
>
> "MAKING PEACE"[1]

Denise Levertov spent decades opposing war. Now in the late 1980s she proposed an alternative — making peace. In the poem by that name, she analogizes peacemaking to poem-making. She calls peace "a presence," "an energy field" that is more than the absence of war. Peace might be realized if "we restructured . . . our lives," "questioned our needs, allowed / long pauses." Peace, like the poem, is possible because of imagination and a willingness to venture into the unknown. It is the poets who "must give us / imagination of peace, to oust the intense, familiar / *imagination of disaster*."

The late 1980s were for Levertov a time of making peace and reconciling. Through imagination she restored a relationship with persons in her past and forged a link between her vocation as poet and Christian. The result was greater personal tranquility and a desire to "clear the decks" and risk a new beginning.

The circumstances of her life were generally positive. She had loyal friends, those she called her "beneficent spirits," and no major crises to derail her. As a consequence she could plumb her interior life in ways she had never done before. Although she claimed to have a "constant" and "primary" preoccupation with religion, this preoccupation did not always nourish her. What did nourish and give satisfaction was poem-making.[2] Writing poems helped her heal her relationships with her parents, her sister, and other friends, and to wrestle with questions of faith.

The years 1985 through 1988 were rich and productive. She continued to live in Somerville and Palo Alto, teach, attend to friends through letters and visits, give readings, travel, garner awards, and create poems. Although the intensity of her romantic life had ebbed, apparently she was content with this turn of events. She wrote that "[t] he pleasure of a chaste well ordered life seems superior to all the turmoil of my sexually active years, I must say! But I suppose I wouldn't feel the one if I hadn't had the other."[3] She reminisced about En Potter, whom she said she loved not more, but more wistfully than any other,[4] and she had an occasional tryst with Stephen Peet. Her engagement with social justice issues continued to be expressed in her poetry, especially in concern for Central and South America, the arms race, the environment, and the spread of AIDS. Although she participated less frequently in public demonstrations, her button inscribed with "Picket and Pray" suggested her new orientation, one which would have been unthinkable ten years earlier.

Levertov's life remained fast paced; the year 1985 was a case in point. After finishing the winter term at Stanford, she was inducted into the American Academy and Institute of Arts and Letters and awarded a Certificate of Recognition by Massachusetts Governor Michael Dukakis. During the early part of the year, she worked hard on some new poems but broke off this writing in order to participate in the Peace Pentecost March in May in Washington, D.C. She then traveled to England where she vacationed on the Devon coast and gave a reading in Norwich. In August she was in Japan to read at the fortieth anniversary of the bombing of Hiroshima and Nagasaki. Arriving back in the United States in October, she gave readings in Santa Fe, Philadelphia, Washington, D.C., and Atlanta. By January she had returned to Stanford ready to teach again.

Now in her early sixties, Levertov was preoccupied with a series of deaths among her friends: Myron Bloy, Episcopal priest and founder of Associates for Religion and Intellectual Life; David Posner and Beatrice Hawley, both of whom were poet-friends; Abbey Niebauer, who was murdered; and Robert Laughlin, son of her publisher, who committed suicide.[5] Levertov herself felt robust and physically strong and hoped, she said, to live into her nineties. Her minor problems were a recent bout with shingles and a diagnosis of Sjogren's Syndrome, an autoimmune disorder that destroys the production of tears and saliva. This latter caused her to use eyedrops and keep a bottle of water always at the ready. She claimed to feel serene and suggested that a sign of her well-being was her new preference for the color blue.[6] But irrespective of her physical and psychological health, by 1987 she wrote that she had had a sense of mortality such as I've never before had; i.e., a *facing*, & with fear, the fact that I am far along in my life, that there is not a vast stretch of likely time before me in which to do, redo, undo; & the terror of the unknown: either grief-laden idea of nothingness, in which one wd not be able to look back, even, at what one's life had been, whatever one made of it — or of the passage into another state (which I cannot believe would be *bliss*, for surely, if not hell, then — more logically than hell or heaven — some form of purgatory must follow the vagaries in this life of all but saints and innocents).[7]

Her concern for the compressing of time left to her did not abate.[8] Convinced that she did not want to fritter away whatever years she had left, she resolved that within the next decade she would create a body of solid poetry that would have an energy similar to that of Pablo Neruda, Robert Lowell, William Carlos Williams, or Wallace Stevens.[9]

This growing awareness of her mortality may help explain her prodigious output. In the period 1985 to 1988 she translated the work of Bulgarian poets Krassin Himmirsky and Liliana Stefanova and the French poet Jean Joubert. Her *Selected Poems* was published in the United Kingdom, and New Directions brought out both *Breathing the Water* and *Poems 1968-1972*, which contain her previous volumes — *Relearning the Alphabet*, *To Stay Alive*, and *Footprints*. She also wrote two essays, "On the Need for New Terms" and "Paradox and Equilibrium,"[10] and the introduction to Baca's *Martin and Meditations on the South Valley*.

Honors and opportunities kept coming too. She was awarded an honorary doctorate by Allegheny College, was named a corresponding member of the Académie Mallarmé, was writer in residence for two months at Lynchburg College, and gave readings at several midwestern colleges and universities — Denison, Ohio State, Earlham, Ohio Wesleyan, and Cleveland State. All this activity increased her correspondence. Overwhelmed by the onslaught of forty pieces of mail a day, she sent a form letter to all her correspondents advising that given this volume, her poetic vocation, and the diminished amount of time she had left in life she would no longer answer their missives.[11] Her resolve was futile. Letters piled up, and she responded, only to necessitate another fruitless attempt to stem the postal tide.

In parallel to this breathless engagement, Levertov carried on a fertile interior life spurred on by the reading of religious commentaries and mystical texts. In her diaries she notes that during this time she was reading *The*

Cloud of Unknowing, works by Pascal, Anthony Bloom, Benedicta Ward, Jean Sulivan,[12] Francois Mauriac, and Jacob Needleman. She read Murray Bodo's *The Way of St. Francis* and interviews with the Helder Camara, Archbishop of Recife, and listened to tapes by the Carmelite monk Basil Pennington. She confessed that although she was exceedingly interested in "mystical experience," it would be "extremely presumptuous" to call her a mystic.[13] She continued to keep abreast of social justice issues and was impressed by the pastoral letters of the U.S. Catholic Bishops Conference on peace and social justice and the leadership on these matters provided by Bishops Hunthausen of Seattle and Gumbleton of Detroit.

In order to sustain her fragile faith, Levertov participated in a wide variety of religious practices. She prayed by meditating on the Psalms, repeating the Jesus Prayer, using the techniques of Centering Prayer, and chanting the Taize service. When she felt a great need for repentance and forgiveness, she would call on Al Kershaw — the pastor of Emmanuel Church in Boston — Murray Bodo, Paul Lacey, or Gerry Pocock.[14] She considered having a spiritual director but decided against this for "temperamental" and "ideological" reasons, concluding she would be her own spiritual director.[15] She made a pilgrimage to the Isle of Iona, which she memorialized in the poem "A Stone from Iona."[16] And she put herself in the company of religious seekers. At Kirkridge, the nondenominational center in the Pocono mountains, she offered a retreat on the topic of "Poetic Language as Spiritual Insight," illustrating her comments with quotes from her favorite poets and transmitting her seriousness of purpose through her presence.[17] Among those attending were friends: Joan Hallisey, Rose Marie Berger of *Sojourners*, and Yarrow Cleaves. She also took on responsibilities with religiously oriented groups, serving on the advisory board of the journal *Cross Currents* and later founding a Peace Group at her beloved Emmanuel Church with the intent of fostering links between contemplation and action. When she gave the Peace Pentecost sermon at the Cathedral Church of St. Paul in Boston in 1988, she emphasized the connection between inner and outer life. "If we neglect our inner lives," she said from the pulpit, "we destroy the sources of fruitful outer action. But if we do not act, our inner lives become mere monuments to egotism." She called on congregants to be like the disciples, who infused with the Holy Spirit, hurried into the streets to begin a life of spiritual action.[18]

Levertov's friendships with religious persons nourished her interior life. Her old friend Eileen Egan of Catholic Relief Services continued to encourage her and again invited her to read at the Catholic Worker House in New

York, and new friends entered her life as well. She met Mary Luke Tobin, a Sister of Loretto, in 1986. A friend of Merton and the prominent Catholic theologians Bernard Haring and Edward Schillebeeckx, Tobin was one of only fifteen women auditors at the Second Vatican Council. Aesthetically appreciative, intellectually astute, and socially committed, Tobin was impressed by *Candles in Babylon* and *Oblique Prayers*. She became a trusted friend, one Levertov referred to as "St. Luke." Levertov's friendship circle also included the Buddhist ecophilosopher Joanna Macy, the Quaker Paul Lacey, and the teacher Edward Zlotkowski, all of whom appreciated and understood her spiritual aspirations.

But it was the Franciscan Murray Bodo who was most helpful. Bodo first heard Levertov read in 1973 in Cincinnati, but that produced no ongoing relationship. They corresponded briefly beginning in 1978, but it was not until 1983 that their friendship began in earnest when Levertov, flummoxed by her relationship with Nikolai, wrote asking if he would serve as her "sounding board."[19] Bodo guided her through both her difficult relationship with her son and the quagmire of belief. By emphasizing the Franciscan care for the earth and the indwelling of God in all things, Bodo helped deepen in her the "Franciscan sense of wonder" she first encountered in the writings of Rilke, Hopkins, and William Carlos Williams.[20] Bodo, who was insightful and courageous enough to reflect back to her some of her own resistance to growth, suggested that one who demonizes others projects one's own evil on them and consciously or unconsciously denies it in oneself.[21] This was advice she needed to hear.

Levertov reciprocated Bodo's generosity. She critiqued his poetry, all the while urging him to greater engagement with issues of social justice. She sent him a subscription to *Sojourners*, and later participated with him in protesting the development of nuclear armaments.

Another source of advice was her friend Bet Mitchell, who both cared for and understood her friend of many years. In response to a letter from Denise, who lamented that she wanted to be cherished by others but thought she was unworthy of such cherishing, Bet offered a sage response. She acknowledged that Denise was loved by her friends, had many wonderful qualities, and was fun to be with, but that she was bossy and demanding: "To me you're still the passionate argumentative girl . . . and you've had to grow as a woman in the limelight — a very very hard thing to do. And of course you've been surrounded by many other strong minded, creative people — you've had to show how strong you are if only you can come through this. . . . Do relax, learn to believe yr. not condemned — only human."[22]

Following a holiday they had together in France, Bet wrote commenting on Denise's odd and "absolutely overbearing" behavior. She opined that although she had spent her life listening to Denise and giving her attention, when she directed her attention to others Denise was jealous and probably did not even recognize this because her jealousy was buried. Bet believed Denise's problems stemmed from the fact that she had no insight into her own basic motives — her need for power, for love, for self-acceptance, and for self-forgiveness. Because Bet believed Denise was unconscious about all of this, she was sure she would take her comments as condemnation. To Bet's lights, what Denise needed was greater inner certainty and not to always be at the center and in charge.[23] Levertov responded as predicted. She felt she no longer had Bet's love and approval and hence her love for Bet diminished. But Bet's comments caused Levertov to ask quizzically in a diary entry: "Is all my love narcissistic and self-referential?"[24] There was little time left for reconciliation. Bet had a stroke and died in 1989. Levertov read at her funeral service and several years later wrote a poem in which she remembered her friend's ability to see beauty, even in the evening of life.[25] In her diary she recorded that Bet "knew rapture"[26] and perhaps that was enough.

Levertov's earnest engagement with perceptive and caring friends began to expose her own complex psyche. It is fair to say Levertov was charming, cosmopolitan, and articulate. She had presence, and as "poet in the world," she was in touch with the great issues of her time. Nonetheless she could be irksome. Empathetic toward those who suffered, she sometimes lacked sympathy for those close at hand. She was oddly formidable and vulnerable all at once. Although never an innocent, she retained the qualities of a child, which endeared her to many; she was full of wonder, joyful, energetic, and fearless. She trusted her own intuition implicitly and said exactly what she thought. By her own account she was impatient and irritable, but she denied the hostility and arrogance others sometimes imputed to her. Although she had an uncanny ability to see into others, especially younger artists, and reflect back to them who they were or might become, she was opaque to herself and had little understanding of how she frustrated others.

Levertov wanted love and loyalty from friends, and if that was not forthcoming, she was capable of closing down a relationship. Perhaps because of her sense of "destiny" as a poet, she guarded her freedom tenaciously. She did not want anyone to "get their hooks in her." Much of her resistance to her mother, and perhaps to Nikolai too, derived from fear of losing her freedom and hence her vocation. Her person was to be poet; the two were one. But during these years it occurred to her that that she might have other obligations as well. "I felt again," she wrote, "that I have that power to give through my work, which is . . . in a certain way what I'm here for — though this does not at all exempt me from trying to be a better person; on the contrary."[27]

The integration of her poet self with a "better" self was a new endeavor for Levertov. She recognized that she was untransformed, yet she was clearly changing. She both experienced intermittent healing and forgiveness and manifested a willingness to deal with her sorrow. She wrote of a "superabundant goodness" flowing over her.[28] In her poem "Zeroing In," she records a conversation about hurt and fear and projects an awareness of the internal damage carried by every person. She compares the self to a landscape, full of "daunting cliffs," "sinkholes," "places of sudden terror," "of malevolent depths" and "quagmires." All this is inside, and if one touches it, one leaps up or "flinches back." "'It's not terror, it's pain we're talking about: / those places in us, . . / that are bruised forever, that time / never assuages, never.'"[29]

Slowly Levertov began to recognize her own "sinkholes" and "quagmires" as she tried to reconcile with the dead — her parents, her sister, and Duncan — and with the living, especially Nikolai. The reconciliation she achieved came in large part through making poems.

Levertov's greatest regret was her abandonment of her mother. The image of Beatrice grimacing on her death bed haunted her, prompting a feeling of remorse that lasted a decade. A breakthrough came in late 1984, when she discovered one of her mother's notebooks in her basement. In it Beatrice had written that there was a cloud of unknowing between God and the self, but that one must go forward without fear, armed only with purity, faith, and fidelity. The suffering in the world could not be understood; it was part of the plan of God, which was vast and unknowable. Denise believed her mother's words were a response to the questions she raised during the period of the Vietnam War. She felt as if her mother, with her strong and resilient faith, was speaking to her across time.[30]

When Levertov expressed guilt about her treatment of her mother, her friends countered that Beatrice was a forgiving person and that one could suspect she would have forgiven her daughter at the end of life.[31] But Denise's remorse waxed and waned. In mid-1988 she wrote that by means of the sacraments, she had come to realize that her mother had forgiven her and that gradually she felt her selfishness and stupidity being washed away,[32] but a month later she again lamented her inability to show greater affection toward Beatrice and for always keeping a stiff upper lip. She concluded that it would be by trying to live a good life and gave up on the idea that she could have any hope of permanent forgiveness.[33] Until the end of her life, Levertov continued to ponder her relationship with her mother. She wrote fourteen poems about this "accidental pilgrim in a strange land," the last composed just prior to her own death.[34]

A breakthrough occurred in her relationship with her father in 1984, when Nikolai found a box of his grandfather's manuscripts and papers and shared them with his mother. Among them was Beatrice's paraphrased recording of her husband's deathbed statement to Denise: "And if you find someday, if you discover someday that God long since found you, how happy that will make me in the place to which I am going."[35] Now more than thirty years after his death, Levertov wrote a poem about a dream in which her father visited her. Having earlier described him as "complex," "vain," "good," and "weak," he now appeared to her in his essence as "an old-fashioned dark-pink garden rose."[36] A few years later in "The Opportunity," she writes of another visitation by her father and her admission that "'[m]uch has happened, over the years. . . . Along the way, / I have come to believe / the truth of what you believe.'"[37] This was her "opportunity" to tell her father of her love, and she seized it. In "The Spirits Appeased," she acknowledges moments of reconciliation with both parents. She describes how they have spoken to her: "I find I have heard you. When I need it, / a book or a slip of paper / appears in my hand, inscribed by yours: messages / waiting on cellar shelves, in forgotten boxes / until I would listen."[38]

A rapprochement was even possible with her sister. In "To Olga," a poem of reminiscences of their early life together, Denise honors the life she and Olga shared. It concludes with Denise's simple yet profound affirmation of a bond that could not be obliterated even in death: "I trusted you."[39]

There was also need of closure with Robert Duncan. He and Levertov last corresponded in 1978 when he wrote in praise of Levertov's newly published *Life in the Forest*, saying that its wonderful poems had been "won in just those 'War poems' I took even rancorous exception to."[40] With his letter he included a copy of his poem "The Torn Cloth," in which he reflects on the "re-weaving" of their friendship. Levertov thanked him for the letter but said that it had come at least two years too late. His expectation of her "unfailing love" was deluded, and she could not respond with gratitude to his praise because "[t]here can be a statute of limitations on emotional commitments."[41] Then in 1980 when she again reread Duncan's comments from his

1969 interview, her bitterness revived. "Imagine," she wrote in her diary, "at a time when we still seemed close friends, when he was seeing me fairly often! It was indeed a nasty betrayal — & reveals his worst homosexual hatred of women, so masked usually. Probably from that betrayal of friendship by such uncalled for, wholly self-projecting malice, dates my distrust of homosexuals of both sexes. . . . [I]n RD's case, jealousy of my attention (given at that time both to politics & to George Q. [Quasha], that absurd infatuation of mine which wd never have happened if Mitch had not been so neurotic & so neglectful of me) plus an underlying fear & hatred of women undoubtedly combined to make him attribute to me his own sado-masochistic fantasies & hang-ups. Uggh!"[42]

Her resentment must have abated somewhat because four years later in 1984 when she and Duncan shared the Shelley Prize, she wrote to congratulate him and express her sorrow about his illness. In a response of gratitude he wrote her a letter but never mailed it.

When Levertov learned of Duncan's death in March 1988, she wrote a poem based on an intense and vivid dream of his visitation. She told Jess Collins that the dream *"really felt* like a reconciliation — the traditional belief in many cultures that the souls of the dead hover around for a little while, especially when there is 'unfinished business.'"[43] Her poem begins with the description of their acrimonious parting:

> You were my mentor. Without knowing it,
> I outgrew the need for a mentor.
> Without knowing it, you resented that,
> and attacked me. I bitterly resented
> the attack, and without knowing it
> freed myself to move forward
> without a mentor. Love and long friendship
> corroded, shrank, and vanished from sight
> into some underlayer of being.[44]

Having put him away like a "folded cloth," she then recounts her dream-vision in which she and Duncan sit together in the Lady Chapel,[45] hand in hand, chosen sister and brother, hearing the strong harmonies filling the arching stone, sounds that had been there through the centuries. Whatever reconciliation Levertov had with Duncan came through poem-making and the images given her by imagination.

Levertov was still in the process of learning to forgive. Among the living, she attempted to reach out to other alienated friends. In 1988, she opened the possibility of a tentative reconciliation with Adrienne Rich. Rich responded warmly, remembering their affirmative talks earlier in their lives.[46] Some years later they would meet face to face.

There was no need to reconcile with Mitch. Ten years after their divorce she continued an episodic relationship with him and his family to whom she sent money and presents. Although Mitch had no emotional hold on her, she cared about his well-being and was glad he had a wife in Sandy, whom she liked, and was affectionate with their son, Matty. Mitch, on the other hand, continued to feel emotionally tied to Denise. He sent his poems for her critique,[47] and he read hers. While Denise had an expansive life, his was constrained. He did not have much to do and considered most people either "corrupt" or "debased."

Levertov's longing for reconciliation with Nikolai was not realized. He remained a part of her life, even though their communication was infrequent, tepid, and usually centered around money.[48] She continued to pay his medical, dental, and mental health bills, and expenses for car repairs, tools, and courses. In Nikolai's scant correspondence with his mother, he indicated that he was full of fear and anger and that his psychological and neurological problems compounded each other, placing him under enormous stress. Although he began a job, he left it because of personality clashes.[49] By 1988, Nikolai had a clean bill of health regarding the brain tumor, but he was considered disabled and no longer held a job, although he continued to paint.[50] He was almost forty years old.

Levertov considered her relationship with her son "blighted," sometimes blaming Nefertiti for Nikolai's negativity toward her. An unpublished poem, "Denise's Blues,"[51] alludes to this, but she also admitted that she had been angry with Nikolai since his childhood.[52] She recorded in her diary that she had been selfish, capricious, and violent toward him and may have "screwed him up psychologically," but she denied actual cruelty toward him.[53] Her attempts to modify her anger were not particularly successful. She was irritated that Nikolai did not appreciate what she did for him, namely that she continually had to scrounge around for money to meet his emergency expenses, and that he often refused to be in communication with her.[54] She concluded she would probably love him more if she felt more certain he loved her.[55] Stymied by their relationship, she consulted Murray Bodo, who responded that one can forgive another, but that it takes two to be reconciled.[56]

This mother-son relationship continued much the same for several years. Although she understood how "unnatural" it was to have one's own child threatened with death, she was nonetheless unable to understand her son. She remained regretful, perplexed, and annoyed by their relationship.

Levertov was preoccupied by forgiveness, not only because of her acknowledged selfishness toward Beatrice and Nikolai but also because of her alleged cruelty toward her nieces and toward a dying child in the hospital during wartime in the 1940s. She accused herself of "crimes" of brutality to others for which she had never atoned or apologized.[57] Although she recognized that her inability to experience forgiveness from either absolution or the Eucharist was to deny God's power to forgive her, her sense of guilt continued, and she blamed this both on her own tepid faith and her inability to forgive herself, believing that self-forgiveness might make her complacent. She explained in her diary: "I've come to the conclusion that atonement consists of continuing consciousness of what one has done, bearing it as a burden, along with behavior (works) that — in the ancient scales — little by little outweigh or compensate for it."[58]

But her need for forgiveness and the feebleness of her faith paled in the face of her fear that she might be "kidding herself" about belief.[59] When she sought the counsel of Al Kershaw, he assured her that doubt was part of spiritual growth and the darkness she encountered might increase her sense of dependence and lead her to God.[60]

Levertov recognized a difference in believing in God and loving God, the latter being that which was necessary to change one's natural greed and selfishness.[61] Her two foundational experiences were awe and gratitude, and she hoped these would lead her to love God. Again, her diary is the place where she explores these confusions:

> And the love of God — what is it? Don't all the writers who speak of it emphasize its basis in God's love for *us*? Few speak of it as a phenomenon that could arise purely out of admiration & awe. The contemplation of God's power & glory gives rise to awe, but it is the idea that we, as a class, & every *I* as a unique creature, *matter* to God that gives rise to love. . . . And this is what binds gratitude *&* love together (& gratitude for my life is what I *do* feel, along with amazement at the existence of anything at all when God could have rested in his own all sufficiency . . .) So perhaps my *gratitude* to God will in time lead me to experience that *love* for God (for Christ) which I['m] aware of lacking.[62]

In the same passage she wrestles with the command to love others, which goes beyond proportional love:

> But does it also imply that my love for persons being based in, or proportional to, their love for me is not an outstanding personal failing, but is the common and natural way? It cannot be so, or we would not have been adjured to love our enemies.[63]

Levertov continued to practice her faith, wagering that through practice she might come to believe. But doubt and intellectual conundrums persisted. This did not mean that she was quiescent when encountering a theological view that diverged from her own. Her wrangle with the Reverend Sam Abbott, a former law professor at Boston University who served as the dynamic priest of St. James Episcopal Church in Cambridge, is a case in point.

Although Levertov liked Abbott, she had deep disagreements with what she construed as his narrow concept of salvation and compassion. She poured out her distress and concern to him in a letter, acknowledging that although Christians had certain advantages — a tradition of prayer, the sacraments, and the Incarnation — this did not mean they had a monopoly on virtue or reward. She considered it a form of "cultural imperialism" to try to convert someone of another tradition who was living a generous, just, and merciful life. Instead, she argued, Christians should attempt to learn from such people.

She went on to berate Abbott for encouraging his congregants to assert abortion as their primary political issue. Although she considered abortion a very real ethical concern that needed to be debated, given the multiple perils facing the human community, abortion was not the most pressing.[64] On the matter of the uniqueness of Jesus as the *only* manifestation of God in history Levertov argued that while he was the fullest and greatest manifestation, all of humankind's great spiritual insights needed to be considered entries of God into human understanding. There were multiple roads to the experience of God, and if Christian parochialism blocked persons from accepting Christianity, it was not their fault. In response to Abbott's misunderstanding of her portrayal of the lamb of God in "Mass for the Day of St. Thomas Didymus," she wrote:

> In it I am speaking about the symbolism of the voluntary defenselessness of God — babe in the manger, suffering servant, crucified, — the Lamb as symbol of the incarnation, if you will. I guess you are right in saying I'm *not* dealing with atonement, exactly — but what I was deal-

ing with was, I think, the challenge the incarnation presents (historically or conceptually or both) to human beings.[65]

She went on to prompt Abbott to encourage his congregation to engage in peace education, oppose militarism, and give sanctuary to immigrants. This was the work of God.

Abbott did not respond immediately to Levertov's missives but called her sometime later. Finally, after three months, what she considered a written pastoral response finally arrived. She was "scandalized" by this delay and let him know it, although she finally apologized for her "roaring" tone. The positive result of Levertov's engagement with Abbott was that it helped her clarify some of her seemingly "unorthodox" views. As she said in an interview at about this time, "[m]aybe my Christianity is unorthodox, but it's still a Christian unorthodoxy, liable to offend both skeptics and members of other faiths."[66]

If Abbott disappointed her, she was also disappointed by the Catholic bishops' statements about birth control and abortion. She lamented that the Catholic church did not recognize the value and dignity of non-procreative sex and that its condemnation of birth control left only abstinence as an option. To her lights, that was unnatural. She embraced the bishops' statement of a "seamless fabric" of social justice but rejected the notion that abortion should be the priority issue. Although repelled by the "feelingless promiscuity" of the times, she did not have remorse for her own abortion and stated that if a really strong Catholic spokesperson did not offer an alternative view on this issue, it would nip in the bud what she called her "secret flirtation with the RC Church."[67] Eileen Egan weighed in with her on this issue and that of papal infallibility. Egan's advice was to not worry about papal infallibility and the "crimes of the churchmen" but to consider the church as a great field in which there were both the "treasures" of the Eucharist and the teachings of Jesus and "the offal and dead men's bones."[68]

Levertov's most pressing theological question was about free will and God's nonintervention in a suffering world. Initially she admitted she could not resolve this paradox, but she came to find a way through:

I began to see these stumbling blocks as absurd. Why, when the very fact of life itself, of the existence of anything at all, is so astounding why — I asked myself — should I withhold my belief in God or in the claims of Christianity until I am able to explain to myself the discrepancy between the suffering of the innocent, on the one hand, and the assertions that God is just and merciful on the other? Why should I for a moment suppose that I or any human mind can comprehend paradoxes too vast to fit our mental capacities and thus, never perceived in their entirely?[69]

Levertov continued to explore these issues with friends. She told Bodo that she thought of God as an artist, one who created humans with freedom. If God exercised omnipotence and eliminated human choice, then God's joy in human achievement would also be nullified.[70] When she queried Robert McAfee Brown about his understanding of this paradox, he suggested that God could not renege on the gift of free will because it was constitutive of human nature, but he also believed the Holy Spirit could enter into the course of events effecting subtle change if humans remained open and receptive.[71] Levertov listened, but in the end she would make her own way through this thicket of theological confusion.

Some years later she was able to deal with her confusion by means of images given her in the process of writing poetry. Imagination was not only the key to poem-making and peacemaking but to theological understanding as well. She explained this connection: "As to my more substantial stumbling block, the suffering of the innocent and the consequent question of God's nonintervention, which troubled me less in relation to individual instances than in regard to the global panorama of oppression and violence, it was through poetry — through images given me by creative imagination while pondering this matter — that I worked through to a theological explanation which satisfied me."[72]

In her work as a poet and as a Christian, imagination was a key. She wrote in her diary: "[W]hen I'm following the road of imagination . . . in the word-by-word, line-by-line decisions of a poem in the making, I've come to see certain analogies, and also some interaction, between the journey of art and the journey of faith."[73]

Breathing the Water (1987), her fifteenth book of poetry, offers examples of the poetic images that made theological explanation possible. The forty-nine poems included in this volume cover a broad range of topics, including poems about injustice, death, nature, myths, and relationships. What distinguishes this collection from previous ones is the absence of violent images or calls to action. In the main its poems are meditative and sensuous. The book opens and closes with poetic variations on themes from Rilke. Like bookends, these variations signal her return to her first mentor, the one who initially inspired her vocation. *Breathing the Water* takes its title from the final

Rilke variation, a poem about timelessness and stillness, which concludes with the lines: "What we desire travels with us. / We must breathe time as fishes breathe water. / God's flight circles us."[74]

Breathing the Water is divided into several sections. Two sections are given over to what she called "Spinoffs," poems written as commentary on photographs.[75] Another section focuses on issues of justice and sorrow and includes the poem "Making Peace." As she frequently did, Levertov concludes the volume with a series of poems that attempt to resolve issues raised in earlier sections. In this case the nine concluding poems have religious themes and are offered as a form of witness.

Conversations with Murray Bodo and a reading of her mother's notebooks[76] inspired Levertov to write "Standoff," one of the major religious poems of *Breathing the Water*. In it she reflects her understanding that once God invested in the Incarnation and bestowed freedom on humans, they would not be forsaken or annihilated; neither would their freedom be annulled. Humans might beseech God and plead with the saints, but their freedom would not be abrogated.[77] God ignores the "gull-screech knifeblades," the "strident or plaintive" pleas of humans gaping at the abyss. God wants them to "fly." She explains that it was this image of a God standing-off that had more power to convince than any theological argument. The inviolability of human freedom was now confirmed for her: In a public address she said, "It's an idea, or theory, undoubtedly familiar to many of you through works of religious philosophy; but *for me* it was original, not only because I hadn't come across such exposition of it but also because the concrete images which emerged in the process of writing convinced me at a more intimate level of understanding than abstract argument would have done."[78]

Breathing the Water contains other poems that manifest an individual's encounter with divine power. The poem "Caedmon" memorializes the seventh-century cowherd whose tongue was unlocked by an angel, earning him the designation of the first English poet.[79] "The Servant-Girl at Emmaus" recounts the meeting of a Moorish kitchen-girl and the "Christ." As she sees the light around her guest, she recognizes him and believes.[80] "Candlemas" recalls the response of the aged Simeon, who when presented with the infant Jesus, knows with surety the meaning of this child:

> With certitude
> Simeon opened
> ancient arms
> to infant light.

Decades
before the cross, the tomb . . .
he knew
new life.[81]

Levertov was inspired to write these three poems based on her life experiences. She read the story of Caedmon as a child in John Richard Green's *History of the English People*. On a trip to Ireland she saw the newly restored Velasquez painting of the servant girl's encounter with and recognition of the Christ. The poem about the revelation to Simeon was stimulated by her experience of a candlelight service in the beautiful Byzantine memorial church at Stanford and the sermon given by a Dominican priest on the occasion of Candlemas.[82]

Of the religious poems in *Breathing the Water* those about Julian of Norwich, the fourteenth-century English mystic, were of central importance. Levertov first read Julian's *Showings* in 1983 when she bought a copy of the book for her niece, Julia. Two years later when she visited Norwich, her appreciation deepened for the wisdom of this anchoress,[83] whose corrupt, violent, and chaotic times Levertov considered much like her own. Julian's question — How can good come out of so much horror? — was also much like her own. Rather than answer this question directly, Julian reminds her readers of the existence of mysteries beyond their intellectual powers. Her message is one of humility: accept paradox as inherent in the human condition. Levertov resonated with her sagacity.

In her rich and evocative Julian poems, Levertov explores pressing theological issues: the value of creation, the powerlessness of evil in the face of the good, the relationship between human suffering and God's mercy, the meaning of the life of Jesus, the Christ, and the role of imagination in experiencing religious truth. As Julian experiences the wounds of Christ through "enacting metaphor," the poet and her reader analogously can experience this reality through creative imagination.[84]

In the poem "On a Theme from Julian's Chapter XX," Levertov asks: Why single out the agony of Christ? What is unique in his suffering? Others have suffered torture for a longer time. Julian's spirit "leapt" to the difference. She saw his "oneing" with the Godhead as opening him to the pain of "all minds, all bodies" "from first beginning / to last day." He was "King of Grief," enduring within history "the sum total of anguish." "*Every sorrow and desolation / He saw, and sorrowed in kinship*."[85]

In her longer poem "The Showings," Levertov acknowledges the vast sweep of history and the heavens, but Julian asks that we consider the world as a little thing the size of a hazelnut lying in God's pierced palm. She does this in order to share the mystery she has been shown: that all creation is "held safe" by God. This powerful image of consolation, given to Julian and shared with Levertov, is passed down to the contemporary reader.

In the second part of "The Showings" Levertov imagines the youth and adulthood of this anchoress, who has one audacious desire: to have the five wounds of Christ. This she achieves by "enacting" metaphor, in order for "flesh to make known / to intellect . . . make known in bone and breath / (and not die) God's agony." With this knowledge Julian is able to laugh, to scorn evil, and to banish the dreaded fiend. She is glad "with *a most high inward happiness.*" The poem ends with a direct petition by the poet to Julian, the one who clung to joy in the midst of agony, the one who like an acrobat, fiercely, and with the certainty of infinite mercy witnessed and desired to share her knowledge that "*Love was his meaning.*"[86]

Julian was Levertov's instructor in faith. From her she learned that love was God's meaning and that because of God's mercy and goodness, human freedom was not abrogated by God's intervention in a suffering world, even though God suffered when humans chose evil.[87] Levertov had come a long way from "Mass for the Day of St. Thomas Didymus" in which she admonished humans to shield "the spark of divine light" lest it be extinguished. The focus here in the Julian poems was on God's loving action in and for the world.

Levertov imagines Julian as a woman who is witness, one whose desire is to "enact" the metaphor of the suffering Christ. This desire for anguish in order to make it "real" is reminiscent of the yearning expressed during Levertov's antiwar protest in 1969: "Wanting it, wanting / with all my hunger this anguish, / this knowing in the body / . . . wanting it real."[88] This reality had now been made known in a way never dreamt of by the younger Levertov.

Through her engagement with the images given her in the creation of poems, Levertov overcame her theological stumbling block. Both art and faith were dependent on imagination; both were "ventures into the unknown." And both were, as she had indicated in an obscure lecture given some twenty-five years earlier, testimonies of the "*participation mystique,*" by which she meant that both art and faith assumed the existence of a spirit and the involvement of the individual in a life beyond itself.[89] The journey of art led Levertov further along the journey of faith. Poetry, she said, was work that "enfaithed."

Breathing the Water clearly announced Levertov as a Christian, although she would eschew the descriptor, Christian poet. A year or so after the book's publication in 1987, she expressed the desire to "clear the decks" and to leave Somerville, the place she had lived for fourteen years. Circumstances soon conjoined to make such a move a reality.

Increasingly she was bothered by the cold climate, the noisy environment, and the remove from nature that characterized life in Somerville. She wanted a place where she would have access to both mountains and water and one less expensive than the Boston suburbs. At first she considered living in Italy on the shores of Lake Garda and commuting from there to Stanford for the winter term, but she realized that arrangement would be prohibitively expensive.

At this point Levertov made about forty thousand dollars a year, including her Stanford salary, royalties, and stipends for poetry readings. But as a single person she was in a high tax bracket, and since she continued to send financial support to Nikolai and Mitch and to make generous donations to peace and justice organizations, she felt strapped for money. She was growing tired of travel and being frequently on the road. If she could find some other source of income, she could cut back on readings. She entered a raffle in hopes of winning and worked in earnest on an anthology of writers' childhood memoirs entitled "I Was Me."[90] She also pursued the sale of her archive to Stanford. Although she had loaned about sixty boxes of her less important materials to Harvard, she retrieved them, ostensibly over some disagreement she had with Harvard's policy on faculty housing. These materials were then included in her offer to Stanford. Negotiations for the sale began in 1988 but were not finalized until 1993. Ultimately the archive yielded approximately half a million dollars, which was to be delivered in increments.

The possibility of Stanford's purchase of the archive meant that in 1988 her voluminous papers were packed up and sent to California. This was no small task given that these materials, as well as those of her parents, were in disarray in the attic. Organization was not Levertov's strong suit, as was evidenced in her method of preserving her extensive correspondence. She would separate important and less important materials, toss them in two large laundry baskets under her desk, and then dump the contents in boxes for storage. Once all of these materials were packed up and sent on their way to Stanford, she felt relieved. She was beginning to "clear the decks."

Although relieved and grateful for Stanford's interest in her archive, she must have had some bit of embarrassment over her statement made in an interview only two years earlier during which she said: "I think it's absolutely awful for people to sell their collections of letters from other people — where we've deposited our souls in them. Many people have done it, . . . but I think it's dreadful, really; it destroys all intimacy when you're writing to your friends."[91] Perhaps she changed her mind. In addition to the financial benefit this sale brought, one might imagine Levertov wanted these materials preserved. In these many boxes was the documentation of her life, and although she continued to be suspicious of biography, her archive would allow for one to be written.

Clearing the decks made the possibility of a move more realistic. She longed to be renewed in a beautiful place, although she knew she would miss Joan Hallisey and Yarrow Cleaves, as well as the Emmanuel Church community. The fact that Al Kershaw was soon to retire as Emmanuel's pastor would mitigate the pain of parting from that community. She was heartened when Nikolai supported the move, but she regretted she would be further away from Mitch, Sandy, and Matty.[92]

The last years of the 1980s had been rich and productive. It was a time of reconciliation, of making peace. She gained greater self-understanding and acceptance, honored the positive aspects of her relationships with the dead, and built a bridge between her art and her fragile faith. All the while Levertov continued to be a "poet in the world," one who would "picket and pray." She was ready to begin a new life. By January 1989, she came to a decision. She would move to Seattle and the wild beauty of the Northwest.

10

The Borderland

1989–1992

The borderland — that's where, if one knew how,
one would establish residence.

. . . .

one almost sees
what lies beyond the window, past the frame, beyond.
"THE LIFE OF ART"[1]

Levertov was a peripatetic who changed residence more than twenty times, not including shuttling from Somerville to Stanford for eight years, fifteen years of summering in Maine, and numerous trips to Mexico to tend to her mother. She traveled abroad often, visiting more than sixteen countries,[2] sometimes multiple times, and was frequently on the road with poetry readings and lecturing. She claimed to be on a journey and to have no home.[3] She was adamant that leaving Somerville would not be difficult; after all, her friendships were long distance.

While her commitment to an artistic journey seemed to make place irrelevant, place nonetheless was important to her. As she said, she was attentive to place. And now in her mid-sixties Levertov approached the move to this new place, Seattle, with relish. She had visited the city previously but knew few people there except her former student Emily Warn; Douglas Thorpe, a faculty member at Seattle Pacific University; and her old friend Eve Triem.

There were pragmatic enticements for this move — a lower cost of living, a more temperate climate, and the possibility of a more reclusive life. The city had its lure: a lively poetry and arts scene, a strong justice and peace community — including the presence of the Catholic Archbishop Raymond Hunthausen, whom she admired — an Anglican Cathedral about which she had heard good things, and proximity to the wilderness of the Pacific Northwest,[4] a place where nature dwarfed the human world. It was this landscape of mist and mountains that would shape her and emerge as a central theme in her poetry. Although she conceived of the "borderland" as a metaphorical destination, the Northwest would become a place where the artist, the pilgrim, and the witness could see "what lies beyond the window, past the frame, beyond."

Her decision to move was made in January 1989. She completed the winter term at Stanford, put the Glover Circle house up for sale, and in late May went to Seattle to look at real estate. On the first day of her search she found a two-story brick house at 5535 Seward Park Avenue South. It was in a middle-class neighborhood and a short walk to Seward Park, a dense forestlike park that jutted out into Lake Washington and provided a vista of four tall poplar trees on its far side. She purchased the house and moved in August.

Perched on top of a steep incline, the house's kitchen and workroom offered a view of the majestic volcanic Mount Rainier towering some fourteen thousand feet above the lake. Entrance to the house required a steep climb up a staircase winding past a fig tree and a cascading grapevine. On the first floor were the kitchen/dining room, an area where she could put the large wooden table that once belonged to Race Newton, her New York City neighbor; a living room that provided space for her "black-cat" piano; and two bedrooms, the smaller of which she would claim for herself, the other to be used as a guest room. The house had a fireplace, a deck at the rear surrounded by abundant foliage, and a cellar in which she could stash some of her more than six thousand books. The second floor had two rooms. One could be used as a workroom, the other as a study in which a large closet would ultimately be converted to an oratory. From the exterior the house was indistinguishable from others on the block; however, the later addition of double mailboxes to accommodate her voluminous mail would set it apart. But the charm of the house was its access to Seward Park, a place for her daily walk on established paths and rabbit trails that could bring her deep into the forest where she could gather mushrooms. She came to consider the park her domain, reminding her of the Wanstead and Valentine parks of Ilford.

Levertov had no regrets about her decision to move to Seattle. She rode shotgun cross-country in a car, with all her possessions stuffed in a Ryder's truck driven by one of the Fussiners' sons. It was a time of personal happiness and public acclaim. She received the Jerome Shestack Prize from the *American Poetry Review* and a coveted fellowship from the Rockefeller Foundation, which provided five weeks in Italy.[5] Her family relationships, except for that with Nikolai, had improved. She thought less about her mother, and she and Mitch wished each other well, although he made episodic requests for financial support. Hoping to visit her in Seattle, he requested she pay part of the airfare for him, Sandy, and Matty.[6] Of course, she obliged. But her central preoccupation was with Nikolai. Levertov was mystified by his wife, Nefertiti, and harbored a strong resentment toward her. In an attempt to deal with this resentment, Levertov took up the mantras — "Divine compassion on Nefertiti," "Divine joy for Nefertiti." By year's end she wrote of her sense of relief after a breakthrough in their relationship.[7] But she continued to be perplexed by Nikolai and repeatedly considered how parental failures might have affected him. She worried that she and Mitch did not enforce limits or establish expectations for him and that their permissiveness was exacerbated by the progressive education he received and the values of the 1960s. Nikolai's claims against his parents were somewhat reminiscent of Levertov's complaints against her own parents, namely that they were unable to parent her. As Levertov saw it, the problem was that Nikolai resisted authority and was selfish. Nonetheless, probably because of her sense of guilt and her realization of his need after his illness, she continued to try to be open toward him and to help him financially.[8]

Over the last few years Levertov's political activism diminished, but it never completely ended. She continued to write and lecture about justice issues. The November 1989 massacre of Jesuits in El Salvador prompted her to give another reading of her Oratorio at Santa Clara University, and her lecture "Poetry and Peace" presented at Boston University signaled her ongoing commitment to peace. She said that it was only through "loving kindness" toward one another and the earth that peace would be sustained. The work of poetry, both as protest and as praise, was to foster such beneficence.[9]

The essential role of art in shaping humanity's moral capacity was cogently expressed in her essay "Paradox and Equilibrium." "We humans cannot absorb the bitter truths of our own history," she wrote, "the revelation of our destructive potential, *except* through the mediation of art. . . . Presented raw, the facts are rejected: perhaps not by the intellect, which accommodates them as statistics, but by the emotions — which hold the key to conscience and resolve. We numb ourselves, evading the vile taste, the stench. But whether neutralized into statistics or encountered head-on without an artist — guide . . ., the facts poison us unless we can find a way both to acknowledge their reality with our whole selves and, accepting it, muster the will to transcend it."[10]

For Levertov, art, working at the level of emotion, gave access to the will and assisted in the development of conscience, potentially opening one to faith. In her next volume of poems, *A Door in the Hive*, she provides evidences of this. Although these poems continue to reflect her Hebraic understanding of reality,[11] their character is more specifically Christian than anything she had written previously. The book's title is laden with meaning and gives a glint of its content. A hive, a place of fullness, is entered through a small door.[12] *Door* is reminiscent of Levertov's Hebrew name, "Daleth," as well as the stance of the poet, the one who lives with the "door of his life open" to the numinous.

All the poems of *A Door in the Hive* were written prior to her arrival in Seattle; some were composed in Somerville, some during her trip to Australia. Much like *Breathing the Water*, this volume opens and closes with poems inspired by Rilke. It includes "Two Threnodies and a Psalm" and "Kin and Kin," which speak of the brokenness of the human condition, and others such as "Two Mountains" and "In Tonga," which describe the chasm between the human and natural worlds. As faint hope for human restoration, Levertov offers "The Mystery of the Incarnation," "Nativity: An Altarpiece," "Calvary Path," and "On the Parable of the Mustard Seed."

Two poems have clear autobiographical resonances. "Flickering Mind" begins in dialogue with God. "Lord, not you, / it is I who am absent." She speaks of her secret joy of stealing alone to sacred places but then laments that her mind, unable to hold still, is like "a darting minnow." It is she who is absent and eludes God's presence. She asks: "How can I focus my flickering, perceive / at the fountain's heart / the sapphire I know is there?"[13] In the poem "St. Thomas Didymus" she recognizes herself as twin of the man who begs Jesus to heal his son. Like him, she cries   I believe, help my unbelief. Like him, she asks why the innocent suffer, this question throbbing in her like "a stealthy cancer." She is twin as well to Thomas the Doubter, and like him, she needs to put her hand in Jesus's wound. The revelation given her at that moment is not of shame or pain but of light, streaming into her, unraveling the knot that had bound her for so long.

> I witnessed
> ....
> my question
> 	not answered but given
> 		its part
> 	in a vast unfolding design lit
> 		by a risen sun.[14]

Two of the most compelling poems of *A Door in the Hive* were first written for services at her beloved Emmanuel Church in Boston. Stimulated by reading Murray Bodo's book on Jesus, she wrote "Annunciation." It is a poem about vocation grounded not in obedience but in courage. In it Levertov challenges the stereotypic view of Mary, rendering her as one free to accept or refuse God's announcement that she would conceive a son. "Called to a destiny more momentous / than any in all of Time, / she did not quail." Mary, the "bravest of all humans" does not plead unworthiness or lack of strength, rather "consent, / courage unparalleled, / opened her utterly."[15] In another poem, "Ikon: The Harrowing of Hell," also written for use at Emmanuel Church, Levertov captures the mystery of Christ's descent into hell to rescue the innocent and just. He enters hell, his "Spirit / streaming through every cell of flesh," his flesh "lit from within, now, / and aching for home." He suffers in order to lead these souls to the Paradise road.[16]

The book concludes with a final "Variation on a Theme by Rilke," a poem of awe and humility addressed to one she calls "You." In this Levertov describes humans as "dustmotes in the cosmos," who from the "rubble of being" construct our "hope of You." She acknowledges that humans cannot conceive the span of "You"; their metaphors shatter, and yet humans hunger

> to offer up
> our specks of life as fragile tesserae
> towards the vast mosaic —...
>
> to be, ourselves, imbedded in its fabric,
> as if, once, it was from that we were broken off.[17]

The poems of *A Door in the Hive* express not piety but the poet's unique experience of the mysteries of faith and of doubt. Images of light, of unraveling knots, of a vast unfolding design, of fragile tesserae become the means by which Levertov both enters and expresses faith. It is imagination, not rational argument, that is her way through.

Soon after her arrival in Seattle Levertov was off to Italy and the beautiful Rockefeller-owned Villa Serbelloni in Bellagio on Lake Como.[18] Her return to the United States was by a circuitous route through Venice, where she steeped herself in the city's art treasures, recording lengthy descriptions of her favorite paintings in her diary. As always, the visual arts were a source of inspiration and nourishment for her.

Compared to her time in Italy, winter term at Stanford was uneventful, at least until March when she participated in the tenth-anniversary commemoration of the death of Oscar Romero held at a nuclear test site in the Las Vegas desert. As part of the weekend event, she and Murray Bodo gave a public reading of "El Salvador: Requiem and Invocation." Bodo also gave a speech in which he explored St. Francis's understanding of the violence inherent in each person and the need both to acknowledge and embrace that potential and allow it to be redeemed by God.[19] It is not known how this affected Levertov, but she was at a stage in her development where she could hear this Franciscan admonition. On return to Seattle, she was back on the poetry circuit giving the Theodore Roethke Memorial Poetry Reading at the University of Washington.

Although she previously had written poem-prayers, Levertov had never spoken autobiographically about the topic of prayer. At this point she felt confident enough to do this. In a little pamphlet, "Why I Pray," she recalls a childhood in which she was introduced to the Anglican prayers of petition and gratitude and subsequently read Buber's *Tales of Hasidim*. But it was the writings of Brother Lawrence and Anthony Bloom that showed her parallels between poetry and prayer. She commented that both required discipline and paying attention and introduced one to the unknown.[20] She speculated that writing poetry might be her own way of praying. Her exploration of this connection between poetry and prayer was continued in "Work That Enfaiths," a lecture given at the Mercy Center in Burlingame, California. In it she described her own gradual coming to faith through the writing of poetry. "Mass for the Day of St. Thomas Didymus," "El Salvador: Requiem and Invocation," "Stand Off," and "The Task" each provided an opportunity to wrestle with doubt and to experience hope. She concluded that for her, poetry was work that "enfaithed."[21]

These considerations of poetry and prayer and the explicitly religious poems of *A Door in the Hive* make it clear that Levertov had arrived in "a new country." Her early lyric, sensual poetry, her political poems, her nature poetry—had made this possible. None of her creative efforts had been lost or wasted. Having come now to an "unorthodox" and "flickering" faith, she resolved to speak from that faith, believing it had positive implications for a secular society. "[A] poet speaking from within the Christian tradition," she wrote, "may have more resonance for our intellectual life than is supposed. The Incarnation, the Passion, the Resurrection—these words have some emotive power even for the most secular minds. Perhaps a contemporary poetry that incorporates old terms and old stories can help readers to reappropriate significant parts of their own linguistic, emotional, cultural heritage, whether or not they share doctrinal adherences."[22]

Levertov continued to read widely in religious literature and was particularly impressed by *Morning Light*, the spiritual journal of the French priest/poet Jean Sulivan. It was Gerry Pocock who had given her a copy of the book with a note from its translator, Joe Cunneen of *Cross Currents*. In *Morning Light* Sulivan suggests that it is not doctrine but the individual's experience of God that is of primary importance. The Christian must find one's own center, experience God oneself, and bring one's faith into being. The result would be that one would belong to the creator and be in communion with all things.[23] For a person who throughout her life sought communion with nature and solidarity with others, this insight must have been experienced as a wonderful revelation.

When she first arrived in Seattle, Levertov thought she would continue her practice of attending various churches, but she also toyed with the notion of becoming a Catholic. She wrote to Murray Bodo to ask his advice:

> I have long thought, off & on, about becoming a Catholic, but as long as I had the quite unique (Episcopal but so different from the more usual ones) Emmanuel church in Boston, with its top-notch music (full-scale Bach cantatas, Boston's best soloists) & its wonderful rector, Al Kershaw (now retired) I didn't need to. The mixture of spirituality, liturgical tradition & dignity, sermons with intellectual & moral content & range & a commitment to peace & justice, which I long for in a church isn't easy to find; but it's easier in Catholic churches than others. Yet the character of the Vatican, the — let's say *variable* politics of the present Pope, and the question of Choice v. "right to life" (I don't think abortion shd be undertaken lightly, but in fact it seldom is . . . and I *do* believe it is sometimes necessary, for several reasons not only extreme medical ones) are stumbling blocks to me, because though I know there are many people who are already Catholics who feel the same way about these issues (& various others, e.g., the possibility of married priests, the role of women, etc. etc.) I feel afraid that the process of *joining* might entail perjuring if one has to accept all of those kinds of things. *Is* one in fact catechized about these topics? I would not want to perjure myself — but by the same token, I feel sometimes (in churches where no one knows me & that I'm not a Catholic, & so takes it for granted that I am) that I am flying under fake colors. What do you think?[24]

Levertov did not share her desire to become a Catholic with many others; it was a private affair.[25] Initially, she attended St. Teresa's Catholic Church, a racially integrated parish. The problem was that the church was five miles from her home. St. Edward's, on the other hand, was less than a mile away, which meant she could walk there. She began to regularly attend services at St. Edward's and got to know its pastor, Gerry Stanley, and Jean Hunter, a nun in whom she confided and with whom she felt great rapport. Hunter consoled Levertov when she said that she did not believe her sharp stabs of guilt were from God. For her part Levertov disclosed to Hunter that without belief her inner life would be desolate.[26]

Irrespective of the support of a church community and new friends, Levertov continued to be unsure about formally declaring herself a Catholic. She asked herself why she would join given her dislike of the church's hierarchy — especially Joseph Ratzinger and John O'Connor[27] — and her dissent from the church's positions on non-procreative sex, abortion, liberation theology, mandatory priestly celibacy, the role of women in the church, and the hypocrisy of many priests' lives. She recorded her reasoning: the largest number of inspiring people she knew were Catholic; the church's liturgical, mystical, and sacramental traditions were more appealing than those she found in other denominations; and she believed the church had great power for good in the world.[28]

In an interview Levertov stressed that becoming a Catholic would not change her politics and that it was the powerful witness to peace and justice by Catholics that attracted her. When asked whether she was a "traditional" or "unorthodox" believer, she answered that she was more orthodox than she once was but that she had had to contend with doubt all of her life and she might never arrive at certitude. She contrasted belief and faith; the former was loving God, the latter believing God loved you. Clinging to the example of St. Thomas Didymus, she prayed that she be cured of her unbelief. Knowing that many Catholics shared her unorthodox views, Levertov felt less dishonest joining the Catholic church and criticizing from within than remaining outside and continuing to participate.[29]

The six-week course to prepare for reception into the church raised concerns, which Levertov shared with her pastor, Gerry Stanley. She said she had difficulty accepting forgiveness for her sins of long ago and was unable to remember any recent wrongdoing, although she was well aware of weaknesses in her character. In sum, she was perplexed as to why she needed to seek absolution.[30] If Levertov had guilt about anything it was for abandoning her mother and her rages against her son in childhood. Other than that, she did not feel personal guilt.

By fall 1990, her decision was made. She would now, at age sixty-seven, join the Catholic Church at St. Edward's on November 18th under the sponsorship of Jean Hunter. Eileen Egan, Gerry Pocock, and Luke Tobin were present at the service, but Murray Bodo, who was in the middle of his doctoral exams, sent regrets. The ceremony was not a dramatic event for her, probably because she had come to Christianity and then Catholicism very gradually and over a long period of time, but she was touched when the entire congregation stretched out their arms to bless her. She said she entered the Catholic church as an act of solidarity. "I believe myself to have thrown in my lot with the tradition of the CW [Catholic Worker] & Tom Merton & Archb Hunthausen et al — & Luke [Tobin]. Perhaps, too without NCR [*National Catholic Reporter*] I would never have done it!" She was now part of an "unbroken chain" of the communion of saints, which she believed included non-Catholics and non-Christians alike.[31]

Although there were many people who influenced Levertov's move toward Catholicism, she specifically credits one person, her old friend Virginia Barrett, with having influenced her through her own faith journey. Barrett and Levertov first met in Guadalajara, after which Barrett's life unraveled. She divorced, married, divorced again, gave up a set of twins for adoption, and lived life on the edge, sometimes sleeping on beaches, hippylike. She acknowledged that her flaws were "money and men"; having a lack of the former and a surplus of the latter. Barrett wrote that Levertov served as her "solid rock," one who lent her money, sent her books, took her in, and grounded her in her nomadic existence. She was one of the many strays Levertov helped through life. Barrett became serious about Catholicism in the early 1980s, attending theology classes at the Graduate Theological Union at Berkeley, meditating, attending mass, and working for Catholic institutions. She claimed the church was her "anchor," although she was frequently disappointed in it. Barrett's search for meaning, admittedly in the midst of a very nontraditional life, inspired Levertov.[32]

Levertov was not a triumphalistic Catholic and did not claim to finally have the truth or to belong to the one true church. In fact she said that if she had lived in England she might be an Anglican of the "left-wing," "high church" sort.[33] Her decision to enter the church was not intellectual, although she was unable to make the move until her intellectual concerns were neutralized. That happened when she allowed her poetic images to take precedence over intellectual doubt about belief. On issues of social justice and aesthetic sensibility, becoming a Catholic was congruent with her past. Where she differed on issues of belief and teaching, she claimed "unorthodoxy." One factor that might have prompted her to move forward with this decision was that she was in a place where her friendships were new. Among old friends she was more circumspect. When friends did find out she had become a Catholic, most were surprised. Others thought it pre-posterous. Hayden Carruth, Robert Creeley, Sam Hamill, and Stephen Peet could make no sense of her decision.[34]

Levertov's first year in Seattle was a great beginning. She felt both wel-comed and acclaimed. In 1990 honors and awards kept coming: the Rob-ert Frost Medal for distinguished lifetime service, the Académie Mallarmé award for publication of Guillevic's *Selected Poems*, and an honorary degree from the Massachusetts College of Art.

She made new friends — younger poets and artists, both women and men — and continued to hope for some romantic engagement. Soon after her arrival she met Mark Jenkins, an actor and teacher, with whom she shared many interests. Jenkins was good-looking, intelligent, and some twenty years her junior. Levertov was delighted and flattered to be with him, al-though she was aware that anything but a platonic relationship with him would create jealousy in her as well as unhappiness, anxiety, shame, and pain. After all, she argued with herself, her libido had declined. She took consola-tion in her conviction that a nonromantic friendship like everything else, could be erotic if it were deep and heartfelt, and involved an active imagina-tion.[35] But the fact was that she wished it were otherwise. Jenkins became a friend, what she called a "great treasure."[36] She wrote two poems — "Ancient Airs and Dances" and "Time for Rivets" — in which she describes her longing for him and the clamoring again of her "shameless heart," when she thought she had learned from "stillness."[37]

Another prospect was Edward Zlotkowski, a close friend who she be-lieved understood her work better than anyone, but who was only very in-termittently in her life. Furthermore he was married, and when they trav-eled together in Austria, their relationship was strictly one of friendship.[38] Of course, Stephen Peet remained in her life. In fact he was scheduled to visit her at Stanford in February 1991, shortly after her formal entrance into the church. Pondering Peet's impending arrival, Levertov recorded that she was not morally concerned about their sexual relationship given that they were past childbearing and that their trysts hurt no one, not even Peet's wife, who knew about them. Furthermore, she did not want to offend Stephen by rejecting him.[39]

Reflecting on her vitality and its implications for both supporting friend-ship and imperiling her romantic life, Levertov wrote: "[M]y unsuccessful romantic life has been affected by on the one hand, the fear men have had of that very vitality — and threat to them — & on the other, has been many times an initial attraction which my own shyness & lack of intuitive erotic sensuality of behavior, along with my naively romantic *emotional* response must have seemed a *false lead* to certain men — the vitality seeming to promise an erotic sensuality which was not forthcoming. (Stephen as always the great exception, the one who with his own uncomplicated sensuality released me, time after time, from the prison of my own shyness & excess of emotion & sentiment.)"[40]

Certainly her personal life was happier. This may be explained in part by her declining libido and her hard-won self-understanding. Her "greenness" had diminished, and she now had a sense of solidarity with fellow believers, both living and dead. This personal happiness did not mean, however, that she was not jarred and depressed by world events.

In January 1991, when the U.S. military attacked Iraq, ostensibly in retaliation for its invasion of Kuwait, she was appalled and horrified. As protests against the Gulf War broke out across the country, she organized Poets for Peace and planned read-ins and demonstrations against the war in Palo Alto, Seattle, New York, and Sacramento.[41] At the University she founded a chapter of the Catholic peace organization, Pax Christi, and recruited the young Jesuit John Dear to launch the chapter and speak to her class.[42] Her English Department colleagues Albert and Barbara Gelpi joined her in this effort and other protest activities. She went on to found another Pax Christi chapter at St. Edward's. This was no mean feat given that parishioners at the church were from a low-income neighborhood where many had links to the military and had little discretionary time for such social activism. But for Levertov peacemaking was a requirement of Christian faith, not an optional commitment.[43]

Her poetry again reflected her concern over war. In one poem entitled "Misnomer" she rejects the notion of the "art" of warfare. It is no art; war "dries up the soul and draws its power / from a dark and burning wasteland."[44] In another poem she describes her "shock" and "shame," at witnessing "the world's raw gash / reopened, the whole world / a valley of streaming blood."[45] In another, reminiscent of her poems about the Vietnam War, she uses the language of military reporting to describe the live burial of Iraqi soldiers. "'Bodycount / impossible.'" "'*What you saw was a / bunch of trenches / with people's / arms and things / sticking out.*'" As in "A Poem at Christmas, 1972," names are named, in this case not Nixon and Kissinger but Cheney and Schwartzkopf.[46]

Horrified and unprepared to take on war again, Levertov gave her energy in subsequent years to opposing the development of nuclear weapons. In March 1991, she returned again to the Las Vegas nuclear test site to participate with several thousand protesters, including the Jesuits Daniel Berrigan and John Dear, and the eighty-two-year-old Helder Camara. This frail, saintly advocate of nonviolence and defender of the poor preached to the gathered crowd. Weeping, he begged God to bring peace to the world and with other protesters, including Levertov, entered the nuclear test site to be arrested, booked, and then released. Levertov memorialized this experience in two poems. In one she remembers Camara, a "wisp" of a man, a "faithful pilgrim" dancing in the desert.[47] In another she directs herself to the desert itself and its destruction by nuclear testing:

> What repelled me here was no common aridity
> unappealing to lovers of lakes and trees,
> but anguish, lineaments drab with anguish. This terrain
> turned to the human world a gaze
> of scorn, victim to tormentor.[48]

But her revulsion at the landscape's ugliness "unstiffened," and she learned to almost love the hostile earth, to bend and kiss its "leper face."

Levertov counted as blessings of the year hearing and receiving the benediction of Camera and having time with Luke Tobin.[49] Although she did not specifically name living in Seattle as a blessing, she professed as much in her lecture "Some Affinities of Content," given in April at Poets House in New York as the Paul Zweig Memorial Lecture. In this she acknowledged that her poetic interests had now turned in a new direction: to the poetry of the Pacific Northwest and the poetry of religious faith, which had "affinities of content." In this lecture she recounts that as a young poet she was preoccupied with technical development and unconcerned with a spiritual quest. However in 1967, when she participated in the symposium on Myth in Religion and Poetry, she realized that such a quest was evident in her work. At this point in her life, however, she was in search of meaning beneath temporal events: a poetry that attests to deep "spiritual longing." She was drawn to the work of poets of the Pacific Northwest — Sam Hamill, Sam Green, Emily Warn, among others. Their poetry was expansive and spoke to the inner life as did that of R. S. Thomas, Czeslaw Milosz, Lucille Clifton, and Kathleen Norris. She lauded the work of the Pole Adam Zagajewski, who believed that humanity's affliction was that persons no longer were present to themselves and therefore could not be present to the divine.[50]

The Zweig lecture set out Levertov's final direction and acknowledged her need to read and to write poems of "wild nature" and of "doubt and faith." She called such poems "testimonies of lived life," poems that "writers have a vocation to give, and readers . . . have a need to receive."[51] The Pacific Northwest provided a vibrant place for Levertov to live, but it also opened a way for her to "witness" to a presence "not behind, but within" the temporal.

Levertov published no major work in 1991. She taught at Stanford and at the University of Washington and learned that she had been granted a National Endowment for the Arts Senior Fellowship worth forty thousand dollars. But the most heartening news came at the end of the summer when Stanford finalized its offer to purchase her archive. She was relieved. She would receive a considerable sum that could be invested, ensuring that she would have money to live on once she stopped teaching. She would use a small amount of this windfall to supplement her Fellowship and travel to Europe. In late December 1991, she left for Prague, Berlin, Rome, and Florence to be "enthralled" by the art treasures she encountered in the museums of those cities.

On her return in March 1992, Levertov lectured at a meeting of the Conference on Christianity and Literature at Seattle University and the Spring Literary Festival at Ohio University. In June she left again, this time for Ireland with Paul Lacey and his wife. She included a side trip to England where she visited her nephew Richard Strudwick in Leeds. By July she was back in Seattle only to leave again for Banff, Canada.

One of the joys of the summer was Paul Lacey's gift of a sock-monkey to replace the lost glove-leather doll she called "Monkey." She was thrilled. When she traveled, this new monkey-doll went with her in her suitcase; when she was at home, he sat propped in the window dressed in clothes made from the academic hoods she received with her honorary degrees. When friends made outfits for Monkey, Levertov was delighted. The incongruity of this grown woman's affection for this animated pet is difficult to explain. In part it may have resulted from her own childlike sense of wonder; in part from her sense of fun and camaraderie. But Monkey was also, as his name "pardoner" indicated, the one who never judged and was "inexhaustibly wise and consoling," always forgiving.[52] He was an embodiment of unconditional love. Until the end of her life, Monkey would serve as Denise's companion.

While she was away in Europe, Nikolai's life became more problematic. Toward the end of 1991 he and Nefertiti parted ways. Their divergent lifestyles and different goals and ambitions seemed to have contributed to their separation. Although Denise worried about her son, she refused to despair. This was a new response. Because Nikolai needed a place to live, he moved in with his father, Sandy, and Matty in Maine, staying for more than a year. In correspondence with Denise, Sandy acknowledged that while there could be spontaneous affection between Mitch and Nikolai, they also fought, each being disappointed in the other. Nonetheless, Sandy, who at this point had been diagnosed with early stage muscular sclerosis, assured Denise that she would be good to her son, as Denise had been to her Matty.[53] Unable to stay in Maine indefinitely, Nikolai left and came to Seattle to visit his mother for about a month. He crossed the country, stopping at his uncle Howard Goodman's home in St. Louis, and arrived in Seattle in August. Apprehensive about the visit, Levertov asked Murray Bodo to pray for them. She felt Nikolai, who was now forty-three, needed to be able to live independently, and she was worried that she could not work effectively if he were living with her. To her relief the visit went better than expected, although she believed there was always an undercurrent of anxiety and potential for misunderstanding when he was around. Nikolai left in early September.[54]

Unable to write poetry during his visit, Levertov worked on a long commentary on the Gospel of John, which had been suggested to her by Jack Costello, the Jesuit she met at the Kirkridge Retreat Center. Because she was feeling bereft of spiritual nourishment at St. Edward's, she was happy to have this opportunity to wrestle with this most mystical of the Gospel narratives. Her commentary was too long for publication, but it provided what she called a "self-guided tour" through the Fourth Gospel, one that was "enthralling" and "fascinating" and "disturbing." This foray into scripture convinced her that her faith was both shallow and weak and that there was an immense gap between what she understood intellectually and aesthetically and what she actually "felt."

Levertov's questioning of her belief was exacerbated by an experience of church priorities. A fund-raising sermon for renovations of the historic Catholic Cathedral of St. James irritated and depressed her. It was not that she was opposed to the renovation itself, but the expenditure of six million dollars was to her mind unjustified given the needs of Seattle's poor. In response, she decided to "shop around" for a new parish church and to find a spiritual director.[55] This latter decision, which she earlier had rejected, was apparently influenced by Murray Bodo, who clarified the notion of "spiritual director" as one who helped discern one's "inscape" and foster one's growth and development.[56] At Stillpoint, the local retreat center, she found such a spiritual director in the person of Jane Comerford, a sister of St. Joseph, who was trained in Jesuit spirituality. Although Comerford was relatively young, Levertov considered her "intellectually sharp" and conversant with literature. Energized by their first meeting, she continued to meet with Comerford for several months.[57]

In an effort to deepen her interior life, Levertov sought more solitude and silence, collected spiritual sayings, and recorded the blessings of each day. She was nourished by her study of religious artists like Giotto di Bondone and poets like George Herbert and Gerard Manley Hopkins and was inspired to an even greater degree by the architecture of great cathedrals. She was especially grateful for her friendship with Luke Tobin and the opportunity to offer a poetry workshop with her at a women's spirituality center in Santa Fe. That experience gave her a sense of how she might transmit the power of faith to others.[58] While longtime friends recognized continuity in Levertov's personality, the reality was that she also had changed. Always poet, always pilgrim, she was now present not only to the world but to herself. She was more forgiving and self-forgiving.

Given her extensive travel in 1992, her professional achievements of the year were remarkable. She published *New and Selected Essays* and *Evening Train*, and continued to work on an anthology of childhood memoirs of prominent writers. When New Directions decided against the publication of *I Was Me*, she was apparently disappointed.[59]

New and Selected Essays, her third prose volume, contained twelve reprints from *The Poet in the World* and *Light Up the Cave* and thirteen new essays.[60] One of these essays, "Biography and the Poet," is illustrative of her abhorrence of both sensationalized life-writing and confessional poetry. Stated positively, the essay is a defense of privacy in various forms of artistic expression. Since Levertov was now back in contact with Adrienne Rich, she sent the essay on to her for critique.[61] Rich responded appreciatively, expressing her gratitude that they were again in conversation about artistic matters. She applauded Levertov's efforts in "Biography and the Poet" for opening up the huge topic of the boundary between public and private life but said she did not think Levertov had fully explored the subject.[62]

Levertov liked autobiographical writing, and was not opposed to biography per se. What she loathed was emphasis on private matters and irrelevant trivia.[63] In her essay she hails Walter Jackson Bate's *John Keats* as exemplary but rants against "dubious, scandalous, sensational" biography. She argues that Bate, like all good biographers, instructs and delights by focusing on the poet's work rather than psychologizing it and emphasizing the intimate details of private life — one's medical history, sexual experience, and states of mind. To her lights, privacy was under siege both because of the availability of personal journals and diaries and the complicity of biographers and confessional poets . She urges one to consider the wisdom of the historian Iris Origio who promotes "enthusiasm" and "veracity" as the virtues of biographers and the temptations "to suppress, to invent, or to sit in judgment" as their vices.[64]

Ironically, her essay on biography was written at the same time she was in final negotiation for the sale of her own archives, voluminous boxes filled with correspondence, notebooks, and diaries in which she recorded her dreams, suspicions, sexual experiences, depressions, and rages and which she had reviewed and was aware would be open to the public.[65] Whether "Biography and the Poet" was a preemptive strike against her own future biographers is unknown, although concern for how she would be remembered in the future could not have been far from her mind. What seems the more proximate stimulus for "Biography and the Poet," although Levertov does not mention it, is her reaction to the 1991 publication of her Stanford colleague Diane Middlebrook's *Anne Sexton: A Biography*, which used Sexton's psychiatric records as source material. The fact that in *New and Selected Essays* "Biography and the Poet" is followed immediately by Levertov's 1974 essay on Sexton's suicide gives some credence to this suspicion.[66]

Levertov claimed she was not anchored in a place, that she was an "air-plant" and rootless, belonging nowhere and everywhere.[67] Yet the move to Seattle reconfirmed her love of place, especially that place. In the poem "Settling" she writes of a place where she was welcomed, where she could "dig in," and live, not merely visit. The fact that she was "London-born" meant that her world was grey and chill. She admits: "Grey is the price / of neighboring with eagles, of knowing / a mountain's vast presence, seen or unseen."[68] There in Seattle on a borderland of "wild nature" and exquisite beauty, Levertov found new communities to sustain her: artists and poets, friends in faith, and social justice allies. Here in sight of the veiled Mount Rainier, "Tahoma" to aboriginal people, she could witness to presences, "elusive," "silent," and "obdurate." Here she could fulfill her need for poetry that is "'on pilgrimage,'" poetry "in search of significance underneath and beyond the succession of temporal events."[69]

Although she continued to have substantial religious doubt, Levertov found that the "knot" that had bound her for so long had unraveled. She had worked through the issues of a double image, of joy and sorrow, of human freedom, and of the mercy of God. These paradoxes were not solved, but were wrapped in "a vast unfolding design lit / by a rising sun." She was aware that something new was being born in her. It was there on the edge of the continent that her intuition, expressed in her earlier poem "Intimation," seemed to be realized. "I've begun to see," she wrote,

> there is something else I must do,
> . . . .
> I know a different need has begun
> to cast its lines out from me into
> a place unknown, I reach
> for a silence almost present,
> elusive among my heartbeats.[70]

Having established residence on the "borderland," Levertov now had an intimation that some new work, some new way of being, was before her.

11

Bearing Witness
1993-1996

I have now, as the task before me, to *be*,
to arrive at being.

"DREAM INSTRUCTION"[1]

Levertov's "intimation" that there might be something else awaiting her was soon affirmed. In early May 1993, after her decision to retire from Stanford, she learned that a biopsy of an ulcer revealed she might have non-Hodgkins lymphoma.[2] Paradoxically this news was energizing and prompted her to resolve to use her time well. She felt grateful she had been given the chance to experience beauty and to enrich the lives of many wonderful friends. Life had not cheated her, and she had no regrets. She was particularly thankful that she had enough financial resources to pass on to Nikolai. Consoled, she nonetheless kept her diagnosis private.[3] A month later she wrote to Steve Blevins telling him the news, and in October she informed Mitch.[4] But few others knew of her malady.

The decision to leave Stanford after twelve years had not been difficult, even though she loved being there. As soon as the 1993 winter term began, she was clear: she wanted to give more time to writing.[5] After all, she would be seventy within the year. Her final three months at Stanford were happy ones. When Hayden Carruth came to speak at the university, she was able to reconnect with Adrienne Rich who, as a longtime friend of Carruth, attended his lecture and an intimate dinner at the Gelpi's. These two former friends continued a congenial, if episodic, correspondence. Levertov also had an opportunity to visit the Camaldolese Benedictine monastery at Big Sur for a week. The rhythm of the place with its daily mass, vespers, and conversations was "blissful," "peaceful," and "refreshing," and she cherished the new friendship she made there with Brother David Steindl-Rast.[6] She wrote Czeslaw Milosz encouraging him to visit this extraordinary place.[7]

Retired, and with looming health problems, Levertov was unwilling to put energy into anything other than writing, poetry readings, and deepening her spiritual life. She did not want to return to protest activity, both because of her disappointment in others and fear of what she called her own "knee-jerk" reaction to political issues.[8] But friendship was life-giving, and consequently she continued to entertain friends from near and far. Hating to use the telephone, she would drop notes in neighbors' mailboxes inviting them over to her home, a form of communication reminiscent of her childhood when she left notes for Jean Rankin in "the rabbit hole" in the local park. Afternoon tea was her specialty. She had an exact method for making it and numerous teapots from which to serve. Neighbors, friends, colleagues, students, fellow poets, and artists all came to her home where they were greeted with exuberance, shared in her bursts of full-bodied laugher, and were sent off with her signature Buddhist bow. Her gift in friendship was to share her endless curiosity and delight in the world. A rapid intake of her breath and a clasp of her hands were her signature responses. Old friends came from England, Europe, the East Coast, and California to stay with her. She made each feel special and at home and then after an intensely "Denny" conversation, would gift her guest with a reading of exactly the right poem for the occasion.[9] Levertov treasured her friends; she needed them, too, both psychologically and practically. She was alone, particularly disorganized, and inept at ordinary life tasks — unable to change a typewriter ribbon or a lightbulb, drive a car, or use a telephone answering machine.

After her teaching ended, Levertov continued to earn revenue from book royalties and advances, this latter only amounting to about two or three thousand dollars per book. Since she could make more by the sale of individual books, she was reluctant to have New Directions bring out her collected works.[10] But poetry readings and artistic residences generated honoraria and helped sell books. Directly after finishing at Stanford, Levertov gave readings in Oregon, in Toronto at the Harbourfront Poetry Festival, and in New York City at the DIA Center where Lucille Clifton introduced her. She claimed that this latter event was a high point of her life and that she did not even mind having her picture taken,[11] something she generally abhorred. She also appeared at Georgetown University, and in November did a two-week residence at Cornell as the Andrew White Professor-at-Large, a post she would hold for several years.[12] While at Cornell she gave readings and participated on panels and interacted with students. She spoke about the responsibility of writers to enlighten readers, but acknowledged that poems cannot convert but only help readers and hearers to see. She insisted that in her case her political poems were not separate from her religious ones.

Although she generally did not speak about religion, in this case she said that "[a]ll religions share that sense of the utter mysteriousness of there being anything at all. Every culture or period has its own way of talking about the divinely poetic aspect of creation and being."[13] After this stint at Cornell she was off for quick trip to London where she read at the Purcell Room on the South Bank of the Thames.

Another high point of the year was being named recipient of the 1993 Lannan Literary Award for Poetry, which brought with it a prize of fifty thousand dollars. The award was given for *Evening Train*, Levertov's eighteenth volume of poetry, which was described as "musical, meditative, humane and transcendent, addressing the nature of faith, the imperiled beauty of the natural world, Eros and politics."[14] Although she was the recipient of many awards, honors, and appointments, Levertov was discriminating about those she would accept. When requests came from old friends, such as Sam Hamill who asked her to join the board of the newly created Copper Canyon Press, she could not say no.[15] But she was leery of using her reputation to advance anything she suspected might be sectarian. She did not hide the fact that she was a religious person — she wore a small cross on a necklace at the Lannan award ceremony, but she declined other awards or engagements if she considered them too parochial. A case in point was her unwillingness to accept the University of Tulsa's Warren Distinguished Catholic Service Award. She demurred by saying she was a "new" Catholic, one who did not want to be "triumphalistic."[16]

If knowledge of a potentially serious health problem had a consequence for Levertov, it was to increase her desire to deepen her spiritual life. She found a resource for this in her new parish church, the Jesuit-run St. Joseph's with its well-heeled congregation. There she encountered splendid music, good liturgy, intelligent sermons, and a congregation committed to social justice. She was attracted by the Jesuits' efforts to reconcile contemplation with social action and was inspired by the church's two amiable pastors, Lee Kapfer and Craig Boly. Although she joined no church organizations, she was invited to give the homily on Mother's Day in May 1995. Realizing her first draft was "sanctimonious," she scrapped it. In the final version she linked the biblical text from the Acts of the Apostles with three of her poems — "Flickering Mind," "Mass for the Day of St. Thomas Didymus," and "The Servant-Girl at Emmaus." Her remarks were wide-ranging and focused on sources for strengthening one's faith. She confessed that attending mass with others made her more receptive and that even though she did not know many in the parish, she had a far-flung community of "seeking and believing friends" who strengthened her. Although she had a "flickering mind" and the doubts of a Thomas, she was sure that a "steady and unwaving conviction" like that of her mother was more valuable than belief. Faith was different from belief, and conversion was not a static event but an ongoing process. She spoke with gratitude of her mother's faith, emblazoned in her memory by the lines from Handel's *Messiah*, "I know that my Redeemer liveth."[17]

After several months of spiritual direction with Jane Comerford, Lee Kapfer agreed to direct her in the Spiritual Exercises of St. Ignatius of Loyola. She liked Kapfer, whom she described as "dignified," "authentic," and "humble," someone who quenched what she called her clever "show-off impulse."[18] She did not speak of her illness either to Comerford or Kapfer.

The Spiritual Exercises are a monthlong activity, but because of interruptions Levertov continued on with them through the early part of 1994. Her voluminous notes from this intense experience illustrate her religious struggles as well as her increased self-understanding. As a poet, she particularly resonated with how imagination was used in the Exercises to conjure Gospel events and the emphasis they placed on observing physical detail.[19] In a later interview she said: "I was really amazed at how close the exercises of St. Ignatius of Loyola were to a poet or novelist imagining a scene. You focus your attention on some particular aspect of the life of Christ. You try to compose that scene in your imagination, place yourself there. If it's the Via Dolorosa, you have to ask yourself, are you one of the disciples? Are you a passerby? Are you a spectator that likes to watch from the side, the way people used to watch hangings? You establish who you are and where you stand and then you look at what you see."[20]

The Spiritual Exercises are specifically constructed to help the participant enter more deeply into the life of Jesus and to realize one's own failings through a program of contemplative practices, including meditation on scripture, examination of conscience, and imaginative exercises. Through this program Levertov was able to identify areas of personal fault. She wrote of her proclivity to selfishness, cowardice, impatience, complacency, sloth, and harsh judgment of others and admitted a sense of pride and feeling of intellectual superiority. She reviewed her failings in regard to Nikolai and prayed for Mitch, hoping he might not be bitter and disappointed in old age, and she acknowledged that she was at fault in not visiting Olga or her father as they were dying. For the first time she named and lamented what she called her "secret" homophobia, acknowledging at the same time that she had many homosexual friends. Although this statement goes unexplored, it appears to be her first admission of this attitude.

Because the Exercises encouraged reflection on one's own death, Levertov was prompted to write that at the end of her life she hoped to have a "steady" and "intense" faith in God, to have written some good poems, to be on good terms with all her friends, to meet her parents and sister in their spiritual essence, and to have all forgiven.[21] This growth in self-understanding was remarkable for a woman who earlier in her life found it extremely difficult to acknowledge her failings.

While the Exercises opened her up to her own brokenness, it was her experience of the love of God that was the basis of faith. In the end, that trumped everything.

> I cannot believe in God's love by looking outside my own experience. That the world — anything — exists at all is matter for wonder but does not prove the *love* of the Creator. Nature is both beautiful & cruel, . . . & so no proof of love. The suffering of others, the endless wars & tortures, . . . (might make us) feel it wd be better not to exist . . . BUT — if I looked at my *own life* I immediately feel the love of God, who has brought me safely *so far*. And then all the preceding . . . is revealed as mere casuistic reasons not to believe. The *reality* is my own experience, and I suppose it is this that enables theologians & mystics to speak with some confidence; each relies on his or her own experience not on generalities & received knowledge.[22]

What remained a conundrum for Levertov was the person of Jesus Christ. She was palpably aware of God's care and felt the reality of the Spirit inspiring good thoughts and actions, but she was incapable of having a colloquy with Jesus as the Spiritual Exercises encouraged. She found the notion of the Incarnation and the life and sayings of Jesus both vivid and meaningful, but the living presence of Jesus Christ was not real to her. Kapfer, in his wisdom, told her not to be concerned.

Levertov's reflection was spurred on by the Spiritual Exercises and by sermons she heard at St. Joseph's parish. What she garnered was an appreciation of a mystical church within the visible, institutional church, which acted to counterbalance it. On a personal level she came to understand that one's sins could not be fully forgiven if one continued to be resentful.[23] But her most important realization centered on the continuity of her vocation as a poet. She wrote: "And all my once-secular sense of being led (The Thread) & of 'having a destiny' . . . I can now see in a religious context as indeed 'bindings' in the *religare* sense. Gracias a la Vida. Gracias a Dios."[24]

If her poetic vocation had religious implications as now understood, she also acknowledged that this vocation had negative consequences for other parts of her life. Reflecting from the vantage point of her seventies, she wrote:

> In my own case, I *was* (unconsciously) conflicted too much of the time. My life in poetry always won out but in many ways at the expense of being a good enough wife and mother. I didn't really realize this until long after I had divorced Mitch. Granted, he was not an easy person to be married to . . . Because I had been dedicated to poetry from childhood I was able to extract "nutriment" (as Thoreau says) "from the stone" of a marriage that was in many ways unpropitious — and I don't *regret* any of my experience, as experience (though of course I wish I had been a better parent when Nikolai was a child). There are many things about which I feel morally culpable, but that doesn't mean I regret my *experience*; I probably would be a poorer writer if I hadn't lived it.[25]

Year by year Levertov gained the resources she needed to follow her newly defined artistic "task" "to be" and "to arrive at being." In one sense there was nothing novel about this orientation. She was, as in the past, "poet in the world," "pilgrim on a journey," and prophet. In the previously published essay "Poetry, Prophecy, Survival," she set out the links between a "poetry of anguish" and prophecy. Like the prophets, poets promise and admonish, but she adds that above all "the prophets provide words of *witness*."[26] This was different from "awakening sleepers"; she intimated a new task, to "*witness*," that is to testify in her poetry to spiritual longing and meaning beyond the temporal.

She begins this work in *Evening Train*.[27] Its eighty-four poems represent the expansiveness of her interests: the earth — its clouds, lakes, rivers, moons, mountains, birds, animals — and the realities of growing old, of the life of the spirit, of the human condition and issues of social justice. These themes were not new, but her rendering of them recognized that "we move through our lives; swiftly," much like the "evening train" moves steadily through the dark, each one of us with "a conscious destination."[28] The poems of *Evening Train* are the work not only of a mature and accomplished poet but also of a woman who herself had now matured. What had been "green" in Levertov was now ripened.

Evening Train contains poems for or about persons Levertov loved or admired: her father and mother, Bet, Steve, Mark, the artist Melanie Peter, the historian Page Smith, the poet Jean Joubert, the artist and longtime friend Howard Fussiner, her childhood maid Becca, and her former secretary Yarrow Cleaves.[29] Other poems, grouped in a section titled "Witnessing from Afar," directly confront the horrors of contemporary life. Although less engaged in active social protest, Levertov continued to write about the tragedies of Central America, war, and environmental degradation. "In the Land of Shinar," written at the time of the 1991 Gulf War, details the construction of the Tower of Babel, a spiraling catastrophe in which all are complicit and for which all will suffer as the tower collapses, engulfing those who live in its shadow.[30]

But the most powerful poems of *Evening Train* are those that seek the presence of spirit within phenomena and those that explore the quest for an encounter with God. In some cases, these two intents are tangled together in the same poem.

The defining image of this collection is the unnamed mountain. Twelve poems explore its many guises. It is always real, commanding, "a vast presence" both "seen" and "unseen," "elusive," coming and going on the horizon. "Veiled," "majestic," "luminous," "obdurate," "unconcerned," it is "massive" but "ethereal," "a vast whisper," perceived as a beckoning "mirage." Portraying the mountain as "presente" and interpenetrated by the spirit, Levertov searches for the spirit within.[31] But she also analogizes the human relationship with the mountain as an encounter with God. This is possible because for her imagination perceives analogies and extends them from the observed to the surmised.[32]

In "Morning Mist" the mountain is described as "absent," much as God is "Deus absconditus," an absent God. It is experienced as "white stillness / / resting everywhere." In the poem "Open Secret" she announces that the mountain is not known by close scrutiny, sense experience, or knowledge of its geology. Its power is in the "open secret" of its remote coming and going, a lofty, lonely apparition. One's relationship with the mountain is not intimacy or communion but awe. It speaks in "a vast whisper." It is hidden sometimes in "veils of cloud," much as the poet "in veils of inattention, apathy, fatigue" is hidden from the mountain's "witnessing presence." "*Respect, perspective, / privacy*" are what it teaches. All that one need know is that the mountain is an "angelic guardian" blessing the city. Its absence is as necessary as silence is necessary to music.[33]

The poems of *Evening Train* are an expression of Levertov's love of all that lives.[34] Poems of chicory and ivy, of herons, coots, doves, chickens, and salmon, attest to her "inseeing" in the natural world, to her sense of being a sibling of every living thing. In the long poem "Embracing the Multipede" she questions and then ponders a creature she calls "repulsive," "vile," "disgusting," and "loathsome." But she is called to a work of mercy, to protect it, to give it her heart. In embracing the multipede through dialogue, she learns it both hides in and seeks God.[35] Even this lowly creature witnesses to "the presence of spirit" within phenomenon itself.

Committed to life and its protection, Levertov laments the human despoiling of the earth. In "The Batterers" she analogizes the earth to a battered woman, and in "Tragic Error" she defines humans as "earth's mind, mirror, reflective source"; they are "those cells of earth's body that could / perceive and imagine, could bring the planet / into the haven it is to be known." Instead, humans, "willful or ignorant," sure of their power, "rooted and pillaged" the earth. The biblical command to subdue the earth was misunderstood; the error was tragic.[36]

The final section of *Evening Train* contains poems with overt religious content. In "The Tide" Levertov speaks of the ebb and flow of faith and of the God she calls "Giver." She asks: "Where is the Giver to whom my gratitude / rose? In this emptiness / there seems no Presence."[37] Some poems contain specific biblical allusions. In "Contraband" she attributes the expulsion of humans from Eden to the fact that they have stuffed and gorged on the "contraband" of "toxic" reason, which separates them from God. God nonetheless squeezes through to them outside of Eden, like filtered light, like a strain of music. In another poem, "What the Figtree Said," she personifies the figtree and has it speak to the "literalists" who claim Jesus cursed it. The figtree counters that Jesus cursed the "literalists" themselves, with their barren hearts, their inability to see or hear or imagine.[38]

In "Salvator Mundi: Via Crucis" she reflects on Rembrandt's rendering of Jesus, a photograph of which she kept in her oratory. She presents him in extremis, a "hero out of his depth," desiring to "let the whole thing go." His heaviest weight is not the torture, betrayal, or anticipation of death but the "desire to renege," to step back from what he had promised. "Ascension" paints a similar agony of Jesus, the relinquishing of his human nature, his liberation from his incarnated self.[39] In "Suspended," the final poem of *Evening Train*, Levertov returns to the simple language of need, doubt and gratitude. "I had grasped God's garment in the void / but my hand slipped. / . . . . though I claw at empty air and feel / nothing, no embrace, / I have not plummeted."[40]

Levertov wrote that everything in *Evening Train* was a prayer.[41] In this volume the reader experiences only a thin membrane between the speaking "I" and the poet herself. In earlier poems the "I" who spoke implied more than Levertov herself grasped. However, these poems reflect great congruence between the poet and the person. Levertov claimed that writing was "work that enfaiths." The poems of *Evening Train* had done just that.[42]

The publication of this volume affirmed Levertov's reputation as a major poet, one who bridged the humanistic, artistic, and religious communities. She continued to receive recognition and invitations. The boundary-crossing journal *Cross Currents* invited her to serve on its advisory board; the Conference on Christianity and Literature recognized her contribution to dialogue among Christian scholars and the secular professional community; and two Jesuit institutions, Santa Clara University and Seattle University, awarded her honorary doctoral degrees.[43] Although she received what must have been a flattering invitation to write a syndicated column for the *New York Times*, she declined, saying she had "other things" to do at this stage in her life.[44] Those "other things" included working to connect art and spirituality.

Levertov had already offered a spirituality and poetry retreat with Luke Tobin and had come away convinced that this might be a means to transmit faith to others. She went on to give retreats on this same topic at the Santa Sabina Center in San Rafael and at other centers of spirituality in Denver and in Santa Fe, again with Tobin. While in Santa Fe she visited the sanctuary of Chimayo, a place of healing from which she sent a packet of its reputedly curative dirt to Steve Blevins, who was near death. At the end of the year when she returned to Seattle from overseas, Levertov gave another retreat at Stillpoint at the request of Jane Comerford. In this she traced her own spiritual development through her poetry from the 1960s onward and explored the origins of both poetry and prayer in the capacities of paying attention, using the senses, and engaging the imagination.[45] In these retreats Levertov always made it clear that she spoke as a poet and not someone with advanced knowledge of the spiritual life like a mystic.

In her poem "Contrasting Gestures," Levertov made a distinction between the two unique vocations of artist and mystic:

> (Though mystics desire submersion
> to transform them,
>
> ....
>
>   And artists
> want not themselves transformed
> but their work.   The plunge itself

their desire, a way to be
subsumed, consumed utterly
into their work.)[46]

She recognized, however, that both artist and mystic share a desire to make something real. Julian of Norwich, of course, wanted to "enact metaphor," to make the suffering of Jesus real for herself in her whole being, her body, and her senses. The poet too wants to make something real, "an autonomous entity," the poem.[47] But Levertov recognized differences between mystic and artist when she wrote: "One truly incompatible endeavor, I think, is to try to be a . . . mystic *and* be an artist (especially a poet). . . . These are 2 quite different modes of being & although a . . . mystic may write beautifully (e.g., St. Teresa) that's just a secondary & inessential occurrence. The mystic really strives to eliminate language, the poet strives to make things out of language, the material he/she adores. Just as the mystic may happen to write well, so the poet *may* be a person of radiant virtue — but that's merely incidental."[48]

Both mystic and artist desired transformation and required subordination of the self to some other end. Both began with a vision, but the nature of the vision and its result were different. The mystic vision was given and demanded in response a transformed self. The poet's vision was arrived at through paying attention, which led to the transformation of sound and music into words. Mystic and artist were singular ways of being and distinctive vocations.

By the mid-1990s Levertov was in her prime. Yet the early months of 1994 proved difficult in terms of her relationship with her son and her own health. Nikolai's desire to move to Seattle permanently caused her anxiety. Her life was peaceful, and she did not think she had the energy to take him on. Ultimately, she persuaded him to delay the move for about six months.[49] But when it was clear he was moving, she resolved to make this an opportunity to deepen their trust and forgiveness and to give herself a second chance as a mother.[50] When Nikolai arrived in February, he moved in with her and she introduced him to fellow artists, but within the month they had two major rows and he moved out with a female friend from his high school days at Putney. Denise paid the rent. Depressed by their wrangle, she sought the counsel of Lee Kapfer, Murray Bodo, and Valerie Trueblood. Although angry about Nikolai's arrival, she realized she could not continue to feel responsible for him even though her bad parenting might have contributed to his problems. She prayed for reconciliation between them.[51]

Levertov was scheduled to be away for more than two months in spring 1994 but considered canceling the trip because of Nikolai's situation. Ultimately, she decided to follow through with her plans. She traveled to England and Ireland and gave readings in both countries, including at the Cuirt Festival of Literature in Galway, which she attended with Eavan Boland.

The trip was a mixed blessing. On the one hand she felt unnourished because she had not prayed much while she was away; on the other, she said that during the trip she had come to realize that she had a particular "ministry" of friendship and listening to others.[52] This form of friendship — paying attention and reflecting back to others their talents — was life-changing, and the recipients, mostly young artists and poets, were profoundly grateful. One can imagine that it was years of practicing her own craft of making poems and probably teaching, too, that prepared her to carry on what she now recognized as a new form of work. She was committed to fostering the "voice" of poets. "To be a poet you must be crazy about language," she said, "and you must believe in the uniqueness of every person, and therefore in your own. To find your voice you must forget about finding it, and trust that if you pay sufficient attention to life you will be found to have something to say which no one else can say. . . . [Y]ou will arrive at writing what you apprehend in a way which embodies that vision which is yours alone. And that will be your voice, unsought, singing out from you of itself."[53]

But if her gift of attentiveness followed from her vocation as a poet, it was undoubtedly strengthened by her own growth in self-understanding, which made her more receptive to others. Although she sometimes had a maternal response to young poets, she mostly acted as mentor. In at least one instance, however, she acted as a religious sponsor for the poet Sam Green when he entered the Catholic church.

During the years after 1994, Levertov's health became more tenuous. She waited more than six months after her initial biopsy to have a second one, which confirmed a low-level lymphoma. Probably unwilling to confront the reality of her illness, she let many more months pass before beginning chemotherapy. To make matters worse, in early 1995 she became aware of a loss of vision. Although her eyesight was never good — she initially wore glasses and then switched to contact lenses — she now feared potential macular degeneration.[54] Additionally, by the end of 1995, she became ill with pneumonia and acute laryngitis while traveling abroad.[55]

Anxiety over these health issues was compounded by the deaths of intimate friends. Her old friend Eve Triem, whom she had saved from penury, died right before the arrival of the new year, and Steve Blevins, her beloved secretary and friend, finally succumbed to AIDS. Her poem "For Steve" expressed her affection for him.[56] Another blow struck in November when she learned of the death of En Potter, her former lover and father of her aborted child. She claimed Potter was the love of her life, and yet said at his passing that she felt something had lifted from her.[57]

Facing her own ill health and the death of friends, Levertov longed to deepen her faith. Believing that faith returns when one prays, just as appetite returns when one begins to eat, she renewed her efforts. Hoping that a concern for others would strengthen faith,[58] she attempted to live more lovingly. But she always returned to the central role of imagination in cultivating faith. She wrote: "It appears to me that faith requires imagination; not in order to deceive ourselves into believing what is not true but precisely in order to grasp what *is* true but is too amazing in its uniqueness to be easily believed. I'm not referring to the cultivation of naive credulity, but of being able to feel as real & personal such concepts as our redemption by Christ's passion & resurrection, which without the faculty of imagination remain abstract, impersonal, and remote."[59]

Having first explored imagination as central to artistic creation, she now found it vital for the cultivation of faith. Imagination was the human capacity that made possible the fusing of intellect and feeling, allowing what Rilke called "inseeing" into the very center of a thing. It also allowed the perceiving of analogies and extending them.[60] Imagination was at the heart of both the artistic and religious response.

Even with the setbacks of 1995, Levertov kept up a routine of readings and residencies. She returned to Cornell as professor-at-large, and gave a reading at Purdue University's Literary Awards ceremony. In March that year she participated in an evening of remembrance of Oscar Romero at Seattle's St. Patrick Church; in mid-April, along with Stanley Kunitz and Gary Snyder, whom she had praised for his simple lifestyle in her poem "Only Connect,"[61] she participated in the Des Moines National Poetry Festival. On one of her trips, she stopped in Cincinnati to visit Murray Bodo at the Franciscan friary where they prayed together for her healing. In the fall she participated in the Welsh Union of Writers Conference in Cardiff, Wales, where she read some of her mother's poetry. It was almost twenty years since she had been in her maternal homeland.

All the while Levertov continued to receive public recognition for her work. The Academy of American Poets awarded her a fellowship worth twenty-five thousand dollars, and New Directions published *Tesserae: Memories and Suppositions*, for which she garnered the Governor's Award from the Washington State Commission for the Humanities. *Tesserae* was a compilation of twenty-seven autobiographical *tesserae*—fragments describing various experiences and people that shaped her artistic life. Its title may well have been inspired by a line from an earlier poem: "our specks of life . . . [are] fragile tesserae."[62] In this, her fourth book of prose, Levertov brought together vignettes about her parents, her childhood and adolescence, and her early friendships and travels. *Tesserae* was motivated perhaps by her interest in the early childhood experiences of artists and her desire to preserve the memories of what she considered her own unique past.

Clearly Levertov was weaker and more frail by 1996, although she neither wrote nor complained of this to others. She continued to carry on with her commitments. In 1996 she gave a workshop at Beloit College, accepted the newly created position of poetry editor of *Cistercian Studies*,[63] published an essay in honor of Daniel Berrigan,[64] received the Seattle Arts Commission's Fellowship Award for Northwest writers, and worked as a consultant to the U.S. Catholic Bishops' Committee on the International Commission for English in the Liturgy. She also prepared two "ponies," small anthologies of her poetry organized around the two most significant interests of her later years, interests alluded to in her lecture "Affinities of Content." In one, *The Stream & the Sapphire*, she traces in a selection of her poems her "slow movement from agnosticism to Christian faith, a movement incorporating much doubt and questioning as well as of affirmation." In the other, *The Life around Us*, she explores the human relationship to nature in poems of celebration, anger, and dread.[65] She prepared these ponies both for herself and her readers. As little anthologies they could be put at bedside or in the pocket or could be used in her retreats. Once they were published, she regretted that she had not also prepared another of her political poems, even though she thought some of those poems might be dated.[66]

By the end of 1996, Levertov was exhausted. Whether to protect her privacy or to not burden her friends, she dismissed her physical maladies as discomfort, a minor problem. Her longtime friend Hayden Carruth complained point-blank in mid-1996 that although he wanted to respect her privacy, he still did not know the nature of her illness.[67] Uncharacteristically she wrote in her diary of being fatigued and lethargic, of feeling her life was shrinking. She slept a lot, did no foreign travel in 1996, saw fewer friends, gave fewer readings, and walked much less in her beloved Seward Park. She was not able to attend the celebratory event at which she was to receive the Governor's Award for *Tesserae*. The fact that Levertov, loyal correspondent that she was, sent no holiday greetings that year was indication of her weakened state. She spent Christmas Day alone, except for a brief visit from a friend who brought her some cinnamon rolls.

Her pleasures were fewer, too, although she was full of gratitude for her friendship with Valerie Trueblood, and for some unrecorded reason, was happier with her relationship with Nikolai. But generally she felt in decline and suspected she might be depressed.[68] At year's end she endured another round of chemotherapy.

Earlier in the year, Levertov learned that Mitch and his wife were having marital problems, but then Mitch wrote to say that although they had suffered, he and Sandy were now back together again. He assured Denise that his marriage was secure and he was happy with what he had made of his life. His missive included no query about her health problems.[69]

Then in December 1996, Mitch himself became ill and was diagnosed with a spinal tumor which had metastasized from pancreatic cancer. He left the hospital and returned home in the middle of the month expecting soon to die. Levertov recorded that Mitch was beautifully resigned, without regrets, and more spiritually open than she thought possible. In reflecting on their many years of marriage, she wrote in her diary: "I think with tenderness of how much growing up & discovering & mutual influence M and I went through together so — clumsily, awkwardly, ignorantly & yet not without its moments of glory and of results in the world."[70]

Nikolai left to visit his father on Christmas Eve, but Denise, although she had been invited by Sandy Gregor to visit as well,[71] decided not to go. She had both her chemotherapy treatment and cataract surgery scheduled and was reluctant to deal with Mitch as he was dying, and with Sandy, Matty, and the world of Temple. It was too much. She stayed in Seattle and talked with him regularly by phone. She was consoled that Mitch had an acceptance of death and a resolve to live well for whatever time remained to him.[72]

The high point in this year of loss and ill health was the publication of *Sands of the Well*, a volume of more than hundred poems. She worried that its length and spiritual content might jeopardize its reception. They did not.

The book opens with the enigmatic poem "What Harbinger?" which begins: "A boat is moving / toward me / slowly, but who / is rowing and what / it brings I can't / yet see."[73] Similar poems follow. There are poems of self-doubt like "Advising Myself" and "For Those Whom the Gods Love Less," in which she asks: "When you discover / your new work travels the ground you had traversed / decades ago, you wonder, panicked, / 'Have I outlived my vocation?'" She answers: "There's a remedy — / only one — . . . Remember the great ones, remember / Cézanne."[74] *Sands of the Well* includes two kinds of poems—those about nature and the presence of spirit *within* phenomena and poems of spiritual longing.

In Levertov's nature poems spirit interpenetrates the landscape, flora, and fauna. Each thing "presents itself" and more than itself.

> Everything answers the rollcall,
> and even, as is the custom,
> speaks for those that are gone.
> —Clearly, beyond sound:
> that revolutionary "*Presente!*"[75]

In "Sojourners in a Parallel World" Levertov holds out hope for the transformation of humans' relationship with nature. When humans enter the world of nature they lose track of their own concerns and "something tethered / in us . . . breaks free. . . . [W]e have changed, a little."[76] Levertov's poems of spiritual longing include a few that have a specific Christian focus, like "On Belief in the Physical Resurrection of Jesus" and "The Conversion of Brother Lawrence." In this latter poem she tracks the dialogue of the seventeenth-century Carmelite monk Brother Lawrence with God. In the midst of the drudgery of kitchen work, Lawrence, in joyful "steadfast attention" to the presence of God, carries on an "unending 'silent secret conversation.'" Levertov opens the poem with the monk's words: "'Let us enter into / ourselves, Time / presses.'"[77] These words must have had particular poignancy, given Levertov's sense that her own life was foreshortened. Other poems reflect an expansive spiritual longing. She writes of "the hospitable silence of God," of God's presence made known in "interventions," and of an ultimate place of sifting, of the rubbing of one's being to a finer substance and then the floating into light, suspended, awaiting the common resurrection.[78] The book's title poem, "Sands of the Well," uses a similar image of sifting, in this case of the golden particles of sand descending in a well. She asks: "Is this / the place where you / are brought in meditation?"[79]

Some of the most compelling poems in the volume center on the notion of clinging and being held by God. In "The Beginning of Wisdom" she describes humans as "so small, a speck of dust / moving across the huge world. The world / a speck of dust in the universe." One knows so little, yet each person and the universe too are held.[80] In "'In Whom We Live and Move and Have Our Being'" Levertov conceives of God as air enveloping the globe of being, while humans "breathe, in, out, in, the sacred."[81] In yet another poem she claims that if one dares to believe, one floats, upheld, living in God's mercy. God's love is not mild or temperate, but a "[v]ast / flood of mercy / flung on resistance."[82]

One senses in the poems of *Sands of the Well* a mature poet at work, one who freely expresses her wisdom. Levertov's freedom and openness in these last years was evident as well in interviews in which she became more self-revelatory. In an interview conducted in September 1996, she responds directly to a number of pointed questions. When queried about her hopes for the future she replied: "I hope to continue to write well and to surprise myself in each poem. I also hope to deepen my spiritual life and to manifest this in my dealings with others." When pressed about what she would do differently if she were to live her life again, she said: "I wouldn't want radical differences in events . . . But I'd like to have been kinder and wiser — doesn't everybody?" She acknowledged that her life was never boring, that she had wonderful friends, and that she had been born with a "definite gift." When the interviewer asked what was the most amazing thing about life, she responded, "That anything exists at all, rather than a void." When queried about how she might face death, she answered: "With awe. With hope that one's faith is not illusory. With the desire to be spiritually ready for it when it comes."[83]

Levertov's brief reference to the need to be "spiritually ready" when death came was also alluded to in her diary jottings. There she laments that she has experienced a loss of faith relative to a few years prior but she will return to the place where her journey began — to gratitude for the blessings of her life.[84] She reviews what she considered the prerequisites of a Christian life: faith that God is paying attention and courage to accept God's love; forgiveness of others and one's self; detachment, but not contempt for the world; generosity, prayer, and persistence.[85] She writes that while she seems to have the power to do good to others, she fails to practice what she preaches; that nonetheless, she needs to "just *get on with* what I am able to do."[86]

It is clear that in her waning years Levertov felt more "under siege" than usual from contemporary society. In a poem written at this time, she addresses "Dear 19th century" and asks for refuge in its sanctuary. She acknowledges that the nineteenth century had its own horrors of dirt, disease, and injustices, but at least there was the illusion of endless time to reform and a beckoning future.[87] She had no such illusion about her own times. She wrote that she hated cyberspace, growth in population, the deterioration of language, the commercialization of poetry, the damming of the Yangtze

River, the talk of ending the monarchy, the increase in racism, and the igno-rance of the young. Convinced these things would not get better in her life-time, she concluded she should count her blessings of friends, books, music, flowers, and her work.[88] But by the end of 1996 she increasingly had a real sense of aging and mortality. She was sleeping a lot and thought she might need to take Zoloft again since her depression had returned.[89]

Although she wanted to be "spiritually ready," Levertov also continued to ponder questions of belief. For her, God's greatest sacrifice was not the Pas-sion and Crucifixion, but the Incarnation. Beginning with the Annunciation, God entered the flawed life of created beings. An ignominious death followed from that, but it was only through that kind of death that the transcendent mercy of God could be revealed in the Resurrection. Incarnation remained for her the first and most important of Christian beliefs.[90] Although she nev-er spoke of a connection between belief in the Incarnation and the founda-tion of her own poetic insight — namely that there was "an abode of mercy" "not behind but within" — these two insights are congruent.

Levertov conceived of the poetry of her later years as witnessing to the double task she set out in "Dream Instruction" — "to be" and "to arrive at being." This last intent is alluded to in "Primary Wonder," the final poem of *Sands of the Well*. In this she reiterates in poetic form her response to the interviewer's question: What is the most amazing thing about life?

> the mystery
> that there is anything, anything at all,
> let alone cosmos, joy, memory, everything,
> rather than void: and that, O Lord,
> Creator, Hallowed One, You still,
> hour by hour sustain it.[91]

Primary wonder. It had been there since the beginning, and it would now carry her through the final year of her life.

12

"Once Only"
1997

All which, because it was
flame and song and granted us
joy, we thought we'd do, be, revisit,
turns out to have been what it was
that *once*, only.
"Once Only"[1]

The deaths of En Potter and Steve Blevins, Mitch's life-threatening cancer,
and her own increasing weakness and worsening health chastened Levertov.
Although she always had a sense of the perishability of life, neither her diaries nor poems of this period show a preoccupation with death. A few of her
closest friends knew of her lymphoma, but most did not. If asked about her
illness, she brushed aside the query. Her sense of privacy kept her guarded.
But mostly she appears to have been incapable of acknowledging that she
would not live. "*You know*," she wrote in 1960, "*I'm telling you, what I love best
/ is life. I love life! Even if I ever get / to be old and wheezy — or limp!*"[2] Levertov
had sucked the marrow of the bone of life. Her laugh, her sense of humor
and playfulness, her ability to be in the moment, her wonderment, were all
aspects of her love of life. The poem "Living," written years before, speaks
of this as well:

The fire in leaf and grass
so green it seems
each summer the last summer.

The wind blowing, the leaves
shivering in the sun,
each day the last day.

. . . .
Each minute the last minute.[3]

216

It was only by an acceptance of the fragility of human life and the earth's life that one could live in the moment and be fully alive. This was, she said, "our open secret of paradoxical delight."[4]

Levertov's self-identity as poet was founded on an intense super-aliveness. When she asked, "Have I outlived my vocation?" her answer was "no," and she proceeded with the only remedy she knew — to continue, much like Cézanne and Bet advised. Poetry was not only her craft but the means by which she gave life to herself and to others. To have stopped writing would mean to stop living, and vice versa. Writing was Levertov's way to survive, as her life experiences were the basis of her writing. She could not imagine the end of either.

As her health deteriorated, she vacillated between the desire to live and a denial of nonliving. Mostly she kept on using her limited energy for writing, giving a few lectures and readings, being with friends, seeing doctors. She kept up her usual activities of knitting, reading novels — especially Jane Austen — and playing her "black-cat" piano as she could. Although she hated to lose the money, she canceled several readings, which were far afield in New York, Washington, and Paris.[5] She needed help, and friends provided it. It was a difficult time, but death was not discussed.

Her last year began with concern for Mitch's impending death and an apprehension about Nikolai's unresolved relationship with his father. She shared these concerns with Lucille Clifton and Murray Bodo[6] and recorded in her notebook that she thought Nikolai was much like herself — able to inspire, hungry for affection, and bitter if rebuffed.[7] She was grateful that at least for the moment, he was able to have some good moments with his father.[8]

Less than two months after his initial diagnosis, Mitch Goodman died on February 1, 1997. Levertov noted in her diary that her grief was not intense, but subdued.[9] After several weeks she wrote affectionately: "[I]n my present sense of loss I *regain* something of the Mitch I *did* love . . . I don't want to sentimentalize & falsify the bitterness & disappointments & frustrations — but the love, & the *lovableness* of Mitch is restored in his loss, in some degree; & that irony is both bitter & sweet."[10]

Over the next month Levertov continued to reflect on their complex relationship. As she saw it, in the early years of their marriage Mitch took on an "insecure" wife, a child, and a mother-in-law, all with very little income. Although both of them were immature, this was masked by their intelligence and creativity. Their sexual life was never satisfying, even though they pretended it was. The rows between them and between Nikolai and her were not conducive to healthy development in Mitch. If Mitch had married an heiress, or not married so young, or if they had not had Nikolai so young, perhaps his life would have been better. Although she thought more money would have made an enormous difference in their lives, it would have deprived them of being "struggling Bohemian artists." If she had been a "kinder," "calmer," and "more devoted" wife, their life might have been better. But she also recognized that Mitch too had his faults. He was lazy, although this went under the guise of anarchism or independence or revolt against the Protestant work ethic. She had this tendency too, but in her case it was mitigated by her conscientiousness and tendency to conformism.[11]

By mid-February Levertov was feeling better again, even though her blood count remained low. And good things were happening. Albert Gelpi, who was preparing the Duncan–Levertov correspondence for publication, reassured her that contrary to her fears, she would not be embarrassed by some of her letters.[12] Christopher McGowan was also readying her correspondence with William Carlos Williams to be brought out as a New Directions book. A symposium on her work had been held at the Institut Catholique in Paris,[13] her foreword to *Writing between the Lines: An Anthology on War and Its Social Consequences* would appear within the year,[14] and she was at work on an essay for a beautiful coffee-table book of the letters and photography of her friend Mary Randlett, which she combined with several of her own poems.[15] In March Levertov received a call from the Library of Congress informing her that she had been nominated by Robert Hass to be the next poet laureate of the United States. She burst out laughing, assuming it was a joke, but when convinced of its authenticity she declined to be considered for the position, claiming she was an "unsuitable choice for many reasons." She demurred probably because of her health and the requirement that the position would put her in the pay of the government,[16] although she had participated in Library of Congress activities earlier in her life.

Given limited energy, Levertov restricted her poetry readings, but she did manage to give two in April: one at Stanford at which she read with Eavan Boland, who had been chosen as her replacement in the Creative Writing Program;[17] and the other at the University of Oregon, Eugene, where composer Robert Kyr, inspired by the poetry of *Sands of the Well*, created Symphony No 7, "The Sound of Light."[18] Later in the summer she read several of her last poems on a return visit to the Port Townsend Writers' Conference, a place she had visited in 1979. For that occasion she bought a new navy blue dress with a French flowered print. Her friend Sam Hamill said she "glowed with life" at that reading.[19] To memorialize her two-day stay with Hamill and his wife, Gray Foster, she wrote "A Clearing." In their "large-windowed house" in the midst of a "paradise of cedars," she was sheltered from an "assaultive world."[20] It was a moment that was once, only.

While she continued to write and make some public appearances, those who were in close contact — her Seattle friends and the many out-of-town guests who came to visit for several days — encountered something different in her response. She was taking prednisone and was tense, edgy, and irritable. Her verbalized preoccupation was not with cancer but with a defect in her retina that seriously threatened her eyesight. Fearful of blindness, she uncharacteristically discussed this problem and the proposed corrective surgery with friends.

One of Levertov's midyear houseguests was Emily Archer, a former graduate student who consulted with her for her dissertation in 1994 and who, at Levertov's request, returned to interview her for *Image*.[21] This interview, which might have been an excuse for Levertov to see Archer again,[22] was wide-ranging and extraordinarily frank. In it Levertov took up a number of her concerns about contemporary society. She was worried about the public's shrinking vocabulary, which she feared would lead to a diminished ability to think about the eternal questions. She worried about technological euphoria and insisted that "virtual experience" was "absolutely anti-incarnational" and needed to be resisted by those who cared about the idea of the "sacred incarnated in the material." Levertov, who always wrote in longhand, feared the implications of computer technology for artistic creativity. In a subsequent interview she said: "The word processor doesn't take as much time as actually forming the letters with your hand at the end of your arm which is attached to your body. It's a different kind of thing. They don't realize that this laborious process is part of the creative process."[23] Her hope was that poets, preservers of language much like Medieval monks, would serve as a kind of invisible counterforce to these trends.

Levertov went on to discuss the moral implications of the diminishment of language and of a sense of the past. She argued that if one lacked understanding of the past, there was no appreciation of sequence, of how one thing led to another, and hence no sense of the future. As a result one had no perception of the consequences of one's actions.

The interview with Archer also contained Levertov's revelatory statements about faith and death. For her, God was an artist, a creator, a giver who in making humans bestowed free will, ensuring nonintervention in their choices. Borrowing from Heidegger, she called man "a conversation," one in dialogue with a maker who would never give up on what had been created and who was desirous of creation's love. When queried about death, Levertov said she was not preoccupied by it; either there was an afterlife or there was not, but she always held out hope for a resurrection, which would give one a chance to take care of "unfinished business" and the opportunity to continue one's development. What did intrigue her was the possibility of "salvation in the here and now . . . actually accepting the Good News" during one's life. She offered as evidence of this hope the "resurrection" of the living she saw shining from the faces of those who have experienced salvation in this life.[24] In the poem "Translucence," she describes the "unconscious light in faces," a "half-opaque whiteness" in the living, who, like Lazarus, are "already resurrected." Theirs is a "great unknowing," a holiness that emanated from their joyful, generous ordinary lives.[25]

The interview with Archer took place in June 1997; atypically, Levertov was pleased with the result.[26] Although she had a chronic cough, she gave Archer no indication that she was ill. In her diary she records nothing of her illness either, although she reflects on death in general, her view that hell is not a place of punishment but perhaps something like being divorced from God. Her faith, she wrote, was in the creator Father and in the Spirit. She admitted she had less of a relationship with the Son — perhaps, she suggests, because the Son demands "works" and she has no impulse to perform them. As a consequence she confesses she does not understand the specifically Christian and Catholic emphasis on Jesus's atonement, redemption, passion, and resurrection.[27]

If the Spiritual Exercises of the previous years did not win her over to a deeper understanding of Jesus, they did seem to leave a residue in her continuing self-examination as she returns to an earlier practice of using her diary as a forum in which to address God and to recount her faults. She mentions that although her friends and public think she is a good person, she knows she is very selfish, even though she tries to do the best she can for friends and for Nikolai. She reminisces with a mixture of regret and relief: "if her friends had only seen her earlier in life."[28] In passing, Levertov mentions that it was Brother David Steindl-Rast's book, *Gratitude the Heart of Prayer*, that confirmed gratitude as the key to faith. Knowing that a distancing from God could be overcome by a return to gratitude, she gives thanks for Craig Boly and Lee Kapfer, for the healing dreams about her parents, for Robert Duncan and Steve Blevins, and for her realization that she must stay alive for Nikolai's sake.[29] This statement, written in February 1997, with its abbreviated reference to the need to "stay alive," is her clearest acknowledgment of the fragility of her life.

From *The Double Image* onward, Levertov's poetry always included poems of "promises" and "fears," of celebration and lament. Although she feared and lamented violence, war, and ecological destruction, death was never a major preoccupation. However, one of her earliest poems, "The Dead," details her experience as a young nurse in World War II. In this she speaks of learning that in death the "music" stops and is replaced only by "a heavy thick silence."[30] During the Vietnam War, especially in her travels to Hanoi, her firsthand experience of military violence made death a subject of some of her poetry. In a 1975 lecture, "Dying and Living," she credits Williams with teaching her that life and death are inextricably linked. His praise was not for "life as *opposed* to death, but for the synthesis, life/death or death/life, the curious embrace and union of positive and negative that is the human condition and indeed the condition of all creation — although we can perceive the condition most readily as conflict, not as synthesis."[31] From Rilke she learned that death was the culmination of the threads of life. If life is unlived, then death could not be lived.[32] Perhaps this is why Levertov's last poems offer few considerations of death, except indirectly as a longing for life.[33]

After the publication of *Sands of the Well*, Levertov continued to write. Forty of her poems, some of which were read at the Port Townsend event, were collected and published posthumously in *This Great Unknowing*. Among these, no theme dominates. In "A Hundred a Day" Levertov decries the demise of millions of species and the sense that there is no longer a beckoning future to be looked to as there was in the previous century. "Roast Potatoes" is a lament as well, a recollection of a time when kindness existed. In the future, she wrote, this human blessedness will become unknown to memory. "Swift Month" pronounces the passage of each day as "too swift."[34]

Some of these last poems are particularly tender. "Enduring Love," based on a dream from which she awoke sobbing,[35] recounts a visitation from her long-dead parents. This hoped-for reconciliation was made possible by their enduring love after she "had been wounded."[36] In the long poem "Feet," she observes that life is begun with small plump and perfect feet and ends with gnarled and twisted ones. She recalls her mother's crooked feet, the aching feet of peasants in the Andes, and the feet of the homeless, all remembered in the foot-washing ritual of Maundy Thursday.[37] Pathos and urgency are captured in her poem "Once Only":

[T]he marvelous
did happen in our lives, our stories
are not drab with its absence: but don't
expect now to return for more. Whatever more
there will be will be
unique as those were unique. Try
to acknowledge the next
song in its body-halo of flames as utterly
present, as now or never.[38]

The themes of her last poems are not new. The mountain reappears in its "lonely grandeur." It offers not intimacy but only a gracious, "measured self-disclosure." Such was its "noblesse oblige." In "Masquerade" the mountain is playful, but its "naïve force" is "dense, unmoving." Its "daily speech is silence," a silence "uninterrupted as the silence God maintains / throughout the layered centuries." The mountain's moods are "frank or evasive," silent, yet "fire seethes in its depths."[39]

Human and divine interaction are revisited. In "Immersion" angry humans reject the silence of God and demand that God speak. But the poet sees this silence as immersing humans in "a different language / events of grace, horrifying scrolls of history / and the unearned retrieval of blessings lost for ever / the poor grass returning after drought, timid, persistent." Language is for humans, a "way to ask and to answer," but God's holy voice is heard rather in "myriad musics, in signs and portents."[40]

In "The Métier of Blossoming," Levertov wrote of human growth by analogizing personal flourishing with the energetic growing and triumphant blossoming of the amaryllis. The poem is reminiscent of both her earlier "Matins," in which the "authentic" is described as that which is fully itself, and "Dream Instruction," which admonishes the reader "to be, / to arrive at being." The human aspiration is expressed in the final lines of the poem: Like the amaryllis, "If humans could be / that intensely whole, undistracted, unhurried, . . . If we could blossom / out of ourselves, giving / nothing imperfect, withholding nothing!"[41] For Levertov, to live fully and to give completely was the pinnacle of human achievement, "the métier of blossoming."

The poems of *This Great Unknowing* return to the juxtaposition of joy and sorrow, hope and despair; "Celebration" begins joyfully with a description of a brilliant day, ablaze with green, but the inherent pathos of the moment is suddenly announced. The sound of a spirited brass band swinging along the street of a dusty town is declared to be "wholly at odds / with the claims of reasonable gloom."[42] In "Mass of the Moon Eclipse," Levertov chronicles the ritual of the waxing and waning of the moon. In this case despair is overcome by hope. In stately fashion "the bright silver inch by inch / is diminished, options vanish." One cannot be sure the moon will move "from death into resurrection." She asks:

> are we to live
> on in a world without moon? We swallow
> a sour terror. Then
> that coppery sphere, no-moon become [*sic*] once more
> full-moon, visible in absence.[43]

Of all the poems of *This Great Unknowing*, the most self-revelatory is "First Love," a poem that defines Levertov's lifetime desire for "secret communion." The poem opens with the child/poet's failure to be in communion with another child, but then suddenly a flower opens:

> It looked at me, I looked
> back, delight
> filled me as if
> I, not the flower,
> were a flower. . . .
> *And there was endlessness.*
> Perhaps through a lifetime what I've desired
> has always been to return
> to that endless giving and receiving, the wholeness
> of that attention,
> that once-in-a-lifetime
> secret communion.[44]

In her memory of a child's experience of "endlessness," there is recognition of being accepted and invited into communion not with another human but with nature. This is the experience that served as the foundation of Levertov's poetic vocation and her lifelong, elusive desire for intimacy. Although she may have tasted "communion" in political solidarity, erotic expression, and friendship, those experiences were fleeting, never sustained.

Her lifelong search for intimacy is linked here with her destiny and her vocation. Giving-and-taking was at the heart of the poetic craft and the way into intimate communion.

Most of the poems of *This Great Unknowing* were probably written by the end of 1996 and certainly not after the summer of 1997.[45] Her calendar indicates that during the fall she was continually trundled off to doctors' appointments, transported principally by her friend Valerie Trueblood. Her physicians apparently were frank with her and indicated the seriousness of her condition. But she had her own ideas. When she was told by one oncologist that there was no more he could do for her, she sought out another, and in September began a third round of chemotherapy. She was a great believer in alternative methods of healing and tried many of these remedies as well. In the next months when she abruptly stopped taking her prescribed steroids, she had dramatic mood changes, and sometimes even became paranoid. She must have sensed some peril because she reviewed her will and literary trust agreement.[46] Nonetheless, in letters to friends, she remained optimistic and hopeful.[47]

Her last major presentation of the year, "Roots and Airplants," was the Yoder Memorial Lecture given at the Mennonite Goshen College in Indiana in late October. On the one hand the lecture is a consideration of the advantages and disadvantages for artists of geographic and cultural rootedness; on the other it illustrates her own position relative to these same phenomena. She begins by saying that many artists — Cézanne, Hardy, William Carlos Williams, and Wendell Berry — are rooted in and nourished by their local geographic environment. But others like Rilke, Conrad, Henry James, and Milosz are by choice or exile not rooted in one place or culture. The disadvantage for the former is that their art can be provincial and sentimental. For the latter, those Levertov calls the "floaters" or "airplants," the disadvantage is they have fewer immediate sources of nourishment to draw from and hence must seek out broader ones. Nonetheless, the "floaters" have a sense of freedom and hence may be more adventurous. Ultimately she concludes that the advantages and disadvantages of being rooted or not rooted are about even. But she quickly counters that the external world, whether experienced broadly or narrowly, is less important than the inner world where the most important changes take place.[48]

As early as 1979 Levertov had characterized herself as an "airplant." Although she identified with the English language and had a great love for the English countryside and English literature, she did not feel as if she were English. She said she was "rootless," except for the roots in the culture and experience of her childhood. In an earlier interview she said: "Perhaps you could say I am a child of the London streets, I am a child of the Victoria and Albert Museum, I am a child of my mother's girlhood memories of Wales, I am a child of my father's Hasidic tales, I am a child of the Christian upbringing that I had."[49]

After exploring the function of geography in the life of the artist, Levertov went on in the Yoder lecture to examine the role of religious allegiance in the artist's life. For poets like George Herbert and Gerard Manley Hopkins, faith is their culture and their emotional and intellectual root. But for others, like herself, religion does not provide a social community; friends are broad and scattered. In either case religion creates a tension for the artist. If one is inside a religious community, one chafes against communal restrictions and self-censorship. If one is outside a community, as she is, the problem is how to divide one's time and energy between the work of religion and service to one's art. In the end the depth one reaches as an artist, irrespective of these various tensions, is determined by the person's unique gift and the strength and persistence with which one pursues it.[50] Although Levertov leaves many aspects of the connection between religion and art unexplored in this lecture, what can be known with certainty is that she considers herself first an artist, one who places herself within a religious community. Art might enfaith her, and her poetry might serve as a means to explore and express her faith, but art was first and always for itself. She was never a Christian poet, but rather a poet who happened to be a Christian.

The experience at Goshen must have been exhausting; she was feeling increasingly weak by the end of October, even though she was animated by a party given by a small circle of her women friends for her seventy-fourth birthday at which she stayed up talking well into the night.[51] No one knew how ill she was. As usual she continued to think of her friends. She wrote Lucille Clifton, who recently had a kidney transplant, and began a poem in honor of her longtime editor, James Laughlin, who died November 12th. Laughlin was enormously important in Levertov's success as a poet, and he had great admiration for her strong defense of principle. In his book of remembrances he writes, I "love and revere her."[52] On Levertov's part she acknowledged Laughlin, along with Mitch and En, as one of the three most important men in her life.[53]

By Thanksgiving 1997, Levertov was seriously ill. She could hardly eat anything other than the custard friends brought in from Eliot Bay Bookstore. She slept with her beloved homunculus, Monkey, who was wise, understanding, and forgiving. In early December she was unable to attend a publication party for her friend Odette Meyer, even though she had written a blurb for her book. She wrote Milosz telling him of her irritation at being sick and having no energy and of a blood transfusion that precipitated an allergic reaction and a bout of pneumonia. But she assured him she had wonderful friends who were helping her and that she was getting better and was not depressed.[54]

Levertov's friends did care for her — drove her to appointments, brought her food, read her poetry and stories, watched her favorite movies with her. In all of this she did not speak of her own dying. At the same time, she was reading the Tibetan Book of the Dead, materials from the Vedanta Center, and Berry's "Pray without Ceasing." Her last diary entry was made on November 23, 1997. In a handwriting that had deteriorated from her big looping script, she recorded that she had been sick almost the entire month. She noted that Nikolai was happy and that Laughlin had died. She confided that her theological confusion had increased and that she needed to talk with Craig Boly and Murray Bodo. She went on to say: "And I'd like to attend a Vedanta Center, just to see. . . . Big problem is now not to 'scandalize' S[am] Green my godson & others who were so glad I became a Catholic. Am I still, & will I be in the future? And what about my 'speaking engagements'? It's all come to a head rather suddenly. . . . This is not about *God* but about the specifically Christian with its exclusivity. Must try to think it out before I discuss with Craig."[55]

As Levertov inched toward death, the categories of faith and doubt that had preoccupied her for so long seemed to become irrelevant. In keeping with the ancient Jewish tradition, she had wrestled with truth, with God. The goddess in Lie Castle, the tree telling of Orpheus, the struggle up the Jacob's ladder, the pull of the thread, the gaping abyss of the standoff, were evidences of her intense struggle. But now at the end, what mattered was depth and inclusivity. She recoiled from religious exclusivity, having had some glint of the light in faces of the already resurrected. She remained a seeker to the end, attesting that she was still on a journey.[56]

The optimism Levertov expressed to Milosz did not hold; she got sicker. Carlene Laughlin, a former student and secretary and wife of James Laughlin's son, arrived in Seattle. It was she who finally convinced Levertov to enter the Swedish Hospital. On admission Levertov claimed: "I feel so old."

Friends came to the hospital to visit and to read her stories like Eudora Welty's "Moon Lake," and her favorite poetry. Her lawyer came for a signature on her will and literary trust. Lee Kapfer came several times and anointed her, but she did not speak of death to anyone. Rather she insisted she would be leaving the hospital shortly. She had assured Gelpi that she would review her correspondence for the edition of the Duncan/Levertov letters as soon as she got out of the hospital, and advised Mark Jenkins not to visit, she would be home soon. Jan Wallace, her former secretary, was sent out to buy Christmas presents for those on her gift list.

She was in the hospital for ten days and after conferring with her doctors, including her friend Rick Rapport, Levertov agreed to a risky exploratory operation to remove part of her bowel. She underwent the operation and never regained consciousness but hung onto life with the assistance of a ventilator. In the chaos of grief, nine friends, unbelieving of what was happening, gathered at her bedside in lament to pray and read poetry. Nikolai spontaneously chanted one of his poems for her. She died on Saturday, December 20, 1997, at 6 P.M. The official cause of death was cardiac failure due to stomach and intestine necrosis, which resulted from lymphoma.[57] As she had written decades previously: the "music" "had stopped, and left / a heavy thick silence in its place." It was the eve of the winter solstice, that borderland in which darkness is gradually overcome by light.

As the world bustled with preparations for the impending Christmas holiday, word of Levertov's death spread quickly. Friends and colleagues, former students, allies of every sort, her devoted "public" were stunned and devastated by the news. Some knew she was ill with some unknown malady, but even to them the announcement of her death was unexpected. It seemed inconceivable that her fierce presence, her super-aliveness, was now gone.

Since she left no directions for a funeral, planning was done ex nihilo. Mark Jenkins took charge of arrangements for the mass at St. Joseph's and the burial at the nearby multifaith Lakeview Cemetery.

Given the Christmas holiday, the funeral was delayed until Friday, December 26th, a cold, gray, rainy day in Seattle. About one hundred people filed in for the 11:30 A.M. mass, a motley group of Christians, Jews, Buddhists, and unbelievers. There were friends and colleagues, former students, local parishioners, artists and poets, and the clutch of strays Levertov always collected. They were all there in their grief, but any other commonality among them was hard to find. Their presence reflected the breadth of her life and her ability to draw together the most diverse of friends. The opening hymn, "Go Down Moses," spoke to her prophetic Jewish ancestry. There were piano and cello music and readings from Isaiah, Paul's Letter to the Romans, Psalm 121, and the Gospel of Matthew. Craig Boly officiated and gave the homily, and Sam Green read his poem "Winter Solstice" as a meditation. David Shaddock, Jan Wallace, and Sam Hamill read poems and gave reflections.[58] On the cover of the program for the funeral mass was Levertov's poem "Poet and Person," a poignant selection for the occasion. It concludes with the words of a departing visitor: "When I leave, I leave / alone, as I came."[59]

After the service, a smaller group, clutching umbrellas and bundled against the cold, traveled to the nearby cemetery. Denise's body, dressed in the lovely dress with the French flower print she wore at the Port Townsend reading, was enclosed in a poplar coffin that was carried to the highest point in the cemetery by a group of pallbearers.[60] Under a sequoia tree and with a view of Lake Washington in the distance, her body was returned to the earth she loved so fiercely.[61] Some mourners left small stones at the site, tokens of their presence at the interment of their friend. It would take several years before the green granite gravestone, inscribed only with her name and dates, would be installed. At one point a friend left a miniature "Monkey" propped against that gravestone. Ultimately, Philip McCracken's sculpture "Stone Poem" would be affixed to the top of the monument, announcing to the passerby that here rested a poet.[62]

A group of mourners repaired to the home of Lou Oma Durand and Ken Patten after the burial, a few houses down the street from Levertov's residence. Some of her books, shards of her life, were passed around. It was all over quickly. Denise had left, and left alone. The gray day, the rain, the hidden mountain were typical of Seattle in December. The ordinariness of the day may have given some consolation to her bewildered friends.

The *New York Times*, the *Times of London*, and many other newspapers carried her obituary,[63] alerting friends across the country and in Europe of her death. Five memorial services were held, beginning with one at Stanford in late January 1998 at which Adrianne Rich, Albert Gelpi, and Eavan Boland gave comments; John and Mary Felstiner sang a motet; and statements were read from Creeley and Al Young. Boland, who organized the event with Gelpi, wrote that Levertov was "bright, definite, humane," "generous, irksome, courageous," a poet who in her works left behind her shining self.[64] The Seattle community turned out to honor her in February at the famed Eliot Bay Bookstore. Nikolai and poets Sam Hamill, Sam Green, Colleen McElroy, Emily Warn, Carolyn Kizer, and Wendell Berry, among others, were present. In March New Directions held a memorial service at St. Mark's in the Bowery, and Emmanuel Church hosted another service for Boston friends. Finally there was a service in San Francisco that included David Shaddock, Carlene Laughlin, Nikolai and his new companion Jalair Box, the Fussiners, Galway Kinnell, and others.[65] Individual poet friends wrote poems to honor her,[66] and Robert Creeley gave an address on her life and work to the American Academy of Arts and Letters describing her as having "presence" and a "stalwart integrity." For him she was "a wide-awake dreamer; a practical visionary with an indomitable will; a passionate, whimsical heart committed to an adamantly determined mind. It wasn't simply that Denise was right. It was that her steadfast commitments could accommodate no error."[67]

Other testimonials appeared in magazines and journals over the next year.[68] Stanford University established the Levertov Poetry Prize to be awarded for the best poem on the environment by a Stanford undergraduate,[69] and Seattle University and *Image* created the Levertov Award for an artist whose work exemplifies engagement with the Judeo-Christian tradition. All her books of poetry and prose were in print at that time, and her poems continued to be anthologized.

Her house was sold; her thousands of books dispersed, including almost four hundred volumes on religious topics; and her personal effects distributed. As if she were following Cézanne's admonition to "proceed," she had made numerous agreements for reading engagements for 1998;[70] all were canceled.

Denise Levertov was gone, but years earlier, intuiting a world of survival, she wrote: "Not farewell, not farewell but faring / / forth into the grace of transformed / continuance."[71] What remained, giving solace to her grieving friends, were their memories and her poetry. *Ars longa, vita brevis.*

EPILOGUE

[W]orks of art . . . are: testimonies of lived life.
"SOME AFFINITIES OF CONTENT."[1]

Denise Levertov wanted to be remembered for her poetry, the "autonomous structures" that would be appreciated on their own terms and would last. In comparison to her art, she considered her life fleeting and insignificant. As a consequence she was suspicious of biography and insisted that if a poet's biography were to be written, it had to focus on the work itself. Even then she was leery of the genre and recoiled from it.

Yet her actions suggest otherwise. She offered her archive to Stanford, although she claimed the sale of personal correspondence appalled her. She believed diaries were tools for self-reflection and hence private, at least while the author lived.[2] Yet she knew her diaries contained reflections and rages, desires and longings, and even revisited them and made sidebar notations. She knew what was contained in her archive,[3] and she surely must have recognized that future researchers would use these sources. In fact, occasionally she indicated she hoped they would.[4]

Ambivalent about biography as an aid to understanding her poetry, Levertov nonetheless claimed repeatedly that her poems emerged from her life experience. While she rejected confessional or self-referential writing, her poems, "testimonies of lived life," reflect her dialogical engagement with the world around her. Two of her Stanford colleagues spoke directly to this issue of the unity of her life and work. "When a poet dies," wrote Eavan Boland, "there is sometimes a rift between what they wrote and who they were. . . . Not so with Denise Levertov. I can think of few contemporary poets whose life and work were so connected."[5] John Felstiner called her one of the leading poets of the late twentieth century, whose influence would be felt for decades to come. "In my mind," he said, "she was a unique presence because in her more than any other poet I can think of, really since Yeats, everything came together in an organic whole — poetry, religion, history and politics, the natural world and people."[6]

Although there is no inherent contradiction between believing that poetry stands independent of a life and is simultaneously inspired by life circumstances, more seems to be at stake in Levertov's reluctance to have her life explored. She was adamant about her privacy, but, of course, she had much to be private about. Although she wrote a few autobiographical pieces and gave many interviews, in these contexts she could manage the outcome, either by limiting what she revealed or refusing to respond to questions posed by her interviewers, which she did on occasion. Because she carefully constructed an interpretation of her life, her ambivalence toward biography in part may have come from her reluctance to have that interpretation challenged. After all, biography, unlike autobiography or interview, cannot be controlled to the same degree by its subject.

A biography tracks the arc of a life over many decades, narrating a story as a subject lived it temporally, appreciating flaws, misjudgments, and achievements. It then translates life into art, and in so doing preserves it. Without the unity biography brings to disparate facts, a life would devolve into its various parts and disintegrate. Biography's mission is to rescue a life and make it accessible for future readers.

The complex life of Denise Levertov is illuminated if one is able to grasp her self-created "myth." That "myth," both consciously and unconsciously, serves as her organizing principle of interpretation, giving unity to her life choices, making them intelligible and significant, and providing both inspiration and consolation. In this sense "myth" is a gloss on a life as well as an aspiration to be lived into and potentially realized by the subject. The leitmotif that runs through Levertov's life is her vocation as poet, one chosen, gifted, and destined. She is not merely artist but "poet in the world," one whose prophetic role is to "awaken sleepers." At midlife this vocation is nuanced: she is a seeker. "I am," she wrote, "by nature, heritage and as an artist, forever a stranger and pilgrim."[7] Her final vocational expression is as witness, one who reveals glints of mystery in persons — Julian, Brother Lawrence, Caedmon, and Romero — or in nature — in the mountain and "the poor grass returning after drought, timid, persistent." It is to these various forms of wonder that she attests.

If vocation is Levertov's life "myth," the organizing principal of her art is the "double image" of joy and sorrow, which arises from her life itself. An early "wound" of rejection meant that she spent a lifetime attempting to understand and discover remedy for this hurt, to find intimate communion. She was propelled to pay attention to that which was around her, and as she brought it into herself it became a basis for wonder and ultimately for gratitude. These experiences of lament and exultation became subject for her art. Her poems were "testimonies" of this, her own "lived life."

A lure of biography, and one reason for its currency, is that it brings into focus the universal — Levertov would say — eternal questions. Although preoccupied with the issues of her times, she believed the most important sphere for exploration was the inner life where one wrestled with these questions. She wrote that it was in the inner life that "the most profound adventures, journeys of discovery, magical transformation take place."[8] She was convinced that this inner terrain was accessible to others through artistic expression. "The act of realizing inner experience in material substance," she wrote, "is in itself an action *toward others*. . . . Just as the activity of the artist gives body and future to 'the mysterious being hidden behind his eyes,' so the very fact of concrete manifestation, of paint, of words, reaches over beyond the world of inner dialogue."[9]

Even though her poetry might give access to her "mysterious being," she nonetheless guarded that access, arguing vehemently that no one, except herself, could know her motivation in writing a poem,[10] or that "[n]o one can ever hear or tell / the whole story"[11] of a life. Privacy was her watchword. Yet a year or so before her death she published the poem "What Goes Unsaid," which gives some evidence that she may have softened on this issue. She wrote:

> In each mind, even the most candid,
> there are forests, . . .
> . . . .
> In these forests there live certain events, shards
> of memory, scraps of once-heard lore, intimations
> once familiar — some painful, shameful, some
> drably or laughably inconsequent, . . .
> . . . .
> There they dwell, . . .
> . . . .
> It is right that there are these secrets . . .
> and these forests; privacies
> and the deep terrain to receive them.

Right that they rise at times into our ken,
and are acknowledged.[12]

While the "rising" of these "secrets" might be for oneself, it is the work of biography to bring these "forests" with their "privacies" into "our ken," not to unmask, but to understand.

This biography was undertaken as an experiment in penetrating the inner life of Denise Levertov. The voluminous raw materials — diaries, written and oral interviews, correspondence, poetry, and essays — allow the biographer to investigate and intuit, patch and paste, imagine and verify. To gain a closer, tauter hold on Levertov is to discover that she remains elusive, much like the mountain — present and absent, her person never fully grasped, but only pointed to and honored.

Denise Levertov will never have a definitive biography because her "inscape" can never be fully grasped. At the center of her own mystery was a vision of another mystery, "a quiet mystery," within all things. Present since childhood, her vision, sometimes inchoate and tangled, was gradually winnowed by life circumstances. Her response was that of "primary wonder." In her beginning was her end.

NOTES

PROLOGUE

1. Denise Levertov was known as Denny, Den, and Deno to friends and family. She was born Priscilla Denise Levertoff, but she never used her first name and changed her last name to Levertov in 1949.

2. The original of Eliot's letter was lost in one of Levertov's frequent moves, but a copy, dated April 24, 1936, was retained by Eliot. Ronald Schuchard, Goodrich C. White Professor of English at Emory University and editor of *The Complete Prose of T. S. Eliot*, forthcoming from Faber and Faber and The Johns Hopkins University Press, has allowed me to see this copy. Levertov consistently maintained that Eliot's letter was "lengthy," but in fact it was fairly abbreviated.

3. Rexroth, *Assays*, 190.

4. She was the recipient of many literary prizes and honorary doctoral degrees from ten American colleges and universities: Southern Connecticut University, Colby College, University of Cincinnati, Bates College, Saint Lawrence University, Allegheny College, St. Michael's College, Massachusetts College of Art, University of Santa Clara, and Seattle University.

5. Notebook, March 11, 1997, Denise Levertov Papers, M0601, Department of Special Collections, Stanford University Libraries, Palo Alto (hereafter DLP), Series 3, Box 11, Folder 8. Her friend and previous occupant of this position, Robert Hass, and others recommended her, but she declined the offer.

6. Pacernick, "Interview with Denise Levertov," 91.

7. "A Poet's View," *New and Selected Essays*, 241 (hereafter *NSE*). When no author is cited, assume that the prose or poetry is by Levertov.

8. "Horses with Wings," *NSE*, 119.

9. "Biography and the Poet," *NSE*, 172–85. In this she offers Walter Jackson Bate's *Keats* as a positive example of a biographical study of a poet and refers to the historian Iris Origo who wrote on the strengths and weakness of biography, 184.

10. "The Poet in the World," *The Poet in the World*, 112 (hereafter *PITW*).

11. Ian Reid, "'Everyman's Land,'" 74.

12. Pacernick, "Interview with Denise Levertov," 90.

13. Maureen Smith, "An Interview with Denise Levertov," 81.

14. Eavan Boland's blurb in support of *Denise Levertov: Selected Poems*. Back cover.

CHAPTER 1. "A DEFINITE AND PECULIAR DESTINY"

1. "The Sense of Pilgrimage," *PITW*, 67.

2. *Rav* means Rabbi, and consequently Zalman's followers would have referred to him as the Rav.

3. "Illustrious Ancestors," *Collected Earlier Poems 1940-1960*,77-78 (hereafter *CEP*). This volume contains early and uncollected poems and poems from *The Double Image*, *Here and Now*, *Overland to the Islands*, and *With Eyes at the Back of Our Heads*. Unless otherwise indicated, all poems cited are those of Denise Levertov.

4. Sources of information on Denise Levertov's ancestors, her family, and her early life are *Tesserae*, 4-11, 12-15, 43-46, 59-64, 65-71, 95-99, 108-9; "Autobiographical Sketch," *NSE*, 258-64. This was first published as "Denise Levertov" in 1984 in *The Bloodaxe Book of Contemporary Women Poets*, edited by Jeni Couzyn ; *Light Up the Cave*, 3-11, 233-37, 238-43, 244-53, 254-61, 279-82, 283-90 (hereafter *LUTC*); "Notes on Family–Paul, Beatrice, Olga," DLP, Series 3.2, Box 14, Folder 7; Quinonez, "Paul Phillip Levertoff," 21-34; *Conversations*, edited by Brooker, includes eighteen interviews with Levertov that contain significant autobiographical material.

5. Years later Denise Levertov wrote "An Arrival" (N. Wales, 1897) commemorating her mother's arrival at the home of the Olivers and her experience of being orphaned and alone. The poem was written for Kenneth Rexroth and first appeared in *For Rexroth*, 274-75.

6. Denise Levertov always made the claim that the connection to Zalman was through the paternal line and that Zalman was her father's great-grandfather. See "The Sack Full of Wings," *Tesserae*, 1. However, Beatrice Levertoff in an "Editorial," the *Church and the Jews*, writes of her husband: "To his father, his grandfather, and to his mother's uncle, the famous Rabbi Shnoer Salman, [*sic*] he felt he owed his own preparation."

7. "A Minor Role," "Denise Levertov," *Tesserae*, 11.

8. *Contemporary Authors Autobiography Series*, 229-46.

9. Ilford has changed substantially over the decades. Today it is a busy and densely populated outer suburb of London with multiple forms of transportation into the city. Its inhabitants represent great ethnic diversity. The Levertov home has now been broken up into four flats, and the front yard, which previously was the site of a garden, is now paved over and used for parking.

10. "Autobiographical Sketch," *NSE*, 259.

11. Pawlak, "Draft from Glover Circle Notebooks."

12. "The 90th Year," *Poems 1972-1982*, 97-98. This volume contains *Freeing of the Dust*, *Life in the Forest*, and *Candles in Babylon*.

13. Wagner-Martin, ed., "An American Poet with a Russian Name," in *Denise Levertov: In Her Own Province*, 79–83 (hereafter *DL Province*).

14. Estess, "Denise Levertov," 94.

15. Block, "Interview with Denise Levertov," 5.

16. "Autobiographical Sketch," *NSE*, 262.

17. "The Sense of Pilgrimage," *PITW*, 63.

18. In this typescript letter, April 24, 1936, Eliot indicated that he would not be publishing any of the poems she sent because, although interesting to him, she would find in a few years that they would be an embarrassment to her. What she needed now was to keep on writing and learning.

19. She refers to her Jewish heritage in two interviews: Andre, "Denise Levertov: An Interview," 61, and Estess, "Denise Levertov," 89–90.

20. In 1931 only 24 percent of girls in England were in fulltime education at age 14. See Todd, *Young Women's Work and Family*, 69. However, a much larger percentage would have been in formal schooling at an earlier age.

21. In *Tesserae* she mentions childhood friendships with Margaret Courtwell, Trixie Burnes, Jean Pilgrim, and Jean Rankin. None of these except Rankin is significant. Her childhood was largely solitary.

22. Levertov denied that she lacked early socialization, but the facts speak otherwise. See Zwicky, "An Interview with Denise Levertov," 111.

23. "The Last of Childhood," *Tesserae*, 59–64.

24. Tassel, "Poetic Justice in El Salvador," 125.

25. Zwicky, "An Interview with Denise Levertov," 111.

26. Specific reference to place are in "A Map of the Western Part of the County of Essex in England," "The Jacob's Ladder," *Poems 1960–1967*, 21, 39. This volume contains *The Jacob's Ladder*, *O Taste and See*, and *The Sorrow Dance*. See also McGowan, "Valentine Park," 3–15.

27. Block, "Interview," 6.

28. "Entertaining Angels Unawares," n.d., DLP, Series 2.2, Box 20, Folder 45.

29. Pacernick, "Interview with Denise Levertov," 91.

30. "Autobiographical Sketch," *NSE*, 260.

31. "Janus," *Tesserae*, 56.

32. "Growing Up, or When Anna Screamed," *LUTC*, 3–11.

33. Diary, September 22, 1980, n.p., DLP, Series 3, Box 7, Folder 1.

34. Notebook, 1967, DLP, Series 3, Box 1, Folder 8.

35. Diary, 1974, DLP, Series 3, Box 5, Folder 8.

36. Diary, 1963, DLP, Series 3, Box 13, Folder 4. See also "August Daybreak," *Breathing the Water*, 5 (hereafter *BTW*).

37. Diary, 1963, DLP, Series 3, Box 13, Folder 4.

38. Notebook, 1967, DLP, Series 3, Box 1, Folder 8.

39. "Autobiographical Sketch," *NSE*, 261.

40. Autobiographical Statement, 1962–65, DLP, Series 2.2, Box 20, Folder 13.

41. Diary, 1974, June 26, DLP, Series 3, Box 5, Folder 7.

42. It is unclear what happened to Olga, although some hints are provided in two archival entries. "Notes on Family — Olga," DLP, Series 3, Box 14, Folder 7, says that when Olga was about twelve and returned home from her partial year in boarding school, she secretly would visit an old priest at the Catholic church and lied about this to her parents. The Levertoffs thought the priest "dishonorable." In Notebook, 1967, DLP, Series 3, Box 1, Folder 8, Denise wrote that Fr. Noel was responsible for Olga's downfall.

43. In addition to Iris, the first born, Olga gave birth to Julian (later Julia), Thomas Richard (later Richard Thomas), and Frances (later Francesca).

44. It is difficult to know the truth of Olga's claims, but, in a long letter to her sister written two years before she died, Olga said that her difficulties during this period stemmed from economic problems resulting from blackmail. She writes that she was unable to expose the blackmailer because "my politics, and Daddy's reputation & fame, were too easily identifiable for the 'Mr. X' lark to have worked. That is why I was a victim, and that is why I had to choose to break Daddy's heart by bad behavior (apparent) & by letting him & Mother think me a worry and a selfish pig — or choose to have him broken much more seriously. I chose the former. I am sure I was right." Olga Levertoff to Denise Levertov, 1962, DLP, Series 1, Box 14, Folder 10.

45. "Notes on the Family — Olga," DLP, Series 3, Box 14, Folder 7.

46. Information from her time at the ballet school is contained in letters from Denise Levertov to her parents. Denise Levertov to Paul and Beatrice Levertoff, DLP, Series 1, Box 1, Folder 3, November–December 1939, Folder 5, July–December 1940, Folder 6.

47. "My Prelude," *LUTC*, 244-53.

48. "Herbert Read Remembered," *LUTC*, 233-37.

49. See Sutton, "A Conversation with Denise Levertov," 21, and Packard, "Craft Interview with Denise Levertov," 36.

50. "Dance Memories," *Poems 1968-1972*, 58. This volume contains *Relearning the Alphabet*, *To Stay Alive*, and *Footprints*.

51. Maureen Smith, "An Interview with Denise Levertov," 79-80.

52. Levertov recalls these years later in the poem "Advising Myself," *Sands of the Well*, 16 (hereafter *SOTW*).

53. See "Chekhov on the West Heath," *Poems 1972-1982*, 85-89, and "On Chekhov," *LUTC*, 279-82.

54. "The Dead," *CEP*, 103.

55. "Three Years," *DL Province*, 60-64.

56. Estess, "Denise Levertov," 88; "Denise Levertov," in *Contemporary Authors Autobiography Series*, 234-36. She mentions meeting Nicholas Moore, Sean Jennet, Alex Comfort, and Tambimmuttu, as well as Dannie Abse, Emanuel Litvinoff, and Keith Sawbridge.

57. Autobiographical Statement, c. 1983-84, DLP, Series 2,2, Box 20, Folder 16.

58. Diary c. 1951, DLP, Series 3, Box 1, Folder 10.

59. "Meeting Miss Noar," *Tesserae*, 77-79.

60. "Meeting and Not Meeting Artists," *Tesserae*, 74-83.

61. "Café Royal," *Tesserae*, 92. "Autobiographical Essay," DLP, Series 2.2, Box 20, Folder 14. In this Levertov confirms that Stephen, her former boyfriend, was in Geneva. Karnow in *Paris in the Fifties* confirms that this is Stephen Peet.

62. Diary, 1974 (separate pages), DLP, Series 3.1, Box 5, Folder 7; Diary, 1989-90, DLP, Series 3, Box 10, Folder 1. Peet remains a lifelong lover. Diary, 1974 (separate papers).

63. Written much after the fact, Beatrice Levertoff recalls in a letter that Denise mentioned that she hoped she was not pregnant after being with Stephen. Mrs. Levertoff indicates that at the time she felt like committing suicide, since this would replicate her experience with Olga. Beatrice Levertoff to Denise Levertov, April 5, 1975, DLP, Series 1, Box 6, Folder 19.

64. "Author's Note," *CEP*, viii.

65. Tassel, "Poetic Justice in El Salvador," 127. There is unwritten lore that she changed the spelling of her last name in order to Russify it.

66. Packard, "Craft Interview," 41.

67. "Childhood's End," *The Double Image*, 9 (hereafter *DI*).

68. Ibid., 24.

69. Ibid., 22.

70. "Primal Speech," *SOTW*, 95.

71. Rexroth, ed., *The New British Poets*.

72. Autobiographical Essay, DLP, Series 2.2, Box 20, Folder 14.

73. Rexroth, *Assays*, 189-90.

74. Notebook, DLP, Series 2.1, Box 1, Folder 4.

75. Levertov misspells the name of the town in her letters.

76. See "Denise Levertov," *Contemporary Authors Autobiography Series*, 236.

77. Denise Levertov to Paul and Beatrice Levertoff, July 22, 1940, DLP, Series 1, Box 1, Folder 5.

78. "Autobiographical Sketch," *NSE*, 263.

CHAPTER 2. IN SEARCH OF VOICE

1. Levertov to Williams, September 21, 1960, *The Letters of Denise Levertov and William Carlos Williams*, ed. McGowan, 100 (hereafter *Letters Levertov/Williams*).

2. Denise Levertov to Paul and Beatrice Levertoff, February 11, 1947, DLP, Series 1, Box 1, Folder 5.

3. Notebook, 1940-42, DLP, Series 2.1, Box 1, Folder 1.

4. "A Woman Meets an Old Lover," DLP, Series 2.1, Box 9, Folder 72, 1978. The final draft appeared in *Poems: 1972-1982*, 90.

5. Diary, c. 1951, January 23, 1952, DLP, Series 3, Box 1, Folder 10. Contains material from other years as well.

6. Diary, c. 1951, March 4, 1948, DLP, Series 3.1, Box 1, Folder 10.

7. "Recoveries," *LUTC*, 12-22.

8. Ibid., 21.

9. Interview with Lee Kafter, S.J. This was said by Levertov not in a confession but in the presence of others in the hospital at the end of her life.

10. "The Pardoner," *PITW*, 206-9.

11. Norman En Potter did subsequently marry Caroline.

12. Betty Mitchell to Denise Levertov, March 27, 1947, DLP, Series 4, Box 17, Folder 37.

13. Lerner, "Ecstasy of Attention," 1-25.

14. Hamalian, *A Life of Kenneth Rexroth*, 192. Hamalian quotes from a letter from Rexroth to Charles Wrey Gardiner, February 28, 1947.

15. Lerner, "Ecstasy of Attention," 13. Quoted from a letter of July 3, 1947, Denise Levertov to Kenneth Rexroth, UCLA Kenneth Rexroth Special Collection: 175, Series 1, Box 7, Folder Denise Levertov.

16. Hamalian, *A Life of Kenneth Rexroth*, 238, quotes from a letter from Kenneth Rexroth to Robert Creeley, July 1, 1951. Lerner, 14, cites this reference to UC Stanford: Robert Creeley Papers c. 1950-97, Collection M0601 Series 1, Subseries 1: 1950-97, Box 128, Folder 32, Kenneth Rexroth, June 30, 1951.

17. N. P. is Norman Potter, or "En" or "Colin," "Solace," *CEP*, 9.

18. Diary, 1988, July 4, 1988, DLP, Series 3, Box 9, Folder 6.

19. Denise Levertov to Paul and Beatrice Levertoff, July 2, 1947, DLP, Series 1, Box 1, Folder 13.

20. Ibid.

21. "The Voice," *Tesserae*, 100-102.

22. Denise Levertov to Paul and Beatrice Levertoff, August 20, 1947, DLP, Series 1, Box 1, Folder 13.

23. Karnow, *Paris in the Fifties*, 11.

24. Diary, c. 1951, December 17, 1950, DLP, Series 3, Box 1, Folder 10. My conjecture is this is 1950.

25. Denise Levertov to Paul and Beatrice Levertoff, August 20, 1947, DLP, Series 1, Box 1, Folder 13.

26. Denise Levertov to Paul and Beatrice Levertoff, October 20, 1947, DLP, Series 1, Box 1, Folder 13.

27. Diary, 1970, January 6, 1971, DLP, Series 3, Box 4, Folder 4. Although the diary is marked 1970, it contains subsequent entries. She is writing to review for herself her marital problems before discussing them with her analyst.

28. "Notes on Family–Beatrice, Paul," DLP, Series 3, Box 14, Folder 6, 54.

29. Mailer, *Armies of the Night*, 6-7.

30. "Some Duncan Letters — A Memoir and a Critical Tribute," *LUTC*, 196.

31. Ibid., 197.

32. "The Instant," *CEP*, 65-66.

33. Denise Levertoff to Paul and Beatrice Levertoff, May 30, 1948, DLP, Series 1, Box 1, Folder 18.

34. Denise Levertoff to Paul and Beatrice Levertoff, n.d., DLP, Series 1, Box 1, Folder 20.

35. Diary, c. 1951, March 4 and 23, 1948, DLP, Series 3, Box 1, Folder 10.

36. "An Innocent," *CEP*, 13-14.

37. "Kresch's Studio," *CEP*, 12.

38. For details on their early life in New York, see "Autobiographical Essay," DLP, Series 2.2, Box 20, Folder 13; Diary, c. 1951, January 7, 1949, DLP, Series 3.1, Box 1, Folder 10; Denise Levertov to Paul and Beatrice Levertoff, January 24, 1949, DLP, Series 1, Box 2, Folder 1.

39. There is no extant evidence that either the Levertoffs or Denise Levertov made any effort to track down these children. Tom Strudwick located them and wrote and visited them occasionally before he emigrated to Australia and then New Zealand.

40. According to Olga, she realized she could not care for her younger children and believed that it was best if she focused on her eldest daughter. Olga Levertoff to Denise Levertov and Mitchell Goodman, March 30–April 4, 1962, DLP, Series 1, Box 14, Folder 10.

41. Included were Levertov's poems: "Christmas 1944," "The Anteroom," "Folding A Shirt," "The Barricades," "Autumn Journey," and "Poem."

42. Hamalian, *A Life of Kenneth Rexroth*, 184-85.

43. Lerner, *Ecstasy of Attention*, 14, and Hamalian, *A Life of Kenneth Rexroth*, 238, quoting from a letter from Rexroth to Creeley, July 1, 1951, Washington University Library, St. Louis.

44. Lerner points out that Rexroth was an avid supporter of the work of Louise Bogan, Babette Deutsch, Mina Loy, Josephine Miles and Kathleen Raine. *Ecstasy of Attention*, 22-23.

45. "Who He Was," *CEP*, 11.

46. Diary, c. 1951, March 26, 1950, DLP, Series 3, Box 1, Folder 10.

47. Diary, c. 1951, December 17, 1950, DLP, Series 3, Box 1, Folder 10.

48. "Pilgrimage," *Tesserae*, 103-7.

49. Archer, "Denise Levertov and Paul Cézanne 'in Continuance,'" 155-76.

50. Creeley recalls their time together in an address to the American Academy of Art and Letters in 1998 reprinted as a preface to *Denise Levertov: Selected Poems*, xiv–xv.

51. See Fass, *Robert Creeley: A Biography*, including excerpts from the memoirs and 1944 diary of Ann MacKinnon, 383-87.

52. The poems that appeared in the 1953 issue of *Origin* were collected in *CEP*.

53. Fass, *Robert Creeley*, 97, 103, 152, 156, 277-80.

54. "15th Street," *CEP*, 16-17.

55. Denise Levertov to Mitchell Goodman, April 1953, DLP, Series 1, Box 4, Folder 29.

56. Denise Levertov to Paul and Beatrice Levertoff, January 19, 1953, DLP, Series 1, Box 3, Folder 14.

57. Denise Levertov to Mitchell Goodman, 1953, n.d., DLP, Series 1, Box 4, Folder 30.

58. The novel was finally published in 1961 by Horizon Press.

59. Sutton, "A Conversation with Denise Levertov," 21.

60. "The Sense of Pilgrimage," *PITW*, 67.

61. O'Connell, "A Poet's Valediction."

62. This was later entitled "Turning" and published in *CEP*, 63.

63. Duncan and Levertov, *The Letters of Robert Duncan and Denise Levertov*, 3-6 (hereafter *Letters Duncan/Levertov*).

64. This was reprinted in *CEP*, 60-61.

65. Creeley, "The Black Mountain Review," 505-14.

66. Some critics construe the Black Mountain poets narrowly. For example, Foster in *Understanding the Black Mountain Poets* includes only Olson, Creeley, and Duncan.

67. Denise Levertov to Paul and Beatrice Levertoff, May 1954, DLP, Series 1, Box 4, Folder 2.

68. Denise Levertov to Paul and Beatrice Levertoff, July 7 and 13, 1954, DLP, Series 1, Box 4, Folder 3.

69. Denise Levertov to Beatrice Levertoff, August 13, 1954, DLP, Series 1, Box 4, Folder 4, and Denise Levertov to Beatrice Levertoff, January–June 1955, Series 1, Box 4, Folder 8.

70. "In Obedience," *CEP*, 67-68.

71. Olga Levertoff, "The Ballad of My Father," *Poems 1960-1967*, by Levertov, 243-44.

72. Denise Levertov to Beatrice Levertoff, December 31, 1954, DLP, Series 1, Box 4, Folder 5.

73. Denise Levertov to Beatrice Levertoff, October–December 1954, DLP, Series 1, Box 4, Folder 5.

74. Denise Levertov to Beatrice Levertoff, January 20, 1955, DLP, Series 1, Box 4, Folder 8.

75. McCarthy, *Washington Post*, February 12, 1974.

76. Levertov to Williams, March 23, 1955, in *Letters Levertov/Williams*, 22.

77. Diary, 1956, June 28, 1956, DLP, Series 3.1, Box 2, Folder 1.

78. This is Levertov's conjecture. It seems unlikely that there was a formal diagnosis of Olga as a schizophrenic.

79. Levertov to Williams, August 25, 1954, in *Letters Levertov/Williams*, 14.

80. Letters from Mitch Goodman to Denise Levertov, 1953 and 1954, DLP, Series 1, Box 11, Folders 13 and 14.

81. Levertov to Bill and Floss Williams, March 12, 1956, in *Letters Levertov/Williams*, 32; and Levertov to Duncan, January 1956, in *Letters Duncan/Levertov*, 32-33.

82. Levertov to Duncan, January 15, 1957, in *Letters Duncan/Levertov*, 54-55.

83. "The Third Dimension," *CEP*, 46-47.

84. Pacernick, "Interview with Denise Levertov," 87.

85. Diary, 1970, DLP, Series 3, Box 4, Folder 4. Although the diary is marked 1970, subsequent entries are included.

86. "Rilke as Mentor," *LUTC*, 283. This essay was first given in 1975 as a conference paper and was subsequently reprinted first in *LUTC* and then in *NSE*. See also Zlotkowski, "Levertov and Rilke," 324-42.

87. "Williams and the Duende," *PITW*, 257.

88. Maureen Smith, "An Interview with Denise Levertov," 83.

89. Reid, "'Everyman's Land,'" 71.

90. "William Carlos Williams, 1883-1963," *PITW*, 254.

91. Reid, "'Everyman's Land,'" 68.

92. Williams to Levertov, March 21, 1956, in *Letters Levertov/Williams*, 36.

93. Adrienne Rich, Carolyn Kizer, Anne Sexton, Maxine Kumin, Sylvia Plath, and Muriel Rukeyser were her most immediate female poet contemporaries, all of whom would gain reputation in the 1960s.

94. In addition to the previous, see "On Williams' Triadic Line," "The Ideas in the Things," and "Williams and Eliot," *NSE*, 22-32, 44-58, 59-66, and "Williams and the Duende," *PITW*, 257-66.

95. "For Robert Duncan's Early Poems," *PITW*, 243, and "Some Duncan Letters," *LUTC*, 196-232.

96. Maureen Smith, "An Interview with Denise Levertov," 84.

97. Packard, "Craft Interview," 41.

CHAPTER 3. THE MAKING OF A POET

1. "Statement on Poetics," in *The New American Poetry*, ed. Allen, 411.

2. "A Meeting of Poets & Theologians," 31. See also "The Prayer," *Poems 1960-1967*, 147-48; "The Sense of Pilgrimage," 79.

3. Williams to Levertov, c. 1957, McGowan, ed., *Letters Levertov/Williams*, 69.

4. Williams to Levertov, April 9, 1960, *Letters Levertov/Williams*, 95.

5. Rodgers, *Denise Levertov: The Poetry of Engagement*, 19. Cited from an interview with William Carlos Williams. Transcriptions by John Thirlwall in *Interviews*, edited by Linda Wagner-Martin, 40. New York: New Directions, 1976.

6. Williams to Levertov, December 31, 1959, *Letters Levertov/Williams*, 92.

7. Appendix B, January 1, 1960, *Letters Levertov/Williams*, 152-53. Levertov applied for a Guggenheim twice and was finally successful in 1962.

8. *Overland to the Islands*, n.p. Duncan's preface was not included in *CEP*.

9. Rexroth, *Assays*, 231-33.

10. She details her early publication history in the author's note to *CEP*, vii-x.

11. Maureen Smith, "An Interview with Denise Levertov," 76.

12. Creeley, "Tribute," 5, and Creeley, "Remembering Denise," 81.

13. Rexroth, *Assays*, 231-33.

14. Mitchell Goodman to Denise Levertov, 1966, DLP, Series 1, Box 11, Folder 28.

15. Denise Levertov to Beatrice Levertoff, June 3, 1975, DLP, Series 1, Box 4, Folder 18.

16. This fresco is no longer extant in this massive Dominican church in Oaxaca.

17. "Five Poems from Mexico," *Poems 1960-1967*, 28-30.

18. "A Supermarket in Guadalajara, Mexico," *CEP*, 70.

19. "Scenes from the Life of the Peppertrees," *CEP*, 72-73.

20. Berger, "Of Love's Risen Body," 2, 50. Berger quotes from a 1961 letter from Merton to Mark Van Doren saying that he has seen this poem and found it "very fine, very spiritual in a broad, Jungian sort of way."

21. "The Artist," *CEP*, 84.

22. "Laying the Dust," *CEP*, 48.

23. "The Way Through," *CEP*, 56-57.

24. "Seems Like We Must Be Somewhere Else," *CEP*, 92.

25. "February Evening in New York," *CEP*, 101.

26. "Notes on a Scale," *CEP*, 103-4.

27. "Come Into Animal Presence," *Poems 1960-1967*, 23.

28. Allen Ginsberg to Lawrence Ferlinghetti, December 7, 1956, *The Letters of Allen Ginsberg*, 147, and Morgan, *The Typewriter Is Holy*, 123. Lafcadio Orlovsky was the brother of Peter Orlovsky, Ginsberg's partner of many years.

29. Levertov to Duncan, January 15, 1957, *Letters Duncan/Levertov*, 54-55.

30. Denise Levertov to Beatrice Levertov, June 3, 1975, DLP, Series 1, Box 4, Folder 18.

31. Mitchell Goodman to Denise Levertov, n.d., DLP, Series 1, Box 11, Folder 19, 1957.

32. Pope, "Homespun and Crazy Feathers," 73-97.

33. "The Earthwoman and the Waterwoman," *CEP*, 31-32.

34. "The Dogwood," *CEP*, 59-60.

35. "The Goddess," *CEP*, 110-11.

36. "Love Poem," "The Lovers," "The Marriage," *CEP*, 35, 44, 47.

37. "The Wife," *CEP*, 114.

38. Levertov to Duncan, January 1958, *Letters Duncan/Levertov*, 98.

39. Davidson, *The San Francisco Renaissance*, 172-74, 193. Davidson claims that Levertov's poem, "Hypocrite Women," was written not only in response to Spicer's poem but also in response to the male homosexual circle that dominated the San Francisco poets. He quotes from an undated and uncharacteristically frank interview with Levertov presumably given to Davidson (no documentation is given), which must have occurred prior to 1988. Davidson quotes Levertov in footnote 41, chapter 6, 239: "So for my poem, what I meant was that women (at that pre-Feminist, or at least pre–late-twentieth-century Feminist period) might also think that genitalia were not pretty, visually-but their *function* was not visual anyway, so why should they be. I said 'hypocrite' because the thought was one not commonly admitted. I

later came to see how much of women's self-deprecation came from macho male attitudes. That occasion was also my first exposure to homosexual males as a group — I had, and continue to have, individual homosexual friends but I find homosexual males and lesbians uncongenial in groups, when they reinforce each other's sexism toward heterosexuals." On this same incident and for an analysis of Levertov's views on female sexuality as expressed in her poetry, see Herrera, "Reappropriating Mirror Appropriations," 37-49.

40. Triem would become a lifelong friend. In 1960 she reviewed *With Eyes at the Back of Our Heads* for *Poetry*.

41. "Seems Like We Must Be Somewhere Else," "The Lost Black-and-White Cat," "The Dead," "Girlhood of Jane Harrison," "Another Journey," *CEP*, 92, 89, 103, 96, 95.

42. Levertov said that when she first came to the United States she tried to Americanize her speech. Later in life she made frequent trips to England and her speech took on a stronger English accent. Crouch, "Interview with Denise Levertov," 153.

43. Rexroth, "The Poetry of Denise Levertov," 11-14.

44. "Interweavings: Reflections on the Role of Dreams," *LUTC*, 34. She indicated that her poem "The Happening" expressed the trauma she experienced when returning to the city.

45. Levertov to Duncan and Jess Collins, March 18, 1958, *Letters Duncan/Levertov*, 102-4.

46. Levertov to Duncan and Collins, August 4, 1958, *Letters Duncan/Levertov*, 129.

47. Levertov to Williams, September 12, 1958, *Letters Levertov/Williams*, 80-81.

48. Carruth, "Review of *Overland to the Islands*," 20.

49. Mills, "Denise Levertov: Poetry of the Immediate," 98-110.

50. For points of similarity among Levertov, Rich, and Rukeyser, see DuPlessis, "The Critique of Consciousness and Myth," 218-42.

51. Albert Gelpi, chair of the English Department at Stanford, was instrumental in arranging Levertov's appointment to that faculty.

52. Hollenberg, "A Poet's Revolution." Hollenberg quotes from a letter from Levertov to Rich, August 17, 1960, held at The Schlesinger Library, Harvard University. Since these archives are not open to the public, my surmise is that Rich allowed Hollenberg to see this letter.

53. Rich's husband, Al Conrad, committed suicide in 1970, soon after the separation.

54. Levertov to Duncan, August 31, 1961, *Letters Duncan/Levertov*, 305.

55. Notebook, November 1957, DLP, Series 3, Box 2, Folder 2.

56. "On Muriel Rukeyser," *LUTC*, 189-95.

57. "The Unknown," *Poems 1960-1967*, 177-78.

58. "In Memory of Muriel Rukeyser," *Poems 1972-1982*, 249-52.

59. Levertov to Duncan and Jess Collins, February 23, 1960, *Letters Duncan/Levertov*, 242.

60. Pawlak, "Where the Highway Ends," 58-69.

61. Notebook, September 28, 1958, DLP, Series 3, Box 2, Folder 5, and Diary, December 1, 1961, Series 3.1, Box 2, Folder 8.

62. Diary, December 1, 1961, and Diary, April 2, 1962, DLP, Series 3.1, Box 2, Folder 8.

63. Denise Levertov to Beatrice Levertoff, March 1957, DLP, Series 1, Box 4, Folder 10.

64. Beatrice Levertoff lived at 313 Crespo with the Abascals. That house is now the Hotel Aitana, a four-star hotel with more than twenty rooms near the Church of Santo Domingo. Several blocks toward the zocalo is the Church of St. Philip Neri where Mrs. Levertoff attended services.

65. Diary, December 1, 1961, DLP, Series 3.1, Box 2, Folder 8.

66. Ibid.

67. "The Jacob's Ladder," *Poems 1960-1967*, 39.

68. "During the Eichmann Trial," *Poems 1960-1967*, 63-67. The only other poem related to Jewish persecution by the Nazis is her posthumously published poem, "Thinking about Paul Celan," in which she celebrates the life of this Jewish Romanian poet who suffered in a Nazi labor camp.

69. "Everything That Acts Is Actual," *CEP*, 43-44.

70. "Origins of a Poem," *PITW*, 53.

71. "A Common Ground," *Poems 1960-1967*, 5.

72. "Matins," *Poems 1960-1967*, 59-62.

73. "Three Meditations," *Poems 1960-1967*, 31-33. For a discussion of this poem see Miller, "Chelsea 8," 99-103.

74. "Origins of a Poem," *PITW*, 45.

75. "Three Meditations," *Poems 1960-1967*, 31-33.

76. "Homage," *CEP*, 42.

77. Duncan to Levertov, November 28, 1961, *Letters Duncan/Levertov*, 324-25.

78. Levertov to Williams, September 21, 1960, *Letters Levertov/Williams*, 99-101.

79. Hollenberg, "Within the World of Your Perception," 247-71.

80. "H. D.: An Appreciation," *PITW*, 244-48.

81. Although Levertov admitted that it had been a privilege to know H. D., after the posthumous publication of the poet's prose, she no longer held her in the same regard as she had previously. At the end of her life, Levertov refused to grant permission for her last letter to H. D., which closed with "I love you," to be published, lest her words be misunderstood. See Hollenberg, "Within the World of Your Perception," 247-71. Hollenberg includes in this article the letters between H. D. and Levertov as well as Levertov's letter to her in August 1997.

82. "A Poet's View," *NSE*, 246.

83. "September 1961," *Poems 1960-1967*, 81-83. After his release from the mental hospital in 1958, Pound returned to Italy where he died in 1972.

84. Levertov to Duncan, August 31, 1961, *Letters Duncan/Levertov*, 303-5.

85. "Overland to the Islands," *CEP*, 55.

86. Although not included in the first edition of Hall's *New Poets of England and America* published in 1957 and reprinted in 1959, Levertov did appear as one of the four women among thirty-nine poets in the 1962 edition published in New York by World.

87. Silliman, "Unerasing Early Levertov," 1. See Sheppard's Blog, June 27, 2008, www.reginaldsheppardblogspot.com/2008, for an exploration of the content and impact of this anthology (accessed December 5, 2011).

88. Shaddock, "Denise Levertov," *Poetry International*, 134-39.

89. Notebook, December 11, 1956, Series 1, Box 2, Folder 2.

90. "Statement on Poetics," *The New American Poetry*, ed. Allen, 411-12.

91. If Levertov made a theoretical contribution to the Black Mountain poets, it was her modification of Olson's dictum that form is never more than an *extension* of content. Her subtle but important restatement was that form is never more than a *revelation* of content.

92. "Denise Levertov," in *Contemporary Authors Autobiography Series*, 243.

CHAPTER 4. "A CATARACT FILMING OVER MY INNER EYES"

1. "From 'Writers Take Sides on Vietnam,' 1966," *PITW*, 119.

2. Ostriker, *Stealing the Language*, 15-58.

3. Notebook, August 18, 1962, DLP, Series 3, Box 2, Folder 10.

4. Ibid.

5. "Interweavings," *LUTC*, 35-36.

6. James Dickey to Denise Levertov, April 19, 1965, May 9, 1965, DLP, Series 4, Box 27, Folder 32 Denise Levertov to Robert Duncan, July 18, 1966; *Letters Duncan/Levertov*, 536-37.

7. Avison, "Interview with D. S. Martin," 334-35. Avison does not recount all details correctly.

8. Denise Levertov to Cid Corman, November 8, 1964, DLP, Series 4, Box 121, Folder 4. November 1966-70, April 8, 1966, May 9, 1966, Folder 5. Denise Levertov to Clayton, October 13, 1969, DLP, Series 4, Box 121, Folder 5. Folders 4 and 5 contain photocopies of Denise Levertov's correspondence from New York University Archives.

9. Hatlen, "Feminine Technologies," 9-14; Oppen, *The Selected Letters of George Oppen*. 57, 79-81; Levertov, "Who Is at My Window," *Poems 1960-1967*, 122. Levertov wrote a review of Oppen's *The Materials* in which she said his craft was in a desperate struggle with the intricacies of his sense of life and that his poems did not always "satisfy but they do stimulate." "Poetry: Pure and Complex," *New Leader*, 25-26.

10. Hollenberg, "'Dancing Edgeways,'" 5-16.

11. Olga Levertoff to Denise Levertov, July 31, 1963, DLP, Series 1, Box 14, Folder 10.

12. "Notes on Family—Olga," DLP, Series 3.2, Box 14, Folder 7, 71.

13. Beatrice Levertoff to Denise Levertov, April 11, 1964, DLP, Series 1, Box 5, Folder 28.

14. "The Untaught Teacher," *PITW*, 149.

15. "An Artist's Life," n.d., DLP, Series 5, Box 24, Folder 53.

16. Pawlak, "Draft: From Glover Circle Notebooks," 10.

17. "Denise Levertov," in *Contemporary Authors Autobiography Series*, 242-43.

18. Denise Levertov to her poetry class, July 15, 1966, Outgoing Correspondence, DLP, Series 4, Box 120, Folder 1. "The Untaught Teacher," *PITW*, 153-57.

19. "The Untaught Teacher," *PITW*, 171-80. Levertov inadvertently recorded incorrect dates for her time at Vassar. Cusac, "Remembering Denise Levertov"; Cusac, "Reading Levertov in Wartime"; Lacey, "Denise Levertov As Teacher," 90-107.

20. Mitchell Goodman to Denise Levertov, 1966, DLP, Series 1, Box 11, Folder 28.

21. Ossman, "Denise Levertov," 1-3.

22. "Origins of a Poem," *PITW*, 55.

23. Ibid., 54.

24. Ibid., 49.

25. "Asking the Fact for the Form," December 6, 1962, Wabash College, DLP, Series 2, Box 20, Folder 10.

26. Denise Levertov to Robert Duncan, August 29, 1962, *Letters Duncan/Levertov*, 368.

27. "Some Notes on Organic Form," *PITW*, 7-19.

28. Ibid., 7.

29. "A Further Definition," *PITW*, 14-15.

30. Albert Gelpi makes the argument that Levertov's clarification, although not fully explored in the early 1960s, would ultimately be an explanatory factor in the profound disagreements between Levertov and Robert Duncan. See Gelpi, "Poetic Language and Language Poetry," 180-98; and Denise Levertov to Robert Duncan, October 25–November 2, 1971, *Letters Duncan/Levertov*, 682.

31. Robert Duncan to Denise Levertov, October 15, 1965, *Letters Duncan/Levertov*, 510-11.

32. Robert Duncan to Denise Levertov, May 13, 1963, *Letters Duncan/Levertov*, 407.

33. "Line-Breaks, Stanza-Spaces, and the Inner Voice," *PITW*, 20-24.

34. Levertov clarifies the importance of the line-break in Crouch, "An Interview with Denise Levertov," 154-55.

35. "On the Function of the Line" and "Technique Tune-up," *LUTC*, 61-69 and 70-77.

36. This appeared in *Poems 1960-1967*, 55.

37. "Line-Breaks, Stanza-Spaces, and the Inner Voice," *PITW*, 20-22.

38. "Work and Inspiration: Inviting the Muse," *PITW*, 25-42.

39. "Notebook Pages," *PITW*, 17.

40. Gelpi, "Two Notes on Denise Levertov, 91-95"; *Poems 1960-1967*, 125.

41. "O Taste and See," *Poems 1960-1967*, 125.

42. "Earth Psalm," *Poems 1960-1967*, 152.

43. "Claritas," *Poems 1960-1967*, 107-8.

44. "The Runes," *Poems 1960-1967*, 155.

45. "The Song of Ishtar," *Poems 1960-1967*, 75. Ishtar is the Babylonian goddess of the moon to whom the pig is sacred. In this poem Levertov personifies Ishtar as sow and the poet as pig copulating together.

46. "In Mind," *Poems 1960-1967*, 143.

47. "Hypocrite Women," *Poems 1960-1967*, 142.

48. "The Ache of Marriage" and "About Marriage," *Poems 1960-1967*, 77, 140-41.

49. The emptiness of their marriage was captured in a short story, "In the Night," which was first published in 1966 and reprinted in *PITW*, 210-13.

50. Diary 1965, DLP, Series 3, Box 3, Folder 4, 38-40.

51. Denise Levertov to Terry Crouch, December 5, 1988, DLP, Series 4, Box 117, Folder 35.

52. Notebook, July 1962, DLP, Series 3, Box 2, Folder 10.

53. Denise Levertov to Robert Duncan, October 21, 1964, *Letters Duncan/Levertov*, 479-80.

54. Robert Duncan to Denise Levertov, November 10, 1964, *Letters Duncan/Levertov*, 481-82.

55. Diary, June 16/17, 1965, DLP, Series 3, Box 3, Folder 4, 86.

56. Denise Levertov to Robert Duncan, April 19, 1966, *Letters Duncan/Levertov*, 525.

57. Denise Levertov to Robert Duncan, August 19-20, 1966, *Letters Duncan/Levertov*, 545-47; "For Robert Duncan's Early Poems," *PITW*, 243.

58. Lorrie Smith, "An Interview with Denise Levertov," 135.

59. FBI file 1143363-000 was declassified and made available under the Freedom of Information Act. From 1962-1974, some of the activities of Goodman were monitored. The file includes articles by him, speeches given, meetings and rallies attended, organizational memberships, and passport information. Levertov's activities are included as part of Goodman's file but include only her letters to newspapers and petitions signed. Sent by David M. Hardy, Section Chief, Records Management Division of the FBI, May 10, 2010.

60. Finn, "Mitchell Goodman and Denise Levertov," in *Protest: Pacifism and Politics*, 463-79.

61. Ibid., 471.

62. "Life at War," *Poems 1960-1967*, 229-30.

63. Diary, June 8, 9, 15, 1965, DLP, Series 3, Box 3, Folder 4.

64. Diary, 1963, DLP, Series 3, Box 13, Folder 5.

65. Diary, 1965 and 1966, DLP, Series 3, Box 13, Folder 6, 62-65.

66. Notebook, 1967, DLP, Series 3, Box 3, Folder 8.

67. Diary, June 15, 1965, DLP, Series 3, Box 3, Folder 4.

68. Denise Levertov to Robert Duncan and Jess Collins, February 5, 1967, *Letters Duncan/Levertov*, 566-67.

69. These sentiments are expressed throughout the archival material. See Notebook, 1967, DLP, Series 3, Box 1, Folder 8; and Notebook, Easter 1982–May 1983, DLP, Series 3, Box 7, Folder 7.

70. Notebook, August 10, 1962, DLP, Series 3, Box 2, Folder 10.

71. Ibid.

72. Notes on Family — "Olga," DLP, Series 3, Box 14, Folder 7, 71.

73. During the last months of her life, Olga was cared for by Harry Green, a warm-hearted, gentle Jew of Russian heritage, whom she met in 1954. They were lovers, but Olga considered their relationship a marriage. It might have been Green who had the Star of David carved on Olga's headstone. Olga Levertoff to Denise Levertov and Mitchell Goodman, March 30–April 4, 1962, DLP, Series 1, Box 14, Folder 10.

74. "Olga Poems," *Poems 1960-1967*, 210.

75. "A Note to Olga," *Poems 1960-1967*, 238-39.

76. In 1967, her work was anthologized, along with that of Rexroth and Williams, in the *Penguin Modern Poets-9*.

77. *In Praise of Krishna: Songs of the Bengali*. See also Dimock, "Levertov and the Bengali Love Songs," 282-87.

78. In addition to this Bengali translation, Levertov would translate the poems of Bulgarian, French, German, Russian, and Spanish poets.

79. "On the Edge of Darkness: What Is Political Poetry?" *LUTC*, 115-29.

80. "The Mutes," *Poems 1960-1967*, 196-97.

81. "Psalm Concerning the Castle," *Poems 1960-1967*, 217.

82. Denise Levertov to George Quasha, February 27, 1969 (misdated as 1968), Outgoing Correspondence, DLP, Series 4, Box 120, Folder 2 (letter was not sent); "City Psalm," *Poems 1960-1967*, 222.

83. Bly [Crunk, pseud.], "The World of Denise Levertov," 48-65.

84. "The Poet in the World," *PITW*, 114.

85. "Grass Seed and Cherry Stones," *PITW*, 249-53. Although Pound died in 1972, as late as 1979 Levertov was defending him as "insane" and hence not responsible for his views. See Zwicky, "An Interview with Denise Levertov," 115-16; and Hollenberg, "'Obscure Directions,'" 737-50.

86. Maureen Smith, "An Interview with Denise Levertov," 85.

87. "A Sense of Pilgrimage," *PITW*, 80.

88. Stoneburner, ed., *A Meeting of Poets & Theologians*, 14-15. See also Wilder, *Theopoetic: Theology and the Religious Imagination*.

89. Mitford, *The Trial of Dr. Spock*, 30-34, and Burrows, "Politics and the Poet," 28-34.

90. To RESIST, December 1967, *Letters Duncan/Levertov*, 597-602.

91. Thomas Merton to Ernesto Cardenal, October 14, 1961, in *The Courage for Truth*, 127.

92. Berger, "Of Love's Risen Body," 50.

93. Merton, *The Other Side of the Mountain*, 7, 22.

94. Denise Levertov to Czeslaw Milosz, May 9, 1997, Czeslaw Milosz Papers, Beinecke Rare Book and Manuscript Library, Yale University, GEN MSS 661, Folder 572 (used with permission).

95. Apparently Merton sent two brief business notes to Levertov, but these are no longer extant. Thomas Merton Correspondence with Denise Levertov, Bellarmine Merton Collection.

96. "On a Theme by Thomas Merton," *Evening Train*, 113 (hereafter *ET*).

97. Burrows, "Politics and the Poet," 30-31.

98. "Advent 1966," *Poems 1968-1972*, 124.

CHAPTER 5. "STAYING ALIVE"

1. Diary, January 18, 1969, DLP, Series 3, Box 3, Folder 9.

2. Diary, January 14, 1969, DLP, Series 3.1, Box 3, Folder 9.

3. Denise Levertov to Robert Duncan, December 2, 1968, *Letters Duncan/Levertov*, 623-24.

4. In 1968 the following were published: *A Tree Telling of Orpheus, A Marigold from North Vietnam, Three Poems*, and *The Cold Spring and Other Poems*. Respectively, these poems were included in *Poems 1968-1972*, 79-83, 65, 28, 60, 6-10.

5. Gallant, "Entering No-Man's Land," 124-25, and Kallet, "Moistening Our Roots with Music," 305-23.

6. "An Interim," *Poems 1968-1972*, 20-27.

7. Mitford, *The Trial of Dr. Spock*, 208; "Mitchell Goodman," Obituary, *New York Times*, February 6, 1997.

8. Diary, August 11, 1968, DLP, Series 3, Box 3, Folder 9.

9. "Mad Song," *Poems 1968-1972*, 47.

10. "July 1968," *Poems 1968-1972*, 62.

11. Diary, July 15, 1968, August 11, 1968, DLP, Series 3, Box 3, Folder 9.

12. George Quasha to Denise Levertov, October 26, 1968, DLP, Series 4, Box 84, Folder 4.

13. Diary, November 17, 19, and 20, 1968, DLP, Series 3, Box 3, Folder 9.

14. Diary, December 2, 1968, DLP, Series 3, Box 3, Folder 9.

15. Denise Levertov to Robert Duncan, December 2, 1968, *Letters Duncan/Levertov*, 622-24.

16. Diary, January 14, 1969, DLP, Series 3, Box 3, Folder 9.

17. Diary, January 18, 1969, DLP, Series 3, Box 3, Folder 9.

18. George Quasha to Denise Levertov, April 27, 1969, DLP, Series 4, Box 84, Folder 6.

19. George Quasha to Denise Levertov, February 2 and 18, 1969, and March 14, 1969, DLP, Series 4, Box 84, Folder 5; April 27, 1969, May 28, 1969, June 21, 1969, and August 17, 1969, Quasha to Levertov, OLP, Series 4, Box 84, Folder 6.

20. Levertov, introduction to *Selected Poems*, by Guillevic; vii–xx. See also Schwartz, "Guillevic/Levertov," 290-98.

21. Levertov's translations of poems by Marina Tsvetayeva and Boris Poplavsky were published in *Poets on Streetcorners: Portraits of Fifteen Russian Poets. Embroideries* pointed to themes in her earlier poetry: the divided self, and joy and sorrow intertwined. These poems were included in *Poems 1968-1972*, 31-36.

22. Lorrie Smith, "Songs of Experience," 177-97.

23. "Relearning the Alphabet," *Poems 1968-1972*, 92.

24. Zweig, "Magistral Strokes and First Steps," 794-95.

25. Contoski, "Review of *Relearning the Alphabet*," 28-30.

26. Quinn, "Review of *Relearning the Alphabet*," 27-28.

27. Gitlin, "The Return of Political Poetry," 375-78.

28. "The Untaught Teacher," *PITW*, 187-99.

29. Denise Levertov to George Quasha, Outgoing Correspondence, February 27, 1969, and March 2, 1969, DLP, Series 4, Box 120, Folder 2. (The February 27 letter is incorrectly cataloged as 1968.)

30. One student of this period was Rae Armantrout who went on to receive the Pulitzer Prize for Poetry in 2010. Armantrout cites Levertov as her teacher, although they came to have divergent views.

31. For a long description of social activism at Berkeley in the 1960s by an eyewitness to the events of People's Park, see Watten, "The Turn to Language and the 1960s," 177-83.

32. Interview with David Shaddock, April 27 and May 18, 2011.

33. "Part III — Staying Alive," *Poems 1968-1972*, 151-53.

34. Shurin, "The People's P***k," in *Robert Duncan and Denise Levertov*, 71-80.

35. Denise Levertov to Robert Duncan, July 5, 1969, *Letters Duncan/Levertov*, 634-35. Quasha went on to become a poet, sculptor, teacher and founder of Station Hills Press.

36. *Summer Poems* was reprinted in *Poems 1968-1972*.

37. *A New Year's Garland for My Students/MIT: 1969-70* was first published in 1970 and reprinted in *Poems 1968-1972*, 212-19.

38. Pawlak, "Where the Highway Ends," 58-69.

39. Introduction to *The Wedding Feast*, by Edelman, 9-10.

40. "'Let Us Sing unto the Lord a New Song,'" *Poems 1968-1972*, 180-81.

41. "At the Justice Department, November 15, 1969," *Poems 1968-1972*, 156.

42. Denise Levertov to Robert Duncan, October 25–November 2, 1971, *Letters Duncan/Levertov*, 681.

43. "Great Possessions," *PITW*, 89-106.

44. Ibid., 97. Levertov gives no source for this quotation from Rilke.

45. "Speech for a Rally, 1970," *PITW*, 121-22.

46. Denise Levertov to Robert Duncan, October 25–November 2, 1971, *Letters Duncan/Levertov*, 681.

47. "The Day the Audience Walked Out on Me, and Why," *Poems 1968-1972*, 220-21.

48. "Part III — Staying Alive," *Poems 1968-1972*, 166-79.

49. Ibid., 179.

50. "The Well," *Poems 1960-1967*, 40-41.

51. Diary, 1970, DLP, Series 3, Box 4, Folder 5.

52. Goodman, *The Movement toward a New America*.

53. Pawlak, "Where the Highway Ends," 58-69. Goodman's insecurity and low self-esteem in his relationship with Levertov are confirmed by Pawlak who knew both of them.

54. Diary, 1970, December 27, January 5, 1971, January 6, 1971, DLP, Series 3, Box 4, Folder 4.

55. Denise Levertov to Richard Edelman, c. 1970, DLP, Series 4, Box 117, Folder 38 (letter not mailed).

56. Ibid.

57. "Conversation in Moscow," *Poems 1972-1982*, 55-61. Interview, Hallisey, July 29, 2009, who explained the importance of this conversation for Levertov.

58. Mitchell Goodman to Denise Levertov, March 29, 1971, DLP, Series 1, Box 11, Folder 30.

59. Denise Levertov to Beatrice Levertoff, September 11, 1971, DLP, Series 1, Box 4, Folder 15.

60. Mitchell Goodman to Denise Levertov, August 23 and 26, 1971, DLP, Series 1, Box 11, Folder 31.

61. See Pawlak, "Draft from Glover Circle Notebooks." In an undated 1975 entry, he refers to Levertov's comment that *To Stay Alive* was like a collage, analogous to a painting of Juan Gris in which he would glue an actual bus ticket to his canvas of a Paris street scene rather than paint the ticket.

62. Gish, "Feminism, Poetry, and the Church," 181.

63. "Author's Preface, 1971," *To Stay Alive*, 105-7.

64. "Part I — Staying Alive," *Poems 1968-1972*, 137-43.

65. Ibid., 191.

66. Carruth, "Levertov," 30-31.

67. Borroff, "Review of *To Stay Alive*," 30-31.

68. Perloff, "Poetry Chronicle, 1970-71," 114.

69. Mersmann, "Denise Levertov," 77-112.

70. Altieri, "Denise Levertov and the Limits of the Aesthetics of Presence," 126-47.

71. Lacey, "The Poetry of Political Anguish," 187-96.

72. Lorrie Smith, "Songs of Experience," 177-97.

73. Carruth, "Levertov," 33-35.

74. Robert Duncan to Denise Levertov, October 19, 1971, *Letters Duncan/Lever-tov*, 669.

75. Herrera, "Linguistic vs Organic," 41-61.

76. Bertholf and Gelpi, eds., Introduction, *Letters Duncan/Levertov*, ix–xxxi, and Gelpi, "Poetic Language and Language Poetry," 180-98.

77. Bertholf, "The Robert Duncan/Denise Levertov Correspondence."

78. Dewey, *Beyond Maximus*, 120-53, and Dewey, "Poetic Authority," 109-25.

79. Felstiner, "The Hasid and the Kabbalist," 81-89; Rudolph Nelson, "Edge of the Transcendent," 96-109, and Aiken, "Denise Levertov, Robert Duncan, and Allen Ginsberg," 132-47.

80. Aiken, "Denise Levertov, Robert Duncan, and Allen Ginsberg," 132-47.

81. Robert Duncan to Denise Levertov and Mitch Goodman, March 30, 1968, *Letters Duncan/Levertov*, 607.

82. Robert Duncan to Denise Levertov and Mitch Goodman, June 19, 1968, *Letters Duncan/Levertov*, 610-13.

83. Denise Levertov to Robert Duncan and Jess Collins, February 22, 1970, *Letters Duncan/Levertov*, 645-47.

84. Duncan, "Santa Cruz Propositions," 237-41.

85. Denise Levertov to Robert Duncan, January 9, 1971, *Letters Duncan/Levertov*, 658.

86. "Part IV — Report," *Poems 1968-1972*, 188.

87. Robert Duncan to Denise Levertov, October 4, 1971, *Letters Duncan/Levertov*, 660-62.

88. Denise Levertov to Robert Duncan, October 1971, *Letters Duncan/Levertov*, 662.

89. Robert Duncan to Denise Levertov, October 16, 1971, *Letters Duncan/Levertov*, 663-64.

90. Robert Duncan to Denise Levertov, October 19–November 3, 1971, *Letters Duncan/Levertov*, 664-74.

91. Denise Levertov to Robert Duncan, October 25–November 2, 1991, *Letters Duncan/Levertov*, 674-86. Here Levertov is appealing not to her own or society's Christian belief but rather to a Christian source for the secular notion of human goodness.

92. Robert Duncan to Denise Levertov, November 9, 1971, *Letters Duncan/Levertov*, 691-92.

93. Denise Levertov to Robert Duncan, November 9, 1971, *Letters Duncan/Levertov*, 692-93.

94. Denise Levertov to Robert Duncan, August 16, 1972, *Letters Duncan/Levertov*, 705-7.

95. Reid, "'Everyman's Land,'" 73.

96. Ibid., 74.

CHAPTER 6. ENDINGS

1. "The Wealth of the Destitute," *Poems 1972-1982*, 73. Levertov borrowed "the

fine art of unhappiness" from William Morris, who condemned his aesthete friends for cultivating this orientation. See "Dying and Living," *LUTC*, 108.

2. "To Kevin O'Leary, Wherever He Is," *Poems 1968–1972*, 220. Kevin O'Leary was a student of Levertov's at MIT.

3. This trip was made in October and November of 1972 at the invitation of the Union of Women and The Committee for Solidarity with the American People.

4. "Glimpses of Vietnamese Life," *PITW*, 129–45.

5. "A Poem at Christmas, 1972, during the Terror-Bombing of North Vietnam," *Poems 1972–1982*, 24.

6. Tassel, "Poetic Justice in El Salvador," 130–31. In this case, Levertov is discussing her essay "Solzhenitsyn Reconsidered," which was written in 1974 at about the same time.

7. "Modes of Being," *Poems 1972–1982*, 64–65.

8. "With the Seabrook Natural Guard in Washington, 1978," *LUTC*, 165.

9. Diary c. December 29, 1972, DLP, Series 3.1, Box 5, Folder 2.

10. Robert Duncan to Denise Levertov, December 13, 1973, *Letters Duncan/Levertov*, 711.

11. Mersmann, "Denise Levertov," 94.

12. Bertholf, "From Robert Duncan's Notebooks," Notebook 47, July 25, 1973, 4:20 A.M.

13. "Some Duncan Letters," was written in 1975 and appeared in Bertholf and Reid, *Robert Duncan*, and was reprinted in *LUTC*, 196–232.

14. "Crosspurposes," *Poems 1972–1982*, 33–35.

15. Diary, January 29–30, 1973, DLP, Series 3, Box 5, Folder 3.

16. Denise Levertov to Beatrice Levertoff, February 23, 1973, DLP, Series 1, Box 4, Folder 16.

17. Pawlak, "Where the Highway Ends," 66–67. I was unable to interview Sandy Gregor, who died in October 2009.

18. Levertov gave the commencement address at the university that year.

19. Pawlak, "Where the Highway Ends," 68.

20. Diary, 1972, DLP, Series 3, Box 5, Folder 3.

21. Richard Edelman to Denise Levertov, DLP, Series 4, Box 32, Folders 19–23.

22. Diary, 1974, n.d., DLP, Series 3, Box 5, Folder 7.

23. "On Friends and Lovers," c. 1975, DLP, Series 2.2, Box 23, Folder 44.

24. Reid, "'Everyman's Land,'" 68–75.

25. Ian Reid to Denise Levertov, DLP, Series 4, Box 86, Folders 27, 32, 33, 34, 35, 36. Special Collections of Flinders University Library, Australia, contains a cache of Levertov's letters to Reid. Although I have not read these materials, I have used Reid's comments contained in two emails sent to me on July 30 and August 3, 2011, as well as Levertov's diaries.

26. This was first published independently in 1977 and then included in *Poems 1972–1982*, 128–47.

27. "Epilogue," *Poems 1972-1982*, 147; Diary, August 7, 1975, DLP, Series 3, Box 5, Folder 8.

28. Diary, August 25, 1974, DLP, Series 3.1, Box 5, Folder 7.

29. Levertov wrote a third-person description of this decision with its accompanying euphoria and pain in "A Woman's Document," *LUTC*, 23-25.

30. Mitch Goodman to Denise Goodman, February 24, 1975, DLP, Series 1, Box 11, Folder 35.

31. Although Levertov frankly admitted several sexual liaisons during this period and although she would have liked to have had one with Edelman, she indicates she did not.

32. Mitch Goodman to Denise Goodman, February 24, 1975, DLP, Series 1, Box 11, Folder 35.

33. Mitch Goodman to Deno, March 4, 1975, DLP, Series 1, Box 11, Folder 35.

34. Diary, Christmas 1974, DLP, Series 3.1, Box 5, Folder 8. In "A Woman's Document," an admittedly fictive piece written in 1974, she discusses a divorce. In this she claims the decision to divorce was made soberly and without rancor and that the decision was mutual. *LUTC*, 23-25.

35. Mitch Goodman to Denise Levertov, July–December 1975, DLP, Series 1, Box 11, Folders 35 and 36. Levertov's income in 1975 was about thirty thousand dollars.

36. Diary, 1974, DLP, Series 3, Box 5, Folder 8.

37. Letters from Jon Lipsky to Denise Levertov, c. 1975- 1986 and 1991-1995, DLP, Series 4, Box 66, Folders 5 and 6; Diary, 1974, DLP, Series 3, Box 5, Folder 8. Jon Lipsky died in March 2011, before I was able to contact him.

38. Diaries, 1974, DLP, Series 3, Box 5, Folders 7 and 8.

39. "The Woman," *Poems 1972-1982*, 32.

40. "Divorcing," *Poems 1972-1982*, 41.

41. "Prayer for Revolutionary Love," *Poems 1972-1982*, 63. This poem was written for Richard Edelman and his intended.

42. "A Woman Alone" was written in 1975 but was not published until 1978 in her next book of poetry, *Life in the Forest; Poems 1972-1982*, 90-91.

43. "A Woman Meets an Old Lover," *Poems 1972-1982*, 90.

44. Diary, 1988, July 4, 1988, DLP, Series 3, Box 9, Folder 6. In this entry she records meeting En in 1976.

45. "By Rail through the Earthly Paradise, Perhaps Bedfordshire," *Poems 1968-1972*, 240-41.

46. "The Life around Us," *Poems 1968-1972*, 251.

47. Mills, "Review of *Footprints*," 219-21.

48. Perloff, "The Corn-Porn Lyric: Poetry, 1972-73," 108. It is debatable whether this characterization of the poems of *Footprints* is appropriate. What is obvious in this review and elsewhere is that Perloff had deep disagreements with Levertov's poetics.

49. Ignatow, "Review of *The Freeing of the Dust*," 35-36.

50. Quoted in Gould, *Modern American Women Poets*, 49.

51. Wagner-Martin, "Levertov As Poet," 6. She offers no evidence for this position although it is not totally suspect.

52. Hoerchner, "Denise Levertov: Review of *The Poet in the World*," *Contemporary Literature*, 435-37, and Woodcock, "Pilgrimage of a Poet," 19-20.

53. These include "The Sense of Pilgrimage," "Great Possessions," "Some Notes on Organic Form," "Origins of a Poem," "The Poet in the World," and "Work and Inspiration: Inviting the Muse."

54. Wagner-Martin, "Matters of the Here and Now," 795-96.

55. Carruth, "Levertov," 30-35.

56. "A Testament and a Postscript," *PITW*, 3-6.

CHAPTER 7. COMING TO A NEW COUNTRY

1. "Beginners," *Poems 1972-1982*, 244-45.

2. Thurston, "'Acts of Faith,'" 130-37. Thurston points out similarities between Weil and Levertov.

3. Diary, 1974, DLP, Series 3, Box 5, Folder 8. Levertov had been at Yaddo, May 8–June 7, 1975, and returned again December 15-30, 1975, when the colony was under the direction of Curtis Harnack.

4. Estess, "Denise Levertov," 100.

5. Mitch Goodman to Denise Levertov, July–December 1975, DLP, Series 1, Box 11, Folder 36.

6. Sandy Gregor to Denise Levertov, July 15, 1978, DLP, Series 1, Box 15, Folder 10.

7. Mitch Goodman to Denise Levertov, n.d., DLP, Series 1, Box 12, Folder 8.

8. Denise Levertov to Nikolai Goodman, June 12, 1977, DLP, Series 1, Box 4, Folder 37.

9. Diary, 1980, July 15, 1980, DLP, Series 3, Box 7, Folder 1.

10. Mitch Goodman to Beatrice Levertoff (Janie), DLP, Series 1, Box 13, Folder 1.

11. The Denise Levertov Papers are open; however, a few letters from this period have been sequestered to protect living family members.

12. Diary, 1974, DLP, Series 3, Box 5, Folder 8.

13. Denise Levertov to Beatrice Levertoff, April 17, 1975, DLP, Series 1, Box 4, Folder 18.

14. Diary, April 29, 1973, DLP, Series 1, Box 28, Folder 5.

15. "Beatrice Levertoff," *LUTC*, 238-43. See also "An American Poet with a Russian Name," *DL Province*, 79-83.

16. Beatrice Levertoff to Denise Levertov, January 14, 1975, DLP, Series 1, Box 6, Folder 19.

17. Diary, Easter 1982–May 19, 1983, DLP, Series 3, Box 7, Folder 7, 36-38.

18. Diary, 1974, DLP, Series 3, Box 5, Folder 8.

19. Beatrice Levertoff to Denise Levertov, April 5, 1975, DLP, Series 1, Box 6, Folder 19.

20. Denise Levertov to Beatrice Levertoff, April 17, 1975, DLP, Series 1, Box 4, Folder 18.

21. "The 90th Year," *Poems 1972-1982*, 97-98.

22. Beatrice Levertoff to Denise Levertov, June 29, 1973, DLP, Series 1, Box 6, Folder 15.

23. "On Muriel Rukeyser," *LUTC*, 194.

24. Adrienne Rich to Denise Levertov, December 21, 1978, DLP, Series 4, Box 87, Folder 23. Adrienne Rich's correspondence with Levertov is housed in the Schlesinger Library at Radcliffe but is not open to the public at this time.

25. Alice Walker to Denise Levertov, DLP, Series 4, Box 104, Folder 39; "The Long Way Round," *Poems 1972-1982*, 119-22. Walker's archive is housed at Emory University but contains no correspondence between her and Levertov. When asked to be interviewed, Walker demurred.

26. "A Daughter (I)," *Poems 1972-1982*, 98-101.

27. "A Daughter (II)," *Poems 1972-1982*, 101-3.

28. "A Soul-Cake," *Poems 1972-1982*, 109-10.

29. "Death Psalm: O Lord of Mysteries," *Poems 1972-1982*, 107-9.

30. "Death in Mexico," *Poems 1972-1982*, 103-5.

31. Diary, 1977-78, DLP, Series 3, Box 6, Folder 5.

32. "Anguish," DLP, Series 2, Box 20, Folder 5.

33. "Chekhov on the West Heath" was first published independently in 1977 and appeared subsequently in *Poems 1972-1982*, 85-89. See also "On Chekhov," *LUTC*, 279-82, and Christensen, "Chekhov in the Poetry of Howard Moss and Denise Levertov," 51-62.

34. "Blake's Baptismal Font," *Poems 1972-1982*, 158-59.

35. "Address to the International Meeting of Writers, Sofia Bulgaria, Sept. 18, 1980," and "Address to the Commission on the Environment and Energy at the World Peace Parliament, Sofia, Sept. 24, 1980," *LUTC*, 181-84 and 178-81.

36. Tom Strudwick, their father, left for Australia and then New Zealand after he and Olga separated five or six years into their relationship. At least episodically, Strudwick kept in touch with his son.

37. Iris Glanville-Levers to Denise Levertov, DLP, Series 1, Box 14, Folders 19-20; Julia Strudwick to Denise Levertov, Box 15, Folder, 21; Richard Strudwick to Denise Levertov, Box 15, Folder 22; Francesca Weaver to Denise Levertov, Box 15, Folder 26.

38. Jeffrey Loomis from Denise Levertov, October 26, 1986, DLP, Series 4, Box 120, Folder 18.

39. "Why I Decided to Resign," DLP, Series 4, Box 120, Folder 10. Diary, February 1, 1979, DLP, Series 3, Box 6, Folder 9.

40. "Craft Lecture," reprinted as "Technique and Tune-up," *LUTC*, 70-77. This should not be confused with Packard's "Craft Interview," 35-51.

41. Haines, "In Memoriam," 11.

42. Maureen Smith, "An Interview with Denise Levertov," 80.

43. "For Chile, 1977," *Poems 1972-1982*, 124-25.

44. "Greeting to the Vietnamese Delegation to the U.N." and "On the 32nd Anniversary of the Bombing of Hiroshima and Nagasaki," *Poems 1972-1982*, 126, 122-24.

45. "On Kim Chi Ha I (1975)" and "On Kim Chi Ha II (1981)," *LUTC*, 136-43, 144-50.

46. "Speech for a Rally on Boston Common, September 15, 1979," *LUTC*, 175-77, and "A Speech: For Anti-draft Rally, Washington, D.C., March 22, 1980," *Poems 1972-1982*, 252-56.

47. Rodgers, *Denise Levertov*, 168-69. Quotation taken from Rodgers's interview with Levertov, October 10, 1982.

48. "About Political Action in Which Each Individual Acts from the Heart," *Poems 1972-1982*, 247.

49. "With the Seabrook Natural Guard in Washington, 1978," *LUTC*, 165-66.

50. Ibid., 174.

51. "For the New Year, 1981," *Poems 1972-1982*, 257.

52. "Beginners," *Poems 1972-1982*, 244-45. Levertov dedicates this poem to Karen Silkwood, an antinuclear activist, and Eliot Gralla, both of whom died in the mid-1970s.

53. Zwicky, "An Interview with Denise Levertov," 111-12.

54. Crouch, "An Interview with Denise Levertov," 162-63.

55. Diary, August 11, 1978, September 3, 1978, January 14, 1979, DLP, Series 3, Box 6, Folder 9.

56. Diary, August 23, 1980, DLP, Series 3, Box 7, Folder 1.

57. "On Sex," DLP, Series 3, Box 18, Folder 5.

58. Diary, December 26, 1980, DLP, Series 3, Box 6, Folder 9, 80-82. She cites a Ken and a Curtis, but gives no last names. However, Ken is Kenneth Aguillard Atchity. Some seventy letters from Levertov to him confirming their affair are contained in the Atchity Collection, Special Collections Research Center, Georgetown University Library. See also DLP, Series 4, Box 4, Folders 21-25. Earlier, Levertov also indicated affairs with K. O. and S. G.

59. Diary, August 23, 1980, DLP, Series 3, Box 7, Folder 1; Stephen Peet to Denise Levertov, November 1, 1974, July 19, no year, September 19, no year, DLP, Series 4, Box 80, Folder 33; Denise Levertov to Steven Blevins, July 21, 1975, DLP, Series 4, Box 117, Folder 8.

60. The DLP contain more than fifty of her introductions, forewords, and blurbs and more than 150 copies of her recommendations.

61. Publication of this book helped Baca win parole and an NEA Fellowship. Baca's voluminous correspondence with Levertov is contained in DLP, Series 4, Box 5, Folders 23-40, and Box 6, Folders 1-18.

62. Denise Levertov to Steve Blevins, February 20, 1983, April 9, 1983, DLP, Series 4, Box 117, Folder 16.

63. Carol Rainey to Dana Greene, August 1 and 5, 2011. Although I have not been privy to them, Rainey has in her possession some fifty letters from Levertov.

64. Diary, July 1980, DLP, Series 3, Box 7, Folder 1.

65. Denise Levertov to Carol Rainey, September 1980, DLP, Series 4, Box 120, Folder 13 (not mailed).

66. Carol Rainey to Denise Levertov, DLP, Series 4, Box 84, Folders 30-31.

67. Rainey claims that she received a final "cruel" letter from Levertov just prior to her death. Rainey to Greene, August 10, 2011. I have not seen this letter.

68. Lacey, *The Inner War*, 110-32.

69. Zwicky, "An Interview with Denise Levertov," 118.

70. Ibid., 117.

71. "Genre and Gender v. Serving an Art." This was first presented at a symposium at the MLA in 1982 and reprinted in *NSE*, 102-3.

72. "Poems by Women," *DL Province*, 98-100.

73. Gish, "Feminism, Poetry, and the Church, 1990," 178.

74. Perloff, in her review of *To Stay Alive,* said it contained "bad confessional verse." "Poetry Chronicle 1970-1971," 97-131.

75. Atchity, "An Interview with Denise Levertov," 105.

76. Estess, "Denise Levertov," 97.

77. "Anne Sexton: Light Up the Cave," *LUTC*, 80-106.

78. "Introductory Note to *Life in the Forest*," *Poems 1972-1982*, 77.

79. "Human Being," *Poems 1972-1982*, 79-80.

80. "On the Function of the Line," *LUTC*, 61-69; "Technique and Tune-up," *LUTC*, 70-77.

81. "The Edge of Darkness: What Is Political Poetry?" *LUTC*, 128.

82. "The Nature of Poetry," *LUTC*, 60 (written in 1975).

83. "Revolution and Poetry: Neruda Is Dead — Neruda Lives," *LUTC*, 130-35 (first published in 1973).

84. Tassel, "Poetic Justice in El Salvador," 133.

85. These six separately published long poems were *Chekhov on the West Heath, Modulations for Solo Voice, Mass for the Day of St. Thomas Didymus, Pig Dreams: Scenes from the Life of Sylvia, Talk in the Dark,* and *Wanderer's Daysong.*

CHAPTER 8. "THE THREAD"

1. "The Thread," *Poems 1960-1967*, 50.

2. Estess, "Denise Levertov," 96.

3. "The Poet's View," *NSE*, 246.

4. Packard, "Craft Interview," 49.

5. "Fragments on an essay on religion, c. 1958," DLP, Series 2, Box 21, Folder 12.

6. Diary, August 11, 1968, DLP, Series 3, Box 3, Folder 9.

7. "The Sense of Pilgrimage," *PITW*, 83. Margaret Avison to Denise Levertov, DLP, Series 4, Box 5, Folder 13-16.

8. Eileen Egan to Denise Levertov, DLP, Series 4, Box 32, Folders 29-31; Sister Bernetta Quinn to Denise Levertov, DLP, Series 4, Box 84, Folders 10-13; Sister Mary Norbert Kob, O.P. to Denise Levertov, DLP, Series 4, Box 78, Folder 15; Fr. Raymond Roseliep to Denise Levertov, DLP, Series 4, Box 89, Folders 1-4; Fr. Gerry Pocock to Denise Levertov, DLP, Series 4, Box 82, Folder 22; Margaret Avison to Denise Levertov, DLP, Series 4, Box 5, Folders 13-16; Wendell Berry to Denise Levertov, DLP, Series 4, Box 10, Folders 5-9; Maureen Smith to Denise Levertov, DLP, Series 4, Box 95, Folders 3-10; Brother Joseph Chvala to Denise Levertov, DLP, Series 4, Box 120, Folder 6; Fr. Murray Bodo to Denise Levertov, DLP, Series 4, Box 12, Folders 15-22; Denise Levertov to Murray Bodo, DLP, Series 4, Box 117, Folder 30; Colman McCarthy to Denise Levertov, DLP, Series 4, Box 70, Folder 35; Joan Hallisey to Denise Levertov, DLP, Series 4, Box 46, Folders 35-41; Tony Stoneburner to Denise Levertov, DLP, Series 4, Box 97, Folders 19-24; "Living What You Believe," DLP, Series 2, Box 20, Folder 8. In a letter to her mother, Levertov mentions that although she did not see eye to eye with Dorothy Day on all matters, she did admire Day's consistently living her convictions. Denise Levertov to Beatrice Levertov (no date, probably Spring 1977), DLP, Series 1, Box 4, Folder 22.

9. Dillon, "Levertov Compares Anti-nuclear Protest with the 1960s."

10. Diary, December 24, 1977, DLP, Series 3, Box 6, Folder 5, 5.

11. Diary, January 14, 1979, DLP, Series 3, Box 6, Folder 9, 23.

12. Foreword to *The Stream and the Sapphire*, vii. See "Human Being," *Poems 1972-1982*, 79-80.

13. "Work That Enfaiths," *NSE*, 249-50; Diary, October 10, 1979, and December 27, 1979, DLP, Series 2, Box 6, Folder 9.

14. Levertov confided to David Shaddock at the time that she thought this poem might be her masterpiece. Personal communication from David Shaddock entitled "The Sudden Angel Affrighted Me: God Wrestling In Denise Levertov's Life and Art."

15. "Mass for the Day of St. Thomas Didymus," *Poems 1972-1982*, 268.

16. Ibid., 272-73.

17. "Work That Enfaiths," *NSE*, 250.

18. Lorrie Smith, "An Interview with Denise Levertov," 141.

19. Diary, December 26, 1980, DLP, Series 3, Box 6, Folder 9, 80-81.

20. "What I Believe" (written for Jan Wallace, July 1985). Privately held.

21. "A Poet's View," *NSE*, 242.

22. Lorrie Smith, "An Interview with Denise Levertov," 141.

23. Fizz, "Denise Levertov: Choosing Our Own Roads," An Interview, 12, 30.

24. "Letter," *Poems 1972-1982*, 165-67.

25. "Candles in Babylon," *Poems 1972-1982*, 183.

26. "Concurrence," "What Could It Be," "An English Field in the Nuclear Age," "Unresolved," *Poems 1972-1982*, 242, 248-49, 242-43, 262-64.

27. "Writing in the Dark," *Poems 1972-1982*, 260-61.

28. "The Many Mansions," *Poems 1972-1982*, 273-74.

29. Diary, July 1980, "The White Crane Dream," DLP, Series 3, Box 7, Folder 1.

30. Levertov taught as a visiting professor at Stanford in 1981, but had a permanent position there from 1982 to 1993.

31. Transcript of tape from Denise Levertov to Murray Bodo, January 6-9, 1985. Privately held.

32. The proceedings of this conference are found in Middlebrook and Yalom, eds., *Coming to Light*. The same year of this conference Levertov presented "Genre and Gender v. Serving an Art," which was reprinted in *NSE*, 102-3.

33. Diary, February 14 and 26, 1982, March 24 and 25, 1982, DLP, Series 3, Box 7, Folder 2. This diary contains both 1981 and 1982 entries.

34. Denise Levertov to Robbie Bosnak, tape of a letter, DLP, Series 8, Box 2, Folder 12.

35. Diary, February 14, 1982, DLP, Series 3, Box 7, Folder 2.

36. Ibid.

37. "A Poet's View," *NSE*, 244-45.

38. The St. Ann's Chapel was a center for Vatican II Catholicism, but it also had a traditional Latin mass at noon. This Catholic community and its choir now are in residence at the St. Thomas Aquinas Church in Palo Alto.

39. Diary, Easter 1982, DLP, Series 3, Box 7, Folder 7.

40. Diary, June 19, 1984, DLP, Series 3, Box 8, Folder 1 (contains entries for 1983 and 1984).

41. "During a Son's Dangerous Illness," *BTW*, 34-35. This poem was first published in "The Menaced World."

42. Diary, July 5–October 15, 1982, DLP, Series 3, Box 7, Folder 7.

43. Diary, October 15, 1982, DLP, Series 3, Box 7, Folder 7.

44. Diary, June 19, 1984, DLP, Series 3, Box 8, Folder 1.

45. Gould, "Denise Levertov," 29.

46. Hallisey, "Invocations of Humanity," 148.

47. Levertov was at the Banff Centre in 1980, 1982 and 1992.

48. "El Salvador: Requiem and Invocation," *A Door in the Hive*, 15-39, 109-10 (hereafter *DITH*); Hallisey, "Invocations of Humanity," 145-51.

49. "Work That Enfaiths," *NSE*, 250.

50. Ibid., 249-52.

51. Kenwood Notebook, 1983, DLP, Series 3, Box 8, Folder 2.

52. Ibid.

53. "Dying and Living," *LUTC*, 98-99.

54. Kathleen Norris to Denise Levertov, DLP, Series 4, Box 78, Folder 20.

55. "Gathered by the River" first appeared in *Two Poems* and was reprinted in *Oblique Prayers*, 40-42 (hereafter *OP*). Earlier she also had written "On the 32nd Anniversary of the Bombing of Hiroshima and Nagasaki."

56. Lorrie Smith, "An Interview with Denise Levertov," 140-41.

57. Gelpi, "Introduction: *Centering the Double Image*," 5-6.

58. " . . . That Passeth All Understanding," *OP*, 85.

59. "Of Being," *OP,* 86.

60. "St. Peter and the Angel" and "This Day," *OP*, 79, 80-81.

61. "The Task," *OP*, 78; "Work That Enfaiths," *NSE*, 252.

62. "The Avowal," *OP*, 76.

63. Other recipients included Arthur Miller and Bernard Malamud. The honor carried a twenty-five hundred dollar award.

64. Dunbar, ed., *In Celebration: Anemos.*

65. "The Ideas in the Things, 1983" and "On Williams' Triadic Line," *NSE*, 44-45, 22-32.

66. "Autobiographical Sketch," *NSE*, 258-64.

67. "Poetry, Prophecy, Survival," *NSE*, 143-53.

68. "Horses with Wings," *NSE*, 107-19.

69. "A Poet's View," *NSE*, 241, 246.

70. Ibid., 242.

71. Ibid., 244.

72. Hallisey, "Invocations of Humanity," 151.

CHAPTER 9. "MAKING PEACE"

1. "Making Peace," *BTW, 40.*

2. Diary, January 5, 1986, DLP, Series 3, Box 8, Folder 10.

3. Diary, February 15, 1987, DLP, Series 3, Box 9, Folder 2.

4. Diary, July 4, 1988, DLP, Series 3, Box 9, Folder 6.

5. Diary, March 8, 1985, and July 19, 1985, DLP, Series 3, Box 8, Folder 7. Levertov wrote poems dedicated to both Niebauer and Hawley. "In Memory: After a Friend's Sudden Death" and "Missing Beatrice," *BTW*, 23, 24. Levertov subsequently edited and wrote an introduction for the posthumously published *The Collected Poems of Beatrice Hawley.*

6. Denise Levertov to Murray Bodo, January 6, 1987. Privately held.

7. Diary, November 12, 1987, DLP, Series 3, Box 9, Folder 2.

8. Diary, July 13, 1988, DLP, Series 3, Box 9, Folder 6.

9. Diary, August 14, 1988, DLP, Series 3, Box 9, Folder 6.

10. These essays were published in *New and Selected Essays*. "Paradox and Equilibrium" is particularly insightful in that it gives Levertov's response to an exhibit by the Japanese painters, Iri and Toshi Maruki, in which she explores the paradox of how beauty can be made from horror and the connective links between art and morality.

11. Correspondence on 65th birthday, October 1988, DLP, Series 4, Box 117, Folder 34.

12. Jean Sulivan is the pen name of Joseph Lemarchand.

13. Crouch, "An Interview with Denise Levertov, 1986," 158-59.

14. Diary, July 13, 1988, DLP, Series 3, Box 9, Folder 6.

15. Diary, January 9, 1986, DLP, Series 3, Box 8, Folder 10.

16. "A Stone from Iona," *DITH*, 68.

17. Levertov included poems by Rilke, Rumi, Hopkins, Williams, Stevens, Yeats, and Berry. The retreat was held in the summer of 1987.

18. "Sermon. Peace Pentecost," 1988, DLP, Series 2.2, Box 26, Folder 8.

19. Denise Levertov to Murray Bodo, November 28, 1983, DLP, Series 4, Box 117, Folder 30.

20. Although Hopkins was a Jesuit, he had been influenced by the thirteenth-century Franciscan theologian, Duns Scotus.

21. Murray Bodo to Denise Levertov, November 5, 1983, DLP, Series 4, Box 12, Folder 19.

22. Rebecca Mitchell Garnett to Denise Levertov, January 30, 1986, DLP, Series 4, Box 40, Folder 14.

23. Rebecca Mitchell Garnett to Denise Levertov, c. mid-1980s, DLP, Series 4, Box 40, Folder 14.

24. Diary, July 10, 1988, DLP, Series 3, Box 9, Folder 6.

25. "For Bet," *ET*, 56.

26. Diary, September 12, 1989, DLP, Series 3, Box 9, Folder 8.

27. Diary, March 24, 1985, DLP, Series 3, Box 8, Folder 7.

28. Diary, July 19, 1985, DLP, Series 3, Box 8, Folder 7.

29. "Zeroing In," *BTW*, 19.

30. Transcript of tape from Denise Levertov to Murray Bodo, January 6-9, 1985. Privately held.

31. Diary, February 17, 1986, DLP, Series 3, Box 8, Folder 10.

32. Diary, June 29, 1988, DLP, Series 3, Box 9, Folder 6.

33. Diary, July 13, 1988, DLP, Series 3, Box 9, Folder 6.

34. "Feet," *This Great Unknowing: Last Poems*, 22-30 (hereafter *TGU*).

35. Denise Levertov to Murray Bodo, Transcript of tape, January 6-9, 1985. Privately held.

36. "August Daybreak," *BTW*, 5.

37. "The Opportunity," *ET*, 59.

38. "The Spirits Appeased," *BTW*, 8.

39. "To Olga," *BTW*, 25.

40. Robert Duncan to Denise Levertov, November 11, 1978, *Letters Duncan/Levertov*, 713-14.

41. Denise Levertov to Robert Duncan, February 19, 1979, *Letters Duncan/Levertov*, 717. Duncan made another overture to Levertov by including a defense of her poems from *The Jacob's Ladder* in "Denise Levertov and the Truth of Myth," 257-59.

42. Diary, July 1980, DLP, Series 3, Box 7, Folder 1.

43. Denise Levertov to Jess Collins, April 17, 1988, *Letters Duncan/Levertov*, 719.

44. "To R. D., March 4th 1988," *DITH*, 4.

45. In 1986 Bet Mitchell sent Levertov a postcard with a picture of the Lady Chapel from Long Melford Church Suffolk suggesting they visit this site the next time she was in England.

46. Adrienne Rich to Denise Levertov, January 22, 1988, DLP, Series 4, Box 87, Folder 23.

47. In the 1980s, Goodman published two books of poetry: *A Life in Common* and *More Light*.

48. Documentation for the relationship between Levertov and her son is lopsided with very sparse evidence for his point of view. Several letters regarding their relationship are not yet available to the public.

49. Nikolai Goodman to Denise Levertov, 1986, 1987, DLP, Series 1, Box 13, Folders 34 and 35.

50. Nikolai Goodman to Denise Levertov, March 24, 1988, DLP, Series 1, Box 13, Folder 36.

51. "Denise's Blues," DLP, Series 2.1, Box 11, Folder 52.

52. Notebook, September 21, 1988, DLP, Series 3, Box 9, Folder 5.

53. Diary, July 15, 1988, DLP, Series 3, Box 9, Folder 6.

54. Diary, June 27, 1988, DLP, Series 3, Box 9, Folder 6.

55. Diary, July 10, 1988, DLP, Series 3, Box 9, Folder 6.

56. Murray Bodo to Denise Levertov, DLP, Series 4, Box 12, Folder 19.

57. Diary, July 15, 1988, DLP, Series 3, Box 9, Folder 6. Levertov gives no details here. Cruelty to Olga's children may refer to the fact that she did not rescue them from their orphanages. Regarding other cruelties, she may be referring to her lack of compassion. There does not appear to be documentation of any actual cruelties she committed.

58. Diary, July 20th, 1988, DLP, Series 3, Box 9, Folder 6.

59. Diary, January 3, 1988, DLP, Series 3, Box 9, Folder 2.

60. Diary, June 13, 1988, DLP, Series 3, Box 9, Folder 6.

61. "I Believe," DLP, Series 2.1, Box 18, Folder 56.

62. Diary, June 8–Sept 21, 1988, DLP, Series 3, Box 9, Folder 6.

63. Ibid.

64. Denise Levertov to Sam Abbott, Saturday, January 8, 1984, outgoing correspondence, DLP, Series 4, Box 120, Folder 16.

65. Denise Levertov to Sam Abbott, n.d., Outgoing correspondence, DLP, Series 4, Box 120, Folder 16.

66. Hallisey, "Invocations of Humanity," 146.

67. Diary, September 8, 1984, DLP, Series 3, Box 8, Folder 7.

68. Eileen Egan to Denise Levertov, August 20, 1985, DLP, Series 4, Box 32, Folder 30.

69. "A Poet's View," *NSE*, 242.

70. Denise Levertov to Murray Bodo, Transcript of tape, January 6–9, 1985. Privately held.

71. Notebook, October 1988, DLP, Series 3, Box 9, Folder 5.

72. "Work That Enfaiths," *NSE*, 251.

73. Ibid., 248-49.

74. "Variation and Reflection on a Theme by Rilke — The Book of Hours, Book I, Poem 7," *BTW*, 83.

75. The photographs were by Peter Brown, son of Robert McAfee Brown, and were published with Levertov's poems.

76. Denise Levertov to Murray Bodo, March 4, 1985. Privately held.

77. "Standoff," *BTW*, 67.

78. "Work That Enfaiths," *NSE*, 251.

79. "Caedmon," *BTW*, 65. This poem, like her earlier "St. Peter and the Angel," describes an angel who frees a subject in order that he might be released for new vocational work.

80. "The Servant-Girl at Emmaus," *BTW*, 66.

81. "Candlemas," *BTW*, 70.

82. Notes, *BTW*, 86. See Giorcelli, "The Servant-Girl at Emmaus," 69-91, and Denise Levertov to Murray Bodo, March 4, 1985. Privately held.

83. *The Rialto*, 1985, DLP, Series 6, Box 28, Folder 12.

84. Block, "Interview with Denise Levertov," 14-15.

85. "On a Theme from Julian's Chapter XX," *BTW*, 68-69.

86. "The Showings: Lady Julian of Norwich, 1342-1416," *BTW*, 75 82.

87. Denise Levertov to Murray Bodo, November 28, 1983, DLP, Series 4, Box 117, Folder 30.

88. "At the Justice Department — November 15, 1969," *Poems 1968-1972*, 156.

89. "Asking Fact for Form," DLP, Series 2.2, Box 20, Folder 10. In this lecture given at Wabash College, December 6, 1962, Levertov refers to art and prayer, the latter is premised on faith.

90. Diary, June 3, 1988, Series 3, Box 9, Folder 2, and June 22, 1988, Series 3, Box 9, Folder 6.

91. Crouch, "An Interview with Denise Levertov," 157.

92. Denise Levertov to Steve Blevins, April 13, 1989, DLP, Series 4, Box 117, Folder 22.

CHAPTER 10. THE BORDERLAND

1. "The Life of Art," *DITH*, 85.

2. From the United Kingdom and the United States, Levertov traveled to Bulgaria, Russia, Vietnam, Greece, Italy, France, Canada, Holland, Australia, Tonga, Japan, Germany, the Czech Republic, Switzerland, Austria, and Yugoslavia.

3. Archer, "A Conversation with Denise Levertov," 69.

4. Denise Levertov to Murray Bodo, May 12, 1989. Privately held.

5. The Rockefeller Center lists Levertov as a Fellow in 1990. Levertov published

several of her poems written at the Bellagio Center in *Evening Train*, a few of which are dedicated to the Center's then director, Roberto Celli, and to Gianna Celli.

6. Mitch Goodman to Denise Levertov, March 1, 1990, DLP, Series 1, Box 12, Folder 23.

7. Diary, September 24, 1989, DLP, Series 3, Box 9, Folder 8, and Diary, January 27, 1990, DLP, Series 3, Box 10, Folder 1.

8. Diary, August 6, 1990, and October 7, 1990, DLP, Series 3, Box 10, Folder 1.

9. "Poetry and Peace: Some Broader Dimensions," *NSE*, 154-71. Also included in this volume is Levertov's 1989 essay "Williams and Eliot," 59-66, in which she explains the differences between them and her own belated appreciation of Eliot.

10. "Paradox and Equilibrium," *NSE*, 141-42.

11. Archer, "Singing the Songs of Degrees."

12. The title of this volume derives from the poem "Dream 'Cello," *DITH*, 104

13. "Flickering Mind," *DITH*, 64.

14. "St. Thomas Didymus," *DITH*, 101-3.

15. "Annunciation," *DITH*, 86-88.

16. "Ikon: The Harrowing of Hell," *DITH*, 105-6.

17. "Variation on a Theme by Rilke," *DITH*, 107.

18. Diary, October 28, 1989, DLP, Series 3, Box 9, Folder 8, and Diary, December 2, 1989, DLP, Series 3, Box 10, Folder 1.

19. Murray Bodo, "Fear and Violence." Typescript. Privately held.

20. "Why I Pray," *Compass*, January 1990, 10. A draft of this appears as "When I Pray," DLP, Series 2.2, Box 27, Folder 34. DLP, Series 2.2, Box 24, Folder 21 contains a draft of a similar article entitled "On the Art of Prayer," 1990.

21. "Work That Enfaiths," *NSE*, 247-57. This lecture was given under the auspices of *Cross Currents*.

22. Ibid., 257.

23. Notebook, January 5, 1989, DLP, Series 3, Box 9, Folder 5. (This is actually included in Notebook, 1988.)

24. Denise Levertov to Murray Bodo, June 5, 1989. Privately held.

25. Albert Gelpi to Denise Levertov, October 23, 1990, DLP, Series 4, Box 40, Folder 27. Apparently in response to her request, Gelpi says he will not mention in his introduction to *Denise Levertov: Selected Criticism* that she had become a Catholic.

26. Blue Notebook, October 21, 1990, DLP, Series 3, Box 10, Folder 3.

27. Cardinal Joseph Ratzinger was then Prefect of the Congregation for the Doctrine of the Faith and subsequently Pope Benedict XVI, and John O'Connor was Archbishop of New York.

28. Diary, June 4, 1989, DLP, Series 3, Box 9, Folder 8.

29. Gish, "Feminism, Poetry, and the Church," 176-80.

30. Blue Notebook, October 30, 1990, DLP, Series 3, Box 10, Folder 3.

31. Blue Notebook, November 24, 1990, DLP, Series 3, Box 10, Folder 3. *National Catholic Reporter* is an independent Catholic national newspaper of liberal persuasion.

32. Virginia (Dana) Barrett to Denise Levertov, DLP, Series 4, Box 7, Folders 26-42, and Box 8, Folders 1 and 2. In October 12, 1986, Folder 39, Barrett quotes from Levertov's letter to her "your spiritual journey influenced mine." This is confirmed independently by Shaddock in "Denise Levertov," 134-39. I was unable to interview Barrett, who died in 2011.

33. Blue Notebook, November 24, 1990, DLP, Series 3, Box 10, Folder 3.

34. The most vocal of these was her long time friend Hayden Carruth who in as late as 1996 made it clear that although he valued her as a poet, he did not share her faith or her respect for organized religion, which he considered "harmful to the species." Hayden Carruth to Denise Levertov, May 4, 1996, DLP, Series 4, Box 18, Folder 8.

35. Blue Notebook, October 30, 1990, DLP, Series 3, Box 10, Folder 3.

36. Blue Notebook, October 21 and 30, 1990, DLP, Series 3, Box 10, Folder 3.

37. "Ancient Airs and Dances," and "Time for Rivets," ET, 31, 32.

38. Diary, October 7, 1990, DLP, Series 3, Box 10, Folder 1 and Blue Notebook, August 30, 1991, DLP, Series 3, Box 10, Folder 3.

39. Diary, October 7, 1990, DLP, Series 3, Box 10, Folder 1.

40. Teal Green Notebook, January 22, 1992, DLP, Series 3, Box 10, Folder 5.

41. Cusac, "'I take up / so much space,'" 103. See also DLP, Series 5, Box 24, Folder 25.

42. Dear, "Denise Levertov's Peacemaking Poetry."

43. "Why Pax Christi?" DLP, Series 2.2, Box 27, Folder 35.

44. "Misnomer," ET, 79.

45. "Witnessing from Afar the New Escalation of Savage Power," ET, 80.

46. "News Report, September 1991: U.S. Buried Iraqi Soldiers Alive in Gulf War," ET, 81-83.

47. "Dom Helder Camara at the Nuclear Test Site," SOTW, 114.

48. "Protesting at the Nuclear Test Site," SOTW, 53.

49. Blue Notebook, May 1991, DLP, Series 3, Box 10, Folder 3.

50. "Some Affinities of Content," NSE, 1-21.

51. Ibid., 21.

52. "The Pardoner," PITW, 206-9.

53. Sandy Gregor to Denise Levertov, July 24, 1992, DLP, Series 1, Box 15, Folder 11.

54. Denise Levertov to Murray Bodo, August 22, 1992, and October 2, 1992. Privately held.

55. Denise Levertov to Murray Bodo, October 2, 1992. Privately held.

56. Murray Bodo to Denise Levertov, September 2, 1992, DLP, Series 4, Box 12, Folder 21.

57. Denise Levertov to Murray Bodo, October 2, 1992. Privately held.

58. Teal Green Notebook, July 12, 1992, October 20, 1992, November 27, 1992, DLP, Series 3, Box 10, Folder 5.

59. *I Was Me* was the title added subsequently. New Directions apparently rejected the manuscript because of length — it was 900 pages — and the difficulty in securing permissions.

60. The most recent of these were "Work That Enfaiths," "Some Affinities of Content," "Williams and Eliot," "Poetry and Peace," and "Biography and the Poet," the last written in 1992.

61. Apparently Levertov wrote to Rich in 1991 when she learned of the brain tumor of one of Rich's sons.

62. Adrienne Rich to Denise Levertov, July 7, 1992, DLP, Series 4, Box 87, Folder 24. Rich thought some of Levertov's language was "highly charged" and that there was a certain vagueness in the essay. She suggested more examples of the kind of thing Levertov was inveighing against. But above all, Rich thought more clarification was needed between social and political boundaries, which cut off discourse, and personal boundaries.

63. Teal Green Notebook, December 28, 1991, DLP, Series 3, Box 10, Folder 5.

64. "Biography and the Poet," *NSE*, 172-85.

65. Levertov read her archival materials prior to 1989. Evidence of this is obvious in her penciled sidebar comments. She probably did not review materials after that date. Post-1989 materials were added to the archive after her death. Her archive, running about 159 linear feet, also contains class lists, lecture notes, departmental memos, student works, hundreds of recommendations, materials on her family of origin and her own family, drafts of poems, clippings about other poets, religious figures, and subjects in which she had interest.

66. In her letter to Levertov, Rich indicates that the newly released Sexton biography had caused her to think about biography as well and to come to some of the same conclusions as Levertov.

67. "Roots and Airplants." Privately held.

68. "Settling," *ET*, 3.

69. "Some Affinities of Content," *NSE*, 4.

70. "Intimation," *DITH*, 5.

CHAPTER 11. BEARING WITNESS

1 "Dream Instruction," *ET*, 60-61.

2. By 1983, Levertov had been diagnosed with Sjogren's Syndrome, an autoimmune disease particularly prevalent among females, which resulted in dry eyes and mouth. Persons with Sjogren's Syndrome have a higher incidence of non-Hodgkins lymphoma, which was her diagnosis. See Tassel, "Poetic Justice in El Salvador," 126.

3. Teal Green Notebook, May 11, 1995, DLP, Series 3, Box 10, Folder 5.

4. Denise Levertov to Steve Blevins, June 16, 1993, DLP, Series 4, Box 117, Folder 26, and Mitch Goodman to Denise Levertov, October 21, 1993, DLP, Series 1, Box 12, Folder 26.

5. Denise Levertov to Murray Bodo, March 25, 1993. Privately held.

6. Levertov subsequently wrote the poem "Wondering," which was dedicated to Steindl-Rast and published in *SOTW*, 9. David Steindl-Rast to Denise Levertov, April 29, 1997, DLP, Series 4, Box 96, Folder 33.

7. Denise Levertov to Czeslaw Milosz, April 8, 1994, Czeslaw Milosz Papers, Yale University Beinecke Rare Book and Manuscript Library, Gen MSS 611, Folder 572.

8. Teal Green Notebook, June 27, 1993, DLP, Series 3, Box 10, Folder 5.

9. McElroy's "Conversations and Tea with Denise," 24-27, illustrates how Levertov tailored her conversations to each person. The "girl talk" between Levertov and McElroy is captured in "Pillow Book," a poem McElroy dedicated to Levertov in *Sleeping with the Moon*, 3-7.

10. Interview with Barbara Epler, editor-in-chief, New Directions Publishing Corporation, June 2010. New Directions will bring out Levertov's complete works in 2013, edited by Paul Lacey and Anne Dewey.

11. Teal Green Notebook, May 10, 1993, DLP, Series 3, Box 10, Folder 5. Since I cannot document any other speaking engagement in New York during this year, I am assuming that Clifton introduced her at this event. Neither the Levertov archive nor the Clifton archive at Emory University give additional evidence of this introduction.

12. This was a six-year appointment allowing Levertov to speak at Cornell up to ten times a year. It appears that Levertov visited Cornell only twice, once in November 1993 and once in March 1995.

13. Cornell University, November 16, 1993, DLP, Series 5, Box 24, Folder 15.

14. *Stanford Report*, October 20, 1993.

15. Levertov joined the Board in 1992.

16. Denise Levertov to Denise Carmody, n.d., DLP, Series 4, Box 17, Folder 13. Carmody was Director of the Warren Center for Catholic Studies at the University of Tulsa.

17. St. Joseph's, May 14, 1995, DLP, Series 5, Box 24, Folder 21.

18. Red Notebook, February 10, 1994, DLP, Series 3, Box 11, Folder 1.

19. Block, "Interview with Denise Levertov," 14.

20. O'Connell, "A Poet's Valediction."

21. Red Notebook, Spiritual Exercises, October 23, 1993–February 3, 1994, Day 44, December 1, 1993 (Xerox copy). Privately held. The archives contains Red Notebook, Spiritual Exercises, Day 72-101, February 7, 1994–April 22, 1994, DLP, Series 3, Box 11, Folder 1.

22. Teal Green Notebook, June 18th, DLP, Series 3, Box 10, Folder 5. Although not indicated, my suspicion is that it is 1993.

23. Blue Notebook, June 13, 1994, and March 26, 1995, DLP, Series 3, Box 11, Folder 3.

24. Red Notebook, Spiritual Exercises, October 23, 1993–February 3, 1994, Day 46 (Xerox copy). Privately held.

25. "Note to Marlene. Poetry vs. Church Activity," n.d. (after 1994). Privately held by Marlene Muller, Levertov's secretary from 1993 through 1997.

26. "Poetry, Prophecy, Survival," *NSE*, 147.

27. *Evening Train* was published in 1992 and reissued in 1993.

28. "Evening Train," *ET*, 62-63.

29. See "The Opportunity," "Link," "For Bet," "Mid-American Tragedy," "Ancient Airs and Dances," "Time for Rivets," "On the Eve," "A Little Visit to Doves and Chickens," "The Composition," "Becca," and "Letter to a Friend."

30. "In the Land of Shinar," *ET*, 85.

31. Although Levertov never used the word, she might be considered a panentheist. Panentheism, unlike pantheism, which makes the divine synonymous with the material world, envisions the divine interpenetrating the world. Levertov read and was impressed by George Steiner's *Real Presences*, which defends the immanentism of the Divine.

32. Although there is no indication Levertov read David Tracy's *The Analogical Imagination* (1981), and she could not have read Andrew Greeley's *The Catholic Imagination*, published in 2000, her work clearly is congruent with the insights of these two authors.

33. "Morning Mist," "Open Secret," "Whisper," "Witness," "Against Intrusion," *ET*, 5, 14, 96, 97, 94.

34. Although Levertov never used the term "biophilia," she would have resonated with the concept. Biophilia was first coined by Erich Fromm in 1964 in *The Heart of Man* to describe an attraction to all that is alive and vital, a love of life and of living systems. It was subsequently popularized by the sociobiologist E. O. Wilson in 1984.

35. "Embracing the Multipede," *ET*, 107-10.

36. "The Batterers," "Tragic Error," *ET*, 71, 69.

37. "The Tide," *ET*, 117-18. An earlier poem by the same title was published in *The Jacob's Ladder*, 1961.

38. "Contraband," "What the Figtree Said," *ET*, 112, 111.

39. "Salvator Mundi: Via Crucis," "Ascension," *ET*, 114, 115.

40. "Suspended," *ET*, 119.

41. Red Notebook, March 24, 1994, DLP, Series 3, Box 11, Folder 1. Levertov refers to "this" book in which the poem on the crucifixion is included. That would be by inference *Evening Train,* which contains, "Salvator Mundi: Via Crucis."

42. Red Notebook, March 24, 1994, DLP, Series 3, Box 11, Folder 1.

43. Santa Clara, where Levertov had given several readings, made the award in 1993. Her longtime friend Judith Dunbar was on the university faculty. Seattle University granted Levertov a degree in 1994. Levertov also had done several readings there prior to her nomination for this award by Edwin Weihe, who was in the process of developing a creative writing program at the university.

44. Blue Notebook, June 12, 1994, DLP, Series 3, Box 11, Folder 3.

45. Stillpoint (On Faith), DLP, Series 5, Box 25, Folder 10.

46. "Contrasting Gestures," *ET*, 100.

47. Block, "Interview with Denise Levertov," 14-15.

48. "Note to Marlene. Poetry vs. Church Activity." Privately held.

49. Teal Green Notebook, July 1 and 15, 1993, DLP, Series 3, Box 10, Folder 5.

50. Red Notebook, Spiritual Exercises, October 23, 1993–February 3, 1994, Day 53, n.d. (Xeroxed copy). Privately held. In other places in Levertov's diaries, she again mentions the desire to have a second chance at motherhood.

51. Red Notebook, March 11 and 13, 1994, DLP, Series 3, Box 11, Folder 1.

52. Blue Notebook, April 31, 1994, DLP, Series 3, Box 11, Folder 3.

53. "The Discovery of Voice," 16.

54. Blue Notebook, January 23, 1995, DLP, Series 3, Box 11, Folder 3.

55. Denise Levertov to Emily Archer, January 10, 1996. Privately held.

56. "For Steve," *SOTW*, 73.

57. Reported in an interview with Lou Oma Durand, Seattle, July 15, 2009. Levertov had only limited contact with Potter over the years. He was a man of considerable charm, although an unconventional free spirit and anarchist. He authored two books on design — *Models and Constructs: Margin Notes to a Design Culture* and *What is a Designer: Things, Places, Messages*, both published by Hyphen Press.

58. Blue Notebook, March 27, 1995, DLP, Series 3, Box 11, Folder 3.

59. Ibid.

60. Brooker, "A Conversation with Denise Levertov," 185.

61. "Only Connect," *Poems 1968-1972*, 209-10.

62. "Variations on a Theme by Rilke," *DITH*, 107. Nikolai Goodman, an artist, suggested that he was the one who advanced the use of the word "tesserae" to his mother.

63. The inaugural poetry page appeared in 1997. Levertov immediately began recruiting friends, including Marlene Muller, her poet secretary, and Lucille Clifton, for submissions.

64. "Living What You Believe," 103.

65. *The Stream & the Sapphire* and *The Life around Us*. The first of these anthologies derives its title from lines in the poem "Flickering Mind," which first appeared in *A Door in the Hive*. The second title is from a poem by the same name, which appeared in *Footprints*.

66. Archer, "A Conversation with Denise Levertov," 67. A collection of these poems was published posthumously as *Making Peace*, edited by Peggy Rosenthal.

67. Hayden Carruth to Denise Levertov, July 15, 1996, DLP, Series 3, Box 11, Folder 8.

68. Red Notebook, December 29, 1996, DLP, Series 3, Box 11, Folder 7.

69. Sandy Gregor to Denise Levertov, February 11, no year given (probably 1995 or 1996), DLP, Series 1, Box 15, Folder 11; Mitch Goodman to Denise Levertov, 1996, DLP, Series 1, Box 12, Folder 30. The marital problems between Goodman and his wife Sandy appear to have begun about 1995. See Robbie Bosnak to Denise Levertov, June 13, 1997, DLP, Series 4, Box 13, Folder 24. Hayden Carruth, a longtime friend and

neighbor of Goodman, wrote to Levertov after her husband's death saying that in the last period of his life, he gave Carruth "such horrendous trouble" that he discontinued their friendship. Carruth allowed that Goodman was "mean," "vicious," "manipulative," and "deceitful," and consequently he did not attend Goodman's memorial service. Looking back, Carruth felt that the pressures that had been evident for years had overcome Goodman, and that he was out of his mind. Hayden Carruth to Denise Levertov, February 12, 1997, DLP, Series 4, Box 18, Folder 8. Because Carruth had bouts of mental instability himself, his description may not be fully objective.

70. Red Notebook, December 29, 1996, DLP, Series 3, Box 11, Folder 7.

71. Sandy Gregor to Denise Levertov, December 17, 1996, DLP, Series 1, Box 15, Folder 11.

72. Red Notebook, January 3, 1997, DLP, Series 3, Box 11, Folder 7.

73. "What Harbinger?" *SOTW*, 3.

74. "For Those Whom the Gods Love Less," *SOTW*, 96.

75. "In the Woods," *SOTW*, 57.

76. "Sojourners in a Parallel World," *SOTW*, 49.

77. "The Conversion of Brother Lawrence," *SOTW*, 111-13.

78. "A Heresy," *SOTW*, 121.

79. "Sands of the Well," *SOTW*, 124-25.

80. "The Beginning of Wisdom," *SOTW*, 109.

81. "In Whom We Live and Move and Have Our Being," *SOTW*, 107.

82. "To Live in the Mercy of God," *SOTW*, 127-28.

83. Pacernick, "Interview with Denise Levertov," 85-92. Questions and answers were submitted in writing.

84. Blue Notebook, March 24, 1996, DLP, Series 3, Box 11, Folder 4.

85. Red Notebook, April 5, 1996, DLP, Series 3, Box 11, Folder 7.

86. Red Notebook, June 6, 1996, DLP, Series 3, Box 11, Folder 7.

87. "A Hundred A Day," *TGU*, 13.

88. Red Notebook, June 29, 1996, DLP, Series 3, Box 11, Folder 7.

89. Red Notebook, December 29, 1996, DLP, Series 3, Box 11, Folder 7.

90. Red Notebook, August 4, 1996, DLP, Series 3, Box 11, Folder 7.

91. "Primary Wonder," *SOTW*, 129.

CHAPTER 12. "ONCE ONLY"

1. "Once Only," *TGU*, 46.

2. "February Evening in New York," *CEP*, 101.

3. "Living," *Poems 1960-1967*, 240.

4. "Dying and Living," *LUTC*, 111.

5. She was unable to appear at the Yara Arts Group in New York; the Library of Congress in Washington, D.C.; and the Paris conference, Rencontres Poétiques du Monde Anglophone.

6. Denise Levertov to Lucille Clifton, January–March 1997, Lucille Clifton Papers, MARBL, Emory University, MSS 1054, Correspondence Box 9; Murray Bodo to Denise Levertov, January 26, 1997, DLP, Series 4, Box 12, Folder 22.

7. Red Notebook, January 3, 1997, DLP, Series 3, Box 117, Folder 7.

8. Notebook, February 12, 1997, DLP, Series 3, Box 11, Folder 8.

9. Notebook, early February 1997, DLP, Series 3, Box 11, Folder 8.

10. Notebook, February 17, 1997, DLP, Series 3, Box 11, Folder 8.

11. Notebook, March 30, 1997, DLP, Series 3, Box 11, Folder 8.

12. Denise Levertov to Czeslaw Milosz, May 9, 1997, Czeslaw Milosz Papers, Beinecke Rare Book and Manuscript Library, Yale University, GEN MSS 661, Folder 572.

13. The proceedings were published as *Rencontres Poétiques du Monde Anglophone*, Paris, 1997.

14. Bowen and Weigl, eds. *Writing between the Lines*, xiii.

15. "The Art of Mary Randlett," *Mary Randlett Landscapes*, 25-33. In 1989, Levertov met Randlett through their mutual friend Eve Triem.

16. Notebook, March 11, 1997, DLP, Series 3, Box 11, Folder 8. Denise Levertov to Czeslaw Milosz, December 6, 1997, Czeslaw Milosz Papers, Folder 572. Robert Hass confirmed that he did suggest Levertov for this position and that, if willing to accept, she probably would have been appointed within one or two years. Ironically, the U.S. Postal Service and the National Portrait Gallery, both government entities, honored Levertov in 2012.

17. Levertov had privately indicated to Albert Gelpi that Boland, Lucille Clifton, and John Haines were poets who would be good replacements for her position.

18. "The Sound of Light," University of Oregon, DLP, Series 5, Box 24, Folder 30.

19. Hamill, "In Her Company."

20. "A Clearing," *TGU*, 54-55.

21. Archer, "A Conversation with Denise Levertov," 55-72.

22. In a letter to Archer dated January 10, 1996, Levertov wrote: "I seldom feel as much regret at the possibility that I never will meet again someone briefly encountered as I do in your case—your visit was really endearing." Privately held. Subsequently, Levertov sent a copy of her newly written poem "First Love" to Archer for her birthday.

23. O'Connell, "A Poet's Valediction."

24. Notebook, March 14, 1997, DLP, Series 3, Box 11, Folder 8. In her diary Levertov attributed this insight to an inspirational sermon she heard at St. Joseph's.

25. "Translucence," *TGU*, 48. Levertov read the fourteenth-century *Cloud of Unknowing,* and this may have inspired her use of the phrase "this great unknowing."

26. Denise Levertov to Emily Archer, September 1, 1997. Privately held.

27. Notebook, February 12 and 17, 1997, DLP, Series 3, Box 11, Folder 8.

28. Red Notebook, March 1, 1994, DLP, Series 3, Box 11, Folder 2.

29. Notebook, February 12, 1997, DLP, Series 3, Box 11, Folder 8.

30. "The Dead," CEP 103.

31. "Dying and Living," LUC 99.

32. Ibid., 110.

33. These poems were published posthumously as *This Great Unknowing*, edited by Paul Lacey.

34. "A Hundred a Day," "Roast Potatoes," "Swift Month," *TGU*, 13, 36-37, 19.

35. Notebook, DLP, Series 3, Box 11, Folder 8, March 14, 1997. Levertov records this dream and the fact that she woke from it sobbing.

36. "Enduring Love," *TGU*, 52.

37. "Feet," *TGU*, 22-31.

38. "Once Only," *TGU*, 46.

39. "Noblesse Oblige," "Masquerade," "*the mountain's daily speech is silence,*" *TGU*, 50, 51, 42.

40. "Immersion," *TGU*, 53.

41. "The Métier of Blossoming," *TGU*, 11-12.

42. "Celebration," *TGU*, 5.

43. "Mass of the Moon Eclipse," *TGU*, 44-45.

44. "First Love," *TGU*, 8-9.

45. This is my surmise. Levertov became increasingly ill after the summer. If the poems are arranged chronologically, one can track the inspiration for the poem and when it was produced. This appears to put most poems as written before 1997 or in the first half of that year. For example, "Once Only" and "First Love" were both written by 1996 when Levertov sent the first to Lucille Clifton and the second to Emily Archer for her birthday.

46. At this point, Levertov added Valerie Trueblood as cotrustee along with Paul Lacey. Although her reasons for this are not documented, Trueblood was living in Seattle and had become a new friend. Lacey had had a heart attack in 1994, and it was at that time that, in passing, Levertov asked Trueblood if she would be willing to take on that responsibility, but nothing was formalized until this point in 1997.

47. Emily Archer to Nikolai Goodman, January 2, 1998. Privately held.

48. "Roots and Airplants," 1-11. Privately held.

49. Atchity, "An Interview with Denise Levertov," 103.

50. "Roots and Airplants," 12-13. Privately held.

51. The party was given by her near neighbor and friend Lou Oma Durand and attended by Grey Foster, Jan Wallace, and Valerie Trueblood.

52. Laughlin, "Denise Levertov," 160.

53. Interview with Lou Oma Durand, Seattle, July 2009.

54. Denise Levertov to Czeslaw Milosz, December, 6, 1997, Czeslaw Milosz Papers, Folder 572.

55. Notebook, November 23, 1997, DLP, Series 3, Box 11, Folder 8. She is referring here to Craig Boly, S.J., pastor of St. Joseph's parish.

56. Interview with Valerie Trueblood, July 2009.

57. Levertov died of a subtype of non-Hodgkin's lymphoma, i.e., MALT (mucosa-associated lymphoid tissue), which arises in the gastrointestinal tract and induces chronic gastritis.

58. Shaddock read "Of Being," and Wallace read "The Hymn."

59. "Poet and Person," *Poems 1972-1982*, 186-87.

60. Pallbearers included Howard Fussiner, Sam Hamill (who because of his arthritis was replaced by Sam Green), Mark Jenkins, Tim McNulty, Ken Patten, and David Shaddock. Honorary pallbearers were Lou Oma Durand, Gray Foster, Sam Green, Rachel Irvine, David Mitchell, Marlene Muller, Doug Thorpe, and Jan Wallace.

61. Levertov is buried in Lot 240B, Grave 5, S/12.

62. McCracken is a Washington state visual artist who studied under Henry Moore and was a friend of Levertov's. Levertov's poem "Southern Cross" (*TGU*, 56) was inspired by a McCracken sculpture.

63. *New York Times*, December 23, 1997, B8; *Times of London*, January 17, 1998; *Chicago Tribune*, December 23, 1997, section 1, 10; *Los Angeles Times*, December 23, 1997, A26; *Washington Post*, December 23, 1997, B7; January 6, 1998, A12; *Time*, January 12, 1998, 31.

64. Eavan Boland, "In her works, poet Levertov leaves behind her shining self," Clippings in the Stanford Creative Writing Program obituary of Denise Levertov, n.d., IC, files of the Creative Writing Program, Stanford University, are probably from the Stanford University newspaper. John Felstiner's "All That Shines Out of Itself: A Recollection of Denise Levertov" is included in this same file and is probably used in his comments at the Memorial Service. See also Stanford University News Release, December 24, 1997.

65. Stanford service, January 27, 1998; Eliot Bay Book Store, February 1, 1998; St. Mark's, New York City, March 14, 1998; Emmanuel Church, Boston, March 29, 1998; San Francisco service, April 19, 1998.

66. Poems in memory of Levertov have been written by Hayden Carruth, Sam Green, Lucille Clifton, Murray Bodo, Wendell Berry, Colleen McElroy, Dick Lourie, Marlene Muller, Ralph Mills, Galway Kinnell, and David Ignatow, among others.

67. Creeley, "Tribute: Denise Levertov." These were the same comments he presented at the Stanford University Memorial Service. See also Creeley's "Remembering Denise," 81-83.

68. See, for example, Berry et al., "In Memoriam — Denise Levertov," 7-11. This includes comments by Wendell Berry, Lucille Clifton, C. K. Williams, and John Haines.

69. See Memorial Resolution, Denise Levertov, www.stanford.edu/dept/facultysenate/archive/1997/reports/10594 (accessed December 5, 2011).

70. Levertov made lecture and reading engagements for 1998 at Western Oregon University, the Folger Shakespeare Library, Claremont McKenna College, Taylor

University, Whitworth College, and Yale University, and had agreed to receive an honorary degree from the University of Essex and the Lifetime Achievement Award from the American Poetry Review.

71. "Relearning the Alphabet," *Poems 1968-1972*, 91-92.

EPILOGUE

1. "Some Affinities of Content," *NSE*, 21.

2. "Why Keep a Journal," Marlene Muller. Privately held.

3. This is the case for the materials up through 1989 when the original portion of the archive was sold to Stanford University.

4. Diary, July 1980, DLP, Series 3, Box 7, Folder 1.

5. Eavan Boland, "In her works, poet Levertov leaves behind her shining self," obituary of Denise Levertov, n.d., 1C, Files of the Creative Writing Program, Stanford University.

6. Quoted in "Poet Denise Levertov Dead at Age 74," by Martin Wolk, Seattle (Reuters), December 22, 1997.

7. "A Poet's View," *NSE*, 245.

8. "Roots and Airplants," 11. Privately held.

9. "Origins of a Poem," *PITW*, 49.

10. Denise Levertov to Emily Archer, June 28, 1994. Privately held.

11. "Complaint and Rejoinder," *SOTW*, 69.

12. "What Goes Unsaid," *SOTW*, 12.

SELECTED BIBLIOGRAPHY

Aiken, William. "Denise Levertov, Robert Duncan, and Allen Ginsberg: Modes of the Self in Projective Poetry." In *Critical Essays on Denise Levertov*, edited by Linda Wagner-Martin, 132-47. Boston: G. K. Hall and Company, 1991.

Allen, Donald M., ed. *The New American Poetry*. New York: Grove Press, 1960. See also under Levertov's writings.

Altieri, Charles. "Denise Levertov and the Limits of the Aesthetics of Presence." In *Denise Levertov: Selected Criticism*, edited by Albert Gelpi, 126-47. Ann Arbor: University of Michigan Press, 1993.

Anderson, Todd. "Denise Levertov." In *Twentieth-Century American Nature Poets*, edited by J. Scott Bryson and Roger Thompson, 214-22. Detroit: Gale, Cengage Learning, 2008.

Andre, Michael. "Denise Levertov: An Interview, 1971-72." In *Conversations with Denise Levertov*, edited by Jewel Spears Brooker, 52-67. Jackson: University Press of Mississippi, 1998.

Archer, Emily. "'Abundant, Multiple, Restless': Levertov and Merton in the 1960s." *Merton Journal* 10 (1997): 131-75.

———. "A Conversation with Denise Levertov." *Image: A Journal of the Arts and Religion* 18 (Winter 1997-98): 55-72.

———. "Denise Levertov and Paul Cézanne 'in Continuance.'" In *Denise Levertov: New Perspectives*, edited by Anne Colclough Little and Susie Paul, 155-76. West Cornwall, Conn.: Locust Hill Press, 2000.

———. "'In the Land of Shinar' by Denise Levertov." In *Poetry for Students*, vol. 7, edited by Mary K. Ruby, 81-95. Detroit: Gale, 2010.

———. "Review of *Evening Train* and *New and Selected Essays*." *Merton Annual* 6 (1993): 219-27.

———. "Singing the Songs of Degrees: Denise Levertov and the Tradition of Psalming." Diss. Georgia State University, 1996.

Atchity, Kenneth John. "An Interview with Denise Levertov, 1979." In *Conversations with Denise Levertov*, edited by Jewel Spears Brooker, 101-8. Jackson: University Press of Mississippi, 1998.

Avison, Margaret. "Interview with D. S. Martin." In *I Am Here and Not There: An Autobiography*, 327-39. Erin, Ont.: Porcupine's Quill, 2009.

Bate, Walter Jackson. *John Keats*. Cambridge: Harvard University Press, 1963.

Beck, Joyce Lorraine. "Denise Levertov's Poetics and Oblique Prayers." In *Denise Levertov: Selected Criticism*, edited by Albert Gelpi, 268-87. Ann Arbor: University of Michigan Press, 1993.

Beebe, Ann. "Levertov's 'Making Peace.'" *Explicator* 63, 3 (Spring 2005): 176-79.

Berger, Rose Marie. "Of Love's Risen Body: The Poetry of Denise Levertov." *Sojourners* 27 (March–April 1998): 2, 50.

Berrigan, Daniel, S. J. "Denise Levertov's Prose." In *Denise Levertov: Selected Criticism*, edited by Albert Gelpi, 173-76. Ann Arbor: University of Michigan Press, 1993.

Berry, Wendell, C. K. Williams, Lucille Clifton, and John Haines. "In Memoriam — Denise Levertov." *American Poet* (Summer 1998): 7-11.

Bertholf, Robert J. "Decision at the Apogee: Robert Duncan's Anarchist Critique of Denise Levertov." In *Robert Duncan and Denise Levertov: The Poetry of Politics, the Politics of Poetry*, edited by Albert Gelpi and Robert J. Bertholf, 1-17. Palo Alto: Stanford University Press, 2006.

——. "From Robert Duncan's Notebooks: On Denise Levertov." *Jacket* 28 (2005). www.jacketmagazine.com/28/2005 (accessed December 5, 2011).

——. "The Robert Duncan/Denise Levertov Correspondence: Duncan's View." *Jacket* 28 (2005). www.jacketmagazine.com (accessed December 5, 2011).

Bertholf, Robert J., and Ian Reid. *Robert Duncan: scales of the marvelous*. New York: New Directions, 1979.

Blaydes, Sophie B. "Metaphors of Life and Death in the Poetry of Denise Levertov and Sylvia Plath." In *Critical Essays on Denise Levertov*, edited by Linda Wagner-Martin, 204-15. Boston: G. K. Hall and Company, 1991.

Block, Ed. "Hans Urs von Balthasar and Some Contemporary Catholic Writers." *Logos: A Journal of Catholic Thought and Culture* 10, 3 (Summer 2007): 151-78.

——. "Interview with Denise Levertov." *Renascence* 50, 1 and 2 (Fall 1997/Winter 1998): 5-15.

——. "Mystery, Myth, and Presence: Concord and Conflict in the Correspondence of Denise Levertov and Robert Duncan." *Renascence* 58, 1 (Fall 2005): 63-89.

——. "Poet, Word, and the World: Reality and Transcendence in the Work of Denise Levertov." *Logos: A Journal of Catholic Thought and Culture* 4, 3 (2001): 159-84.

——. "Poetry, Attentiveness and Prayer: One Poet's Lesson." *New Blackfriars* 89, 1020 (March 2008): 162-76.

Bly, Robert [Crunk, pseud.]. "The World of Denise Levertov." *Sixties* 9 (Spring 1967): 48-65.

Bodo, Murray. "Denise Levertov: A Memoir and Appreciation." *Image: A Journal* 27 (Summer 2000): 82-93.

———. "Last Visit — Poem." *Sojourners* 28 (July/August 1999): 4.

———. *Poetry As Prayer: Denise Levertov*. Boston: Pauline Books, 2001.

Boland, Eavan. "Denise Levertov: Letters to a Broken World." *In a Journey with Two Maps: Becoming a Woman Poet*, 181-93. New York: W. W. Norton and Company, 2011.

———. "A Visionary Element." *Renascence* 50, 1 and 2 (Fall 1997): 153-59.

Borroff, Marie. "Review of *To Stay Alive*." In *Denise Levertov: Selected Criticism*, edited with an introduction by Albert Gelpi, 30-31. Ann Arbor: University of Michigan Press, 1993.

Bowering, George. "Denise Levertov." In *Denise Levertov: Selected Criticism*, edited by Albert Gelpi, 243-54. Ann Arbor: University of Michigan Press, 1993.

Breslin, James E. B. "Denise Levertov." In *Denise Levertov: Selected Criticism*, edited by Albert Gelpi, 55-90. Ann Arbor: University of Michigan Press. 1993.

Brooker, Jewel Spears. "A Conversation with Denise Levertov, 1995." In *Conversations with Denise Levertov*, edited by Jewel Spears Brooker, 182-89. Jackson: University Press of Mississippi, 1998.

———. Introduction to *Conversations with Denise Levertov*, edited by Jewel Spears Brooker, xi–xvii. Jackson: University Press of Mississippi, 1998.

Buber, Martin. *Tales of the Hasidim, The Early Masters*. New York: Schocken Books, 1947.

Burrows, E. G. "Politics and the Poet: An Interview, 1968." In *Conversations with Denise Levertov*, edited by Jewel Spears Brooker, 28-34. Jackson: University Press of Mississippi, 1998.

Carruth, Hayden. "An Informal Epic." In *Denise Levertov: Selected Criticism*, edited by Albert Gelpi, 25-27. Ann Arbor: University of Michigan Press, 1993.

———. "Levertov." In *Critical Essays on Denise Levertov*, edited by Linda Wagner-Martin, 30-35. Boston: G. K. Hall and Company, 1991.

———. "Review of *Overland to the Islands*." In *Critical Essays on Denise Levertov*, edited by Linda Wagner-Martin, 20. Boston: G. K. Hall and Company, 1991.

———. "What 'Organic' Means?" *Sagetrieb* (Spring 1985): 145-46.

Christensen, Peter G. "Chekhov in the Poetry of Howard Moss and Denise Levertov." *South Atlantic Review* 54, 4 (November 1989): 51-62.

Clifton, Lucille. "Some of the Bone Has Gone Missing." In *Denise Levertov: New Perspectives*, edited by Anne Colclough Little and Susie Paul, 1. West Cornwall, Conn.: Locust Hill Press, 2000.

Collecott, Diana Surman. "Inside and Outside in the Poetry of Denise Levertov." In *Critical Essays on Denise Levertov*, edited by Linda Wagner-Martin, 61-73. Boston: G. K. Hall and Company, 1991.

Contoski, Victor. "Review of *Relearning the Alphabet*." In *Critical Essays on Denise Levertov*, edited by Linda Wagner-Martin, 28-30. Boston: G. K. Hall and Company, 1991.

Creeley, Robert. "The Black Mountain Review." In *The Collected Essays of Robert Cree-ley*, 505-14. Berkeley: University of California Press, 1989.

——. "Remembering Denise." In *Denise Levertov: New Perspective*, edited by Anne Colclough Little and Susie Paul, 81-83. West Cornwall, Conn.: Locust Hill Press, 2000.

——. "Tribute: Denise Levertov." *Poetry Society of America: Crossroads Online* 51 (Spring 1998). www.poetrysociety.org/journal/articles/tributes/levertov (accessed December 5, 2011).

Crouch, Terrell. "An Interview with Denise Levertov, 1986." In *Conversations with Denise Levertov*, edited by Jewel Spears Brooker, 152-63. Jackson: University Press of Mississippi, 1998.

Cusac, Anne-Marie. "'I take up / so much space': Denise Levertov As Teacher." In *Denise Levertov: New Perspectives*, edited by Anne Colclough Little and Susie Paul, 99-105. West Cornwall, Conn.: Locust Hill Press, 2000.

——. "Reading Levertov in Wartime." *Jacket* 36 (2008). www.jacketmagazine.com (accessed December 5, 2011).

——. "Remembering Denise Levertov." *Progressive* (March 1998): 17-18.

Dargan, Joan. "Poetic and Political Consciousness in Denise Levertov and Carolyn Forché." In *Critical Essays on Denise Levertov*, edited by Linda Wagner-Martin, 236-45. Boston: G. K. Hall and Company, 1991.

Davidson, Michael. *The San Francisco Renaissance: Poetics and Community at Mid-Century*. New York: Cambridge University Press, 1989.

Dear, John. "Denise Levertov's Peacemaking Poetry." *National Catholic Reporter* 1, 24 (January 30, 2007).

Dewey, Anne. "'The Art of the Octopus': The Maturation of Denise Levertov's Political Vision." *Renascence* 50, 1 and 2 (Fall 1997/Winter 1998): 65-81.

——. *Beyond Maximus: The Construction of Public Voice in Black Mountain Poetry*. Palo Alto: Stanford University Press, 2007.

——. "Denise Levertov." *American Poets since World War II*, Fourth Series, edited by Joseph Mark Conte. *Dictionary of Literary Biography*, 165. Detroit: Gale Research, 1996.

——. "Gender Difference and the Construction of Social Space in Levertov's Writing after the Duncan-Levertov Debate." *Jacket* 36 (2008). www.jacketmagazine .com (accessed December 5, 2011).

——. "Poetic Authority and the Public Sphere of Politics in the Activist 1960s: The Duncan-Levertov Debate." In *Robert Duncan and Denise Levertov: The Poetry of Politics, the Politics of Poetry*, edited by Albert Gelpi and Robert J. Bertholf, 109-25. Palo Alto: Stanford University Press, 2006.

Dillon, Millicent. "Levertov Compares Anti-nuclear Protest with the 1960s." In *Campus Report*. Stanford University, March 17, 1982.

Dimock, Edward C. "Levertov and the Bengali Love Songs." *Twentieth Century Literature* 38, 3 (Fall 1992): 282-87.

Dougherty, Edward A. "Toward a Poetry of Witness." *Mid-American Review* 11, 1 (Fall 1990): 238-46.

Dougherty, James. "Presence, Silence and the Holy in Denise Levertov's Poems." *Renascence* 58, 4 (Summer 2006): 305-28.

Driscoll, Kerry. "A Sense of Unremitting Emergency: Politics in the Early Work of Denise Levertov." In *Critical Essays on Denise Levertov*, edited by Linda Wagner-Martin, 148-56. Boston: G. K. Hall and Company, 1991.

Duddy, Thomas A. "To Celebrate: A Reading of Denise Levertov." In *Critical Essays on Denise Levertov*, edited by Linda Wagner-Martin, 111-23. Boston: G. K. Hall and Company, 1991.

Dunbar, Judith. "Denise Levertov: 'The Sense of Pilgrimage.'" *America* 178, 19 (May 30, 1998): 22-25.

———, ed. *In Celebration — Anemos*. Palo Alto, Calif.: Matrix Press, 1983.

Duncan, Robert. "Denise Levertov and the Truth of Myth." In *Denise Levertov: Selected Criticism*, edited by Albert Gelpi, 257-59. Ann Arbor: University of Michigan Press, 1993.

———. "Santa Cruz Propositions." *Poetry Review* 62 (1971): 237-41.

Duncan, Robert, and Denise Levertov. *The Letters of Robert Duncan and Denise Levertov*, edited by Robert J. Bertholf and Albert Gelpi. Palo Alto: Stanford University Press, 2004.

DuPlessis, Rachel Blau. "The Critique of Consciousness and Myth in Levertov, Rich and Rukeyser." In *Denise Levertov: Selected Criticism*, edited by Albert Gelpi, 218-42. Ann Arbor: University of Michigan Press, 1993.

Entwistle, Alice. "'At Home Everywhere and Nowhere': Denise Levertov's 'Domestic' Muse." In *Women's Writing 1945-1960: After the Deluge*, edited by Jane Dowson, 98-114. New York: Palgrave, 2003.

Estess, Sybil. "Denise Levertov, 1977-78." In *Conversations with Denise Levertov*, edited by Jewel Spears Brooker, 87-100. Jackson: University Press of Mississippi, 1998.

Fass, Ekbert. *Robert Creeley: A Biography*. Hanover, N.H.: University Press of New England, 2001.

Felstiner, John. *Can Poetry Save the Earth?: A Field Guide to Nature Poems*. New Haven: Yale University Press, 2009.

———. "The Hasid and the Kabbalist: Denise Levertov, Robert Duncan." In *Robert Duncan and Denise Levertov: The Poetry of Politics, the Politics of Poetry*, edited by Albert Gelpi and Robert J. Bertholf, 81-89. Palo Alto: Stanford University Press, 2006.

———. "Poetry and Political Experience: Denise Levertov." In *Coming to Light: American Women Poets in the Twentieth Century*, edited by Diane Wood Middlebrook and Marilyn Yalom, 138-44. Ann Arbor: University of Michigan Press, 1986.

———. "'that witnessing presence': Life Illumined around Denise Levertov." *Jacket* 36 (2008). www.jacketmagazine.com (accessed December 5, 2011).

Fernández, Cristina María Gámez. "'Help Thou Mine Unbelief': Perception in Denise Levertov's Religious Poetry." *Renascence* 60, 1 (Fall 2007): 53-76.

Finn, James. "Mitchell Goodman and Denise Levertov." In *Protest: Pacifism and Politics: Some Passionate Views on War and Nonviolence*, 463-79. New York: Random House, 1967.

Fischer, Kathleen. "The Imagination in Spirituality." *The Way* Supplement 66 (Autumn 1989): 96-105.

Fizz, Robyn. "Denise Levertov: Choosing Our Own Roads." An Interview. *Sojourners* (August 1982): 12, 30.

Foster, Edward Halsey. *Understanding the Black Mountain Poets*. Columbia: University of South Carolina Press, 1995.

Fuchs, Karen Marie. "Setting Denise Levertov's High Drama to Music for High Liturgy." In *Denise Levertov: New Perspectives*, edited by Anne Colclough Little and Susie Paul, 225-31. West Cornwall, Conn.: Locust Hill Press, 2000.

Gallant, James. "Entering No-Man's Land: The Recent Religious Poetry of Denise Levertov." *Renascence* 50, 1 and 2 (Fall 1997/Winter 1998): 123-34.

———. "'In the Black of Desire': Eros in the Poetry of Denise Levertov." In *Denise Levertov: New Perspectives*, edited by Anne Colclough Little and Susie Paul, 51-61. West Cornwall, Conn.: Locust Hill Press, 2000.

Gardner, Geoffrey, ed. *For Rexroth*. New York: The Ark, 1980.

Gelpi, Albert. "Centering the Double Image." In *Denise Levertov: Selected Criticism*, edited by Albert Gelpi, 1-8. Ann Arbor: The University of Michigan Press, 1993.

———. "The Genealogy of Postmodernism: Contemporary American Poetry." *Southern Review* (Summer 1990): 517-41.

———. "O Taste and See." *Southern Review* (Autumn 1968): 1032-35.

———. "Poetic Language and Language Poetry: Levertov, Duncan, Creeley." In *Robert Duncan and Denise Levertov: The Poetry of Politics, the Politics of Poetry*, edited by Albert Gelpi and Robert Bertholf, 180-98. Palo Alto: Stanford University Press, 2006.

———. "Two Notes on Denise Levertov and the Romantic Tradition." In *Denise Levertov: Selected Criticism*, edited by Albert Gelpi, 91-95. Ann Arbor: The University of Michigan Press, 1993.

Gilbert, Alan. "Exquisite Balances." *Denver Quarterly* 27, 1 (1992): 22-42.

Gilbert, Sandra. "Revolutionary Love: Denise Levertov and the Poetics of Politics." In *Denise Levertov: Selected Criticism*, edited by Albert Gelpi, 201-17. Ann Arbor: University of Michigan Press, 1993.

Ginsberg, Allen. *The Letters of Allen Ginsberg*, edited by Bill Morgan. Philadelphia: Da Capo Press, 2008.

Giorcelli, Cristina. "The Servant-Girl at Emmaus (After a Painting by Velazquez): Denise Levertov's Religious Ekphrasis." *Sources* 12 (2002): 69-92.

Gish, Nancy K. "Feminism, Poetry, and the Church, 1990." In *Conversations with*

Denise Levertov, edited by Jewel Spears Brooker, 171-81. Jackson: University Press of Mississippi, 1998.

Gitlin, Todd. "The Return of Political Poetry." *Commonweal* 94 (July 23, 1971): 375-78.

Gitzen, Julian. "From Reverence to Attention: The Poetry of Denise Levertov." In *Critical Essays on Denise Levertov*, edited by Linda Wagner-Martin, 123-32. Boston: G. K. Hall and Company, 1991.

Goldstein, Laurence. "Politics by Parable: Denise Levertov and the Gulf War." *Tri-Quarterly* (Fall-Winter 2009): 105-22.

Goodman, Mitchell. *The End of It: A Novel*. New York: Horizon Press, 1961.

———. *A Life in Common*. Brunswick, Maine: The Dog Ear Press, 1984.

———. *Light from under a Bushel*. Mount Horeb, Wis.: The Perishable Press, 1968.

———. *More Light: Selected Poems*. Brunswick, Maine: The Dog Ear Press, 1989.

———. *The Movement toward a New America: The Beginnings of a Long Revolution: A Collage — A What?* Philadelphia: Pilgrim Press, 1970.

Gould, Jean. "Denise Levertov." *Modern American Women Poets*, 29-50. New York: Dodd, Mead and Company, 1984.

Green, Sam. "Winter Solstice, 1997." In *Denise Levertov: New Perspectives*, edited by Anne Colclough Little and Susie Paul, 79. West Cornwall, Conn.: Locust Hill Press, 2000.

Greene, Dana. "Denise Levertov: Poet and Pilgrim." *Logos: A Journal of Catholic Thought and Culture* 13, 2 (Spring 2010): 94-108.

———. "The Vocation of Denise Levertov." *The Way* 46, 1 (2007): 65-75.

Griffin, John Howard. *Follow the Ecstasy: The Hermitage Years — Thomas Merton*, edited by Robert Bonazzi. Maryknoll, N.Y.: Orbis Press, 1993.

Haines, John. "In Memoriam: Denise Levertov." *American Poet* Summer (1998): 11.

Hall, Donald, and Robert Park, eds. *New Poets of England and America*. New York: World, 1962.

Hallisey, Joan. "Denise Levertov — . . . 'Forever a Stranger and Pilgrim.'" *Centennial Review* 30 (1986): 281-91.

———. "Denise Levertov's 'Illustrious Ancestors.' The Hassidic Influence." In *Denise Levertov: Selected Criticism*, edited by Albert Gelpi, 260-67. Ann Arbor: University of Michigan Press, 1993.

———. "Denise Levertov's 'Illustrious Ancestors' Revisited." *Studies in American Jewish Literature* 9, 2 (Fall 1990): 163-75.

———. "Denise Levertov Sings 'The Unheard Music of That Vanished Lyre.'" *Renascence* 50, 1 and 2 (Fall 1997/Winter 1998): 83-95.

———. "Denise Levertov's 'Mass for the Day of St. Thomas Didymus.'" *Religion and Intellectual Life* 2 (Winter 1985): 127-33.

———. "Invocations of Humanity: Denise Levertov's Poetry of Emotion and Belief, 1986." In *Conversations with Denise Levertov*, edited by Jewel Spears Brooker, 143-51. Jackson: University Press of Mississippi, 1998.

———. "Themes in Denise Levertov's Poetry." *Modern American Poetry*. www.english
.illinois.edu (accessed December 5, 2011).

Hamalian, Linda. *A Life of Kenneth Rexroth*. New York: W. W. Norton and Company,
1991.

Hamill, Sam. "In Her Company: Denise Levertov." *Jacket* 36 (2008). www.jacket-
magazine.com (accessed December 5, 2011).

———. "Salt and Honey: On Denise Levertov." In *Denise Levertov: New Perspectives*,
edited by Anne Colclough Little and Susie Paul, 187-98. West Cornwall, Conn.:
Locust Hill Press, 2000.

Hamilton, Jeff. "Wrath Moves in the Music: Robert Duncan, Laura Riding, Craft and
Force in Cold War Poetics." *Jacket* 26 (2004). www.jacketmagazine.org (accessed
December 5, 2011).

Hampl, Patricia. "A Witness of Our Time." In *Denise Levertov: Selected Criticism*, edited by Albert Gelpi, 167-76. Ann Arbor: University of Michigan Press, 1993.

Hanson, Katherine, and Ed Block. "Gender, Nature, and Spirit: Justifying Female
Complexity in the Later Poetry of Denise Levertov." In *Denise Levertov: New Per-
spectives*, edited by Anne Colclough Little and Susie Paul, 63-76. West Cornwall,
Conn.: Locust Hill Press, 2000.

Harris, Victoria. "Denise Levertov and the Lyric of the Contingent Self." In *Denise
Levertov: New Perspectives*, edited by Anne Colclough Little and Susie Paul, 17-34.
West Cornwall, Conn.: Locust Hill Press, 2000.

———. "The Incorporative Consciousness: Levertov's Journey from Discretion to
Unity." *Exploration* 4, 1 (December 1976): 33-48.

Hatlen, Burton. "Feminine Technologies: George Oppen Talks at Denise Levertov."
American Poetry Review 22, 3 (May/June 1993): 9-14.

———. *George Oppen: Man and Poet*. Oronco, Maine: National Poetry Foundation, 1981.

Hearn, Tammy, and Susie Paul. "Denise Levertov's Variations on Rilke's Themes: A
Brief Explication." In *Denise Levertov: New Perspectives*, edited by Anne Colclough
Little and Susie Paul, 177-86. West Cornwall, Conn.: Locust Hill Press, 2000.

Herrera, José Rodríguez. "In Homage to Levertov: Translating *Sands of the Well*."
Jacket 36 (2008). www.jacketmagazine.com (accessed December 5, 2011).

———. "Linguistic Versus Organic, Sfumato Versus Chiaroscuro: Some Aesthetic Differences between Denise Levertov and Robert Duncan." *Renascence* 58, 1 (Fall
2005): 41-61.

———. "Musing on Nature: The Mysteries of Contemplation and the Sources of Myth
in Denise Levertov's Poetry." *Renascence* 50, 1 and 2 (Fall 1997/Winter 1998): 109-
21.

———. "Reappropriating Mirror Appropriations: Female Sexuality and the Body in
Denise Levertov." In *Denise Levertov: New Perspectives*, edited by Anne Colclough
Little and Susie Paul, 37-49. West Cornwall, Conn.: Locust Hill Press, 2000.

———. "Revolution or Death: Levertov's Poetry in Time of War." In *Robert Duncan and Denise Levertov: The Poetry of Politics, the Politics of Poetry*, edited by Albert Gelpi and Robert J. Bertholf, 148-60. Palo Alto: Stanford University Press, 2006.

Hewitt, Avis. "Hasidic Hallowing and Christian Consecration: Awakening to Authenticity in Denise Levertov's 'Matins.'" *Renascence* 50, 1 and 2 (Fall 1997/Winter 1998): 97-107.

Heyen, William, and Anthony Piccione. "A Conversation with Denise Levertov." *Ironwood* (1972): 2-34.

Hoerchner, Susan. "Denise Levertov. Review of *The Poet in the World.*" *Contemporary Literature* 15, 3 (Summer 1974): 435-37.

Hollenberg, Donna Krolik. "'Dancing Edgeways': Robert Creeley's Role in Denise Levertov's Post-war Transition." *Renascence* 58, 1 (Fall 2005): 5-16.

———. "Denise Levertov's Ambivalence about Feminist Poetry: Biographical Context, Interpretive Possibilities." *Renascence* 62, 2 (Winter 2010): 141-55.

———. "'History as I desired it': Ekphrasis As Postmodern Witness in Denise Levertov's Late Poetry." *Modernism/Modernity* 10, 3 (2003): 519-31.

———. "'Obscure Directions': Interpreting Denise Levertov's Ambivalence about Ezra Pound." *Biography: An Interdisciplinary Quarterly* 27, 4 (Fall 2004): 737-50.

———. "A Poet's Revolution: The Life of Denise Levertov." *Jacket* 36 (2008). www.jacketmagazine.com (accessed December 5, 2011).

———. "Visions of the Field in Poetry and Painting." In *Robert Duncan and Denise Levertov: The Poetry of Politics, the Politics of Poetry*, edited by Albert Gelpi and Robert J. Bertholf, 43-59. Palo Alto: Stanford University Press, 2006.

———. "Within the World of Your Perception: The Letters of Denise Levertov and H. D." *Paideuma* 33, 2 (2003): 247-71.

Howard, Richard. "Denise Levertov." *Tri-Quarterly* 7 (Fall 1966): 133-43.

Ignatow, David. "Review of *The Freeing of the Dust.*" In *Denise Levertov: Selected Criticism*, edited by Albert Gelpi, 35-36. Ann Arbor: University of Michigan Press, 1993.

Jackson, Richard. "A Common Time: The Poetry of Denise Levertov." *Sagetrieb* 5, 2 (1986): 5-46.

Janssen, Ronald R. "Dreaming of Design: Reading Denise Levertov." *Twentieth Century Literature* 38, 3 (Fall 1992): 263-80.

———. "Evening Train." *Twentieth Century Literature* 38, 3 (1992): 353-60.

Kallet, Marilyn. "Moistening Our Roots with Music: Creative Power in Denise Levertov's 'A Tree Telling of Orpheus.'" *Twentieth Century Literature* 38, 3 (Fall 1992): 305-23.

Karnow, Stanley. *Paris in the Fifties.* New York: Times Books, 1997.

Kinnahan, Linda A. *Poetics of the Feminine: Authority and Literary Tradition in William Carlos Williams, Mina Loy, Denise Levertov, and Kathleen Fraser.* New York: Cambridge University Press, 1994.

Kouidis, Virginia M. "Denise Levertov: Her Illustrious Ancestry." In *Critical Essays on Denise Levertov*, edited by Linda Wagner-Martin, 254-72. Boston: G. K. Hall and Company, 1991.

Lacey, Paul. "Denise Levertov As Teacher." *Renascence* 58, 1 (Fall 2005): 90-107.

——. "Denise Levertov: Testimonies of the Lived Life." *Renascence* 53, 4 (Summer 2001): 243-303.

——. *The Inner War: Forms and Themes in Recent American Poetry*. Philadelphia: Fortress Press, 1972.

——. "The Poetry of Political Anguish." In *Critical Essays on Denise Levertov*, edited by Linda Wagner-Martin, 187-96. Boston: G. K. Hall and Company, 1991.

——. "'To Meditate a Saving Strategy': Denise Levertov's Religious Poetry." *Renascence* 50, 1 and 2 (Fall 1997/Winter 1998): 16-33.

——. "The Vision of the Burning Babe: Southwell, Levertov, and Duncan." In *Robert Duncan and Denise Levertov: The Poetry of Politics, the Politics of Poetry*, edited by Albert Gelpi and Robert J. Bertholf, 161-79. Palo Alto: Stanford University Press, 2006.

——. "Wanderer and Pilgrim; Poet and Person." In *Denise Levertov: New Perspectives*, edited by Anne Colclough Little and Susie Paul, 241-52. West Cornwall, Conn.: Locust Hill Press, 2000.

Laughlin, James. "Denise Levertov." *The Way It Wasn't*, edited by Barbara Epler and Daniel Javitch, 160. New York: New Directions, 2006.

——. "For the Record." *Twentieth Century Literature* 38, 3 (Fall 1992): 280-82.

Lerner, Rachelle K. "Ecstasy of Attention: Denise Levertov and Kenneth Rexroth." *Jacket* 36 (2008). www.jacketmagazine.com (accessed December 5, 2011).

Levertoff, Beatrice. "Editorial." *Church and the Jews* 180, 4 (Autumn 1954): 1-7.

Levertoff, Olga. *The Jews in a Christian Social Order*. London: Sheldon Press, 1942.

——. "Paul Levertoff and the Jewish-Christian Problem." In *Judaism and Christianity/Essays Presented to the Rev. Paul P. Levertoff, D.D.*, edited by Lev Gillet, 93-111. London: J. B. Shears and Sons, 1939.

——. *The Rage of Days*. London: Hutchinson and Company, 1947.

Levertoff, Paul. *Love and the Messianic Age in Hitherto Untranslated Hasidic Writings with Special Reference to the Fourth Gospel*. London: The Episcopal Hebrew Christian Church Publications, 1923.

——. *The Messianic Hope: The Divine and Human Factors*. London: Thomas Murby and Company, 1935.

Little, Anne Colclough. "Old Impulses, New Expressions: Duality and Unity in the Poetry of Denise Levertov." *Renascence* 50, 1 and 2 (Fall 1997/Winter 1998): 33-48.

Little, Anne Colclough, and Susie Paul, eds. Introduction to *Denise Levertov: New Perspective*, xiii–xxvii. West Cornwall, Conn.: Locust Hill Press, 2000.

Long, Mark C. "Affinities of Faith and Place in the Poetry of Denise Levertov." *Interdisciplinary Studies in Literature and Environment* 6, 2 (1999): 31-40.

Lynch, Denise. "Denise Levertov and the Poetry of Incarnation." *Renascence* 50, 1 and 2 (Fall 1997/Winter 1998): 49-64.

——. "Denise Levertov in Pilgrimage." In *Denise Levertov: Selected Criticism*, edited by Albert Gelpi, 288-302. Ann Arbor: University of Michigan Press, 1993.

——. "Seeing Denise Levertov: Tesserae." In *Denise Levertov: New Perspectives*, edited by Anne Colclough Little and Susie Paul, 201-13. West Cornwall, Conn.: Locust Hill Press, 2000.

Mailer, Norman. *Armies of the Night*. New York: The New American Library, 1968.

Mariani, Paul. *William Carlos Williams: A New World Naked*. New York: McGraw Hill, 1981.

Marten, Harry. "Exploring the Human Community: The Poetry of Denise Levertov and Muriel Rukeyser." In *Critical Essays on Denise Levertov*, edited by Linda Wagner-Martin, 215-24. Boston: G. K. Hall and Company, 1991.

——. "'To Take Active Responsibility': On Teaching Denise Levertov's Poems." In *Denise Levertov: New Perspectives*, edited by Anne Colclough Little and Susie Paul, 107-18. West Cornwall, Conn.: Locust Hill Press, 2000.

——. *Understanding Denise Levertov*. Columbia: University of South Carolina Press, 1988.

Martin, Clarence Anthony. "The Projective Verse Movement: Its Influence upon American Poetry Since 1950." Master's thesis. Middle Tennessee State University, 1971.

Mazzaro, Jerome. "Denise Levertov and the Jacob's Ladder." In *Denise Levertov: New Perspectives*, edited by Anne Colclough Little and Susie Paul, 215-23. West Cornwall, Conn.: Locust Hill Press, 2000.

——. "Denise Levertov's Political Poetry." In *Critical Essays on Denise Levertov*, edited by Linda Wagner-Martin, 172-87. Boston: G. K. Hall and Company, 1991.

McCarthy, Coleman. "Interview with Denise Levertov." *Washington Post* (February 12, 1974).

McCaslin, Susan. "Pivoting toward Peace: The Engaged Poetics of Thomas Merton and Denise Levertov." *Pacific Rim Review of Books* 10 (Fall/Winter 2009). www.prrb.ca (accessed December 5, 2011).

McElroy, Colleen J. "Conversations and Tea with Denise." In *Page to Page: Retrospectives of Writers from the "Seattle Review*," edited by Colleen J. McElroy, 24-27. Seattle: University of Washington Press, 2007.

——. "Pillow Book." In *Sleeping with the Moon. Poems by Colleen J. McElroy*, 3-7. Urbana: University of Illinois Press, 2007.

McGowan, Christopher, ed. *The Letters of Denise Levertov and Williams Carlos Williams*. New York: New Directions, 1998.

——. "Valentine Park: 'A Place of Origin.'" In *Denise Levertov: New Perspectives*, edited by Anne Colclough Little and Susie Paul, 3-15. West Cornwall Conn.: Locust Hill Press, 2000.

Mersmann, James. "Denise Levertov." *Out of the Vietnam Vortex: A Study of Poets against the War*, 77-112. Lawrence: University Press of Kansas, 1974.

Merton, Thomas. *The Courage for Truth: The Letters of Thomas Merton to Writers*, edited by Christine M. Bochen. New York: Farrar, Straus, Giroux, 1993.

——. *The Other Side of the Mountain: The End of the Journey*. Vol. 7 of *The Journals of Thomas Merton,* edited by Patrick Hart. San Francisco: Harper San Francisco, 1998.

Middlebrook, Diane, and Marilyn Yalom, eds. *Coming to Light: American Women Poets in the Twentieth Century.* Ann Arbor: University of Michigan Press, 1985.

Middleton, Peter. *Revelation and Revolution in the Poetry of Denise Levertov.* London: Binnacle Press, 1981.

Millier, Brett. "Chelsea 8: Political Poetry at Midcentury." In *Robert Duncan and Denise Levertov: The Poetry of Politics, the Politics of Poetry*, edited by Albert Gelpi and Robert J. Bertholf, 93-108. Palo Alto: Stanford University Press, 2006.

Mills, Ralph J. "Denise Levertov: Poetry of the Immediate." In *Critical Essays on Denise Levertov*, edited by Linda Wagner-Martin, 98-110. Boston: G. K. Hall and Company, 1991.

———. "Review of *Footprints.*" *Parnassus* 1, 2 (1973): 219-21.

———. "What / Calm." In *Denise Levertov: New Perspectives*, edited by Anne Colclough Little and Susie Paul, 253. West Cornwall, Conn.: Locust Hill Press, 2000.

Mitford, Jessica. *The Trial of Dr. Spock.* New York: Knopf, 1969.

Mlinko, Ange. "Craft vs. Conscience: How the Vietnam War Destroyed the Friendship between Robert Duncan and Denise Levertov." www.poetryfoundation.org/archive/18/1959 (accessed December 5, 2011).

Moffet, Penelope. "Levertov: A Poet Heeds the Socio-Political Call, 1982." In *Conversations with Denise Levertov*, edited by Jewel Spears Brooker, 120-22. Jackson: University Press of Mississippi, 1998.

Morgan, Bill. *The Typewriter Is Holy.* New York: The Free Press, 2010.

Muller, Marlene, and Dennis Vogt. "In the Service of Hope — A Conversation with Wendell Berry." In *Conversation with Wendell Berry*, edited by Morris Allen Grubbs, 201-13. Jackson: University Press of Mississippi, 2007.

Narbeshuber, Lisa. "Relearning Denise Levertov's 'Alphabet': War, Flesh, and the Intimacy of Otherness." *Canadian Review of American Studies* 36, 2 (2006): 131-48.

Nelson, Cary. "Levertov's Political Poetry." In *Denise Levertov: Selected Criticism*, edited by Albert Gelpi, 162-66. Ann Arbor: University of Michigan Press, 1993.

Nelson, Rudolph L. "Edge of the Transcendent: The Poetry of Levertov and Duncan." In *Critical Essays on Denise Levertov*, edited by Linda Wagner-Martin, 225-35. Boston: G. K. Hall and Company, 1991.

Nielsen, Dorothy. "The Dark Wing of Mourning: Grief, Elegy and Time in the Poetry of Denise Levertov." In *Denise Levertov: New Perspectives*, edited by Anne Colclough Little and Susie Paul, 119-37. West Cornwall, Conn.: Locust Hill Press, 2000.

———. "Prosopopaeia and the Ethics of Ecological Advocacy in the Poetry of Denise Levertov and Gary Snyder." *Contemporary Literature* 34, 4 (Winter 1993): 691-713.

Norris, Kathleen. "Denise Levertov: Work That Enfaiths." *Christian Century* 116, 5 (February 17, 1999): 185.

Norris, Keith S. "Openmouthed in the Temple of Life: Denise Levertov and the Post-modern Lyric." *Twentieth Century Literature* 38, 3 (Fall 1992): 343-53.

Obituary. "Mitchell Goodman." *New York Times*, February 6, 1997.

O'Connell, Nicholas. "A Poet's Valediction." *Poets and Writers* (May/June 1998). www.pw.org (accessed December 5, 2011).

O'Leary, Peter. "Duncan, Levertov and the Age of Correspondence. Review of *Letters of Robert Duncan and Denise Levertov*." *Chicago Review* 51, 1 and 2 (Spring 2005): 231-39.

Oppen, George. *The Selected Letters of George Oppen*, edited by Rachel Blau DuPlessis. Durham, N.C.: Duke University Press, 1990.

Ossman, David. "Denise Levertov, 1963." In *Conversations with Denise Levertov*, edited by Jewel Spears Brooker, 1-3. Jackson: University Press of Mississippi, 1998.

Ostriker, Alicia Suskin. *Stealing the Language: The Emergence of Women's Poetry in America*. Boston: Beacon Press, 1986.

Pacernick, Gary. "Interview with Denise Levertov." In *Denise Levertov: New Perspectives*, edited by Anne Colclough Little and Susie Paul, 85-92. West Cornwall, Conn.: Locust Hill Press, 2000.

———. "The Question of Denise Levertov's Gift." In *Denise Levertov: New Perspectives*, edited by Anne Colclough Little and Susie Paul, 93-98. West Cornwall, Conn.: Locust Hill Press, 2000.

Packard, Williams. "Craft Interview with Denise Levertov, 1971." In *Conversations with Denise Levertov*, edited by Jewel Spears Brooker, 35-51. Jackson: University Press of Mississippi, 1998.

Pawlak, Mark. "Draft from Glover Circle Notebooks, 10/31/75." *Jacket* 36 (Fall 2008). www.jacketmagazine.com (accessed December 5, 2011).

———. "Where the Highway Ends: Sketches of Denise Levertov and Mitchell Goodman." *Hanging Loose* 90 (2007): 58-69.

Perloff, Marjorie. "The Corn-Porn Lyric: Poetry, 1972-73." *Contemporary Literature* 16, 1 (Winter 1975): 108-25.

———. "Poetry Chronicle, 1970-71." *Contemporary Literature* 14, 1 (Winter 1973): 97-131.

———. "Poetry in Time of War: The Duncan-Levertov Controversy." *Poetry On and Off the Page: Essays for Emergent Occasions*, 208-21. Evanston: Northwestern University Press, 1998.

Pinsker, Sanford. "Finding, Discovering, Pursuing: Poets on Poetry. Review of *New and Selected Essays*." *Gettysburg Review* 7, 1 (Winter 1994): 165-73.

Pope, Deborah. "Homespun and Crazy Feathers: The Split-Self in the Poems of Denise Levertov." In *Critical Essays on Denise Levertov*, edited by Linda Wagner-Martin, 73-97. Boston: G. K. Hall and Company, 1991.

Quinn, Bernetta. "Review of *Relearning the Alphabet*." In *Critical Essay on Denise Levertov*, edited by Linda Wagner-Martin, 27-28. Boston: G. K. Hall and Company, 1991.

Quinonez, Jorge. "Paul Phillip Levertoff: Pioneering Hebrew-Christian Scholar and Leader." *Mishkan* 37 (2002): 21-34.

Reid, Ian. "'Everyman's Land': Ian Reid Interviews Denise Levertov." In *Conversations with Denise Levertov*, edited by Jewel Spears Brooker, 68-75. Jackson: University Press of Mississippi, 1998.

"Review of *The Poet in the World*." *Commonweal* 101 (December 6, 1974): 246.

Rexroth, Kenneth. *Assays*. New York: New Directions, 1961.

———, ed. *The New British Poets*. New York: New Directions, 1949.

———. "The Poetry of Denise Levertov." In *Denise Levertov: Selected Criticism*, edited by Albert Gelpi, 11-14. Ann Arbor: University of Michigan Press, 1993.

———. *With Eye and Ear*. New York: Herder and Herder, 1970.

Rexroth, Kenneth, and James Laughlin. *Selected Letters*, edited by Lee Bartlett. New York: Norton and Company, 1991.

Rich, Adrienne. "Dialogue and Dissonance: *The Letters of Robert Duncan and Denise Levertov*." In *The Human Eye*, 70-81. New York: W. W. Norton, 2009.

Rodgers, Audrey T. *Denise Levertov: The Poetry of Engagement*. Rutherford, N.J.: Fairleigh Dickinson University Press, 1993.

Rogers, Bobby C. "Denise Levertov's Poetics of Process." In *God, Literature and Process Thought*, edited by Darren J. N. Middleton, 207-25. Burlington, Vt.: Ashgate, 2002.

Ross, Jean W. "An Interview with Denise Levertov, 1988." In *Conversations with Denise Levertov*, edited by Jewel Spears Brooker, 164-70. Jackson: University Press of Mississippi, 1998.

Rukeyser, Muriel. *How Shall We Teach Each Other of the Poet?: The Life and Writing of Muriel Rukeyser*, edited by Anne Herzog and Janet E. Kaufman. New York: St. Martin's Press, 1999.

Sadoff, Dianne T. "Mythopoeia, the Moon, and Contemporary Women's Poetry." In *Critical Essays on Denise Levertov*, edited by Linda Wagner-Martin, 245-54. Boston: G. K. Hall and Company, 1991.

Sakelliou-Schultz, Liana. *Denise Levertov: An Annotated Primary and Secondary Bibliography*. New York: Garland Publishing, 1988.

———. *Levertov's Poetry of Revelation—1988-1998: The Mosaic of Nature and Spirit*. Athens, Greece: George Dardanos, 1999.

Schloesser, Stephen. "'Not behind but within': Sacramentum et Res." *Renascence* 58, 1 (Fall 2005): 17-39.

Schwartz, Leonard. "Guillevic/Levertov: The Poetics of Matter." *Twentieth Century Literature* 38, 3 (Fall 1992): 290-99.

Shaddock, David. "Denise Levertov: A Remembrance and an Appreciation." *Poetry International* 3 (1999): 134-39.

———. "Opening the Gates of the Imagination. Review of *The Letters of Robert Duncan and Denise Levertov*." *Poetry Flash* (Winter/Spring 2006): 296- 97.

Shapiro, David. "Denise Levertov: Among the Keys." *Twentieth Century Literature* 38, 3 (Fall 1992): 299-305.

Sheppard, Reginald. "Reginald Sheppard's Blog," June 27, 2008. www.reginaldsheppardblogspot.com/2008 (accessed December 5, 2011).

Shurin, Aaron. "The People's P***k: A Dialectical Tale." In *Robert Duncan and Denise Levertov: The Poetry of Politics, the Politics of Poetry*, edited by Albert Gelpi and Robert J. Bertholf, 71-80. Palo Alto: Stanford University Press, 2006.

Silliman, Ron. "Unerasing Early Levertov." *Jacket* 36 (Fall 2008). www.jacketmagazine.com (accessed December 5, 2011).

Sisko, Nancy. "To Stay Alive: Levertov's Search for a Revolutionary Poetry." *Sagetrieb* 5, 2 (Fall 1986): 47-61.

Slaughter, William. "Con-versing with Denise Levertov." *Kalliope: A Journal of Women's Art* 1-2 (Spring/Summer 1979): 36-48.

———. *The Imagination's Tongue: Denise Levertov's Poetics.* Isle of Skye, Scotland: J. C. R. Green Publishers Ltd., 1981.

Smith, Lorrie. "An Interview with Denise Levertov, 1984." In *Conversations with Denise Levertov*, edited by Jewel Spears Brooker, 135-42. Jackson: University Press of Mississippi, 1998.

———. "Songs of Experience: Denise Levertov's Political Poetry." *Denise Levertov: Selected Criticism*, edited by Albert Gelpi, 177-97. Ann Arbor: University of Michigan Press, 1993.

Smith, Maureen. "An Interview with Denise Levertov, 1973." In *Conversations with Denise Levertov*, edited by Jewel Spears Brooker, 76-86. Jackson: University Press of Mississippi, 1998.

Stepancher, Stephen. *American Poetry since 1945.* New York: Harper and Row, 1965.

Sterling, Eric. "The Eye As Mirror of Humanity: Social Responsibility and the Nature of Evil in Denise Levertov's 'During the Eichmann Trial.'" In *Denise Levertov: New Perspectives*, edited by Anne Colclough Little and Susie Paul, 139-53. West Cornwall, Conn.: Locust Hill Press, 2000.

Stoneburner, Tony. "Denise Levertov: The Poet Standing between Life and Words." *Anglican Theological Review* 50, 3 (July 1968): 270-75.

———, ed. *A Meeting of Poets and Theologians to Discuss Parable, Myth and Language.* Cambridge, Mass.: Church Society for College Work, 1968.

Sutton, Walter. *American Free Verse: The Modern Revolution in Poetry.* New York: New Directions, 1973.

———. "A Conversation with Denise Levertov, 1965." In *Conversations with Denise Levertov*, edited by Jewel Spears Brooker, 4-27. Jackson: University Press of Mississippi, 1998.

Tassel, Janet. "Poetic Justice in El Salvador: Denise Levertov Brings Her Poetry and Politics to the Oratorio Form, 1983." In *Conversations with Denise Levertov*, edited by Jewel Spears Brooker, 123-34. Jackson: University Press of Mississippi, 1998.

Thorpe, Doug. "A Celebration of Denise Levertov's Comings and Goings." *Cross Currents* (Summer 1993): 247-52.

Thurley, Geoffrey. *The American Moment: American Poetry in the Mid-Century*. New York: St. Martin's Press, 1977.

Thurston, Anne. "'Acts of Faith': The Poetry of Denise Levertov." *Doctrine and Life* 47, 3 (1997): 130-37.

Todd, Selina. *Young Women's Work and Family in England, 1918-1950*. New York: Oxford University Press, 2005.

Trueblood, Valerie. "A Fellow Feeling. Review of *The Letters of Denise Levertov and William Carlos Williams*." *American Poetry Review* 6 (November/December 1999): 31-33.

Valdes, Carmen. "Candles in Babylon: The Imagination of Hope in the Religious Poetry of Denise Levertov." Diss. Graduate Theological Union, University of California, Berkeley, 2005.

Villanueva, Tino. "Poet in the World: A Tribute to Denise Levertov." *Jacket* 36 (Fall 2008). www.jacketmagazine.com (accessed December 5, 2011).

Waggoner, Hyatt H. *American Poets from the Puritans to the Present*. Baton Rouge: Louisiana State University Press, 1984.

Wagner-Martin, Linda. *Denise Levertov*. New York: Twayne Publishers, 1967.

———, ed. *Denise Levertov: In Her Own Province*. Introduction. New York: New Directions, 1979.

———, ed. *Interviews*. New York: New Directions, 1976.

———. "Levertov As Poet." In *Critical Essays on Denise Levertov*, edited by Linda Wagner-Martin, 1-14. Boston: G. K. Hall and Company, 1991.

———. "Levertov: Poetry and the Spiritual." In *Critical Essays on Denise Levertov*, edited by Linda Wagner-Martin, 196-204. Boston: G. K. Hall and Company, 1991.

———. "Matters of the Here and Now." *Nation* 218 (June 22, 1974): 795-96.

Waldman, Anne. "Wisdom Hath Built Her House." In *Denise Levertov: New Perspectives*, edited by Anne Colclough Little and Susie Paul, 233-40. West Cornwall, Conn.: Locust Hill Press, 2000.

Warn, Emily. "The Almost Wilderness: Remembering Denise Levertov." *Poetry Northwest* (Fall and Winter 2011-12). www.poetrynw.org (accessed February 15, 2012).

Watten, Barrett. "The Turn to Language and the 1960s." *Critical Inquiry* 29, 1 (Autumn 2002): 139-83.

Wilder, Amos Niven. *Theopoetic: Theology and the Religious Imagination*. Philadelphia: Fortress Press, 1976.

Woodcock, George. "Pilgrimage of a Poet." *New Leader* 57, 5 (March 4, 1974): 19-20.

Woodruff, Keith, and Brent Goodman. "Transformation of the Experienced: A Craft Interview with Denise Levertov." In *Delicious Imaginations: Conversations with Contemporary Writers*, edited by Sarah Griffiths and Devin J. Kehrwald, 131-40. West Lafayette: Purdue University Press, 1998.

Yore, Sue. *The Mystic Way in Post Modernity: Transcending Theological Boundaries in the Writings of Iris Murdoch, Denise Levertov and Annie Dillard.* Bern, Switzerland: Peter Lang, 2009.

Young-Bruehl, Elizabeth. *Creative Characters.* New York: Routledge, 1991.

——. *Subject to Biography: Psychoanalysis, Feminism, and Writing Women's Lives.* Cambridge: Harvard University Press, 1998.

Younkins, Ronald. "Denise Levertov and the Hasidic Tradition." *Descant* 19, 1 (Fall 1974): 40-48.

Zlotkowski, Edward. "In the Garden — A Place of Creation." In *Denise Levertov: Selected Criticism,* edited by Albert Gelpi, 303-20. Ann Arbor: University of Michigan Press, 1993.

——. "Levertov and Christianity: A Journey toward Renewal." *Christianity and Literature* 41, 4 (Summer 1992): 443-71.

——. "Levertov and Rilke: A Sense of Aesthetic Ethics." *Twentieth Century Literature* 38, 3 (Fall 1992): 324-42.

——. "Presence and Transparency: A Reading of Levertov's *Sands of the Well.*" *Renascence* 50, 1 and 2 (Fall 1997/Winter 1998): 135-51.

Zweig, Paul. "Magistral Strokes and First Steps." *Nation* 212 (June 21, 1971): 794-95.

Zwicky, Fay. "An Interview with Denise Levertov, 1979." In *Conversations with Denise Levertov,* edited by Jewel Spears Brooker, 109-19. Jackson: University Press of Mississippi, 1998.

SELECTED WORKS BY DENISE LEVERTOV
Arranged Chronologically

The Double Image. London: Cresset Press, 1946. (*DI*)

Here and Now. San Francisco: City Lights Pocket Bookshop, 1957. See *CEP.*

5 Poems. San Francisco: White Rabbit Press, 1958. See *CEP.*

Overland to the Islands. Highlands, N.C.: J. Williams, 1958. See *CEP.*

With Eyes at the Back of Our Heads. New York: New Directions, 1959. See *CEP.*

"Statement on Poetics." In *The New American Poetry,* edited by Donald M. Allen, 411-12. New York: Grove Press, 1960.

The Jacob's Ladder. New York: New Directions, 1961. See *Poems 1960-1967.*

"Poetry: Pure and Complex." *New Leader* 46, 4 (February 18, 1963): 25-26.

City Psalm. Berkeley: Oyez, 1964. See *Poems 1960-1967.*

O Taste and See. New York: New Directions, 1964. See *Poems 1960-1967.*

Psalm Concerning the Castle. Mount Horeb, Wis.: Perishable Press, 1966. See *Poems 1960-1967.*

In Praise of Krishna: Songs from the Bengali, translated by Denise Levertov and Edward C. Dimock. Garden City, N.Y.: Doubleday, 1967.

Supervielle, Jules. *Selected Writings*, translated by James Kirkup, Denise Levertov, and Kenneth Rexroth. New York: New Directions, 1967.

The Sorrow Dance. New York: New Directions, 1967. See *Poems 1960-1967*.

Out of the War Shadow: An Anthology of Current Poetry, edited by Denise Levertov. New York: War Resisters League, 1967.

Penguin Modern Poets-9. London: Penguin Books, 1967 (contains poems by Levertov, Rexroth, and Williams).

The Cold Spring and Other Poems. New York: New Directions, 1968. See *Poems 1968-1972*.

A Marigold from North Vietnam. New York: Albondocani Press and Ampersand Books, 1968. See *Poems 1968-1972*.

A Tree Telling of Orpheus. Los Angeles: Black Sparrow Press, 1968. See *Poems 1968-1972*.

Three Poems. Mount Horeb, Wis.: Perishable Press, 1968. See *Poems 1968-1972*.

Embroideries. Los Angeles: Black Sparrow Press, 1969. See *Poems 1968-1972*.

Tsvetayeva Marina, and Boris Poplavsky. *Poets on Streetcorners: Portraits of Fifteen Russian Poets*, edited by Olga Carlisle, translated by Denise Levertov. New York: Random House, 1969.

Guillevic, Eugene. *Selected Poems*, translated by Denise Levertov. New York: New Directions, 1969.

Introduction. *The Wedding Feast*, by Richard Edelman. Berkeley: Oyez, 1970.

A New Year's Garland for My Students/MIT: 1969-70. Mount Horeb, Wis.: Perishable Press, 1970. See *Poems 1968-1972*.

Relearning the Alphabet. New York: New Directions, 1970. See *Poems 1968-1972*.

Summer Poems, 1969. Berkeley: Oyez, 1970. See *Poems 1968-1972*.

To Stay Alive. New York: New Directions, 1971. See *Poems 1968-1972*.

Footprints. New York: New Directions, 1972. See *Poems 1968-1972*.

The Poet in the World. New York: New Directions, 1973. (*PITW*)

The Freeing of the Dust. New York: New Directions, 1975. See *Poems 1972-1982*.

Modulations for Solo Voice. San Francisco: Five Trees Press, 1977. See *Poems 1972-1982*.

Chekhov on the West Heath. Andes, N.Y.: Woolmer/Brotherson, 1977. See *Poems 1972-1982*.

Life in the Forest. New York: New Directions, 1978. See *Poems 1972-1982*.

Foreword. *Where Silence Reigns*, by Rainer Marie Rilke, translated by T. G. Craig Houston. New York: New Directions, 1978.

Collected Earlier Poems 1940-1960. New York: New Directions, 1979 (contains poems from *The Double Image, Here and Now, Overland to the Islands, With Eyes at the Back of Our Heads*, and some uncollected earlier poems. (*CEP*)

Light Up the Cave. New York: New Directions, 1981. (*LUTC*)

Mass for the Day of St. Thomas Didymus. Concord, N.H.: William B. Ewert, 1981. See *Poems 1972-1982*.

Pig Dreams: Scenes from the Life of Sylvia. Woodstock, Vt.: Countryman Press, 1981. See *Poems 1972-1982*.

Talk in the Dark. San Francisco: Square Zero Editions Broadside, 1981. See *Poems 1972-1982*.

Wanderer's Daysong. Port Townsend, Wash.: Copper Canyon Press, 1981. See *Poems 1972-1982*.

Candles in Babylon. New York: New Directions, 1982. See *Poems 1972-1982*.

Poems 1960-1967. New York: New Directions, 1983 (contains *The Jacob's Ladder, O Taste and See*, and *The Sorrow Dance*).

Two Poems. Concord, N.H.: William Ewert, 1983. See *OP*.

El Salvador: Requiem and Invocation. Concord, N.H.: William B. Evert, 1983. (*DITH*)

"Denise Levertov." *The Bloodaxe Book of Contemporary Women Poets*, edited by Jeni Couzyn, 74-79. Newcastle upon Tyne, U.K.: Bloodaxe Books, 1984.

"Denise Levertov." *Contemporary Authors Autobiography Series*, 19, 229-46. Detroit: Gale Research Company, 1984-99.

Oblique Prayers: New Poems with 14 Translations from Jean Joubert. New York: New Directions, 1984. (*OP*)

The Menaced World. Concord, N.H.: William B. Ewert, 1985. See *BTW*.

Selected Poems. Newcastle upon Tyne, U.K.: Bloodaxe Books, 1986 (contains selected poems from 1957 through 1982).

Introduction. *Martin and Meditations on the South Valley,* by Jimmy Santiago Baca. New York: New Directions, 1986.

Poems 1968-1972. New York: New Directions, 1987 (contains *Relearning the Alphabet, To Stay Alive*, and *Footprints*).

Breathing the Water. New York: New Directions, 1987. (*BTW*)

Poets of Bulgaria, edited by William Meredith and translated by John Balaban and others, including Denise Levertov. London: Forest, 1988.

Bosquet, Alain. *No Matter No Fact,* translated by Denise Levertov, Sam Beckett, and Edouard Roditi. New York: New Directions, 1988.

Joubert, Jean. *Black Iris: Selected Poems by Jean Joubert*, translated by Denise Levertov. Copper Canyon, Wash.: Copper Canyon Press, 1988.

A Door in the Hive. New York: New Directions, 1989. (*DITH*)

Hawley, Beatrice. *The Collected Poems of Beatrice Hawley*, edited by Denise Levertov. Cambridge, Mass.: Zoland Books, 1989.

Joubert, Jean. *White Owl and Blue Mouse*, translated by Denise Levertov. Cambridge, Mass.: Zoland Books, 1990.

New and Selected Essays. New York: New Directions, 1992. (*NSE*)

Evening Train. New York: New Directions, 1992. (*ET*)

"The Discovery of Voice." *Signals: The Chapbook of the Olympic College Writers' Conference* 2, 1 (December 1993): 9-16.

Tesserae: Memories and Suppositions. New York: New Directions, 1995.

"Living What You Believe." In *Apostle of Peace: Essays in Honor of Daniel Berrigan*, edited by John Dear. Maryknoll, N.Y.: Orbis Books, 1996.

Sands of the Well. New York: New Directions, 1996. (*SOTW*)

Introduction. *Dreams That Wake As Words,* by Steven Blevins. Berkeley: Tangram, 1997.

The Life around Us. New York: New Directions, 1997.

The Stream and the Sapphire. New York: New Directions, 1997.

Foreword. *Writing between the Lines: An Anthology on War and Its Social Consequences,* edited by Kevin Bowen and Bruce Weigl. Amherst: University of Massachusetts Press, 1997.

This Great Unknowing: Last Poems, edited by Paul Lacey. New York: New Directions, 1999. (*TGU*)

Denise Levertov: Poems 1972-1982. New York: New Directions, 2001 (contains *The Freeing of the Dust, Life in the Forest,* and *Candles in Babylon*).

Denise Levertov: Selected Poems, edited by Paul Lacey. New York: New Directions, 2002.

Making Peace, edited by Peggy Rosenthal. New York: New Directions, 2006.

"The Art of Mary Randlett." In *Mary Randlett Landscapes,* 25-33. Seattle: University of Washington Press, 2007.

MANUSCRIPTS

Czeslaw Milosz Papers GEN MSS 661, Folder 572. Beinecke Rare Book and Manuscript Library, Yale University, New Haven, Conn.

Denise Levertov Papers (DLP). M0601. Dept. of Special Collections, Stanford University Libraries, Stanford, Calif.

Kenneth Aguillard Atchity Collection Series 1, Box 20. Special Collections, Georgetown University, Washington, D.C.

Lucille Clifton Papers MSS 1054. Manuscripts, Archives and Rare Book Library, Emory University, Atlanta, Ga.

INDEX

Oppen, George, 75
"The Opportunity" (Levertov), 170
"Origins of a Poem" (Levertov), 78, 159
Orlovsky, Lafcadio, 55
Orlovsky, Peter, 55
Ossman, David, 77-78
Ostriker, Alicia, 152
O Taste and See (Levertov), 43, 81-82, 85
"Out of the War Shadow" (Levertov), 90
"Overland to the Islands" (Levertov), 69-70
Overland to the Islands (Levertov), 50

"On the Parable of the Mustard Seed" (Levertov), 185
"Paradox and Equilibrium" (Levertov), 165, 184
"participation mystique," 179
Pavese, Cesare, 142
Pax Christi, 145, 192
Peet, Stephen, 22-23, 30, 120, 123, 164, 191, 193
Pennington, Basil, 166
Perloff, Marjorie, 152
Pocock, Gerry, 146, 166, 188, 189-90
"A Poem at Christmas, 1972, during the Terror-Bombing of North Vietnam" (Levertov), 114
"Poet and Person" (Levertov), 228
"Poetic Language as Spiritual Insight" (Levertov), 166
poetic sources and themes: antiwar poetry, 85, 101-2; autobiographical poetry, 141-42, 185, 196-97, 211, 223; biographical poetry, 232; borderland, 197-98; communion in solidarity and common action, 153, 223-24; "confessional" poetry, 140-41; divided self theme, 82, 120-21; double image theme, 23-24, 151, 160-61, 193-94, 197, 222-23, 232-33; free verse, 79; geography in poetic life, 224-25; inner life exploration, 233, 234; life-death linkage, 221; life experience, 78-82, 102-3, 217, 223, 231; lyric poetry, 120-21; mountains, 34, 205, 222, 234; mystery celebration theme, 144-45; nature, 153, 182, 193-94, 197-98, 205-6, 211, 213, 222; organic poetry, 78-82; painters, 36, 91; peacemaking/poem-making theme, 163; poem-prayers, 187; poetry and Christianity, 225; poetry of relationships, 204-5; political poetry, 88-89, 90-91, 94-96, 100-101, 102-4,

132-35, 143, 205; prayer-poems, 157-59, 206-7; religious poetry, 185-86, 201, 211, 213-14, 222; shock poetry, 72; women's issues, 138-39; work that enfaiths, 179-80, 187, 206-7
The Poet in the World (Levertov), 113, 121-22
"Poetry, Prophecy, Survival" (Levertov), 159, 204
"Poetry and Peace" (Levertov), 184
Poetry Quarterly (Gardiner, ed.), 22
poetry readings: Academy of American Poets, 83; Alabama, 164; Arizona State Prison, 136; Cardiff, Wales, 210; Choate, 77; Cleveland State University, 165; Colby College, 77; Colgate University, 77; Cornell University, 200; Dartmouth College, 77; DIA Center, New York City, 200; Earlham College, 165; England, 209; Goucher College, 77; Harbour Front Festival, Toronto, 200; Harvard University, 60; Ireland, 209; Montreal Poetry Conference, 89-90; New York University, 60; Ohio State University, 165; Ohio Wesleyan University, 165; Oregon, 200; Philadelphia, PA, 164; Port Townsend Writers' Conference, 218; Princeton University, 60; Purcell Room, London, UK, 201; Purdue University, 210; San Francisco Poetry Center, 57, 60; Santa Clara University, 184; Santa Fe, NM, 164; Stanford University, 218; St. Theresa's College, 92; Theodore Roethke Memorial Poetry Reading, 187; Tucson, AZ, 92; Union College, 92; University of Chicago, 92; University of Kentucky, 92; University of Oregon, 218; University of Washington, 187; Vancouver Poetry Conference, 75, 78; Washington, DC, 164; Wesleyan University, 77; Yale University, 60
Poets for Peace, 192
"A Poet's View" (Levertov), 161
Posner, David, 164
Potter, Norman (En), 24-25, 26, 120, 164, 210
Pound, Ezra, 68-69, 89-90
In Praise of Krishna: Songs from the Bengali (Levertov), 88-89
"Prayer for Revolutionary Love" (Levertov), 120
"Primary Wonder" (Levertov), 215
prizes. See awards and prizes
"Psalm Concerning the Castle" (Levertov), 88

Taylor, Carolyn, 128

teaching: Beloit College, 211; Brandeis University, 132; City College of New York, 77; Cornell University, 200, 210; Drew University, 77; Goucher College, 103; Hendrix College, 132; Kirkland College, 104; Lake Forest College, 132; Massachusetts Institute of Technology, 101-2; New York City YM-YWCA Poetry Center, 76, 77; New York Poetry Center Workshop, 77; Ohio State University, 194; Santa Clara University, 207; Seattle University, 194, 229; Stanford University, 132, 151, 180-81, 194, 199, 218, 229; Tufts University, 113, 131; University of California, Berkeley, 98-101; University of Cincinnati, 113, 116-17; University of Oregon, 218; University of Sydney, 132; University of Washington, 187; Vassar College, 77

"Technique and Tune-Up" (Levertov), 142

"Tenebrae" (Levertov), 92

Tesserae: Memories and Suppositions (Levertov), 210-11

"On a Theme by Thomas Merton" (Levertov), 92

"On a Theme from Julian's Chapter XX" (Levertov), 178

"This Day" (Levertov), 158

This Great Unknowing (Levertov), 221, 224

Thomas, R. S., 193

Thorpe, Douglas, 182

"For Those Whom the Gods Love Less" (Levertov), 212

"The Thread" (Levertov), 144

"Three Meditations" (Levertov), 65-67

"Time for Rivets" (Levertov), 191

Tobin, Luke, 167, 189-90, 193, 196, 207

"In Tonga" (Levertov), 185

"Tragic Errors" (Levertov), 206

translations: "The Artist," 54; Eugene Guillevic, 98-99; in general, 1, 88, 99; Jean Joubert, 158; "In Praise of Krishna: Songs from the Bengali," 88; "The Sorrow Dance," 88

"Translucence" (Levertov), 220

travels and temporary settlings: Australia, 130; Banff, Canada, 194; Boston, MA, 101-6; Boulder, CO, 104; Brookline, MA, 106, 106-13; Bulgaria, 130; Canada, 130; England, 130;

164; France, 130, 168; Geneva, 30-32; Greece, 50, 72; Holland, 25-28; Ilford (London,) UK, 8-25, 104, 106; Italy, 38, 104, 130, 183, 186; Japan, 164; Maine, 60, 73, 89, 101, 114; Mexico, 44, 45, 52-57, 106, 123; New England, 37, 58; New York City, 30-32, 34-44, 35-49, 57-98; Palo Alto, CA, 151-81; Paris, 28-29, 28-33, 33-34; Provence, 30, 37-38; Puerto Rico, 86; San Francisco, 57; Saratoga Springs, NY, 123; Scotland, 166; Seattle, WA, 181-229; Somerville, MA, 113-51; Soviet Union, 106; Tonga, 130, 185; Vermont, 41-42, 44; Vietnam, 114; Wales, 210; Yugoslavia, 104

"A Tree Telling of Orpheus" (Levertov), 96

Triem, Eve, 57, 146, 182, 209

Trueblood, Valerie, 212, 224

"The Tulips" (Levertov), 80

"Twain." See Levertoff, Beatrice Spooner-Jones (mother); Levertoff, Paul Philip (Born Feivel) (father)

"Two Mountains" (Levertov), 185

"Two Threnodies and Psalm" (Levertov), 185

"Variation on a Theme by Rilke" (Levertov), 186

Vietnam War, 113-15

Wabash College, 78

Wales, 5-6, 7-8

Walker, Alice, 128

Wallace, Jan, 227-28

Warn, Emily, 182, 193

War Resisters League, 90

Waveren, Ann van, 74

Weaver, Francesca, 131

"What Goes Unsaid" (Levertov), 233

"What Harbinger?" (Levertov), 212

"What is a Poet?" (Levertov), 160

"What the Figtree Said" (Levertov), 206

"In Whom We Live and Move and Have Our Being" (Levertov), 213

"Why I Pray" (Levertov), 187

"The Wife" (Levertov), 56

Williams, Jonathan, 51

Williams, William Carlos: on cost of life as female poet, 47-48; death, 75-76; first reading, 33-34; friendship, 40, 46; on Levertov, 50-51; Levertov relationship, 67-68; mentor, 36, 44

Dana Greene is Dean Emerita of Oxford College of Emory University. Her other books include *Evelyn Underhill: Artist of the Infinite Life* and *The Living of Maisie Wood.*

THE UNIVERSITY OF ILLINOIS PRESS
is a founding member of the Association of American University Presses.

Designed and typeset by Carrie House, HOUSEdesign llc
Composed in 10/14 Emigre Tribute with You Work for Them Jute display
Manufactured by Sheridan Books, Inc.
University of Illinois Press
1325 South Oak Street
Champaign, IL 61820-6903
www.press.uillinois.edu